I WANNA
BE YOURS

Also by John Cooper Clarke

The Luckiest Guy Alive

JOHN COOPER CLARKE

I WANNA BE YOURS

PICADOR

First published 2020 by Picador
an imprint of Pan Macmillan
The Smithson, 6 Briset Street, London ECIM 5NR
Associated companies throughout the world
www.panmacmillan.com

ISBN 978-1-5098-9610-3

7 9 8 6

A CIP catalogue record for this book is available from the British Library.

Typeset by Palimpsest Book Production Ltd, Falkirk, Stirlingshire
Printed and bound by CPI Group (UK) Ltd, Croydon, CRO 4YY

Visit **www.picador.com** to read more about all our books
and to buy them. You will also find features, author interviews and
news of any author events, and you can sign up for e-newsletters
so that you're always first to hear about our new releases.

In memory of my late nephew Paul James Clarke

CONTENTS

THE STAR OF MY OWN MOVIE

Poetry is my first language, so forget the static data: I'm not on trial for murder. Rather than a ponderous trudge through the turgid facts of an ill-remembered life, to fleetingly call up various events that best illustrate the flavour of my existence at any given point, this is my aim. It's a tough call, but somebody's gotta do it.

Thank God it's me.

All my life, all I ever wanted to be was a professional poet. To me being a professional poet was better than notching up a hat trick at Old Trafford. It was better than living above a candy factory. Better even than starring in a screwball romance opposite Liz Taylor.

You get to wear fine clothes and perfume and nobody pulls you up on it. You get out of bed late in the day and nobody calls you a lazy bastard. A state of reverie and the virtue of idleness are paramount. Any poet will tell you this.

Women hold men like this in great affection: it's a well-known fact.

The life of a useless flâneur, however, was not encouraged in the 1950s, especially among the blue-collar population of a heavy-industrial metropolis like Manchester. There was the often unpleasant necessity of financial buoyancy, for a start. Circumstances had dealt me a cruel blow in this matter. Given my lack of provenance in the world of English letters, a generous stipend was out of the question. Why, even a monthly emolument of ten shillings or less would have been beyond any reasonable expectations.

Poetry has never been regarded as a reliable engine of wealth – quite the reverse. It is rather the province of scoundrels, aristocrats, and wasters: the squanderers of fortunes, the usurpers of husbands, and the ruin of families. The poet is at best an upsetting presence among the lumpen bourgeoisie. Either that or a crackpot mystic leading a hermetic life of self-imposed destitution. In any event, not the life that George Frederick Clarke would have recognised as in any way advisable.

His attitude, which seemed to be unanimous in the adult world, could be summed up in three words: get a job.

Chapter One

THE EDGE OF DIFFERENT WORLDS

I was a mystery to my mum and dad, and they were a mystery to me. There was the world of kids, the world of women, and the world of men, with certain points of overlap: Easter and Passover, Christmas and Hanukkah, summer holidays, the usual annual set pieces of the Judaeo-Christian family calendar.

The prevalent attitude to parenting in my family was a form of benign neglect; there was never really any high-volume aggro with my mum and dad. In fact, the only things they ever said I *couldn't* do were get a bike and make a living out of poetry. Other than that, they were quite encouraging.

My dad really only ever gave me four pieces of advice, which I've never taken the trouble to forget. Number one: 'All the vitamins you'll ever need are in the head of a beer.' Number two: 'Never leave a bookie's with a smile on your face.' Number three: 'You'll never get food poisoning from a chip shop – what could live in that temperature?' Number four: 'Never enter a game of cards with a man whose first name is Doc.'

My parents, George Clarke and Hilda Barnes, were both from Salford. Before that, who knows where anyone in my large and neglected family came from: County Tyrone, Vilnius, Kraków,

Oldham, possibly even Wales! But we all had one thing in common – we were English.

My dad worked at Metropolitan-Vickers, a heavy-engineering firm in Trafford Park, as an electrical engineer – switchgear specialist. Twenty thousand people worked at Metro-Vicks, and that was just one factory among any number of a comparable size in Trafford Park. I don't even know what they made there, nor exactly what my dad's work entailed, but I imagine that during the Second World War they were involved in the manufacture of engines for Lancaster bombers. In any case, his work was certainly deemed in the national interest, and that's why he wasn't called up. He did his bit, however, in the Home Guard: Dad's Army, literally.

In 1949, the year I was born, Dad was promoted to the position of foreman; he proved a charismatic leader of men, popular with his gang. Later, during my schooldays, he was often away during the week, working on the construction of substations and the consequent electrification of those benighted pockets of Scotland and Wales that were still in thrall to the steam age, delivering clean labour-saving energy to their erstwhile gloomy, unenlightened homes.

Before she married, my mum had several jobs here and there. As a cleaner; putting the pastry lids on mass-produced meat pies; and as a shop assistant in a high-end confectioner's. During the war, she worked in the Manchester Metal Works munitions factory near our home making shells, bullets, and bombs. She also worked part-time as a barmaid. I'm no detective (unless you count those thirty years I spent working in Scotland Yard's Forensic Division), but I imagine that's how she met my dad.

When they got married, my mum became a professional house-wife. My dad was on good money, and it was a badge of honour to have your wife at home. Owing to his absence during the working week, however, she retained a couple of her cleaning jobs, for the social aspect more than anything else: she liked the company.

There were a great many fatalities in my early life. Within one year, my mother lost her mother, her younger brother Sid, who died in a motorbike accident on his way to their mother's funeral, and her sister Irene. It was heartbreak upon heartbreak – it seemed like a time of constant sorrow. That left my mum, her sister Winifred, and their cousin Dennis, who was brought up as their brother: his parents couldn't afford to bring him up, so they just handed him over to my grandma, no questions asked. Uncle Dennis was quite a bit younger than my mum. He was in the RAF, then when I was about ten he was demobilised and for a short period came to live with us.

Aunt Winifred was married to Uncle Frank. They had two kids: my cousins Sid and Frankie. Sid's real name was Dennis, but to avoid any confusion with Uncle Dennis, he was known by his middle name. They lived in Ordsall, down near the docks, and we regularly hung out together.

My mother's Uncle Sid, a confirmed bachelor, was the manager of the Manchester branch of Jackson's, the high-street tailor. He was quite an elderly chap, and was very popular in the pubs round about because he could play the piano. Not a bad bloke, but a real arch-snob, with a waspish, withering humour.

Nobody ever saw Uncle Sid other than at family set pieces: weddings, funerals, twenty-first parties. He would swan in for half an hour, immaculately attired, not a marcelled hair out of place, a pair of snooty-looking tortoiseshell glasses on the end of his beak, nursing a Scotch and soda, never a pint. Image-wise, think Clifton Webb circa *Three Coins in the Fountain*. If anybody wore a cravat with his pyjamas, it was Uncle Sid.

He didn't like us kids much: you could tell he just thought we were a messy, noisy, bothersome presence to be tolerated but not encouraged, although he would always cough up a couple of bob for Sid, Frankie, and me. In this he was, as in every other depart-ment, extravagant. Uncle Sid had none of the tweed-'n'-flannel dependability of the professional dad; he favoured an inner-city sharpness. Blazers in previously unseen fabrics. A mauve pocket square here, an undone cuff button there. He was, after all, in the business – strictly front-of-house. Frankie reckoned he smelled like a lady's handbag.

On my dad's side, there was Auntie Marjorie, her husband Uncle George, and their daughter, my cousin Mary, who looked a lot like the late Princess Di. His other sister, Irene (popular name), was married to Uncle Dick. Uncle Dick was atypical of our family: a teetotal, white-collar motorist. He owned a Ford Popular, but he never went over four miles an hour in it. He was the first motorised family member since the demise of my maternal granddad, who drove a van for Lovells Confectionery. I never met the guy, but my mum backs up the photographic evidence: her father was a ringer for the late Spencer Tracy.

My paternal grandfather, George, had been a regular soldier in India until chucking-out time in 1948, and funnily enough bore an uncanny resemblance to Mahatma Gandhi (who apparently suffered from corns and bad breath, in other words a supercallousedfragilemysticplaguedwithhalitosis, as Julie Andrews and Dick Van Dyke almost sang). Seriously, though, my granddad gave me my first peach – even now my favourite fruit – and introduced me to the remarkable adventures of Rupert Bear and his immense social circle.

There was a whole load of neglected peripheral family that I never even met. We weren't too fussy about that sort of thing. We did our best, but you know . . . lack of transport.

There was my mum's cousin, Uncle Charlie, Dennis's brother, for example. He was a bit of a charmer with lavishly pomaded hair and a million-dollar Pepsodent smile, a born schmoozer whose social finesse, although attractive, was not enough to keep him from utter penury. He was however in possession of a tuxedo and a pair of cufflinks the size of jaybird eggs. Despite being the schnorrer of the family, whenever Uncle Charlie showed up at any crucial birthday, funeral, baptism, or betrothal, draped in the finest Continental suitings, he impressed the fuck out of us kids; but then, he wasn't hitting *us* up for any money. The only surviving visual evidence of the late Charlie Barnes is a single monochrome photograph which accurately captures his prodigious elegance and laid-back allure: clad in the aforementioned tuxedo, he is standing at a microphone fulfilling some indeterminate showbiz engagement.

Given his ignominious end, in Salvation Army hostels and flophouse bedsits, this photograph introduced a note of seldom-heeded caution to my embryonic world view: an unwelcome reminder of the possibility of failure and disgrace. The passing years have elevated this portrait to the status of cautionary iconography.

Finally, next door to Grandma Barnes's old house, there was my unofficial Uncle Stan, Auntie Edie, and the rest of the Shepherd family: i.e. my mate Baz and his two teenage sisters, Florence and Joan, commonly known as Cat and Dog, owing to their mutual animosity.

I was born in Hope Hospital, Salford, in 1949, four years after the end of the Second World War. This was austerity Britain, but although I never saw a banana until I was five, I had no real sense of deprivation. To be honest, I'm hard-pressed to remember much at all from that early age – I was just five when rationing ended in 1954.

I'm from Higher Broughton. Higher Broughton is not the roughest part of Salford. A number of trees could still be found in one of the several Victorian municipal parks in the area, but posh would be pushing it a bit. Even today, in spite of Media City, Salford is not posh.

The front of our home looked out on the junction of two of

the city's main arteries: running north to south was Bury New Road, the Scotland to London road, and east to west, Great Cheetham Street, part of the A57, which goes from Liverpool all the way to the Lincolnshire coast, through Derbyshire and the Pennines via the Snake Pass, a biker's rite of passage, strewn with hairpin bends and precipitous inclines.

Salford was bombed very heavily in the Blitz, especially in our area. From the cockpit of a Heinkel He111, our building would have looked very close to Salford Docks, and the munitions factory where my mum worked was only about a hundred yards away. Bury New Road, therefore, received more than its fair share of Teutonic ordnance: target number one. Bomb craters and collapsed buildings, real unsafe shit, that was our adventure playground.

Our apartment was contained in a villa built in the Italianate style befitting the taste of the affluent Victorian high bourgeoisie: a mock-Palladian edifice notable for the crumbling splendour of its applied ornamentation and the flaking stucco of its lavishly fenestrated facade. What would once have been an entire three-storey dwelling had been hastily and badly converted into three self-contained apartments. Slums to anyone who didn't live in them, perhaps, but grandiose nevertheless, and at some point, we lived in each one of them.

At the rear of the building, the exterior was zigzagged by a fire escape. Its iron steps and balconies provided the setting for any social intercourse and it was out here, back of house, where most of my dealings took place. When I was an infant we occupied the top-floor apartment, but then one day I fell down the fire escape, saved only by the wooden drying rack, which prevented any further descent. My near-death experience must have left my mum in trauma, and we consequently exchanged with Mr and Mrs Korn, the elderly, childless couple on the ground floor.

The middle apartment was occupied by a chap called Jack Jordan, one of my dad's regular drinking pals. Jack had achieved a measure of celebrity as a professional pianist and the composer of 'Little Red Monkey', the main title theme to the 1955 Cold War espionage thriller of the same name starring Richard Conte. He was resident pianist on the popular radio programme *Have A Go*, starring Wilfred Pickles and his wife Mabel. On his fortnightly professional visits to tweak the finer points of the show, Pickles would occasionally join Jack and my dad in the pub, where he adroitly managed to avoid ever getting a round in. Rightly or wrongly, my father put his meanness down to the traditional tight-fisted nature of the Yorkshireman. 'He wouldn't give you the steam off his piss, that bloke,' was his considered verdict.

At some point after Jack moved out, we took over his vacant apartment, where my parents remained until they were rehoused in a modern high-rise in the early Seventies.

It was a kind of Three Bears situation: top floor, too dangerous; ground floor, too dark; central floor, just right. In spite of its grandiose floor-to-ceiling windows, the acreage of our gargantuan front room in the first-floor flat required the illumination of not one but two chandeliers, which hung from a stratospheric ceiling. A picture rail encircled the walls three feet below the elaborate plasterwork cornicing.

Each of the utility rooms, however, was an ergonomic fiasco. The kitchen wasn't even a kitchen, merely a passage from one area of the apartment to the other, with a four-ring electric stove, a grill for toast and bacon, and a sink bodged in. Somehow my mum managed to cook a Sunday dinner there every week and a Christmas dinner every year. It's a mystery how she did it.

Downstairs, as well as Mr and Mrs Korn was Mr and Mrs Freedman's chemist's shop. Next to that was our communal front door, which opened onto an expansive spiral stairway with filigree ironwork banisters, punctuated on each landing by a finial in the form of a torch-bearing nymph. The hallway, ill-lit by the grime-bespattered skylight, was painted in a dismal pre-war drab, and housed bas-relief statuary, friezes, and a fabulous bestiary of gargoyles – the furniture of most people's nightmares and a place of dread foreboding to anyone in their right mind. Welcome home.

I hated having to come in through the front door of our building. I was a nervous kid, and the profusion of possible hiding places coupled with its easy accessibility from the street made our stairwell the ideal lurking spot for kidnappers and child-murderers, so I always used to go round the back and up the fire escape. Later, at school, whenever I mentioned the fire escape for any reason, the other kids had no idea what I was talking about until around 1961 and the movie *West Side Story*. I could then refer them to the publicity posters featuring Natalie Wood and Richard Beymer running hand in hand through the Hispanic streets of New York, and prominent in the background the familiar iron zigzags of the tenement fire escapes. In the movie most of their romantic close-ups take place on these structures.

I remember instantly recognising that world because I was living in my own little bit of Manhattan, right there, in Higher Broughton. I felt I had more in common with those characters in *West Side Story* than the children I went to school with. Later, when Nico and the Beat poet Gregory Corso moved from New York to Higher Broughton, they too would comment on the familiarity of the neighbourhood ambience.

That was my very early view of the world: fire escapes, traffic lights, commercial transport, and Haredi Jews. Higher Broughton and Broughton Park were and remain a largely Jewish area. The Salford Jewish community was well established: merchant families had first come from Germany in the boom years of the nineteenth-century cotton industry; Hasidic sects had migrated from Russia, Lithuania, and Poland; and, of course, the most recent arrivals were those fleeing Europe and the horrors of National Socialism. Considering I went to a Catholic school, I was by virtue of my address regarded by my largely Polish classmates as a rootless cosmopolitan and one of Josef Stalin's useful idiots: aka a Jewish Bolshevik. I don't want to wave the victim flag, but the banter, at times, got savage.

The more assimilated of their number were all quite glamorous. Have I seen *Schindler's List*? I was *on* Schindler's list – Dr Schindler my dentist that is. He was a recent arrival from Germany and would say 'goodbye' in lieu of 'hello', and vice versa, but he remains nevertheless the only dentist I ever met who wasn't an arsehole (apart from the late Dougie Green).

Mr and Mrs Freedman, who owned the chemist's on the ground floor of our building, were a significant fixture in my life. Leonard Freedman was an extremely suave individual. A wearer of cravats, a drencher of colognes, he even affected a beard, meticulously topiarised into the then popular Vandyke style. Mrs Freedman, also a trained apothecarist, was pretty hot: picture an off-the-shoulder Breton-style matelot top, paired with pastel pedal-pushers and a pair of espadrilles, all totally St Trop. Given the location, this look occasionally seemed incongruous, even in the summer months. The dichotomy, however, worked in her favour.

Everyone's home, for better or worse, has an odour, and the smell of one's own home can never be known. This source of olfactory anxiety was obviated in our case, however, by the proximity of Freedman's pharmacy, which meant that our place reeked of cocaine, its ethereal omnipresence at once aseptic, astringent, and clean. At that time most people would have recognised the smell of cocaine due to its use in dental procedures: you could choose a general anaesthetic in the form of nitrous oxide gas that put you in a coma, or you could opt for a local anaesthetic – invariably cocaine, injected into the gums – and remain conscious. Typically, I took the coma option.

As kids back then, we didn't recognise cocaine as the recreational rock and roll stimulant we know today. No, for us cocaine was synonymous with the worst-case scenario in the world – the dentist. Each school was allocated a dentist: ours was called Dr Frankenstein. I'm not kidding. A date with Dr Frankenstein – the horror, the horror.

Back of house, from my vantage point high atop the fire escape, it was *Coronation Street* for a million miles, with sporadic church spires poking out of the smoky distance. These fading streets were home to almost everybody I knew.

But from the front windows of our various apartments I had a very different view of life. I would look out and see the busiest intersection of the entire pre-motorway North of England teeming with traffic from all over the UK, an endless stream of trucks, cars, coaches, buses, and bikes, all heading to destinations unknown: Glasgow, Leeds, Liverpool, London, Hong Kong.

Rather than looking out of my front door and seeing another front door, I saw a parade of grand, if decaying, architecture. Nobody else that I knew lived on a main road unless their parents had a shop. And even though we lived in a succession of crummy apartments, to me they were superior to the other houses: we had a fridge, a bath, an indoor lavatory, *and* a fire escape.

Aunt Winifred and Uncle Frank lived in Ordsall, near the docks, two bus rides away from our gaff. Even though they had a TV before we did, my cousins Sid and Frankie used to have to come to my house every Friday for a bath, whether they needed it or not.

My only experiences of split-level living coincided with episodes of family illness. For a short time we'd lived at my grandma Barnes's in the immediate period before her death. Later, when my mum went into hospital, I had to live with Aunt Winifred and Uncle Frank in Ordsall, where I was horrified to discover that Sid and Frankie were required to do the washing up after tea. One washed, the other dried. I was appalled.

'What the hell are you doing?' I yelped in a tone of sincere inquisitiveness.

'We're washing up,' they explained.

'What's Auntie Winnie doing that's so important that she can't do the washing up?'

That was my line of thinking, but they said it was only fair because she did all the cooking. 'Of course she cooks your tea!' I protested. 'She's your mother, for God's sake. It's a legal obligation.'

This allocation of labour seemed a pretty rum deal in my opinion – you know, child exploitation, or something. I don't think I ever recovered from that.

Upon her return home from hospital, I regaled my mother with this tale of injustice, and made it clear that although I was very fond of Sid and Frankie, any future sleepovers were out of the question until they reformed their regime.

By contrast, on another occasion when my mum had to go into hospital, I went to stay at my Auntie Marge and Uncle George's house, where I was treated like fucking gold. It was a novelty for Auntie Marge to have a lad in the house, and I was consequently spoilt rotten. The most lavish prefabricated desserts were served up on a daily basis: Bird's Instant Whip (a precursor of Angel Delight), Betty Crocker's Pancakes, Symington's Table Creams, and, my favourite, Royal Lemon Meringue Pie. These delights had one thing in common: they all came out of a box and were heavily advertised, with flattering full-colour serving suggestions, in women's magazines.

My short stay at Auntie Marge's was like what they said in the After Eight Wafer Thin Mints advert: 'Luxury – pure, unashamed luxury' – and with no help from me, dishwashing or otherwise.

When it was time for my mum to leave hospital on that occasion,

I wondered whether it would be best all round if they kept her in for further observation. In so doing, I cleverly convinced myself of my own altruistic concern:

'They're not letting her out yet, are they? What? No aftercare? Shouldn't they keep her in another week?'

Chapter Two

THE MOVIES

Alma Cogan had a hit record in 1956 with the verse 'The railroad runs through the middle of the house', which from where I was sitting seemed entirely possible.

The crossroads outside our building was a really happening place. Garment factories; various one-man entrepreneurial dealerships; three barber's shops; Millicent's the ladies' hairdressers; snooker halls; two cabaret joints; two dispensing pharmacies; three medical practices; several movie theatres; various car showrooms; two gentlemen's outfitters; several patisseries; Freda Sieff's bagel joint; Barclays Bank; a launderette; three pubs; three coffee bars; countless confectioners/tobacconists/newsagents; a wine shop; a valet service – that is, a guy, usually a qualified tailor, who carried out invisible mending, steam pressing, miscellaneous alterations, and, where necessary, button replacement; plus the UCP, United Cow Products, which although specialising in many of the less popular ruminant organs was known throughout the industrial North-West as the Tripe Shop . . . All these attractions, just beyond the communal front door.

Next door but one was Harry Davis's Hotel Amanda, the hang-out of Manchester's drag mafia, including club owners such as Frank 'Foo Foo' Lammar, Bunny Lewis, and Jackie Carlton, and from Blackpool, Diamond Lil (baptismal name unknown). After I started school, my mum got a cleaning job there that came with a warning from Harry that she'd have to be 'broad-minded'. 'More like women than women,' was my mum's verdict. I was sceptical about this.

Every weekend there would be a party at the Hotel Amanda, which would always degenerate into a punch-up in its backyard. Up on the fire escape I had a ringside seat, and, take it from an eyewitness, these guys were no ladies. Some of them were rock hard and bad-tempered with it.

The opposite block, dominated by the faience-tiled facade of the majestic Rialto Super Cinema built in the 1920s, housed a parade of shops in the same ornate style: Sid and Aubrey's barber shop, for example, and the Higher Broughton Assembly Rooms.

The Assembly Rooms was a high-end functions venue, available for weddings, bar mitzvahs, twenty-first-birthday celebrations, etc. It boasted a Louis XIV interior featuring indoor fountains picked out by magenta spotlights, and a sprung dance floor in the ballroom. At some point the Assembly Rooms, under new management, was renamed The Whisky-a-Go-Go.

On a Friday night it became The Disc-a-Go-Go, a pre-Beatles teenage nightspot, sometimes involving a local group in the manner of Cliff Richard and the Shadows, but more often it was the first example of something I'd never heard of: a discotheque. The resident DJ was the monstrous Jimmy Savile, who lived nearby.

There were quite a few fires there (possibly insurance related; we will never know), which I observed from our front windows (we made our own entertainment in those days), but the place always rose from the ashes, even exceeding its former splendour.

Occupying the upper floors of this busy commercial parade was Potter's Snooker Club, where all the world-class players from the Barry Hearn stable of the 1980s practised their games. The possession of a Yale key in lieu of a membership card meant that, for them, the club never closed. Since it was on Great Cheetham Street, otherwise known as the A57, it was a straight road to Sheffield and the Crucible Theatre, then as now the national arena of snooker excellence; Potter's, therefore, became a second home to the likes of John Virgo, Alex 'Hurricane' Higgins, John Spencer, Steve 'Interesting' Davis, Dennis Taylor, Jimmy 'Whirlwind' White, and the Canuck contingent featuring the devilishly handsome Cliff Thorburn, Kirk Stevens, and of course Bill Werbeniuk, a man of aboriginal Canadian descent who had somehow finagled an NHS prescription for eight pints of lager, to be taken daily in order to combat the career-threatening effects of the betablockers he took for his high blood pressure.* He was a lager-than-lime character. It was a shame he didn't live long enough to be older Budweiser (geddit?).

The block was dominated, as I said, by the Rialto picture house. When my mum went shopping, she'd stick me in the Rialto and pick me up on the way back. That was my babysitter: the movies.

There were at least half a dozen movie theatres within walking distance. Movies were my life. This enthusiasm was mainly due to my mum. My dad's interest in motion pictures began and ended with Jimmy Cagney, and he was in good company: when Orson Welles was asked to name his three favourite screen actors, he replied, 'That's easy. James Cagney, James Cagney, and James Cagney.' When the emblematic lion came up at the beginning of an MGM feature, it was my dad's cue to stand up and say, 'Seen it . . .' That was his get-out clause.

In fact, my dad only ever took me to see two movies, both in 1956. The first was *The Searchers*, directed by John Ford, starring

---

* These facts can't be entirely verified, but have nevertheless entered the realms of urban mythology. As James Stewart said in *The Man Who Shot Liberty Valance*, 'Print the legend.'

John Wayne, Jeffrey Hunter, and Natalie Wood. The second was *Moby Dick*, directed by John Huston and starring Gregory Peck as Captain Ahab and Richard Basehart as Ishmael.

He took me to see *The Searchers* as a treat for my seventh birthday. It was showing at the Odeon, the hyper-luxurious picture house in Manchester city centre, Odeon being an acronym of Oscar Deutsch Entertains Our Nation – Oscar Deutsch was the entrepreneur responsible for this ubiquitous cinema chain. (Not many people know that, as Sir Michael Caine apparently never said.)

The Odeon was the venue for the Big Night Out – bigger screen, softer seats, stereophonic sound, and a much greater variety of snacks available in the foyer. Rather than the standard popcorn, Paynes Poppets, and peanuts, at the Odeon you could get things like hot dogs, ice-cream floats, various partially gelatinated non-dairy gum-based snack beverages (milkshakes to you), and a profusion of refrigerated fizzy drinks, my choice, as ever, a glass of Pemberton's* – Coca-Cola, that is. Wow! What a flavour – the lightning pick-me-up of the jet age, refreshment guaranteed. Delicious with or without Bacardi, and did you know you can cook with it?

At the smaller local cinemas like the Rialto you could still only get room-temperature, flat fruit squash – give it a name, Kia-Ora! Even so, the Rialto was no slouch: it was a luxury cinema in every other way. The staff were smartly uniformed: the chaps were in fitted burgundy dress jackets with gold-braided *Sgt. Pepper* epaulettes, bareheaded apart from one fella whose job description was 'Fireman' – he wore a peaked military-style cap. For the ladies, i.e. the box-office operative, the usherettes, and the ice-cream girl

---

* Colonel John S. Pemberton, 1831–88, manufacturer of America's premier beverage and nerve tonic – brain food. John Pemberton, we salute your technical expertise.

(the Rialto was an equal-opportunity employer), the livery was a rather attractive, though even then slightly anachronistic, 1940s boogie-woogie-style blouse in cream parachute silk with ballooning diaphanous sleeves that gathered at the wrist – a style popularised by Stewart Granger in the movie *Scaramouche*. This was worn with a neat pencil skirt in the same burgundy cloth as the gentlemen's uniforms, and a little burgundy felt pillbox hat perched on the side of the head. It was all very old school at the Rialto: the women looked like the Andrews Sisters and the men dressed like some sort of military personnel.

When my dad was working away, I was required to accompany my mother on her thrice-weekly visits to the flicks. Two of them would be her choice, and the third, usually a Western, would be mine. More often than not, in spite of myself, I found something to enjoy in her 'women's pictures': the killer dialogue, the cars, and the gents' tailoring provided adequate distraction, not to mention the amplified attractiveness of the leading ladies in such films as *The Best of Everything*, *Peyton Place*, *The Opposite Sex*, and anything involving Doris Day.

Doris Day was a great favourite of ours. A dream girl in every sense, she existed in her own golden microclimate of glamour. Her singing voice alone justified every ounce of her stardom. She was without doubt the most beautiful woman I had ever seen at that point, and as a screen actress, utterly convincing. I can't be the only guy for whom Doris Day was the first ideal woman. 'The Black Hills of Dakota' is a constant on my daily-revised *Desert Island* playlist.

With a couple of exceptions, I consider the hours spent watching these 'women's pictures' to be golden, the first exception being *Gone with the Wind*, which I saw under sufferance. The only light relief from Vivien Leigh's capricious toings and froings between Leslie Howard and Clark Gable was the Civil War massacre scene. 'This is more like it,' I thought. It started to look like a cowboy film for a bit, with all the dead bodies. But no, it was over in ten minutes! The Civil War was a mere backdrop to this fickle woman's ups and downs. There was no lifestyle advice whatsoever to be gleaned from this depiction of the secessionist Southern states. The message I took from that three hours and thirty-one minutes was this: 'Ah, perfidy. Thy name is Woman', a sentiment reinforced by every *Popeye* cartoon.

What is it with Vivien Leigh? She also starred in *The Deep Blue Sea*, the second exception, and the film I blame for my ongoing nervous disposition. Its opening shot of Vivien's head in a gas oven introduced me to the idea of suicide.

'She's trying to kill herself? What the . . .? Huh? What's the matter with this woman? She's got it all. A pretty face, fine gowns, and a nice apartment in London.'

It seemed to me the dumbest thing anybody could possibly do.

'What? Is she insane?'

My mum tried to close down this line of enquiry by telling me that Vivien's character had had a nervous breakdown.

'What's one of them?' I asked. 'Is she retarded or something, or is she a nutter?'

'No, no, it's her nerves. She had a nervous breakdown. She's not a nutter: a nervous breakdown can happen to anyone.'

That was the worst thing she could have said. (NB: Be careful what you say to your kids, even if you're a nice person, it could be the wrong thing.)

'What, anyone? Just suddenly, like? So everything is normal, and it can just happen to anyone? What are the symptoms?'

I figured that any minute now I was either going to have a nervous breakdown myself, or a nuclear war would break out in the wider Cold War world. One way or another, these factors militated against any future contentment. Even when everything seemed to be going in my favour, my thoughts would inevitably turn to the possible foreshortening of that situation. I don't think I've ever lost this fear. It turned me into a default existentialist by the time I was six: I quickly learned that the pursuit of happiness is largely pointless, happiness being the only target one merely has to aim at in order to miss. And you know what planted that seed? Not Jean-Paul Sartre, not Albert Camus, not Søren Kierkegaard, but the idea that I might lose control of my mental faculties, at any time, in any situation, any minute now.

Movies were the cause of, and the antidote to, most of my personal anxieties. What better distraction than the messed-up lives of others played out beneath the big skies of Montana? America featured big in my imagination, and I was a willing recipient of this cultural hegemony. Divorce, for example, was an American import that I discovered from the movies. It seemed to me that over there it was possible to get married in Las Vegas, get a quickie divorce in Tijuana on the same day, and wake up the next day like it never happened. Back then, divorce was something I only associated with Americans – over here, meanwhile, divorce was inevitably seen as a personal catastrophe, and marriage remained a life sentence. That situation persisted until the mid-Seventies with only rare exceptions.

Divorce aside, movie dialogue raised many other questions for me. What is *ravioli*? What is *our* ZIP code? What is a *pizza*? Is *garbage* the same as rubbish? Why don't our policemen have guns? What is *7-Up*? When will the electric chair replace the hempen noose for the dispatch of murderers? Then there was the matter of water management, and the American superiority in that field. They had showers; no sitting around in their own filth for them. And while we're at it, where was our swimming pool?

Most Saturdays I went to the kids' afternoon matinee at the County, a movie house less than two minutes from the fire escape. The County had a two-tier pricing policy: the best seats in the rear stalls cost ninepence, the front stalls just sixpence, owing to the stiff neck one would acquire and the perspectival distortion of the on-screen action. My friends' and my MO was to purchase sixpenny tickets, wait for the lights to go out, and then, much to the annoyance of all the people settling down to watch the movie, crawl commando-style under the seats, all the way to the comparative luxury of the ninepennies: anything for a buck.

Whoever put those kids' matinee programmes together really had their finger on the collective pulse: something for everyone. Before the main feature, usually a Western featuring the likes of Roy Rogers, Johnny Mack Brown, or Gene Autry – that or the Bowery Boys – you'd have half a dozen cartoons: the whole Looney Tunes crowd, *Bugs Bunny*, *Tweety and Sylvester*, *Road Runner*, and my favourite, I say my favourite, *Foghorn Leghorn*, along with *Popeye*, *Tom and Jerry*, *Mr Magoo*, and several two-reelers featuring the Three Stooges. The sound effects to the hilarious violence of the Stooges were right up our street.

The programme ended each week with a serial. *Flash Gordon*, *Congo Bill* (a pith-helmeted detective whose beat happened to be the perilous snake-ridden jungles of Central Africa), *Hop Harrigan* (a P.I. in possession of a biplane), and *The Batman* (directed by Lambert Hillyer in the 1940s, featuring Lewis Wilson as the caped crusader and J. Carrol Naish as his sinister arch-nemesis Dr Daka). Each episode concluded with a cliff-hanging situation, the resolution of which guaranteed further attendance next Saturday.

Then there were the afore-referenced Bowery Boys, who started out as the Dead End Kids in possibly the greatest motion picture of all time, *Angels with Dirty Faces*, the 1938 crime drama directed by Michael Curtiz for Warner Brothers, with Jimmy Cagney taking star billing over Humphrey Bogart, along with the saintly Pat O'Brien as Father Jerry Connolly.

The Dead End Kids played a gang of street urchins who congregated around the New York waterfront, captivated when Cagney's character, the notorious gangster William 'Rocky'

Sullivan, alights from a Duesenberg, accompanied by a swell broad draped in silk, wrapped in mink, jacked up on high heels. He's got it all, that Rocky. The swell broad. The big car. The pale suit. What impressionable punk wouldn't want a piece of that? It had a very contemporary message. In some poor quarters, crime is still regarded as the fast track to the big life.

The Tatler News Theatre on Oxford Street was one of a chain of movie theatres called Jacey, which ran Movietone newsreels. The rest of the programme included the Three Stooges, Laurel and Hardy, and Warner Brothers cartoons: *Road Runner*, *Bugs Bunny*, *Tweety Pie* – a bumper programme on a loop. It was cheaper than most movie houses, so I went there a lot.

If you bought a ticket at 2pm you could sit there and watch the whole programme over and over until the theatre closed down at ten o'clock. People used to arrive in the middle of a movie, then leave when the programme reached the point where they came in.

Chapter Three

LACK OF TEAM SPIRIT

Nobody is born with the ability to read, but I have no memory of the pre-literate life. And so it is here that I must grudgingly thank the teaching profession. I assume I acquired the rudiments quite rapidly, when at the age of four I took my place at St Thomas's Roman Catholic Primary, a short bus ride from home.

I fucking hated school right from the start. The only thing that got me in there was when, as some kind of blackmail technique, my mum told me that, apparently, the school board sent these guys, like detectives, around the streets, and if they saw a school-age child at large, they took him home and then arrested his mum. The very idea of my mum in a jail house was so abhorrent that I couldn't let it happen. What kind of lousy kid would want that on their conscience? So, school it had to be.

An ongoing issue at school was my 'lack of team spirit', a personality disorder, which was assiduously pointed out in every end-of-term report.

You make the best of things when you know there isn't any escape, and when it came to the three Rs — well, two out of three ain't bad, and I quickly learned that writing and arithmetic do not begin with the letter 'R'.

The acquisition of a library card and the profusion of comic books in the local newsagents souped up my enthusiasm, but in their absence, I would read anything in sight: Mary Grant's problem page in *Woman's Own*; the *Football Pink*; processed food ingredients (I started that craze); and, of course, cereal box information: Niacin – check, Thiamine – check, Riboflavin – wadda you think?

It was just such a box that provided an early glimpse of the outside world. Of Welwyn Garden City, that is. Home of the Welgar Shredded Wheat Factory. The bright yellow carton showcased its go-ahead, extravagantly glazed factory building with adjacent grain silo, a gigantic Shredded Wheat hovering overhead like an edible Zeppelin.

'Well Wyn Garden City, eh?' I didn't know how to pronounce it, nor its geographical position. Somewhere near London, perhaps.

'A city? In a garden? . . . What the . . .? Huh?'

The National Breakfast, Shredded Wheat has been around since 1893 – part of the spartan nutritionist movement spearheaded by Dr Kellogg and the unfortunate guinea pigs at his Battle Creek Sanitarium in Michigan, USA, where he disseminated the then fashionable ideas of vegetarianism, exercise, nudism, and racial purification (beginning in the large intestine). The field of eugenics was gaining traction among the social improvers of the age – George Bernard Shaw, H. G. Wells, Francis Galton, Sidney and Beatrice Webb, and Bertrand Russell (who advocated the issue of 'procreation tickets'). It wasn't until the proactive policies of the Nazis that these so-called progressive ideals were discredited. Terrible. On the other hand, weird manifesto aside, who doesn't like Cornflakes? And have you tried Frosties? They're grrrrreat.

Like most wheat-based breakfast foods (and Shredded Wheat is whole wheat – nothing added, nothing taken away!), the promotional artwork featured a child, in this case brandishing a wooden sword and wearing an origami pirate hat made from a sheet of newspaper. The use of children in the promotion of breakfast foods probably harks back to 1902 and Sunny Jim, the public face of Force Flakes, depicted in all his supercharged vitality on every box, wearing some kind of crackpot jug hat, accompanied by the following verse:

High o'er the fence leaps Sunny Jim,
Force is the food that fortifies him.

This health emphasis still persists in the less sugar-centric side of the industry, where flavour takes second place to fibre, the front runner being Kellogg's All Bran. And don't forget those also-brans like Raisin Bran, Sultana Bran, Bran Flakes, Crunchy Bran, and, my least favourite of all, Weetabix.

My mum had this special-occasion hat, one of those Fifties items – basically a piece of moulded velveteen with a touch of netting, a bit like the fascinators you see at modern weddings. It was a kind of one-size-fits-all matador style.

We had somehow inherited the last of the wind-up gramophones, which was housed atop a Queen Anne-style cabinet, with a cupboard below for the storage of shellac 78s. Why we had this, I do not know, because it was an antique even then. My mum kept her special matador hat in the gramophone cabinet. Once while we were looking after Auntie Winnie's cat I grabbed the matador hat, the better to go into my usual routine involving a red rag, a wooden sword, and an imaginary bull, and found it full of what I thought to be Weetabix.

It was *Death in the Afternoon*, almost, when my mum told me that I was mistaken and it was actually semi-calcified cat shit. I'd never seen cat shit before, but as I discovered, in its desiccated format it was exactly the same colour and consistency as Weetabix that had been hanging around for a while. I guess the proximity of the main road rendered outdoor defecation hazardous to the beast, so God knows how long it had been using Mum's hat as a litter tray.

Thanks to this early lesson in the dangers of pet ownership, I've never eaten Weetabix since, even though the serving suggestions in *Woman's Own* were really quite attractive. A strawberry perched on top of a blob of crème fraiche is, however, purely cosmetic. It's still Weetabix underneath, the brutalist breakfast of the worried well, with all its colon-scouring virtue intact. And if it can be mistaken for cat shit, I'm not interested: it's off the menu.

In that respect, I'm a Shredded Wheat guy all the way, although it is only made edible by the addition of hot milk and sugar. For some reason, cold milk will not assist its swallowability. At some point the Welgar marketing department tried to introduce exciting new serving suggestions which, if the full-colour illustrations on the side panels of the box were any indication, required no milk at all. One was a fried egg on a neat row of Shredded Wheat. Imagine eating that with a knife and fork. Given the consistency of an unadulterated Shredded Wheat – kind of springy and brittle at the same time – it would be flicking egg all over the place.

As soon as I could, I read the newspapers. Every day the paperboy delivered the *Daily Mirror* and the *Daily Worker/Morning Star*, except Sundays, when we got the *News of the World* and the *Sunday Express* on account of its superior football coverage. When the *Express* arrived, I'd go straight to the comics page and 'The Adventures of Rupert Bear'.

Comic books and cartoons were an important early source of reading matter. The Rupert Bear strips were ingenious in that they offered three speeds of reading: you could read just the one-line heading at the top of the page; the full story text in prose underneath the pictures; or a simple rhyming couplet beneath each illustration that summed up everything in the text . . . ideal for the beginner reader. I got the hardback annual for Christmas every year.

The weekly comics were delivered with the papers, in my case the *Dandy* and the *Beano*, both of which had the kind of delinquent energy so necessary to any publication aimed at children, with a house style that was *Viz* without the filth. Other weekly comics were swapped with my pals at school, so that one way or another it was possible to read them all: the *Beezer*, the *Topper*, the *Tiger*, the *Victor*.

I used to collect cowboy comics published by a company called L. Miller & Son based in Hackney Road in London. They did reprints of Marvel titles like *Gunsmoke*, *The Human Torch*, *Captain Marvel*, *Rawhide Kid*, *Kid Montana*, and some original Western titles including *Colorado Kid*, *Davy Crockett*, *Kid Dynamite*, *Pancho Villa*, *Rocky Mountain King*, and *Marvelman*. When I got spends, I'd buy sweets and one of these comics which cost a shilling or sixpence. My favourite was *Kid Colt Outlaw*, whose hero was a sort of misunderstood teenager on the run on account of a murder he didn't commit.

Later on, I got the *Eagle*, which was a bit more grown-up, and distinctly imperialistic in tone. It featured serialised articles, such as the life of Winston Churchill, on its back page, and I think my parents bought it for me in hopes that I'd grow up into some sort of responsible citizen or something. It also had some handy bits – for example, fishing advice straight from the river bank, courtesy of George Cansdale; a page with useful table-tennis pointers from Johnny Leech; and 'Stay Safe', road-safety tips from motorcycle champion John Surtees, e.g. 'I notice some herberts are still riding their bikes without a skid-lid, this has to stop, blah, blah, blah' – that I found interesting, but although I liked it, I never really grew out of the *Beano*. That, and later, *Mad* magazine, another of my all-time favourites.

Every ten years or so, a type of humour comes along that seems designed to alienate the older generation. In the Fifties, *The Goons*; in the Sixties, *Around the Horne*; in the Seventies,

Monty Python's Flying Circus; in the Eighties, the excellent Vic Reeves and Bob Mortimer; and more recently, I would suggest, *The Mighty Boosh.*

Similarly, in the world of comics, the arrival in Britain of the American *Mad* magazine around 1958 was a defining moment. For a start, it was aimed at adults as well as children, and not just any adults, but those who were socially aware and media-literate before these terms existed. In other words, *Mad* took the cultural piss, establishing in me a ready appreciation of the new 'sick' American comedians like Mort Sahl and Lenny Bruce. Before I actually read it I'd seen it on the news stands, and had been immediately impressed by the emblematic features of ultra-nerd Alfred E. Neuman, the very face of *Mad* magazine – with his jug ears, freckles, and goofy anarchic dentition, this seemed to me the most stupidly happy face I'd ever seen. In fact, if I ever get a tattoo, he will be it. I first read the magazine in hospital after having my tonsils removed at the age of about ten, when the guy in the next bed lent me his copy. Whenever the voice of the editor, Al Feldstein, made itself known, he took care to give the impression that, in his opinion, the fact that you were even reading his publication marked you out as a clod, a moron, a schlemiel.

While I was still at primary school, I used to get *Modern Screen* magazine from Mr Korn downstairs. He had a brother in Chicago who would occasionally send him parcels of American goods, and having no interest in any of this stuff, Mr Korn would hand it straight over. In one such parcel I got a two-tone bowling shirt, duck-egg blue with a canary-yellow stripe running down either side. It was a generous fit for me at the age of nine, but I'd recently seen Gene Vincent in the movie *The Girl Can't Help It* wearing this very style. A precious gift from that wonderland of treasures, the USA.

Mainly, though, there'd be American comic books: cowboy

stories, like *Johnny Thunder*, a rebel gunslinger in a buckskin bolero jacket; graphic true-crime series, including *Justice Traps the Guilty* and *District Attorney*, which had sensationalist stories of low-rent punk mobsters; and various movie-related magazines including *Photoplay* and the aforementioned *Modern Screen*.

Photoplay and *Modern Screen* dominated the fanzine market, the main attraction being their constantly feuding star gossip columnists. *Photoplay* had Hedda Hopper and Walter Winchell, while *Modern Screen* had Faith Baldwin and Hopper's sworn enemy, Louella O. Parsons, a former Hollywood actress who liked to boast that she was 'the first movie columnist in the world'.

With stories such as 'Doris Day's Summer Wardrobe', 'My Love Affair with Brigitte', 'When will Rock Hudson Finally Quit his Wild Ways and Settle Down with That Special Girl?', and 'Debbie Rebuilds her Shattered Life: A Story of Courage Every Woman Should Read', these magazines played a big part in my education. I liked to keep up to date with the antics of the Rat Pack and the ringside commentary on Frank Sinatra and Ava Gardner's tempestuous romance. I was equally entranced by the back-cover advertisements, often featuring Frederick's of Hollywood's Foundation Garments, with artists' impressions of ladies who all seemed to be modelled on Lucille Ball clad only in pointy brassieres and corsets with adjustable arse panels in that horrible Germolene, artificial-limb colour.

In between Mr Korn's sporadic packages, there was the weekly appearance of my mother's *Woman's Own*, providing an update from planet female. I was always quite excited when it arrived each Wednesday.

I'd pay a lot of attention to the full-colour adverts. There'd always be a picture, usually an artist's idealised rendition of the product in question, contextualised in a manner bespeaking a quality of life that anybody in their right mind would aspire to. If the product was soup, you'd see it steaming in a bowl on a gingham tablecloth next to a window through which a heavy storm or a blizzard is visible, and two perishing schoolkids coming up the garden path. What a cosy world awaits them. As they'll tell you at any business college: don't sell the steak; sell the sizzle.

Certain products called for a more exotic approach, evoking a level of sophistication that it seemed to me was known only beyond these shores. There was Cadum soap, for instance, or Camay as it was later known: 'Cadum for Madam, enriched with a Parisian perfume, worth nine guineas an ounce'; Fry's Turkish Delight was 'full of Eastern promise'; meanwhile, they came in search of paradise, and found it in the new Bounty bar, 'by far and away the most exotic chocolate treat', stuffed with 'South Sea island magic' – i.e. desiccated coconut.

And then there were the underwear adverts, specifically those which played on the Freudian anxieties of the modern woman. Try this one: a board meeting (all-male, natch), each attendee around the table staring in open-mouthed acknowledgement of the sudden entrance of one of their wives, clad only in her foundation garments. And, in an anxious font, the shock horror strapline, 'I dreamed my husband saw me in my Maidenform bra.'

For a young fellow the romance stories were a great insight into that eternal, internal question that has perplexed mankind since forever: 'What do women want?' There were more questions than answers, as Johnny Nash pointed out in his song, 'There Are More Questions Than Answers' – especially when it came to the rudiments of reproduction. These I pieced together from the snippets of ill-comprehended information I found in the medical columns.

Whenever I sought further enlightenment from my mother – e.g. 'What's a sanitary pad? What is a period?' – she deftly wriggled out of the embarrassing occasion with the promise of a 'special book' when I was old enough, which would explain everything. But it turned out that I would never be old enough, and then all of a sudden I was too old. One way or another, that book never arrived. But my equally ignorant pals proved to be more than helpful, particularly Broono.

Broono, real name Dennis Brown, was the class's self-appointed sexpert. One of our number had an older sister who had recently started her periods and, concerned, he had turned to Broono for clarification. Broono gave her six months to live.

Despite these regular fake news bulletins, I eventually reached a measure of comprehension. But when Broono first explained the mechanics of sex to me, I reacted with appalled incredulity: 'You dirty bastard! I know my parents, and they would never do something like that!'

The idea of a frank discussion with either of my parents on this matter still creeps me out, beyond the grave. I'm glad it never happened.

'I'll get you that book' – my arse. My mum was always at the library, but she never returned with that book.

Literacy was the solution to every problem at home, and I can't remember a time when I wasn't in possession of a library card. The same went for everybody in the family, apart from Uncle Dennis, who moved in with us just before I started secondary school. While serving his country in the trouble spots of the dying empire, far from the benign reach of the public library system, he had acquired a predilection for the more transportable pulp fiction writers of the day. Dennis and I shared a room, so his rich paperback collection found its way onto my shelves. The fact that these novels were deemed unsuitable for children, given the level of sensational violence and depersonalised sex, only added to their allure, and I read them all.

More wholesome sentiments could be found in the frontier values of the Westerns by the likes of Zane Grey, Luke Short, Jack Schaefer, and Ernest Haycox, in which clear moral values were reinforced. There were no anti-heroes in the pre-psychological universe of the Wild West, where only three conditions applied: good, bad, and dead.

It was also thanks to Uncle Dennis and his softback archive that I became immersed in the morally ambiguous milieu of modern espionage to be found in the adventures of James Bond. The unfathomable nature of the arcane titles alone spoke to my burgeoning poetical sensibilities: *Live and Let Die, For Your Eyes Only, Thunderball, Dr. No, You Only Live Twice* . . .

The deceitful opulence of Bond's lifestyle, with its early stirrings of label snobbery and brand loyalty, instilled in me a desire for a degree of international sophistication. Bond wore only Sea Island cotton shirts; his suits, made by Benson, Perry & Whitley of Mayfair, came with a full chest (not applicable in my case), gently suppressed waist and, round the back, a centre vent (side vents not yet being an option on a single-breasted coat). Roped sleeve heads and gauntlet cuffs also featured. Even his cigarettes were bespoke, a Macedonian blend of Balkan and Turkish tobaccos from Morelands, lit with an oxidised Ronson lighter. He washed his hair with Pinaud's 'Elixir' – 'that Prince of shampoos' – and drank strong black coffee from De Bry in New Oxford Street. Mention is also made of Floris, although the use of cologne is not entirely approved of.

In 1962, when Bond finally made it to the screen in *Dr. No*, I was thus already furnished with the particulars of his appearance and Sean Connery was so visually perfect that I could even discount the inappropriate Scottish brogue. Only a pedantic detail-freak like me would have picked up on the one lapse of sartorial accuracy: Connery's tie was fastened in a Duke of Windsor knot, and although that was my own preference, it was regarded by Bond to be the mark of vanity in a man.

Crime fiction also became inordinately important, providing a glossary of British and American underworld slang. When I discovered a writer I liked, I would exhaust their entire back catalogue: John Creasey's *The Toff*, Leslie Charteris's *The Saint*, *Flesh of the Orchid* by James Hadley Chase, *The Big Sleep* by Raymond Chandler, who created one of the great existential heroes of all time in Philip Marlowe, a tough guy who exemplified Chandler's philosophical musings on the detective story, 'Down these mean streets a man must go who is not himself mean . . .'

Such sentiments would never have occurred to Mike Hammer, Mickey Spillane's hard-nut hero of titles such as *My Gun is Quick*, *The Girl Hunters*, *Kiss Me, Deadly*, *Vengeance is Mine!*, *The Big Kill*, *Murder Never Knocks*, *Kill Me, Darling*, and *I, the Jury*.

Spillane's lurid covers invariably featured a dame in some kind of trouble immediately prior to the timely arrival of Hammer, her knight in tarnished armour. The age of chivalry, twentieth-century style. Forensics, fingerprints, fuhgeddaboudit. Hammer was more the bourbon, bribery, and beatings type.

Meanwhile, on the other side of the tracks, a great favourite of mine, Simon Templar aka The Saint, was part of the gentleman sleuth tradition. Unlike others of his ilk, like Sherlock Holmes or the Honourable Richard Rollison, aka The Toff, Templar's field of operation had a global reach involving transatlantic jet travel, plutocratic yachts, and oligarchic Maltese villas.

And, of course, there were also the police procedurals, as they are now known, highlighting the often humdrum life of the journeyman copper. These usually stuck to the pattern established in 1841 by Edgar Allan Poe in his story 'The Murders in the Rue Morgue'. It was Poe who invented the genre of the omniscient detective with his slightly less intelligent sidekick as narrator. What better device to convey the full marvel of his master sleuth Chevalier C. Auguste Dupin, and his exquisite powers of deduction?

Before the entrance of Uncle Dennis and his collection of pulp fiction, I had acquainted myself with the cream of European and

New World letters courtesy of Gilberton Company, Inc's Classics Illustrated, an improving comic-book imprint from America 'Featuring stories by the world's greatest authors', with great covers and illustrations in very diverse graphic styles.

As a result, at twelve years old, I was conversant in the works of, among others, Alexandre Dumas, Victor Hugo, Samuel L. Clemens, Charles Dickens, and Jules Verne. I was particularly taken by the work of Dostoevsky, specifically *Crime and Punishment*. When Dostoevsky came up in an adult conversation I was all, 'Ah, yes, Raskolnikov. Marvellous. Searing indictment of pre-revolutionary Russia. Yes, yes, Dostoevsky. Giant of Russian literature. You must read him.' Even though I'd only read the sixty-four-page comic-book versions, it didn't matter: they gave you a flavour of the original tome, and the final frame carried the Classics Illustrated line of intent, 'We strongly urge you to read the original.'

The titles were carefully chosen for their suitability to be transformed into the comic-book style: *Ivanhoe* by Sir Walter Scott; *The Black Knight*, *The Black Arrow*; Cyrano de Bergerac (you can see why I identified with him: a romantic swashbuckling poet with an absurd nose); *The Spy* by James Fenimore Cooper; *Frankenstein*; Edgar Allan Poe's *Tales of Mystery and Imagination* and *The Gold Bug*; *Oliver Twist*; *Jane Eyre*; *The Downfall* by Émile Zola (crikey, that was hard going: I used to think thank God I don't live a hundred years ago – the shit that could happen to a guy). I was a sucker for a seafaring yarn: *Moby Dick*, *Two Years Before the Mast*, *Mutiny on the Bounty* taken from the court transcripts of Nordhoff and Hall; and lots of Alexandre Dumas: *The Black Tulip*, *The Man in the Iron Mask*, *The Three Musketeers*, *The Count of Monte Cristo* – I can still see the cover of that one: a man in a striped jailbird's outfit crouched in front of a glowing chest overflowing with bullion, clutching fistfuls of diamond necklaces, a look of deranged greed on his gold-fevered face.

Wherever you could buy *Batman*, *Superman*, and the usual array of comic books, there would always be a selection of Classics Illustrated. They were slightly more expensive, and each one listed all the other available titles on its back cover. Nobody ever had the full set, but there was a bit of that collecting frenzy involved, because my friends and I wanted to read them all. We all traded comic books all the time. In my case, a large cache could also be exchanged for other luxuries – firearms and daggers, for example.

Chapter Four

LISTENING TO THE RADIO

Prior to the demobilisation of Uncle Dennis and his subsequent, though temporary, residence at our place, our only source of music was the Queen Anne wind-up gramophone (minus cat shit) and the ever-present radio.

Sunday lunchtime gave us *Two-Way Family Favourites*, a BBC Light Programme request show on which soldiers stationed in various parts of the disintegrating empire dedicated songs to their sweetheart or 'the best Mum in the world'.

Family Favourites reflected the diverse tastes and the generational span of the armed forces, so for every up-to-the-minute pop hit there might be several requests for the pre-rock-and-roll crooners of the requester's courtship years: Edmund Hockridge, Dennis Lotis, Lita Roza, Pearl Carr and Teddy Johnson, Ella Fitzgerald, Mario Lanza, Jo Stafford, Jane Morgan, Josef Locke, Teresa Brewer, Perry Como, Dean Martin, Sinatra, Johnnie Ray, Mel Tormé, or the King's College Cambridge choir doing Allegri's *Miserere*, or something.

What it had going for it was variety, and I was therefore introduced to the repertoire of songs from the rich history of the English music hall: recordings by performers such as Harry Champion with numbers like 'I'm Henery the Eighth, I Am', 'Any Old Iron', and 'Boiled Beef and Carrots'; Gus Elen, the singing costermonger, with 'Arf a Pint of Ale', 'It's a Great Big Shame', 'Down the Road', and 'Put a Bit of Treacle on My Puddin', Mary Ann'.

My dad and I shared an enthusiasm for one particular classic, 'The Spaniard That Blighted My Life' by Billy Merson.

> When I catch Alfonso Spadone the toreador
> With one mighty swipe I shall dislocate his bally jaw
> I'll catch that bullfighter I will
> And when I do the blighter I'll kill.
> He shall die, he shall die [. . .]
>
> [. . .] And I'll raise a bunion on his Spanish onion
> If I catch him bending tonight. Olé.
> When I get Spadone
> He shall wish he had never been born
> And to this very purpose
> My stiletto I fetched out of pawn
> It cost me five guineas to fetch it
> The cost of it caused me much pain
> But the pawnbroker said
> When I've killed Spadone
> He'll take it in pawn once again.

The romantic superiority of the Latin male had long been a source of public anxiety to Anglo-Saxons, as this Hispanophobic opus perfectly illustrates. Try the version by Al Jolson and Bing Crosby – seldom has homicidal intent been so amusingly expressed.

I had a soft spot for any artiste who delivered lyrics without actually singing, *Sprechgesang* being the Teutonic term for this particular style, exemplified by the likes of Stanley Holloway, who specialised in music hall-style monologues, 'Albert and the Lion', 'Brown Boots', etc. Higher up the social scale, there was Rex

'Sexy Rexy' Harrison, the darling of Broadway with his 'Why Can't a Woman be More Like a Man' from *My Fair Lady*.

Stateside, there was Phil Harris with numbers such as 'Darktown Poker Club', 'That's What I like About the South', and his fabulous rewrite of a sentimental nineteenth-century eco-poem by George Pope Morris, 'Woodman, Spare that Tree'. Harris's version has no pretensions to conservation, however – he wants the tree spared for less altruistic reasons.

> Go chop a birch, an elm or a pine
> But leave old slippery there,
> That's mine.
> That's the only tree my wife can't climb,
> Mr Woodman, spare it for me.

But I was there for the rock and roll.

I was eight in 1957, when 'Diana' by Paul Anka became an ongoing favourite of mine as it hit the international number one spot.

Anka was a schoolboy from Ottawa (Ottawhat???), who by virtue of his songwriting skills and prodigious singing voice became the first teenage pop tycoon, a millionaire sensation.

He'd started a hometown vocal group called the Bobbysoxers when he was only thirteen and won himself a trip to New York by collecting Campbell's soup-can labels for three months; he mithered his parents until they agreed on a trip to Los Angeles, where he rang every record label in the phone book, finally landing an audition with Modern Records.

He was no Elvis – who could be? Elvis was the king of the world – but Paul Anka was the first actual *child* to conquer this world for young people that Elvis had created.

In the pictures I saw in the magazines, with his Semitic good looks and the elegance of his raiment, Paul Anka looked like a lot of the kids in my neighbourhood, and because of this I always assumed he was Jewish. He wore these Rat Pack-style short, boxy, bum-freezer Neapolitan suits that were just becoming available in the high-street ready-to-wear shops. I imagined that there were loads of connections between me and Paul. And yet there he was, dressed like a little prince, chicks falling all over themselves to get next to the guy. Female company was always important, and if a chubby kid from Ottawa could get it . . . Why not me?

That was the point of identification: the status of Elvis was obviously unassailable, existing as he did in a position of supremacy that no other man could possibly inhabit. But maybe Paul Anka's level, remote as it might have appeared, was more accessible.

'Lonely Boy', the follow-up to 'Diana', became the incidental music to my protracted exile in North Wales (of which more in Chapter Six). What with my flair for self-dramatisation, the lyrics fed right into my overwrought view of my condition: 'I'm just a lonely boy, lonely and blue, I'm all alone, with nothing to do . . .'

See what I mean? Fucking tragic.

'Lonely Boy' was also a great favourite of World Heavyweight Champion Cassius Clay: Muhammad Ali to you. In 1963 the two men would meet by chance in the lobby of the Sahara Hotel, Las Vegas, resulting in an a cappella duet of the song. The pugilist was himself in possession of a fine singing voice – I would refer you to his version of the Ben E. King hit 'Stand by Me', recorded earlier that year.

But back in 1957 or 1958, everyone was convinced that rock and roll would be over in two years; the phenomenon of the teenage idol was unprecedented, and there was no reason to believe that the whole shebang wasn't just a flash in the pan. Even if it did outstay its welcome, nobody over twenty-one would be singing it. Bobby Darin, Sam Cooke, Frankie Avalon, Bobby Rydell, and all the real big hitters of the late Fifties teen-pop world truly believed that they had an imminent sell-by date, and with that in mind they perfected a more lounge-friendly, more adult repertoire.

From about 1958 onwards, I went to see every rock and roll star possible: Jerry Lee Lewis, Little Richard, Eddie Cochran, Gene Vincent, the Everly Brothers, Dion, Freddy 'Boom Boom' Cannon, Joey Dee and the Starlighters, Del Shannon; all courtesy of the capo di tutti capi of Manchester's music business, Don Arden, with a little help from Harvey Lizberg, Rick Davis, and Danny Betesh at Kennedy Street Enterprises.*

Don Arden (born Harry Levy, Cheetham Hill, Manchester) was responsible for bringing all the big stateside acts to Manchester. He was himself a recording artist, having released albums of Hebrew and Yiddish songs and, more recently, two versions of 'Sunrise, Sunset' from the Broadway musical *Fiddler on the Roof*. He was in fact a gifted cantor with a voice that could charm the birds out of the trees.

Having said that, don't go mistaking Don Arden for some whole other body. He was a Hightown hard nut, the archetypal two-fisted pop impresario with a reputation for having dangled some troublemaker by his ankles from a high window. He is remembered not only for this, but for his claim 'I never exploited anybody who didn't want to be exploited.'

Mr Arden's package shows would be advertised months in advance via the entertainment section of the *Manchester Evening News* and on fly-posters all around town. They would sell out immediately. The shows, usually at the Apollo Theatre, which is still in operation today, ran from 7 to 10pm. I would arrive in the afternoon, when all the equipment was being delivered, slide into the loading bay, then slip round to the front-of-house and select a seat. As long as I didn't make a nuisance of myself or get under anybody's feet, I was in for the duration.

* Kennedy Street Enterprises was the North-West's key music promoter and artist management company, founded by hotshot lawyer Danny Betesh.

I saw all those shows, and I never paid the admission. Mr Arden wouldn't have been happy about that. With customers like me, who needs creditors? The basic social skills, plus a degree of personal charm, seemed to work in my favour, and I've continued in that vein ever since – now, sometimes I even get an invite.

Chapter Five

A SPLASH OF COLOUR

When I first saw *Coronation Street* on a colour television, it seemed utterly wrong and unrealistic. I would always turn the colour off; you could do that then.

I feel the same way about Cumbria. In the collective imagination the Lake District is a place of outstanding natural beauty, the acme of poetical inspiration, what with William Wordsworth and his daffodils. Granted, the sighting of a daffodil would be an explosive sensual assault in the Romantic poets' sodden universe of grief. Let's face it, it's either raining, or dripping off the trees. No wonder they were all on the Black Drop.

Until around 1955, it seemed to me that colour itself was on the ration books. There were very few daffodil moments – maybe the odd lavishly festooned hearse. Other than that – nish.

Well, not entirely nish. There was the fishmonger's; the green-grocer's; three neighbourhood municipal parks with the odd herbaceous border; my mum's women's magazines, specifically *Woman's Own* and *Woman*; travelling fairgrounds; tropical fish; comic books; and, of course, Technicolor movies were Paramount (no pun intended).

At the time I'm talking about, however, drapers, haberdashers, and outfitters stocked only forty-eight shades of grey, with the odd fleck of bottle-green or lovat thrown in here and there. Similarly, cars, like footwear, were available in black, brown, or a kind of dull burgundy, and had all the visual allure of a magnified bedbug.

The packaging of household items – scouring powder, carbolic soap, various tracklements and canned goods – was mostly monochrome, worthy, and utilitarian. No pictures. Apart from the over-excitable breakfast-food market, there was a studious avoidance of hype: Petroleum Jelly, BP. Andrews Liver Salts. California Syrup of Fig. ACDO Detergent.

Other than apples, I thought every fruit with any colour in it was imported from the empire. Everything I saw on a packet of fruit pastilles – lemon, lime, orange, blackcurrant, raspberry, strawberry – I couldn't believe that any of that could grow in this country. I wouldn't have seen a blackberry bush, or raspberries, or strawberries growing in Salford, ever. You didn't see them in greengrocers' either, or at least I didn't, except occasionally maybe a punnet of gooseberries.

It was only thanks to Jerry Lewis and Dean Martin in those fabulous Frank Tashlin movies that I realised that colour was even possible in everyday life. The hyper-bright American Technicolor world depicted in *Who's Minding the Store* or *Hollywood or Bust* exposed me to the synthetic colours and general level of overstimulation only available stateside.

Sure, Technicolor had been around for a while by then – used to great effect by Walt Disney and in films of the 1930s such as *The Wizard of Oz* and the hateful *Gone with the Wind* – but up until the mid-Fifties it had really only been seen to its best advantage in outdoor movies, Westerns notably, in which, irrespective of the main guy, the co-star was always the endless expanse of America itself. And while Technicolor was essential in conveying this land of natural promise, it really came into its own in the post-war world of revolutionary new dyes and the boom in conspicuous consumption – soda fountains spouting neon-raspberry pop; the metallic iridescence of America's space-age cars; the scratch-your-eyes-out aniline colours of their resort wear. Technicolor alone could capture this.

Movies really were America's shop window, a great opportunity to show off the kind of consumer durables that were becoming generally available at that time: pop-up toasters, fridges, spin-dryers and Hoovers, all with a candy-coloured showroom patina, dressed in the finest chrome. In any *Tom and Jerry* cartoon these household appliances attain the magnitude of architecture.

Pretty soon the world around us began to brighten up for real, and quite swiftly too. Prior to Manchester's post-war redevelopment, the city's many bomb craters were obscured by gigantic billboards advertising confectionery, soap powder, cigarettes, booze, and, of course, an ever-expanding range of breakfast cereals, with a bowl of the Sunshine Breakfast being amplified a million-fold, pop art before the event.

The products depicted therein began to jazz up the shelves of the pre-supermarket corner shops. It seemed that everything was in ascendance; there were perceptible improvements year after year, and there was no reason to suspect that this trajectory of excellence would ever be curtailed.

Car ownership was aggressively recommended. Pastel shirts gained respectability in the world of menswear, and the sporting of suede shoes ceased to be an arrestable offence. The short back and sides, with its unwelcome reminder of military life, was so last decade, and a wider range of tonsorial options was now presented to the modern man. It was bananas all round, and at last, my first taste of 7-Up.

This wasn't all down to the Americans. Thanks in no small part to Cinecittà studios, a bequest of the late Benito Mussolini, the competitive cost of film production in Italy helped to postpone the decline of the American movie industry, then suffering from the effects of mass television ownership. A state-of-the-art

studio and an infinite supply of extras willing to work for four
meals a day provided an added attraction. Hollywood on the Tiber,
hence that era's preponderance of Biblical epics and any historical
feature requiring multitudes.

Italy began to inform the styles in America, and by extension,
the world. For a while, La Bella Figura was the main thing in
town, even in Hollywood, where all the leading ladies were now
dressed by Fontana, Brioni, and Gucci. In William Wyler's 1953
Roman Holiday, a monochrome travelogue taking in the landmarks
of the eternal city by way of Audrey Hepburn and Gregory Peck
on board a Vespa, Peck's character is shown clad in an early
approximation of the Continental suit: single-breasted, minimal
structure, tight arm holes and scooped-out breast pocket, natural
shoulder, narrow lapels, three buttons, all in a pale summer-weight
fabric. This would later be exaggerated in the thirty-eight-gram
suits affected by the Modernists of Soho circa 1958, or as it was
known in America, the 'jivy Ivy look'.

La Dolce Vita: scooters and cars and Gaggia espresso machines
in chrome, cream, and sky blue: the colour scheme of the Via
Veneto. The first local stirrings of this Italian style supremacy
became evident at the barber's I frequented in the parade of shops
adjoining the Rialto. At some indeterminate point around 1958,
Sid and Aubrey, the brothers Silverstein, had a big revamp and
went totally Italian, what with the Tony Curtis quiffs and their
matching new three-quarter-length work jackets. Although it
seemed that their former Jewish knockabout cynicism had given
way to a jaunty life-affirming Johnny Baloney-type bonhomie, it
remained the number-one source of irreverent off-colour humour.
For example:

'Two Jewish lads are walking past a Catholic church. There
is a sign nailed to the door: *Introductory offer, one week only.*
Anyone converting to Catholicism gets £25.

One lad says to the other, "I'm going to have a word with this guy. I'm very interested in comparative religions. Come with."

To which his friend Howard replies, "Stuart, it's a free country. You can do what you like but count me out. I'll wait here. Don't be too long."

Twenty minutes later Stuart returns. "Did you go ahead with it?" says his friend.

"Yes, he was a very persuasive man."

"Did you get the twenty-five quid?"

"Howard, is that all you people think about?" '

Prior to the Silversteins' makeover, small children would be perched on a plank across the arms of a normal barber's chair. Now they had these space-age pneumatic jobs, in ribbed chrome with candy-apple red, wipe-clean leatherette seats, and pump-action height-adjustment apparatus fitted as standard.

Sid and Aubrey's new three-quarter-length jackets were custom-made in matching candy-apple red. They had a scooped-out breast pocket to house scissors, razors, clippers, and combs, with a styl-ised half-belt at the back, and sleeves truncated just below the elbow: 100% pure nylon. You'd hear the static swish of the fast-moving thermoplastic as they zipped around, snipping away.

After this complete Continental makeover, you'd see any number of trainee playboys and residual spivs wanting in on the crucial Italianate look, all heading to Sid and Aubrey's for the full hot-towel treatment, not to mention the opportunity to purchase any one of the new array of unguents, tonics, astringents, and pomades, and, lending its fragrance to the entire saloon, the cologne du jour, Acqua di Selva by Visconti di Modrone.

All the 'Something for the weekend, sir?' schtick went straight over my left shoulder, although the meaning of the 'Durex for Family Planning' sign invited curiosity, as did a complimentary calendar promoting 'Veribest Surgical Rubber Wear', which was apparently 'Sensitol lubricated' and 'electronically tested'.

Further afield, the beautification process extended to architecture and, around 1959, the introduction to Manchester of the skyscraper in the form of office blocks and apartment buildings. I had a friend (Georgie Williams, of whom more later) who lived on the fifteenth floor of one of the very first of its kind, in Silk Street, Salford. The foyer featured a huge primary-coloured abstract mural in the manner of Fernand Léger. Modern art: get used to it. The apartments themselves were amenable to solar illumination, airy, hygienic, easily maintained, with 100% Enkalon fitted carpets throughout. This was luxury you could afford – by Cyril Lord.*

I left home three years before my family was rehoused in the Seventies, so I never experienced this much-anticipated domestic utopia. Still, you can't have everything – where would you put it?

My mum fancied herself as the female equivalent of Percy Thrower, but the nearest thing she ever got to a garden was the balcony of her new ninth-floor apartment, which proved to be a sun trap facilitating the cultivation of tomatoes, beans, and geraniums. Just add water.

---

* Cyril Lord, aka the Carpet King, purveyor of the revolutionary wall-to-wall fitted carpet in 'virtually indestructible', deep synthetic nylon pile, direct from the Donaghadee, N. Ireland factory, at factory prices. The full TV advertising jingle went like this:

> This is luxury you can afford by Cyril Lord –
> Squash it, and it just springs back,
> Wash it, and the colour stays fast,
> Give it the treatment, the family treatment,
> Enkalon is made to last for years and years and years and years . . .
> This is luxury you can afford by Cyril Lord!

Chapter Six

THE CAPTAIN OF ALL THESE MEN OF DEATH

As a seasoned didaskaleinophobe, I was always eager for any excuse to skip school. Luckily, at the age of eight, escape came in the form of affliction. It was a case of tuberculosis to the rescue.

My mum's youngest sister, Irene, who lived in North Wales, had recently died of the disease. Did she get it from me, or did I get it from her? Or neither of the above? The source of infection remains unclear, but I was taken out of school and returned to the very hospital where I had been born.

Sadly, in Auntie Irene's case her condition was too advanced for her to survive, but for a newcomer like me, there was never a better time to have tuberculosis. One year earlier it would have been curtains, but the timely discovery of streptomycin, isoniazid, and all manner of other delicious pharmaceuticals, along with the newly established National Health Service, guaranteed my ongoing staying-alive-type situation.

Other than the night sweats and the hacking up of much arterial claret, alarming though that was, I don't actually remember feeling particularly inconvenienced. It's not as though I had a glorious sporting career that had been cruelly foreshortened, or anything. And did I mention morphine on tap?

What with the medication and the elasticity of time in the

young mind, I have no idea how long I spent in hospital, but while I was there my parents arranged the apartment swap with the Korns, the better to avoid any further fire escape accidents, and so it was that on my discharge I found everybody and everything was in flux.

I returned to unfamiliar territory, a gloomy set of unestablished rooms, much more disturbing than being in Hope Hospital. In the eye of this storm of confusion sat my granddad, the one still-reassuring presence, with his stack of Rupert books and a pack of cards with which to teach me pontoon, rummy, and snap.

Unlike the upper floors, the new apartment was a place of permanent shadow, and we had to keep the lights on all day. No sooner had I grown accustomed to finding my way around in the dark than I was sent to live with Auntie Irene's widowed husband Eric, their daughter, Estelle, and her two older brothers, Johnny and Billy. They lived in Rhyl, a North Wales seaside resort where it was thought that the fresh sea air might benefit my recovery. In order for my lungs to heal, it was important that I try not to cough. If I ran for any reason I would bring forth all these pints of gunk and scar tissue, so I had to take cough-suppressant medicine for a while, some morphine solution or other in a big bottle.

Uncle Eric lived close to the seafront, in a brand-new corporation settlement called the Marsh Road Estate, which to me seemed like Hollywood or somewhere: pristine white houses, front gardens with flower beds, wide traffic-free streets lined with clean trees.

In the holiday period he was a bus driver. Off-season, a casual labourer, working around the coast repairing the sea defences. Uncle Eric was always in employment, which meant that my cousins were looked after by their grandma, who lived in a big house a few streets away. I, however, was left entirely to my own devices. To send a sickly eight-year-old to live with his recently widowed uncle and his motherless children in a seaside town around which he would be allowed to wander alone in the dead of winter might seem casual by today's standards, but there wasn't much more anybody could do for me, as long as I took whatever medication I had, as and when. It could have been traumatic, but it wasn't. I don't remember feeling homesick, not in the least. Fresh air took priority over everything.

What I remember most about that time with Uncle Eric in Rhyl is that it was utterly liberating: that sense of being taken out of the world, kept off school, being on my own. It was a life unlike that of almost anyone else my age.

I would leave the house at 10am, and wasn't expected back until it was getting dark, even out of season when it was pissing down all the time. Ten in the morning till teatime, that's a helluva lot of 'me time' . . .

It was a lonely existence at first, but there was no shortage of diversion. It was fascinating to see Rhyl deserted like that, stripped of its gaudy, sugary summer-seaside clobber. Then, as spring gave way to summer, and the days lengthened and the temperature rose and, perhaps, the rain held off, I saw it bloom into a place devoted to the pleasures of working-class people (give 'em a name – Scousers). And I'd see the holidaymakers come and the holidaymakers go. It was very poetic, that sense of a town that wakes up in June and then goes back to sleep in September, the facilities of the promenade now idle: the creaking swing, the stagnant paddling pool, invalids of every sort.

There was always somewhere to go to get out of the rain; I just schlepped around the amusement arcades, hung about under the awnings at the pleasure beach, or in the many shops and department stores. Even at home in Manchester I used to do much the same.

Then there was the public library, and of course the movies. Rhyl's showpiece picture theatre was the Odeon, its frontage dominated by an elegant glazed rotunda. Other available cinemas were

the Plaza and the Regal, which would open at 2pm with a con-
tinuous performance through to around 10.30pm. If I was at a loss
for any other form of entertainment, there was always that default
activity of all children – whacking at vegetation with a stick.

The semi-feral life of the solitary trainee boulevardier is all
very well, but for a lonely person, social interaction can sometimes
become a pressing need. At the fairground on the promenade,
where the gypsy operatives were engaged in off-season maintenance
work, I made myself useful by running errands and fetching the
pie and chips at dinner time. In return, I'd get a bottle of Coke
and the odd free dodgem ride. I even acted as unpaid test pilot
on the spanking-new Hurricane Jets, a white-knuckle thrill ride
fitted with a joystick allowing the occupant full altitude control.

Fairgrounds were the great early disseminators of rock and roll.
The first time I heard Elvis it was through the sonic distortion of
Radio Luxembourg, but it was at the fairground in Rhyl that I
heard Elvis's 'All Shook Up', 'Shakin' All Over' by Johnny Kidd
& the Pirates, and 'Cathy's Clown' by the Everly Brothers on a
big sound system for the first time – that was where most people
first heard rock and roll at an actual ear-bursting decibel level that
would have been impossible on any domestic equipment available
at the time. The rackety fairground rides generated a nerve-
jangling clamour all of their own, but the music would always prevail.

It was a zone of full-on sensory overload: the food had too
much flavour, the light was too bright, the music too loud, the
smell of onions all-pervading; everything was drenched in sugar
and colour. What a way to be introduced to rock and roll as a
too-young, restless, hyperactive, overstimulated kid.

Teatime back at Uncle Eric's was altogether more wholesome fare.
Uncle Eric was a proto food crank: although not a vegetarian, he
had a mistrust of refined foods and was an early proponent of

wholemeal bread and brown sugar. I'd never seen brown sugar before. Obviously, I didn't know what it was, but once I found out I was eating it by the dessertspoonful, and sprinkling a generous serving of demerara on top of my Shredded Wheat. As well as baking all his own bread, Uncle Eric dished up home-made curry and rice. I was already a big fan of rice pudding but this savoury option was again something new.

Eric was a real handyman, and was interested in nature and the cosmos. He even had a high-powered telescope trained on the moon from an upstairs window, so I got to see the craters on its surface for the first time.

In Rhyl, I also learned to ride a bike — what a thrill, to stay upright on two wheels — and tasted my first hamburger — cheese-burger, even — from Wimpy, the gold standard in British food at that time. I'd seen hamburgers in American movies and been struck by this most democratic of portable snacks. My mum had occasionally tried to fob me off with something that looked like one: slabs of Fray Bentos corned beef, slices of Spam, deconstructed sausages, slapped inside a banjo with a bit of mustard . . .

Though these sad approximations never fooled me, she would attempt to bottle it out: 'It's a hamburger, I tell you.'

Then somebody like Fray Bentos, or Tom Piper, anyway one of the many canned-meat firms, started making tinned hamburgers: four of them, one atop the other, jammed into a can, about the same size as a small tin of tuna. Now that was the real deal: top-quality reclaimed meat expertly minced and ingeniously stuck back together in hygienic factories. My mum even induced some caramelisation around the edges for that all-important crispy finish.

Chapter Seven

TELEVISION

Upon my return from Rhyl, I found school to be even worse than I remembered it. At an age when one should be vigorous, adventurous, and bold, there was I, the model of opiated detachment in a realm that insisted upon itself.

In the school playground, everybody but me was singing ditties from the TV adverts. Thanks to the Cadbury's Drinking Chocolate commercial, there was now a new reply to the simple question 'What's the Time?': 'It's chocolate time.' This caught on like wildfire, as did many of the TV punchlines and jingles of the day.

'Omo washes not only white, not only white but bright.'
'Go, go, go, never, never go. Never go without, never go
    without a Capstan, Capstan, Capstan. Wherever you go,
    never go without a Capstan!'
'You'll wonder where the yellow went, when you brush your
    teeth with Pepsodent.'
'Silvikrin for lovely hair, Silvikrin for lovely hair, Silvikrin
    shampoo.'
'Bel Air, Bel Air, Bel Air, Bel Air
    Bel Air has a flair for hair.'

If you think that's emphatic, try this one:

'Morton, Morton, Morton, Morton, Morton, Morton garden
peas. Morton, Morton, Morton, Morton, Morton, Morton
garden peas. Why does everyone love Morton garden peas?
Because Morton taste better. Morton taste better. Morton
taste better.'

As you can see, stylistically speaking, detailed product analysis
took second place to repetition.

Due to our lack of a television set, I was cruelly excluded from
these little sing-songs. This situation was rectified when we finally
acquired a rented Phillips 23-inch in 1958, the year Pope Pius XII
died. I remember the precise date of this momentous event because
anybody in our school whose family had a telly was allowed to
go home in order to watch the funeral of the outgoing pontiff.
From the first day, TV ownership was paying out. I got the rest
of the afternoon off, but I didn't watch the funeral of Pius XII
– I watched *Popeye the Sailor*.

Popeye was on at six o'clock every evening. Unmissable. Each
episode reaffirmed my growing comprehension concerning the
true story of men and women since year zero. Fickle Olive,
whose affections are constantly veering between, on the one
hand, Popeye, the spinach-munching embodiment of all civilised
values, tough, well-meaning, kind; and on the other, Bluto, the
ugly mug of unfettered nature, lustful, deceitful, and cruel. These
nightly cartoons, coupled with the invaluable insights of Broono,
the class sexpert, rendered the non-appearance of 'that book'
irrelevant.

Every weeknight, over on the BBC there was *Tonight*, a magazine programme that went round the provinces reporting on
strange stories, odd phenomena, and the like, presented by Cliff
Michelmore, launching the career of Alan Whicker and featuring

such quirky observers of modern life as Fyfe Robertson, Derek Hart, Julian Pettifer, and Kenneth Allsop.

Whicker is the one that people remember most from *Tonight*, because he seemed to cream off all the most glamorous gigs: Barbados rather than Barnsley, Bermuda rather than Bermondsey . . . (you see where I'm going with this). His meeting with 'Papa Doc' Duvalier and the Tonton Macoute in Haiti was not the sort of cushy number he was accustomed to. In that zone of pure menace there was Whicker, cravated up in his double-breasted navy blazer, his personal charm alone keeping him out of harm's way.

The *Tonight* show also featured guests from the world of folk music – Robin Hall and Jimmie Macgregor from Scotland, for instance, Cy Grant, performing topical calypso, and even an early British appearance by Bob Dylan.

It became a cliché among the usual doom-mongers of the social-improvement industry that television 'destroys the art of conversation', as if every pre-TV family had been a hotbed of informed debate. If anything, owning a telly promoted conversation: at last we had something to talk about. Even with your friends you would say, 'You going to watch "blah blah blah" on telly?'

The concept of the curatory approach to movie history was unknown in 1950s Manchester, and apart from a couple of city-centre venues, the Classic (now the Cornerhouse) and the Cinephone (which featured some of the racier Continental art movies), box-office receipts were the only concern. Movies were entertainment, and to be a cinema goer did not mark you out as 'artistic'. There was a fresh movie every week, and to be interested in a film beyond its normal run would have seemed weird.

From 1958 on, however, I got to see a whole generation of fantastic movies that without a TV I wouldn't even have known about. A film had to be at least five years old before it could be shown on TV, so you'd get some real classics, notably those great Warner Brothers gangster flicks from the Thirties and Forties featuring George Raft, Edward G. Robinson, and Humphrey Bogart, not to mention Jimmy Cagney, Jimmy Cagney, and Jimmy Cagney. These films, intended to highlight the problem of urban delinquency, had instead introduced the idea of the anti-hero and a degree of psychological nuance to cinema goers in the Depression and war years.

No such moral ambiguity was allowable in the popular TV Westerns of the late Fifties: *Cheyenne, Bronco, Maverick, Sugarfoot, Lawman, The Deputy, The Rifleman*, all with complex central characters faced with some kind of spiny ethical situation.

Cheyenne, played by Clint Walker, is shown to be a virtuous drifter, a half-breed saddle-tramp who roams the West, a force for justice in the lawless hick towns, righting wrongs, solving mysteries, and moving on.

Ty Hardin as Bronco, the clue is in his name: a peripatetic, self-employed horse-wrangler from the Texas Panhandle.

Sugarfoot features Will Hutchins as Tom 'Sugarfoot' Brewster, an aspiring lawyer who, forsaking the gun, seeks resolution via the courtroom, thus heralding the end of the Old West.

Lawman starred John Russell as Marshal Dan Troop, whose luxuriant moustache was obviously modelled on the Wyatt Earp handlebar, and Peter Brown as his teen-idol-style deputy, Johnny McKay. Of them all, *Lawman* had by far the best theme song.

All of the above embodied the manly virtues of physical strength, marksmanship, courage, and stoic fortitude in a savage landscape. All of them except every member of the Maverick family.

These were Bret Maverick, played by James Garner; Bart Maverick, played by Jack Kelly; and later Beau Maverick, played by our very own Roger Moore. The Maverick brothers introduced a healthy note of cowardice into the usual proceedings. They were clean-shaven dandy gamblers, lounge lizards who preferred casinos, saloon bars, or the elegant parlours of high-class hotels to the lawless prairies and the perils of the cowboy life. They weren't your usual tobacco-chewing roughnecks, but were accordingly attired in ruffle-shirts, brocade vests, silken neckties, and frock coats. If push came to shove, however, the Mavericks could all handle a gun.

Each complete episode of these Westerns affirmed liberal values. Racial discrimination, whenever it presented itself, was invariably shown to be foolish and wrong. Morality plays, certainly, but done with a light touch, with any social lessons the natural consequence of the overarching human story.

Chapter Eight

THE BLUE ORCHID GANG

When I was about eleven I fell in with a group of lads who lived in the same back-to-back street as my recently departed Grandma Barnes. Barry Shepherd, Dave Ankers, and Billy Smethurst were all nice kids, if not the toughest guys on the block by any means. But as we were all loafing about during the holidays with nothing much to do, we decided to form our own gang.

In some parts of Salford, if you took a wrong turn the rival gangs would be on you like a shot: people would be tied to lamp posts and have bricks thrown at them, just for walking down another gang's street. I don't know what gives rise to that small-area xenophobia, and I didn't live in a street like that, so I didn't really feel it in my bones, but you gotta have a gang, and this was the nearest I got to it.

We'd all seen *The Young Savages*, starring Burt Lancaster, a pre-*Kojak* Telly Savalas with hair, Shelley Winters, and an actor called John Davis Chandler, who had the ultimate weasel face and always played baddies. It was about two rival New York teenage gangs – the Horsemen (Puerto Ricans) and the Thunderbirds (Italian-/Irish-American greasers) – pitted in a deadly turf battle in East Harlem. Things come to a head when the brutish Thunderbirds murder a blind Puerto Rican kid in broad daylight.

We were naturally on the side of the Horsemen, because they all wore these sharp-as-fuck sharkskin suits with their gang emblem, a chessboard paladin, embroidered on the back of their jackets. Thus inspired, we thought we'd better come up with a name for ourselves. Let me first explain that the thing with our gang was that everybody in it was ill. I don't just mean we had the measles or something, there was something certifiably medically wrong with each and every one of us: me, recovering tubercular; Barry Shepherd, epileptic; Dave Ankers, chronic asthma; and last, but best, of all, Billy Smethurst, haemophiliac. Billy looked pretty hard, but he had an ambulance more or less permanently parked outside his house; the slightest knock and it was an instant fucking internal haemorrhage.

It was Billy who came up with our name: the Blue Orchid Gang. Poncy name, poncy gang. He got the idea from a *Dick Tracy* comic in which some Chicago Mobster sent his girlfriend a blue orchid. None of us had ever heard of an orchid before; it was a fascinating word, especially with a spelling like that. For all we knew, it could have been a rocket ship, or a jet plane, or a racing car. We didn't have a clue. We had to look it up in the dictionary, and then go and get a library book out to see what an orchid even looked like so we could make a flag with our emblem painted on it. Ever since then I've always had a thing for orchids. Anyway, thanks to his *Dick Tracy* fixation, Billy had inadvertently hit on a very appropriate gang name: delicate flower, delicate kids.

We were just fucking about, really; we didn't tie anyone to a lamp post or throw bricks about. We just hung out together and tried to avoid trouble. In the summer holidays we'd be out from 10am until teatime. We never went home to get anything to eat, and never had any money, so we were always starving in the daytime. I'd take a couple of slices of bread in my pockets to feed the ducks at Heaton Park and usually finished up eating them myself. I even turned fucking hunter-gatherer – once I found out that you could eat nasturtiums, we were all at it. On the rare occasions that we saw some fruit on a tree, we'd eat it. When we found some gooseberries on one of our foraging expeditions we ate them all, obviously. Fucking hell, that was a bit of a shock; the lot of us got diarrhoea.

We used to go into town, and we'd often end up in the fancy-schmancy deli department of Lewis's food hall, where they always had free samples of this, that, and the other. We'd help ourselves to all the specialities on offer: a couple of cubes of some posh French cheese, a slice of Tuscan salami, maybe a few Greek Kalamata olives. Then we'd go into the gents and swap clothes, and go round again for second and third and fourth helpings, changing clothes each time in case anyone was being observant. None of us wanted the embarrassment of being kicked out on our ear.

Chapter Nine

THE BOOKIE'S, THE BOOZER, THE BARBER'S, THE BIKE, AND THE BEAUTIFUL GAME

'Are you, or have you ever been, a member of the Communist Party?' Personally, I'm taking the Fifth, but I'll tell you who was: my dad. We were a working-class family, but with my dad's job as an electrical engineer, we were now high-end working class. Not quite lower-middle-class, though, because they were paid a salary each month whereas the workers on a wage were paid weekly – 'very weakly', as my dad would have said. Nevertheless, his work was highly skilled and it wasn't going to be automated any time soon.

He didn't share the general public's dim view of the late Joseph Stalin. It should be remembered that engineers were the blood royal of the proletariat, and enjoyed a life of comparative privilege in the Soviet Union. I don't want to paint my dad as any kind of political activist, he certainly wasn't that: if push came to shove and politics came into it, George Clarke's concerns didn't go far beyond wages, working hours and conditions, paid holidays and sick leave.

He was live and let live, within reason, but never a Liberal. In the Thirties he had fought Oswald Mosley's Blackshirts in pitched battles in Ancoats and Collyhurst, where a typical weapon was a raw King Edward studded with razor blades. Even so, he thought that people who went on demonstrations were troublemakers. 'Get 'em in the army,' would have been Dad's recommendation. 'What, the one you were never in?' being my unuttered cheeky riposte.

To be fair, my dad, a premature anti-fascist, would have done his bit had his work not been so vital to the war effort. As I've said, he was enlisted in Dad's Army, 45th Lancashire (Trafford Park) Battalion. Occasionally, they would show footage of the Home Guard on a programme called *All Our Yesterdays* that dealt with life as it was in the recent past. There they would be, each with a mop, broom, or a billiard cue in lieu of his yet-to-be-issued rifle, to which my dad would come on like the traumatised vet with all that, 'Yeah, we had it rough. You weren't there, man. My God, we had it rough,' kind of thing.

You didn't have to do much to be left wing then, and a great many working-class people were in the Communist Party, or at the least sympathetic to it, and would certainly have been in a trade union: it was simply a default position that was more to do with economic fairness than reinventing humanity. As I've mentioned, Dad bought the *Daily Worker*, or the *Morning Star* as it became in 1966, but also the *Daily Express* for its superior sports coverage and the racing pages.

He was a tall guy, six foot three, bad posture: I inherited his slouch. A full head of iron-grey hair worn in an American-style buzz cut. If I were to call Dad to memory, he would be wearing a charcoal-grey suit, and a three-quarter-length mackintosh three hundred and sixty-five days per year. This was Manchester, remember. He looked like he was in the upper echelons of Scotland Yard – or a gangster. I used to tell all my school pals he was a detective.

I thought the world of my dad and vice versa. Not that we were ever in each other's pockets, because he wasn't in the house much, and when he was home for the weekend he spent a lot of time in any one or other of several all-male environments: the boozer, the bookie's, and the barber's.

He was a sociable fellow who genuinely didn't understand any guy who didn't drink; that's why he fucking hated Wales. He couldn't understand why miners would sacrifice a whole day of their precious weekend not having a pint. For that reason he thought the Welsh were beyond the pale − sneaky, shifty, and snide. And worst of all, miserable. That's why he cried off any holidays in Rhyl. All this because the pubs shut on a Sunday.

On a weekend my dad and his pal Wilf would go to the Devonshire Sporting Club, run by Bill 'Man Mountain' Benny, a twenty-stone wrestler and borderline gangster. Mr Benny had done well for himself; well enough to own, in partnership with fellow 'businessman' Dougie Flood,* three gentlemen's nightclubs: the Dev, the Levenshulme Sporting Club, and the Cabaret Club on Oxford Road. He was also in possession of three state-of-the-art American cars − a Chevrolet Impala, a Ford Fairlane, and a Cadillac Eldorado. That's nothing, though. The fucker had actually met Elvis. Bill Benny had tried unsuccessfully to get him over here for a charity concert. He flew to the States with a million pounds, organised a meeting with Colonel Parker, who said, 'That's fine for me. What about for Elvis?'

Back in those days, most clubs had their own signature song. Until his ill-timed demise in 1963,† at some point in the evening Bill himself would get up on stage with his bull neck, bald head, and big cigar, then he'd get a grip of the microphone. The guv'nor was in the house, so what could possibly go wrong? An evening

---

* Benny and Flood were allegedly members of the Quality Street Gang, of which more later.
† Aged forty-four, the larger-than-life Bill Benny died of a heart attack while getting a blowjob off a prostitute. The police had to batter down the door to his flat and lift his corpse off her flattened body.

of top-flight entertainment awaited. Then he'd burst into the club anthem:

> The friends you will meet there,
> The stars you will greet there,
> You know that Bill Benny is always at his best.
> So why not come and join him and be one of his guests
> At the Devonshire Sporting,
> Married or courting,
> The Devonshire Sporting Club.

My dad would often come back from a night out at the Devonshire singing the club song and enthusing about the great acts he'd seen that evening, people like Shirley Bassey, Lena Horne, Lena Martell, Toni Dalli, Dennis Lotis, Buddy Greco, and Sugar Pie DeSanto. What the . . .? Huh? I never expected to hear those three words coming out of my dad; it was like he'd invaded my turf. I was all like, 'What do you know from Sugar Pie DeSanto all of a sudden? Stick to Bing Crosby, old man, and leave this stuff to us newer fellows.'

Dad also became a member of the Albion Casino, which was attached to Salford Dog Track and run by a guy called Gus Demmy, the William Hill of his day. Christ knows what my dad was playing at in there, but he was punching above his weight with those hot shot high rollers and he got in over his head. Thanks to just one unlucky night at the tables, he had to cough up a whole week's wages, which meant that we couldn't pay the electricity bill and were consequently cut off. The irony wasn't lost on my mum; Dad was away all year, wiring up the country, and there we were in the pre-electric gloom, cooking on an open fire.

I wasn't as perturbed about this as my mother. In fact, I thought it was quite funny. I enjoyed the cowboy ambience of heating up a can of beans on the fire. Then we got one of those paraffin lamps like they had out on the prairie, so it didn't interfere with my reading habit. It was quite an adventure.

After Dad's Albion Casino wipeout, it would take my parents nearly a year to get back on track financially. He learned his lesson early. It never happened again and henceforth his gambling was confined to the horses.

Where I lived, people didn't ask, 'Do you like football?' The only question was: 'United or City?' My dad supported United, so naturally, me too. On match days, Salford City Transport provided a fleet of Football Specials, destination: Old Trafford. Dad took me to all the home games, plus the occasional not-too-distant away game, and on Wednesdays we went over to the Cliff to watch the reserves.

Going to the match at Old Trafford with my dad was a hot date, not least because of the railroad in the middle of the street. Buses and normal traffic ran down either side of the road, while rumbling right down the middle, a fucking great steam train carried coal, sheets of steel, and what have you from one part of Trafford Park to the other.

For us kids, this railroad was almost as much an attraction as the football match because of its role in the manufacture of daggers. Instructions as follows: you got a nine-inch steel nail, placed it on the track, and waited for the next train to come along and completely flatten it out into a blade, the shape of which made it easy to attach to the wooden shaft of an old hammer. You then soaked this under a tap, and as the wood dried it would contract and tighten to grip the dagger shaft. A real class act for the price of a nine-inch nail. Everybody did that. Again, we made our own entertainment in those days.

Our skills didn't stop at bladesmithery. We were also self-taught fletchers. When the rag-and-bone men came round on a horse and cart, blowing a trumpet, people would emerge with various tattered remnants, redundant coats, pullovers, and so on. These could be exchanged for either a goldfish in a plastic bag which died within a week, a balloon on a string, or a bow and arrow, the last being the most popular. In the summer months, we would take the melted tar from the road and use it to attach our Trafford Park-sharpened panel pins to the ends of the arrows. This, and the application of cardboard flights on the other ends, resulted in deadly missiles – if you fired them at a wooden door they would actually stick. What larks . . . until somebody loses an eye.

The main thing about going to the football then was the unique opportunity to use profane language at a very high volume. There were very few other situations where that would have been allowed. Profane language, even in pubs, was confined to a particular room called the vault, where the beer was a penny cheaper and there was no carpet on the floor. If you swore in any other part of the pub, they'd say, 'Eh, we've got a room for that language.' The vault was strictly men only; there would have been uproar if a woman had gone in there.

Barber shops were another all-male 'safe space'. Sid and Aubrey Silverstein used to have the woman from the chip shop come round with their pies at 12.30 every day. She would just stand on the doorstep with the pies; she never crossed the threshold.

The other comparable situation was a factory in which the machinery was very loud. But even in a factory, if a woman came onto the shop floor with the tea, the language of the male work-force would be regulated accordingly.

The football, therefore, was the one situation where you could actually shout out the worst profanities available, as loud as you possibly could without fear of arrest. A social safety valve? Perhaps, but a very enjoyable one.

It was all a bit of a thrill, but when they replaced the terraces with seats and the ladies started joining in, that's when the rot set in, in my opinion. Of course, there had always been women at football matches – I wouldn't go so far as to say it was an equal-opportunities situation, and I'd better not go into this too much or I'll get death threats – but they weren't the kind of women that you'd worry about swearing in front of. Some of them were worse than blokes, sample conversation: 'Fucking blind cunt.'

I was extremely young when I started going to Old Trafford with my dad. There was invariably a brass band from some mill or other, or as was often the case, the Manchester Metropolitan Police Silver Band, doing a medley of tunes before the game and later at half-time. While the match was in progress, the band members occupied a special bench on the edge of the pitch. Before kick-off, Dad would lift me over the picket fence (it was about three feet high!!!) so I could sit alongside the band members. There was a limited amount of space on the band's bench for us kids, so the trick was to get there early. Now I had an uninter-rupted view of the action, but because I was on the same level as the players, it meant that I could only really see what was going on right in front of me. You needed to be up higher in the terraces to properly see the sweep of the pitch. Luckily, to my mum's bewilderment, Dad and I would watch the highlights again later on *Sports Special* anyway.

On the way back home, occasionally, if my dad met someone he knew, they'd break the journey for a pint, parking me outside on the pub doorstep with a packet of crisps and a bottle of pop along with all the other kids whose dads were inside. Once in a while, the dads would stick their heads round the door to ask if we needed any crisp reinforcements. Usually, though, we got on the special bus and Dad would drop me off home, then go to the pub.

The main deal on our outings to the football was pies. At some point in the early Sixties, they introduced hot dogs, but for my dad and me it was always pies. The pie stall at Old Trafford offered a choice of meat and potato, meat, steak and kidney, or cheese and onion. I was a meat and potato pie* guy all the way. A sustaining winter snack, the meat and potato pie is the more portable choice and, in my opinion, the ideal outdoor hand pie: mainly potato done in stock, just a threat of meat (i.e. one flake of mince), onions, and, the big secret, white pepper – all packed in there, no gravy about it. Gravy can be troublesome if you're standing up and walking about: that's why the steak pie – with its hot, wet, loose contents – never really made it as a hand pie.

When I first started going to see United, it was the Matt Busby pre-Munich 1958 air-disaster side, the Busby Babes: David Pegg, Dennis Viollet, Bill Foulkes, Johnny Berry, Geoff Bent, Roger Byrne, Eddie Colman, Duncan Edwards, Bobby Charlton, Jackie Blanchflower, Tommy Taylor. The goalie was either Ray Wood or Harry Gregg.

They were a glamorous, world-class club even then, with a bestselling calypso record dedicated to them, 'Manchester United

---

* Even now, Holland's meat and potato is my favourite pie. When I was in my twenties, I used to warn anyone thinking of moving south to pack a lifetime's frozen supply, because in those days you couldn't buy them south of Birmingham. Happily, they're now available all over the country in packs of four in the freezer department of most good supermarkets. To conform with The Meat Products (England) Regulations 2003, due to the minimum meat requirement, however, they've had to change the name to Potato and Meat. Give them a go. However, you would never hear anyone in the Greater Manchester area asking for a 'Potato and Meat' pie. To do so would single you out as an invader from another planet who had taken human form and inadequately learned our local customs. It isn't 'Potato and Meat' any more than it's Tonic and Gin, Chips and Fish, Bowser and Callard, Costello and Abbott, Roy and Siegfried, Large and Little, Wise and Morecambe, or Vinegar and Salt. You see where I'm going with this?

Calypso', that was often played on the aforementioned *Two-Way Family Favourites* radio programme:

> Manchester,
> Manchester United.
> A bunch of bouncing "Busby Babes",
> They deserve to be knighted.
> If ever they're playing in your town,
> You must get to that football ground.
> Take a look and you will see,
> Football taught by Matt Busby.

It was the full production, a steel band going on behind the singer Edric Connor, who sounded a lot like Edmundo Ros. Many of my readers will remember him.

My favourite player was the twenty-one-year-old centre forward Duncan Edwards. He was a prodigious talent, a fantastic player with a very promising career ahead of him, but he died in the Munich air crash. This was a tragedy that went beyond Manchester. The grief seemed universal.

That evening the *Manchester Evening News* issued a Late Final edition with the devastating news. It was the lead item on the national news, and throughout the evening the scheduled programmes were interrupted with reports of another death, or about the condition of the few known survivors, including Bobby Charlton, Bill Foulkes, Dennis Viollet, Johnny Berry, and Matt Busby himself.

The following morning, just before I left for school, the *Daily Mirror* arrived with photographs of the wreckage on the front page. A pall of doom hung over the whole neighbourhood. At school all the priests, nuns, and teachers were very concerned about the recovery of the injured passengers. Entire masses and church services were dedicated to the wellbeing of the surviving team members. In the cinema, the Movietone News carried regular reports. It was a very gloomy time.

The human interest element of manager Matt Busby's eventual recovery coupled with the resurrection of the team seemed to be of national importance. How do you rebuild a side after something like that? It wasn't until the mid-Sixties, with the reign of Georgie 'El Beatle' Best, Denis Law, et al., that United started climbing back up to the top.

Some people are a tough act to follow. Matt Busby was one of them; Alex Ferguson is another. After Busby's departure in the early Seventies, and before Ferguson's reign, United laboured under a succession of muppets under the collective title Frank O'Farrell. We had great hopes for Tommy 'The Doc' Docherty, but he wasn't there long enough to make any difference, to be fair.

This miserable period culminated in the relegation of Manchester United.* Match days were often upsetting, especially since arch-rivals Manchester City were enjoying quite a moment with players like Colin Bell, Francis Lee, Mike Summerbee, and Rodney Marsh.

City were the worst, although Liverpool and Leeds United were in the same bag. While United was in the khazi, Leeds were also in their heyday under Don Revie. I'd like to say for them it was the days of wine and roses, but knowing the house style of Leeds United it was more brown ale and pork scratchings. Revie had this anti-glamour policy – none of the Leeds side were allowed to get their suits from anywhere other than Burton's, or to drive a car beyond a mid-range Vauxhall Viva. His rigour extended onto the pitch, too. Revie's boys played that kind of tactical European game: get an early goal and then play it safe. It was unexciting: nobody got their money's worth, but in spite of their

---

* For the full sorry tale, I would refer you to the excellent documentary *Too Good to Go Down* based on the book by Wayne Barton, directed by Tom Boswell, and narrated by your humble scribe.

no-thrills game, they were winning everything. Where are they now, though? Leeds haven't been in the top division since 2004 and I'd like them to put that right. Like Sir Alex, I miss those Trans-Pennine skirmishes.

Enemy No. 3 – I mean Liverpool obviously, although to be honest, I liked Bill Shankly. After Matt Busby, he was the ideal manager. I had a sneaking regard for Shankly's dedication to his Liverpool side and his utter conviction – he simply couldn't see the point of any other team. He would go to the ends of the earth for his squad and defend them to the hilt: 'That wasnae a goal!' In Shankly's eyes, any booking of a Liverpool player was unjust; every penalty against his side was a mistake – the referee was either blind or an idiot, but his boys never put a foot wrong. I admired his steadfast defence of his players, in the face of all evidence, and thought every manager should be like that. My team, right or wrong.

The football terrace chant, as it was then, was the last reposi-tory of true folk music. It's amazing how quickly snippets of topical import would make their way into the baying derogatory chorus, but it was usually inflammatory insults aimed at the opposing fans and indeed the town they lived in. One ghetto having a go at another. Take this favourite anti-Liverpool chant of mine, the classic 'Kop Twats', to the tune of 'Top Cat':

Kop Twats,
You thieving bastards
Kop Twats,
You thieving bastards
We all know you sign on the dole,
And you live in a fucking shit 'ole.

It was all about how they were worse off than us – an accu-sation, largely, that could equally be levelled at ourselves. As well as everything else, days out at Old Trafford were an invaluable introduction to the delights of crowd-poisoning.

Having been a sick child with a short life expectancy had its downside. My mum refused to get me a bike, for example. I begged and pleaded, but she was steadfast in her refusal. I can understand her reticence; it was very sweet and I belatedly thank her for caring enough to want to prolong what little time she thought I had left – mothers are like that – but it was a serious deprivation for me.

As I've said, I had learned to ride on a rented pushbike on Rhyl's off-peak promenade and my mother would point this out, indicating the busiest crossroads in the entire North-West just outside our window.

In the end, when I was about ten or eleven, my dad helped me out and talked my mum into letting me get a bike. 'Well, I'm not buying it,' she said. 'I'm not subscribing to your early death.' I had to buy it myself. To this day, I can't think of anything else I have ever saved up for. After so much self-denial, odd jobs, hard work, and opposition, my first bike was a big event. It was a Phillips lightweight racer, dull gold with drop handlebars.*† It cost me £4.50, which was quite a prohibitive sum back then, but it made a big difference to my lifestyle.

The deal was that I stick to the backstreets, suburban avenues and parks, avoiding the terraced streets with their haemorrhoid-inducing cobblestones. But, of course, I craved the main road and

---

* In *Austerity* (or *Modernity?*) *Britain* by the excellent David Kynaston there is a photograph by Shirley Baker of a boy on a drop-handlebar bike in a cobbled terraced street in Salford. It could so easily be me: the bike is just like mine, I had that Tony Curtis haircut, and I wore a suit exactly like the one the boy is wearing to my Uncle Dennis's wedding in 1961.

† Nan Levy, Shirley Baker's granddaughter, keeps the archive of Baker's great images of Salford in the time of its most dynamic changes.

in no time at all I had broken my promise. Turning right outside the front door, I headed north towards Prestwich, Whitefield, and beyond. I had prepared a halfway snack of my own design – a pork-pie doorstep. Here's the recipe: take one white loaf (unsliced), hollow it out, place three pork pies and eight pickled onions into the vacant space, then flatten the whole thing out. Thus sustained, I explored the austere stone streets and the Pennine slopes of various mill towns where the shops all had strange names: Hardcastle, Arkwright, Holroyd, Hollerenshaw, Ackroyd, Shufflebottom, Eckerslike, and such. Through the forty-watt gloom of the interior I could discern that the shops themselves seemed poorly stocked with brands I'd never heard of. There wasn't a movie theatre anywhere in sight, and the chip shops didn't even sell meat and potato pies. 'Thank God, I don't live here,' I thought, as I headed homeward.

Since moving to Essex, I have recently rediscovered the joy of cycling thanks to the flat topography of the area and the acquisition of a classic 1959 Hercules Roadster in an attractive shade of British racing green.

Chapter Ten

BOOKIE'S RUNNER

Of all the major national and international sociopolitical issues of my childhood years (the NHS aside), the most significant was not the all-encompassing fear of the mushroom cloud – there was nothing that I, as a citizen, could do about that.

No: the thing that really fucked up my life was the successful passage through Parliament of the 1960 Betting and Gaming Act.

During my convalescence in Rhyl, I'd precociously acquired the habits of the independent young man about town. Back in the old neighbourhood, the need for dosh was more pressing than ever. After all, what cunt doesn't want money? I had to get a part-time job.

Paper round? Forget about it. I had once deputised for a kid with a paper round for a week while he was away on holiday. Never again! Who knew paper could weigh like that? I tried doing it on a bike, but the tonnage of the newspaper sack rendered balance impossible.

That was the hardest job I've ever had in my life, I swear to God: up at six, and even after you've got rid of all the morning papers it's still not over. No, after school it's back to the newsagent for the evening editions. Sisyphean or what?

I was always on at my dad about making money. I loved the

records of the American singer and bandleader Louis Prima, everybody did. They were a regular feature on the radio, songs like 'Embraceable You', a duet with his wife, the lovely Keely Smith; 'Angelina'; 'Just a Gigolo'; and 'Luigi', a fine example of the Americanisation process, the story of a Sicilian-American bookmaker revered in his neighbourhood, dressed like a dude with amplified cufflinks and a bejewelled pinkie ring.

Prima's song evoked such a vivid picture of a charmed life that the cautionary denouement went unheeded in my case. My father often had a financial interest in the outcome of various equestrian events, and with this in mind I mooted the possibility of a position of trust in the field of turf accountancy. What with his dry sense of humour and his social finesse, my dad knew people all over town, many of whom were unreformed spivs, bookies, club owners, chancers, and the like. He put the feelers out, and Bob's your uncle, soon after my eleventh birthday I landed my first proper job in the then-illegal world of off-track betting. So long, suckers. Not for me the daily back-breaking toil of the paperboy: I was a bookie's runner.

My job description was pretty straightforward: to make the rounds of several all-male environments around our block – the billiard hall, a couple of pubs, three barber shops, the guys at Green and Zonis, a nearby Ford dealership – and collect the illegal bets, mainly on the horses but sometimes the dogs, and the odd fight. I simply did the pick up. The punters would have the money ready in envelopes with fake names on them, which I then delivered in a larger brown envelope to the local backdoor bookie's.

The HQ was up a back alley, running parallel to the main road, which was accessible from our fire escape. A sheet-metal roof had been put over the whole of the backyard so it was now a big shed – that was the bookie's. Cut into its door at eye level was one of those speakeasy sliding hatches – you know, 'Knock twice and ask for Jacky.' Somebody would pull open the hatch and I handed over the envelope. At 5pm-ish I went back and collected any winnings in the same pseudonymously marked brown envelopes.

Twelve-year-old kids had the monopoly on this work due to their immunity to any serious prosecution. Worst-case scenario, if I ever got pulled by the law, I was advised to wax moronic and claim to be ignorant of the contents of this brown envelope, and indeed of the purpose of my errand. It was an unnecessary precaution though, because owing to the betting habits of the local constabulary themselves this area of the law was not rigidly policed.

On each corner stood a number of other hirelings whose sole purpose was to dog out for any police activity, but as I've said, this never happened. It was in everybody's interest to keep the operation going; it generated some disposable income in an otherwise poor area. We're not talking payday loans and death threats here: if you didn't have the Cadbury's* you couldn't place the bet. There were no markers or anything like that. No IOUs, or any unpleasantness where some no-neck had to be sent round to collect. Not that I knew of, anyway. It may have gone on, but that part of the operation was kept well away from any kids.

It was a good earner. I got a bit for delivering the envelopes in the first place, but law of averages, a few of the punters got lucky, and when somebody got lucky it was considered good form to duke the runner. So I was on perhaps £2 a week, the same wage as an apprentice mechanic or similar. In the words of Huey 'Kingfish' Long, the former Governor of Louisiana, 'Every Bum's a King'. Well, that was certainly true in my case. I was pissing pure gold, and still at school already! Stash those Paynes Poppets where the sun don't shine, buster! Every trip to the movies now involved a half-pound box of Black Magic. I was forever festooning

---

* In Cockney rhyming slang, Cadbury's Smash = cash.

my mother with costume jewellery she'd have to pretend to like. I hadn't started smoking yet, but if I had, it would have been Cohibas all the way.

Some of the people I was dealing with were degenerate gamblers from the insalubrious part of Higher Broughton and this early glimpse of their chaotic lives was educational. I was a wise-guy by the time I was twelve.

Where I come from, a victimless crime is punching a guy in the dark. But here's another example. There was a household-goods pitch every Saturday afternoon at Cross Lane market run by Barmy Mick, the insinuation being that to sell his stuff at such knock-down rates he must have been certifiably insane. A punter on my round had acquired a gross crate of hundred-watt Osram pearl light bulbs at cost from Barmy Mick, who was a mate of his apparently, and with this initial outlay, he went into business.

He went round knocking on doors and offering to change every light bulb in the house for a pound. It was a really good deal: even if you didn't need any bulbs changed, sooner or later one was going to blow, so it seemed well worth a quid for a complete household illumination update.

So, he goes round the houses and starts changing people's light bulbs, but here's the genius of it: he puts the old bulbs he's taken out into the cardboard sleeves from his stock of new bulbs, sticks them back in his crate, and off he goes to the next house, where he plays the same trick. Genius! Everybody was happy, even if it was a fool's paradise.

He wasn't even really doing anything illegal, because all he was saying was, 'I'll change every light bulb in your house for a pound.' He's not claiming that these bulbs are new, so, technically, no one could nobble him under the Trade Descriptions Act.

What a scam, or possibly scamola. The neat circularity of it: all the principles of capitalism in place. Easy money *and* it was an ongoing fucking gig. I felt privileged that he let me in on it; he obviously thought, 'Here's a lad who can keep his trap shut.'

He had it made, or so you'd think. Who would kiss that off? But then, because of some urgent financial pressure, he had to sell his lucrative recycled light-bulb business to some other idiot who was never heard of again. I've said it before, and I'll say it again: you can't educate a mug.

My personal Wall Street Crash came in January 1961, when thanks to the implementation of the previous year's Betting and Gaming Act and the consequent immediate appearance of legitimate bookies on every high street, I was made redundant.

The bookie job was irreplaceable, and I didn't have any steady income for the next couple of years. The only comparable earner that I knew of was caddying for local golfers, but that was hard graft, involving a lot of walking about in the outdoors, and would have written off the entire weekend. I went with a mate of mine, Razzer, once. His granny lived in Wythenshawe, and on a Saturday afternoon, he would put in a few hours at the nearby Baguley Golf Club on the outskirts of Cheshire.

That was the first time I ever went to Wythenshawe. Although it was a showcase post-war overspill estate, it was considered to be a bit on the rough side. Maybe I was easily impressed, but to me it looked like Beverly fucking Hills. Mature trees, no factories, acres of pastureland, meadows even. Front and back gardens with flowers and shrubbery! And a fucking golf course. And this is the place I'm supposed to believe is a deprived-fucking-juvenile-delinquent-ridden hellhole?

There's no pleasing some people.

Chapter Eleven

MALDANO'S LATE NIGHT FINAL

In the top-floor apartment, which we had vacated some years before, lived a kid called Mike Partington with his mum and his grandma, Mrs Cook. Mrs Partington and my mum came to be long-time pals. I never met his dad – perhaps owing to the temporal proximity of the Second World War, paternal absence was never a comfortable subject.

Mrs Partington worked full-time for Ward and Goldstone, a local firm that made plastic electrical components such as switches, adapters, and plugs. Like any member of the national workforce, she liked a drink of a weekend. She had some quite exotic clobber, including several fake leopardskin items that Mike and I used to muck about with. My mum, a stay-at-home bookworm and more restrained in her wardrobe, had nothing so ostentatious.

Given that I was a full two years older than Michael, I became the Saturday night designated babysitter while his mum and grandma went out to the Conservative Club. They weren't politically aligned, but the club had a piano player, they knew how to treat a lady there, and the rigid dress code kept the riff-raff out. The ladies' intake didn't end when they got home, obviously, and Mrs Partington had a piece of furniture formerly unknown to me: a cocktail cabinet. It was one of those fabulous Fifties

pieces, sort of art deco, with blue lights all along the top, and
sliding doors that when opened revealed peach-coloured mirror
tiles and glass shelves laden with jars of maraschino cherries, a
flagon of Emva Cream Cyprus sherry, and a bottle of a cocktail
called Maldano's Late Night Final ('A Glow in Every Glass'): it
was like a shrine to booze, a ritual altar to the God of ethanol.

Apart from a snifter of port on Christmas Day, our house was
a booze-free zone. My dad liked a drink, but only in the context
of the pub, the exception being Cup Final day, when a few of
his pals would come round with a crate of beer. The Partingtons'
cocktail cabinet proved to be my introduction to the world of
hard liquor. One Saturday night I assumed the role of sympathetic
bartender, and set about fixing a couple of drinks: two generous
tumblers of the aforementioned, aptly named Maldano's Late
Night Final.

The suspension of all civilised inhibition is a widely desired state.
In my case, however, the suspension of all reason and its attendant
derangement brought only borderline gender confusion, nausea, and
eventual collapse. It was way past our bedtime anyway, and my only
memory is of a period of aimless laughter followed by the rapid
onset of enforced slumber. We regained consciousness in a ransacked
room amid various fake leopard accessories we had accessed from
Mrs Partington's wardrobe. File under 'The Lost Weekend'.

Maldano's Late Night Final: Late Night Kibosh more like.
Welcome to the world of urban sophistication. They used to advertise it at the movies: an elegant late-night couple, the guy in a
tuxedo and the chick in slinky evening attire – people of obvious
discernment – enjoying this delicious, high-end nightcap. The reality
was more like an over-the-counter cough preparation. The
Chloroform of the Cocktail World. Make sure you've put your
pyjamas on.

Mike's mum and his grandma must have noticed the missing
Maldano's Late Night Final, and known we'd given it a whirl. Far

from drawing any serious rebuke, our antics met with universal adult hilarity. Incidents such as this, after all, were the stuff of light relief on the teatime news. You know the kind of thing: '. . . before turning the gun upon himself. And finally, it's not all doom and gloom. In Wigan, a three-year-old drank a bottle of Johnnie Walker. Happily, he's made a full recovery.'

Cheers!

Chapter Twelve

UNCLE DENNIS

As I've mentioned, after National Service in the RAF, Uncle Dennis came to live at our place. He had been serving in Cyprus, and it had been going off royal out there, what with Johnny Turk and the Bubbles at each other's throats.

Like all my uncles, I called him Unc, but being half the age of any of my older relatives, he was more like an older brother. He was a cheerful presence, but he wasn't a soft touch by any means. Spends were earned: he used to give me a couple of bob a week if I polished his shoes.

As we were pushed for space, Uncle Den shared my room, where we slept Morecambe and Wise style. He brought with him a kitbag full of rare and desirable swag. I blagged a couple of choice pieces: a pair of steel-framed aviator sunglasses with Zeiss lenses in their own stainless-steel case; a pair of tropical-weight RAF-issue pyjamas, pale blue Egyptian cotton with darker blue piping around a lido collar, crying out for the addition of a silken night cravat; and a bayonet in a scabbard. What he was doing with a bayonet in the RAF, I don't know.

But his greatest contribution to the household was the gift of music, by virtue of his beautiful pale blue and cream Dansette record player, auto-change even. Long-players and vinyl records were a new thing, and he had a bunch of them: Sinatra, Nat King Cole, Mel Tormé, Peggy Lee, Jo Stafford, and an EP by the Goons featuring the 'Ying Tong Song'. He also brought his aforementioned paperback library.

Dennis had hoped to resume his previous employment at L. Gardner and Sons, a light engineering firm in nearby Patricroft, where he had operated some dangerous machinery, probably a lathe. However, since leaving the RAF, he had suffered several blackouts, and could no longer work in his former role. Nevertheless, Gardner's took him back, and by virtue of night school and day release, he retrained as a draughtsman and became a white-collar worker.

The RAF, universally known since the war as the Brylcreem Boys, were regarded in the popular imagination to have a bit more cachet than the other armed forces. So Dennis was getting a lot of action in the dating world, which gave me a glimpse into the exciting life of the eligible young bachelor. One pretty girl after another would come knocking at the door: Barbara, slender, pallid, and quiet; Pearl, curvaceous and a keen cyclist; and then there was Margaret – all in search of the dashing Dennis Barnes in all his brilliantined pomp.

Speaking of hair products, take my advice. Don't ever ingest them.

Uncle Dennis had a chest of drawers in which he kept shirts, colognes, gentlemen's depilatory requisites, and what I thought was booze. One day I was rooting around like the professional nosey-parker I am, and came across a hip flask-sized bottle of Bay Rum. The label featured a galleon, so there was no reason to suspect that this wasn't the well-known buccaneers' beverage.

Glug, glug, glug. And, what the . . . ? Huh . . . ? Projectile nausea! Don't make my mistake: Bay Rum is a hair tonic.

Upon his return, noticing the crustless pizza at my feet, Dennis quickly guessed the sequence of events. No sympathy.

My predicament was greeted with the humour-free sarcastic laugh he saved for such occasions.

'*You bloody necked it, didn't ya? Well, you'll do me . . . it's for your hair, you daft sod.*'

The bayonet that had come my way via Dennis was a prize possession. It had been blunted – you couldn't have cut a slice of bread with it – but it was a beautifully made piece of kit, which looked good and made a satisfying *shlang!* sound as it was unsheathed.

I was crazy about swords and fancied myself as quite the swash-buckler. It's a good weapon for me. I present a narrow target and I've got quite a reach, what with my legs. Consequently, I feel that I have some claim to the title 'the finest swordsman in all England'; if I'd taken up fencing, I think I could have been an Olympic gold-medal contender.

The acquisition of weaponry was very important for me and the other kids in our neighbourhood: dangerous times. I got a double-barrelled popgun one Christmas. It was a Tri-ang, a really solid number made out of steel with a wooden stock. Each barrel had a breech-loading piston that shot out corks attached to a string, so you wouldn't have anybody's eye out. What was the point of that? I wanted to actually hit something or someone, so I cut the string off. Then I thought, why stop at corks? Any missile could be discharged from the barrels by means of the spring-loaded pistons, at quite a velocity. Why not ball bearings? With just a pair of scissors I converted my gun into a weapon with which I *could* have actually taken someone's eye out. It came into its own particularly in the run-up to Bonfire Night, when I could buy bangers; I put one down each barrel so the gun fired with a satisfying explosion. The trick was to shoot them out so they detonated in mid-air; a truly terrifying thing to witness. It looked like I was packing a real shotgun. 'Fuck off! Bang! Fuck off! Bang!' We were always getting up to no good with explosives. Tooled up. You had to be.

In the 1950s, there had been a breakdown in parental authority owing to the absence of dads during the Second World War, the mums struggling at home, and kids going feral. This was the generation that became Teddy Boys, as is evidenced in the preamble to *The Blue Lamp*, which featured Dirk Bogarde as a proto-Ted with a gun, and launched the TV career of Jack Warner as Constable George Dixon.

At this time, there was a massive problem with un-decommissioned firearms. Demobbed soldiers had returned from the war with portable souvenirs, including Nazi daggers and Luger pistols swiped off dead Germans. The Luger, being a very attract-ive sidearm, quickly became a staple of any discerning criminal's wardrobe. With a rise in armed robberies and growing concern about Luger-toting Teddy Boy gangs at large on the streets of Britain, an arms amnesty was put in place in 1960. One day when I was off somewhere else, some government official came round the houses collecting any outstanding weaponry, and my mum bottled it and handed over my treasured bayonet.

I went fucking mad. 'You did what? You surrendered my sword to the authorities? Blimey, what did you do that for?'

'I'm not having weapons in the house,' she said.

My every attempt to expand my arsenal was thwarted by my parents. I had a mate at school called Kevin Dynes whose older brother Jim, the last Teddy Boy standing, was the owner of a pump-action Webley pistol, a beautiful silver thing modelled on the aforementioned Luger. It only fired slugs, so you couldn't kill anyone with it unless you really made a point of it: if you shot them up the throat from two inches away, possibly; or maybe in the eye socket or the temple; or perhaps if you went for that soft bit near the submandibular glands.

Jim had recently acquired a Diana air rifle much like the one used by Albert Finney in *Saturday Night and Sunday Morning*, so this rendered his pistol superfluous. I swapped all my American comics for it, but when my dad clocked it, he went crazy. '*Bloody hell, you are not having a bloody gun! Give it back to him. Bloody hell.*'

I told him that I couldn't reverse the deal because I'd touched black, and as the ritual has it, 'Touch black no back.'

Dad said he didn't care, and Jim could keep my comics, but I wasn't having the gun.

'But, Dad, everybody's got one!' I protested feebly.

'I don't bloody care, it's not the bloody Wild West.' Mutter, mutter, mutter. 'Bloody gun in the 'ouse!'

He wasn't having any of it, so I returned the Webley unconditionally, but Jim, decent cove that he always was (deep down), gave me my comics back.

Chapter Thirteen

MR MALONE

At secondary school the pals I hung out with were Fred Fielder, a Polish kid called Nick Kanuk, John Tyson, Kev Dynes, occasionally Broono (in an advisory capacity), and the two Mos, Maureen Mellor and Maureen Logan.

Some people grow up quicker than others at school and we were the 'bad' brigade. We aspired to the reputation of two older kids in the form above us, namely Raymond Ball and Arthur 'Archie' Waterhouse, a habitual wearer of sunglasses and the possessor of a steel comb, sharpened into a weapon. This was pre-Beatles, and everybody had a comb. Quiff adjustment was necessary, possibly every ten minutes. I blame Edd 'Kookie' Byrnes.*

We weren't evil, but all our interests seemed to be disapproved of: we listened to pop music with our hands in our pockets, slouched around chewing bubble gum, and quickly adopted the smoking habit, spending our dinner money on cigs. Five Park Drive cigarettes cost the same as a meat and potato pie. No wonder I lost weight.

I would also save money on bus fares by jumping on the back

* See *77 Sunset Strip*.

of any passing truck heading in the direction of school. The traffic had to slow down at the crossroads outside our house, giving me the perfect opportunity to hop on. It slowed down again at a particular bend just fifty yards from the school gate, where I would disembark, thus enabling me to rake in yet more cigarette funds.

Terrible. Risking my life so that I could risk my life further. In truth, though, the traffic never went above five miles an hour on that stretch, so we're not talking Evel Knievel here. I always thought that riding on the backs of trucks was one of the great pleasures of life. I'd see road gangs going to work and think, *They've got it all.* I couldn't wait to leave school. When my dad's pal Arthur MacNicholl told me that the best years of your life are your schooldays, it was the worst news I'd ever had from an adult. *Christ, they've got the perspective and they're saying that?* Were it not for my zest for life, I think I would have opened a vein.

As I said, the prospect of my mother doing bird was the only thing that kept me in continued education. I believed all that about the school-board detectives, everybody did, largely thanks to the positive propaganda of Edgar Lustgarten's *Scotland Yard*, a series of low-budget second features drilling home the message of the far-reaching hand of the law.

If you were thinking of shoplifting, for instance, the internal dialogue would run thus: 'Go ahead, steal that Mars Bar. You will eat that Mars Bar and then you'll go to bed tonight and forget all about that Mars Bar. But the guys at the Yard work in shifts, and when you go to sleep, having forgotten all about that delicious Mars Bar, the wheels of justice will be relentlessly turning, and as sure as night follows day, you will pay for that crime.'

Justice traps the guilty. I wasn't inordinately gullible, but like most sentient would-be criminals at that time, the myth of the omniscient detective was uppermost in my mind.

School was a mixed Catholic secondary modern. The head-mistress, Sister Geraldine, and many of the teachers had taken

Holy Orders. It had all the facilities one would expect of a school: qualified teachers, blackboards, forty children per class. It was a tough school. Put it this way – we had our own coroner!

Ever since the advent of the comprehensive system, people hark back to the perceived injustice of throwing eleven-year-old children who failed their eleven-plus on the 'scrapheap' of secondary modern education. Believe me, I was there, and nobody thought of our school like that, and we certainly weren't encouraged to regard ourselves in those terms: it was shut up, pay attention, and you might learn something. That was the deal.

I got a fairly solid education at my school. If nothing else, I was introduced to literacy, poetry, and the parables of Our Lord Jesus Christ. There was no excuse for ignorance of any occurrence prior to one's birth, which I've heard invoked as a mitigating factor on *University Challenge*: 'The Magna Carta? A bit before my time.' Yes. Yes, that is true. However, there *is* written evidence and you *are* studying history.

The cane, the plimsoll, the flying blackboard duster, and the fists of Sister Geraldine were the routine instruments of control, but non-violent coercion via sarcasm was preferred. Who at that age really wants to look like an idiot, especially when there are girls around? There's nothing worse.

I wouldn't say I got into any real trouble apart from on my very first day, the time I truanted for the small matter of a fortnight, and, of course, the incident that led to my boxing injury. The first time was for a dress-code violation. I was wearing jeans, and any long trousers were non-regulation, so me and this other kid who was also wearing jeans, who I'd obviously never met, were accused of being a gang and punished accordingly. I was very self-conscious about my physique, and there was no way I was wearing shorts, so my canings persisted for a week. They quit before I did.

My second major breach of discipline involved a new kid at

school. I can't remember his first name, but because his surname was Crosby, naturally, we all called him Bing. He had an older sister, and the two Mos, Bing and I, obviously without parental consent, skipped school and hung out at Bing's place, where they had a radiogram. His sister had a pile of records, and we spent two weeks doing the jitterbug and smoking cigs. Call it an unofficial holiday. We got in dead lumber over that: six swipes, three per hand, in front of the whole fucking school.

The third incident constituted a miscarriage of justice. Towards the end of my schooldays we got a new teacher, Mr Durcan, in charge of sport, who introduced a new policy to deal with playground brawls. He would break up the fight, and then, at the end of the day, the guilty parties had to settle their differences like gentlemen: duke it out, Marquess of Queensberry style, in the ring. I wasn't a scrapper, but just because you're not a scrapper doesn't mean you don't occasionally lose your rag, and on this day I was involved in a minor fracas with a boy called Joe Corrigan. No, not the fucking piss-useless Manchester City goalkeeper, but an equally large Irish Traveller lad, with whom, naturally, I wasn't exactly spoiling for a punch-up.

Under normal circumstances our little argy-bargy would have been forgotten by the time the bell rang, and Corrigan and I would have returned to our unspoken mutual hostility. Unfortunately, that day, Mr Durcan was on yard duty. Along he came: 'You know the drill, boys, break it up. We will settle this later in the ring.' I couldn't believe what I was hearing. I don't know who was supposed to be taught a lesson in this exercise. This guy was going to fucking marmalise me! I mean, where's the kudos in beating up a seven-stone fucking consumptive? I was a self-confessed coward, then as now. My coat of arms has been detailed elsewhere: four white feathers on a field of yellow. Nothing for me is more terrifying than physical pain, so the coming ordeal hung over me all day.

It was all over in less than a minute. We got in the ring, danced around for a bit, and then BANG went my aquiline profile! As I have bemoaned, the old Cooper Clarke hooter is a pretty large target, and Corrigan hooked me right on the conk. It wasn't technically a KO, but as soon as my nasal fracture and the ensuing claret became apparent, Mr Durcan signalled an end to the contest.

The match wouldn't have been allowed in a real boxing arena; we would have been in completely different weight categories. I would have preferred swordplay. I'm fucking lousy in a punch-up, whereas, as I've said, I'm great with a blade.

Unlike Mr Durcan, some of the teachers were morally opposed to violence, eschewing corporal punishment, and by testing their patience, we rapidly found out who they were.

'Really? Mr Donnelly doesn't condone corporal punishment? What a mug.'

Not 'What an enlightened man'. Nobody thought that.

The deputy head, Gerry Garvey (Mr Garvey to you), was terrific, a master of sarcasm, and our English teacher Mr Malone didn't cane anybody but used to whack them round the arse with a gym shoe, and that was the end of it. Just: 'Come 'ere!' Whack. 'Don't do it again. Sit down, behave yourself.' It was out of the way in no time.

Mainly, though, like Gerry Garvey, Mr Malone preferred the verbal take-down.

'You're an idiot. What are you?'

'An idiot, sir.'

'What? I didn't hear you. Who's an idiot?'

'Me, sir.'

'Well, say it then.'

'*I'm* an idiot, sir.'

The world is full of idiots, but who among them would care to admit it in front of witnesses? You learn early on: these people are always going to have the last word.

Everyone in our class had an amphetamine habit, but we didn't see it like that. Most of my classmates seemed to have a reliable source of uppers, pep pills pinched from their mum's perfectly legal stash: 'Mother's Little Helper', smoothing her way through the busy modern world, while simultaneously maintaining that much-sought-after slimline silhouette.

The number-one appetite suppressant was Tenuate Dospan, or Tombstones, massive torpedo-shaped pills about the size of a piece of blackboard chalk, with a score down the middle the better to break them in half; indeed, you had to break them in half or you could kill yourself trying to swallow them. We used to crunch them up, but the stated dose had to be exceeded for maximum effect.

These preparations were manufactured by white-coated experts in Switzerland, hyper-qualified scientists in ultra-hygienic labora-tories, all working in the public interest. A priestly class for a Godless age. Thanks to these amphetamines, Class 4A were card-carrying members of the wide-awake club, but if anyone had accused us of drug addiction we would have been horrified. The world of the drug addict was 3,334 miles away in the New York of Frankie Machine, the hero of Nelson Algren's 1949 bestseller *The Man with the Golden Arm*, played by Frank Sinatra in Otto Preminger's 1955 movie of the same name. Frankie's world involved hard jail time, gangsters, and hypodermic syringes: a far cry from anything to be found in our mothers' handbags.

We generally assumed that in order to become a qualified teacher, one must first become the repository of the sum total of all human knowledge; minimum requirement, surely? To hear a teacher say, 'I don't know,' was a shocking experience. Who do they think they are?

In the same vein, unhealthy doctors, barmy psychiatrists, and halitotic dentists provided a further source of puzzlement.

I've always found teachers to be rather unworldly people. After all, they go to school, they leave school, go to another school, leave that school, and for the rest of their lives they work in a school. So, to them – you see where I'm going with this – life is a school.

To be fair, I've met the odd exception, the best example being our English teacher John Malone. I'd first heard of Mr Malone from Mrs Forshaw, who along with her husband Charlie ran our local corner shop, a grocer's/off-licence. Mr Malone had been their lodger.

Mrs Forshaw was your typical blowsy Elsie Tanner type; she was a very gifted pianist,* and used to play the joanna at the pub. One day when I was in the shop, she alerted me to Mr Malone's forthcoming appearance that night on *The Carroll Levis Discovery Show*, a forerunner of *Opportunity Knocks*, and also featuring a Canadian MC. I duly tuned in, and there was Mr Malone in this vocal group, a doo-wop outfit: him and three other guys in co-ordinated tuxedos, doing an excellent version of the 1957 smash hit 'At the Hop' by Danny & the Juniors.

Mr Malone was a rugged outdoors type, fond of rock-climbing, skiing even, surfing, skin-diving, and other subaquatic pursuits. Nobody in our neighbourhood at that time was involved in anything like that, with the possible exception of Lenny Freedman, the pharmacist.

I'm not saying Mr Malone was one of those 'down with the kids' teachers you get today; there was none of that spooky nonsense. He wasn't trying to be our pal. Nor was he a fierce disciplinarian who frightened the fucking life out of us, but you wouldn't mess him around.

We'd done poetry with other teachers, but with them it was the whole 'dismantle this poem' approach: turn to page xxx, what

---

* Mrs Forshaw probably could have been a concert pianist in another life. She had pretensions that were slightly beyond the denizens of the back-to-backs: she owned the corner shop.

do you think he meant by blah? In other words: kill it. Analyse it to death.

Mr Malone was different. For a start, his own interest in the poetry was palpable. He had an instinct. His choices, selected from *Palgrave's Golden Treasury*, were inspiring.

At that time, what every school-age child had in common was *Palgrave's Golden Treasury*, the standard poetry anthology issued to every school in the country no matter what denomination. It encapsulated the gamut of English poetry, from Andrew Marvell, John Donne, and the Metaphysicals, right up to what was then regarded as modern verse, with W. H. Auden, T. S. Eliot, and Louis MacNeice representing the moderns.

Naturally enough, given Mr Malone's energetic lifestyle, he had a preference for those verses that featured military exploits: 'The Charge of the Light Brigade' by Alfred, Lord Tennyson; 'Vitaï Lampada' by Sir Henry Newbolt; 'Tommy' by Rudyard Kipling; and 'The Highwayman' by Alfred Noyes, a verbal gallop of a poem recording a gentleman of the road's last ride.

Not every poem was an imperial shoot-'em-up; Mr Malone also had a soft spot for the Romantics of the nineteenth century, 'The Lady of Shalott' by Tennyson, Wordsworth's daffodil number, natch, and 'The Bells' by Edgar Allan Poe.

Arousing or romantic, we had to learn them off by heart. Most importantly, Mr Malone read them out loud. He seemed to know instinctively that poetry has always been a phonetic medium, and dynamically so. He read in a very spare way. He didn't ham it up, there was no need: he let the language do the talking. Take 'The Bells', for instance. The metric precision leaves no room for personal interpretation.

The main consideration is what a poem sounds like. If it doesn't sound any good, it's because it isn't any good. That is the big lesson I learned from Mr Malone.

When it came to writing our own poetry, we were encouraged

to commandeer the stylistic methodology of the superstars, while still conveying our own personal perspective. I tended to write myself in as the hero of the piece. In this regard the exquisite poetry of the young Cassius Clay was my guide, with lines such as 'I done wrestled with an alligator, I done tussled with a whale; handcuffed lightning, thrown thunder in jail; only last week, I murdered a rock, injured a stone, hospitalised a brick; I'm so mean I make medicine sick.'

To my mind, self-mythology was what it was all about.

Somehow, Mr Malone's classes became a feverish hothouse of literary endeavour. Unbelievable though it seems, an effeminate pursuit like poetry had brought about a hyper-competitive atmosphere of linguistic combat. It wasn't just me and the rest of the nerds either; some of the toughest guys I ever knew were all vying for attention with million-dollar words, the slickest of rhymes, and ever more arcane vocabulary.

Ours was a mixed school, and we were just entering the age when that mattered, so this pursuit of one-upmanship through verbal dexterity acquired a hormonal charge. I imagine that's why the rap world is like it is: all about braggadocio. Don't watch that, watch this. Everybody sucks but us.

From that day to this, poetry has kept me from hanging around on street corners.

Chapter Fourteen

FLAT TOP WITH FENDERS

1961 was quite an eventful year. Life-changing, in fact. The arrival of my brother Paul when I was twelve cruelly usurped my position as the solitary heir to the Clarke fortune. My empire in ruins, I would seek distraction on the unforgiving rain-swept streets of the city, a perilous and aimless milieu.

I had acquired a coterie of friends from the year above with whom I shared several nameless loathings and various existential anxieties. Mike Cawley was the prodigiously gifted owner of a solid-body electric guitar and the older brother of Eddie, one of my cleverer classmates. Then there was Dennis Walkden, aka Woggy, or Wog. This nickname was often met with mystification. There was, however, a nearby suburb called Walkden, pronounced locally as 'Wogdon', thus Dennis became Woggy. Apart from being broke, we were each independently, at all times, in a state of violent alienation. We seemed to be constantly under the cosh for some reason, and the avoidance of trouble was our top priority the minute we left the house.

Sanctuary was provided at last in the spanking form of a twenty-eight-lane all-American-style bowling alley right there in Cheetham Hill, where the old Odeon building had been expertly transformed by a state-of-the-art refit complete with jukebox, refrigerated

Coca-Cola machines, hot dogs, milkshakes, and a Gaggia. Half a dollar,* returnable on exit, gained admittance to this wonder-land of treasures. The entry fee was just to keep the riff-raff out. We didn't even do any bowling, but that entitled us to unlimited residence. A significant upgrade on the streets outside.

We would sit for hours in that coffee bar, buying the odd Coca-Cola and listening to other people's jukebox selections. It was all bright and lively, modishly tricked out in that post-Sputnik atomic-era fashion, involving chrome, candy-stripe draperies, wipe-clean primary-coloured surfaces, leatherette soft furnishings, and recurrent sci-fi reference points here and about. All the luxury and the leisurewear of the not too distant future – *right now*. At last I could walk like a man in my two-tone bowling shirt without fear of derision.

Clothes were very important. You were judged. To go to school in any shirt that wasn't white singled you out for universal oppro-brium, as I discovered to my cost. Coloured shirt – big deal! The way they went on about it you'd think nobody had ever seen a movie, but if your mother washed your white shirt with something red, it would inevitably acquire a pink tinge: in every case this tainted garment would have to go. With few exceptions, there was no way a bloke could possibly get away with wearing anything pink.

At that time, men's shirts came in three shades: white, grubby, and filthy. In my highly polluted neighbourhood, that was the available colour scheme. Coloured shirts carried the stigma of delinquency: spivs, queers, Latinos, and worst of all, Teddy Boys, who by virtue of their hard-nut reputation as blade artists could wear whatever they liked.

I myself was not immune to the influence of this reprobate

---

* A half crown, or two shillings and sixpence.

subgroup. With their relentless rude humour and swaggering airs, the Teds personified a kind of feral elegance, and for a while I wore my hair in a Tony Curtis: quiffed up at the front and smarmed back at the sides with copious quantities of Fixo, Woolworth's own-brand pomade, available in art deco jars the shape of an Aztec temple.

At Sid and Aubrey's you could have one of four stylings for the back of the head.

One: the fourpenny-all-off, or short back and sides. This un-attractive army style was favoured by the parents of schoolchildren, presumably as a hedge against scalp infestation.

Two: the Boston, a more stylish military haircut, introduced to these shores by American servicemen. This was gradually tapered into the nape and was the first choice of the more stylish post-war adults, e.g. my dad.

Three: the square neck, the collegiate clean-cut-kid look, which I was anxious to cultivate for a while.

And, finally, number four: the DA, the only serious rock and roll option. The DA owes nothing to the District Attorney, that patrician figure of American law enforcement, none of whom, to my knowledge, wore their hair in this fashion. In this instance DA equals Duck's Arse, a fair description of this greasy delta of tonsorial topiary.

In the song 'Beauty School Dropout', sung by Frankie Avalon in the movie *Grease*, there is a memorable chunk which goes thus:

Baby don't sweat it.
You're not cut out to hold a job.
Better forget it,
Who wants their hair done by a slob?

You know, like they say: never trust a thin chef, or a doctor with leprosy. With that in mind, I was always more inclined to

trust the judgement of Aubrey over Sid, on account of his superior
personal style. He was a safer pair of hands: very important when
handling sharps. Even so, call me Mr Fusspot, but I could never
get exactly what I wanted. And me with my extensive vocabulary
and superlative descriptive skills! The look I wanted was a sort of
suedehead, but a bit more spiky on top, smarmed back at the
sides with the DA aft. Dream on, buster. Although he never sent
me out of there looking like a schnorrer − I was, after all, a
walking advert − Aubrey didn't fully embrace my specific ideal.

Help came from Chicago, Illinois, via the brother of Nat Korn
and the back issues of *Modern Screen* magazine. On the inside back
cover of one of them I discovered a whole page detailing all the
haircuts available to the modern American gent.

They all had names inspired by the automotive industry: the
Convertible, the Detroit Jeepnik, the Studebaker Wedge, and the
one I was after, the Flat Top with Fenders. Finally, I could give
it a name. I took the *Modern Screen* to the barber shop and ordered
up a Flat Top with Fenders.

Aubrey had no idea what I was talking about, and directed me
to Green and Zonis, the nearby Ford dealership.

'It's a hairstyle, Aubrey,' I said, referring him to the illustration,
to which he replied, 'Is that an American magazine? Well, this is
England and we call it a Semi Crew.'

Now he tells me. If only I'd known! Given my ignorance, I
can't help feeling partly responsible for my own disappointment,
although to be fair, Aubrey should have kept up to speed with
the stateside nomenclature. I mean, for this they sent him to barber
college?

It never stops hurting.

Chapter Fifteen

WE ARE THE MODERNS

From a very young age, my physical appearance has always been a matter of great concern. Apart from my weediness, many of my anxieties revolved around my nose and the dimensions thereof. I intended to get a bit of aesthetic moderation about the mosh, but my mum was always talking me out of it: 'Well, it suits your face,' she'd say.

She would say that, though, because she had a sizeable hooter herself. 'Everybody gets the nose they're given,' she'd insist. 'The one that God intended, and it usually suits their face.'

Later, I realised my mum was right, but as an anxious teenager, I wasn't convinced. 'No film stars have big noses,' I argued. 'Everybody gets a nose job in show business. Why not me?'

'Plenty of film stars have a big nose,' she'd say, usually citing Jimmy Durante in the same breath, not like anyone would want to look like Jimmy Durante. 'Great. Thanks a lot,' I'd huff. 'Is that what I've got to look forward to?' So then she'd start trying to think of some other names. 'No, not just Jimmy Durante. What about Danny Kaye, then?' By this point, she was a bit exasperated, and only said that because she knew I liked Danny Kaye. I told her I didn't want to look like Danny Kaye either. What I actually said was, 'Fucking hell, I like Danny Kaye but I don't want to look like him! I mean, Mum, I like the Three Stooges but I wouldn't want to look like any one of them.'

Then, when The Beatles appeared, she alighted on Ringo. 'Look, Ringo, the fourth most popular man in the world, and he's got a right conk on him.' 'Yeah, but . . .' I sighed. 'I wouldn't mind looking like George Harrison, but I wouldn't swap faces with Ringo, no offence.'

Likewise, I was always borderline obsessive about my clothes. At Auntie Marge's, apart from the many enticing desserts on offer, the main attraction was my cousin Mary, a very pretty girl two or three years my senior. Mary was extremely fashion-conscious and au fait with the ever-changing pop world, subscribing to several teen-girl magazines, for instance *Mirabelle* and *Boyfriend*, which featured romantic picture stories, problem pages, and centrefold Technicolor pin-ups of the current late-Fifties dreamboats: Elvis (at the time serving his country in Germany), Ricky Nelson, Bobby Rydell, Frankie Avalon, Fabian, etc. Then there were the home-grown derivatives from the stable of Larry Parnes, usually named after some human quality: Johnny Gentle, Lance Fortune, Billy Fury, Vince Eager, Duffy Power, Dickie Pride, Marty Wilde. You get the idea. The stars would usually be presented in a triple-photo feature – kitted out for a gig; engaged in some indeterminate outdoor activity involving a shovel while wearing a pullover; and lastly, unwinding at home, their home being some fabulous residence with a double garage in Kingston upon Thames or some other perpetually sun-lit Home Counties idyll. They always made it look like a branch of the Riviera anyway.

Pre-1962, i.e. before The Beatles, I was just wearing variations on the jeans, windcheater, and winklepickers (or, as we called them, Italians) ensemble – anything else, forget about it. Meanwhile, here was this eighteen-year-old, living the big life, lounging beside his swimming pool in a pair of outré lemon-coloured jeans. Where did he get those jeans?* A candy-stripe resort shirt. Where did he get that shirt? That seersucker blazer, where did he get it? A pair of cyclamen loafers, where did he get them? Those septicaemia-coloured socks, where from?

The first reference to the 'young modernists' appeared in *Town* magazine in October 1962 in an article by Peter Barnsley featuring photographs by Don McCullin. The article quoted a young Terence Stamp, the upwardly mobile son of an East End tugboat skipper, with the memorable line, 'We are the Moderns. We wear elastic-sided boots,' the implication being, smart young man in a hurry. Shoelaces? *Phneh!* Leave that for the web-foots, Jack!

A fifteen-year-old Mark Feld of Stamford Hill (Marc Bolan to you) was also cited, discussing how he financed his wardrobe and where he got certain items, in particular an American Ivy League treasure of a gingham button-down shirt. His access to some of the finest schneiders in the capital meant that his short stature did not hinder his discerning standards of personal elegance. In the words of the late Lou Rawls, 'I gotta maintain my front so's I can keep on making my game.'

This was a look that I was already familiar with via *The Small World of Sammy Lee*, a 1963 monochrome masterpiece featuring Anthony Newley, who also had a pop career and an offbeat weekly TV series, *The Strange World of Gurney Slade*. Many of Newley's fellow pop stars (Adam Faith and Jess Conrad, for instance) were going for this neat urban vibe that seemed a world away from the predominant rock and roll template. And no wonder: its roots belonged in the rarefied world of modern jazz and the movies of the French nouvelle vague.

Like any teenager, I was the star of my own movie, and the production values were very important to me. Image came into

---

* The answer, I found out later, was Vince in Newburgh Street in Soho, about which more later.

it all the time. The *Town* article confirmed that I wasn't entirely alone in my preoccupations.

That same month, October 1962, the 'look' was consolidated and broadcast by The Beatles, when they made their TV debut on Granada's nightly teatime magazine programme *People and Places*, with a live performance of 'Love Me Do', their first self-composed single. At the beginning of November they were on again, doing a cover of 'A Taste of Honey', an earlier stateside hit for Lenny Welch, and then after that, they seemed to be on Granada teatime telly every other week until 'Please Please Me' took them to world domination.

John, Paul, George, and Hilda were the names of myself and my immediate family. How I begged my mum to change her name to Ringo. She was not that keen.

'Bugger off, you're not calling me Ringo.'

'Go on, Ma. Dad doesn't mind. Hey, Dad: call Mum Ringo.'

To which my dad replied, 'Bingo? That's a bloody dog's name.'

'No Dad, RINGO.'

I gave it one more shot.

'Go on, Ma. Nobody's called Hilda any more. Name one.'

'Bugger off. I don't like being called Ringo.'

My mother seemed inordinately attached to her baptismal name, and the matter was never spoken of again.

At first, The Beatles were kitted out in the existentialist strip of black polo neck, dark drainpipes, and of course the revolutionary elastic-sided flamenco boots of Anello and Davide. This would soon be supplanted by the group uniform best illustrated by a joke told to me by a local tailor, Abe Sachs:

'A young man came in here the other day, asking, "Can you do me one of those Beatles suits?"

"Never heard of them," I said. "Describe the suit."

"OK, the jacket: no lapels. No breast pocket. No flaps on the
side pockets. The trousers: no pleats. No pockets. No
turn-ups. How much for a suit like that?"
"Well," I said, "normally for a two-piece gentleman's made-to-
measure suit, £25. But with all these extras . . ." '

These radical suits were accredited to Pierre Cardin, although
in reality they were made by Tin Pan Alley's in-house costumier,
the late Dougie Millings, who set up shop in a salon above the
famous Two I's coffee bar on Old Compton Street, Soho, the
better to serve his prospering pop clientele.

The Beatles looked fabulous in a strange way, like the chairmen
of some new kind of board. The corporate get-up absolved each
member from the onerous responsibility of individual personal
fabulousness. The alienated romanticism of the solitary heart-throb
(see 'Teenage Idol' by Ricky Nelson) was replaced by this cheeky
good-time gang you longed to be a part of. They had a readily
identifiable monochrome house style that somehow legitimised
the malnourished silhouette. Before then, you were better off
being a bit on the beefy side, as was evidenced by the flourishing
body-building industry personified by Charles Atlas. Thanks to
this spindle-shanked combo in their dandy-ish Little Lord
Fauntleroy suits, weediness was instantly a desirable attribute. The
Look: I already had it by default, and everything was fabulous.
For a while.

It was the same for women. The pneumatic fertile sex bombs
of yesteryear gave way to the coltish, androgynous look of Françoise
Hardy and the Jeans Shrimpton and Seberg. We still thought
Marilyn Monroe was sexy, obviously, but our eyes were opened
to a different idea of what was desirable. This expanded the playing
field, and gamine, flat-chested girls with choirboy hips became
an additional attraction. A new kind of people, a new kind of
beauty was being invented on the fly.

Suddenly the UK was calling the sartorial shots, and for three short years, Swinging London was the style capital of the world. Meanwhile, America looked comparatively antique. When The Beatles invaded the States in '64, it became apparent that American girls remained hopelessly out of step. The girls screaming at JFK Airport were all dressed like their moms: frou-frou lace collars sticking out of pullovers, floral poplin skirts with multiple petti-coats, little white gloves, and matching handbags. Cute enough, but cinched in and constricted. Not Modern.

Over here, our girls' clothes were cut like their hair: sharp. No gatherings, ruchings, or darts, or if there were, they were minimal and just at the right spot. Now it was people wearing clothes, and not the other way round. Gone were the torturous foundation garments of yesterday; ease of movement was paramount in this high-speed age.

To me and my pals, even Dusty Springfield looked old-fashioned: like your older sister who didn't know what was going on any more. Dusty was all elaborate syrups and hairpieces done up in rollers, back-combed, lacquered, and sprayed into solid cottage-loaf bouffants as opposed to the asymmetrical bob, the Mary Quant one-eye, the famous Vidal Sassoon five-point cut, the last word in cranial beautification.

The modern young gent got a barnet makeover too. The 'Beatles haircut' was simply a longer version of the College Boy, itself a slightly longer, unkempt version of a Perry Como with a higher than average side parting (obfuscated), slightly layered and very, very short and neat. No pomade necessary. This giant step for mankind was a real generational signifier; for the quiffed-up commandos of the old guard, the clue was in the name: Greasers.

The Flat Top with Fenders was so five minutes ago. Its ante-diluvian taint had to be brutally addressed. 'Enough already with this, give me a College Boy, Aubrey.' This wasn't a problem; the barber-shop window display featured photographic evidence of its availability. I had kinky, thick hair as a kid, however, and some kind of process was de rigueur: lustrous and straight was the desired effect. Happily, there were several non-greasy unguents available for men, mainly Tru-gel and Vitalis. Later, when my hair had grown to the desired length, brown paper and a Morphy Richards steam iron would also be employed.

There was only two years' age difference between us and the Greasers, yet we were like a new species. For about eighteen months, an uneasy stylistic hostility between Mods and Rockers prevailed: they thought we were effeminate, London-centric upstarts; we thought they were, well, slobs. But the hair thing was the main difference, and in my experience, it never went much beyond taking the piss.

Chapter Sixteen

THE BEATLES OR THE STONES?

'The weekend starts here.' Is there a more cheerful sentence in the English language? This is the catchphrase that introduced *Ready Steady Go!* on ITV at teatime every Friday, accompanied by its theme tune, 'Wipe Out' by The Surfaris, and introduced by Dusty Springfield, who, as it later turned out, was enjoying a moment with the show's producer Vicki Wickham.

On the very first show, on 9 August 1963, The Rolling Stones made their debut live appearance with a clipped, no-nonsense version of 'Come On', the B-side of 'Go, Go, Go', the current single by their idol Chuck Berry.

For some reason, my mother was an instant fan. Later, in 1965, as their career was taking off, the Stones were arrested for pissing in the forecourt of an East London gas station. 'We'll piss anywhere, man,' said Mick Jagger, with a note of swaggering insouciance, at once establishing the group's outlaw credentials. My mum was very sympathetic about this injustice, however, and bemoaned the evident lack of public conveniences around our capital.

'Well, they needed the lavatory, it's not their fault. Try to see it from their point of view.' That was my mum all over, she was very generous-spirited like that – probably the only member of our family that ever was. My dad was less forgiving: 'Lock 'em up. Bloody awful, that. Bloody hell.'

Many people had a downer on the Stones anyway, and this incident just consolidated their reputation as the anti-Beatles. If such forecourt unpleasantness had ever befallen the Mop Tops, Brian Epstein would have paid cash money to shut that grease monkey up about it. That's the difference.

The Stones' young manager, on the other hand, was the exotic, Phil Spector-obsessed Andrew Loog Oldham, who had worked for a while as Epstein's publicist and seen how it was done. Realising that The Beatles were unassailable, and the Stones couldn't compete on a level pitch, his masterstroke was to amplify the antisocial, morally compromised decadence of his young charges. To this end they ditched the group uniforms and all the trappings of the Merseybeat craze – except for the flamenco boots, that is.

The irony is that just a few years before, when the Stones were swotting for their exams in the leafy Kent suburbs, The Beatles were living a completely degenerate life in Hamburg, fucking whores, taking drugs, and fleecing the odd drunken sailor for cig money. They were sustaining eight hours at a stretch at the Star Club, playing requests from drunkards who would get belligerent if they couldn't oblige. Most of them wanted to hear the American hits of the day: show tunes, comedy records, rock and roll and R&B, country music, plus pre-rock and roll pop by the likes of Tennessee Ernie Ford, Peggy Lee, and Doris Day.

On their return from Germany, The Beatles' musical scope knew no limits. Versatility was their friend. If The Beatles wanted to give a song a bit of a late-night feel, they knew which chord would do that; if they wanted to try a country flavour, each one of them had a microphone and would finesse his harmonies accordingly. The chords in their songs are not like any others, diminished sevenths and minors. Real sophisticated shit. There's

no shortcut to success and it was no accident why it was The
Beatles first, and then everybody else.

The Stones were primitive by comparison, often sticking to
the shave-and-a-haircut-ten-cents riff popularised by the great Bo
Diddley. Their second single and first big hit was 'I Wanna Be
Your Man' – a Lennon and McCartney song (that's gotta hurt).
It was crucial for them to write their own material, otherwise
they were just going to be a blues band forever, with no publishing
royalties. To this end Loog Oldham locked Mick Jagger and Keith
Richards in a room and told them to get on with it, which they
did with creditable results.

Beyond the music, *Ready Steady Go!* provided the increasingly
fashion-conscious provinces with up-to-the-minute glimpses of
the metropolitan crowd and their attendant styles. At this point
it was all Italian cycling shirts with ring-pull zips, PVC raincoats,
Clarks desert boots, Madras blazers, imported Levi's and Farahs,
plus Converse high-top sneakers.

Here were the early stirrings of label snobbery. Having read
all the James Bond books, in which brands were paramount, this
was not a new thing for me. I was all too conscious of Burberry,
Fred Perry, Austin Reed, Cecil Gee, and houses like that. People
were even snarky about Clark's – anybody who wore any other
brand of desert boot was seen as certifiable. Like Levi's (which
became the generic term for jeans), it absolutely had to be Clark's,
because *they invented them*.

The Modernist ethos was exclusive, judgemental, and wrong.
Virtues almost entirely absent today. It appealed to a snobbish part
of our identity that defied easy definition. And yet, we would never
have dreamed of calling ourselves Mods: although we all looked like
each other and it was obvious that we were falling into some pattern,
if the media could sum you up in three letters, there was something
wrong with your personality. Give anything a name and very quickly
its more obvious elements will be plundered by the plebs.

People who want to seem deep say that appearances aren't important, but I say, *always* judge by appearances. In the very Mod town of Manchester, what you looked like was everything. It was all about standing out, and being confident in the knowledge that no matter what anybody said, you looked better than they did.

I had a specific idea of what I needed to achieve the Look, but there were no outlets to supply it. In that interim period between 1963 and 1965, until boutiques started opening in the city, the immaculate, sleek threads as seen on TV remained elusive.

The magazines I read made reference to King's Road boutiques which catered to the 'Chelsea Set', or their cheaper fast-fashion equivalents on Carnaby Street for the more disposable stuff. At that time, a couple of shops in London's West End, Vince in Newburgh Street and later His Clothes in Carnaby Street (the brainchild of former Vince employee John Stephen), seemed to be the only outlets for the Neapolitan resort clothes, hipster pants, and imported sportswear affected by anyone in the immediate orbit of The Rolling Stones.

At first, Vince catered mainly for the Soho gay underworld, but there was a certain overlap with the modern jazz crowd at Ronnie Scott's, which had recently moved from Gerrard Street to nearby Frith Street. Their suits were purchased at Cecil Gee or Austin Reed, but their casual requirements were met by Vince, and later by John Stephen, who was rapidly colonising nearby Carnaby Street with his boutique empire. Before long, the less edgy items began to catch on with the Young Turks of that new thing, the Media, who quickly introduced these striking fashions to the more discerning of the Modern provincial public.

The first places in Manchester to sell the clothes I liked were to be found in St Ann's Square: the Boston Man's Shop, Smart Weston, Cecil Gee, and Austin Reed – far beyond the means of a penniless schoolboy. The default wardrobe of the Modernist male was the thirty-eight-gram three-button suit – the wide-awake image of the pepped-up urbanite, the cylindrical uniform of the fast-buck meritocracy. Whatever your build, whatever your age, whatever your social station, the three-button suit will make the best of any man. A made-to-measure suit, however, only concerned the over-twenty-ones. Before that, a suit on the drip might be outgrown before the cessation of its weekly payments. How miserable would that be? Your first made-to-measure suit on your twenty-first birthday, therefore, was a major rite of passage.

For a while, finding satisfactory off-the-rail clobber gave your imagination a full-time job. At first, all the covetable American workwear labels – Levi's, Wrangler, Lee, or Dickies – just weren't available over here, except for some reason at the Army and Navy Surplus stores, of which there were many all over town. There you could buy seconds at knock-down rates, so the first pair of Levi's I bought had a bit of a twisted seam or some other minor defect.

The same applied to Converse Chuck Taylor All-Star basketball shoes, a highly unavailable brand. When they first appeared, they were only on sale in sports shops, of which there weren't that many, and even though they were substandard seconds, they were five times the price of a pair of cheap leather shoes. When I told people what they cost, they couldn't believe I was stupid enough to pay that kind of money for what they saw as unacceptable footwear.

We would also find the odd thing in the Army and Navy that would catch on with the burgeoning Mod crowd: cotton double-twist chefs' pants that came in a shade just darker than sky blue with a white railroad stripe, for example. We took them to a valet service for modification: removal of pleats and turn-ups and the seams taken in for a slimmer leg. They also had these waistcoats in a complementary shade called Hospital Blues, which were originally worn by wounded soldiers in a battle situation to indicate the urgent need for medical help according to the tenets of the Geneva Convention.

Close-fitting skinny-rib sweaters, often with a crew or polo neck, called for a degree of cross-dressing, as for some reason men's pullovers were always cut more generously than the ladies', so my knitwear requirements could only be met by Woman at C&A, Etam, Van Allen, and Marks and Spencer's women's department, where the perfect cylindrical fit could be obtained. Coloured shirts for men were now here to stay, and thanks to Patrick Macnee as the dandified semi-Ted John Steed in *The Avengers*, pastel or Bengal-stripe shirts with a white collar were *it*.

After working out what was or wasn't *it*, the problem was one of acquisition. I wasn't made of money, but I was the owner of several threadbare white shirts. Enter Dylon cold-water dyes, available at the haberdashery counter of any department store or reputable high-street drapers. Bingo. The colour of a shirt could be cheaply transformed any number of times, becoming progressively darker with each fresh treatment. Another little job for my mum. The collar was tucked under and an auxiliary button attached to the back of the neckband, the better to affix the detachable Bond Street collar, which my new pal Terry Irvine had introduced me to.

The Bond Street collar, 'For that Savile Row look', was purchased from Woolworth's, which had been selling them since the days before collar-attached shirts became widely available. The packet had a picture of a well-dressed guy in a gleaming collar standing in either Savile Row or the titular Bond Street. They came in three styles: short point, spear point, and cutaway. I went for the spear point, which I would round off with a pair of scissors and the edge of a saucer to achieve the much-sought-after crescent collar worn by The Beatles. Terry preferred the more severe, really high and unyielding white cardboard Mobster version, which went right up to the chin, so his posture was always perfect.

For nearly nothing, I now had an ever-changing array of pastel shirts, each with a white collar that never got dirty. Thanks to the miracle of plastic, the Bond Street collar could be removed and washed at any time, and dried immediately. Although they were a bit sweaty and uncomfortable, I could now enjoy a level of patrician smartness unachievable to most of my fellow citizens. Anyway, from an aesthetic point of view, comfort made me feel uneasy: it was the antithesis of *sharp*.

At some point, the Mod look had a short-lived *Country Life* moment, when the gorgeous mohair sheen of the three-button suit gave way to matte autumnal earth tones. Give it a name: fucking brown. It was all a bit bucolic for my taste.

Nothing too itchy and scratchy, but you know, salt and pepper Donegal, Irish thornproof, cavalry twill, the whole array of hounds-tooth, window pane, pinhead, tattersall, and Prince of Wales checks, even Harry Fenton was knocking them out.

I blame the Downliners Sect.

Chapter Seventeen

LEMONHEAD AND THE LANNY

I was never a scrapper and avoided fights like the fucking plague, but that didn't keep me out of them. It was a good month that only featured a couple of punch-ups.

Me and my friends had to get out of the house in order to smoke cigarettes and swear, and since none of us ever had any money we used to mooch about at the bowling alley, or more often than not we'd just head into the centre of Manchester, a twelve-minute power walk past Strangeways jail, boarded-up wholesale warehouses, cash and carry outlets, and a Salvation Army men's hostel, its immediate vicinity haunted by meths-drinking tramps and newly released prison inmates, all of them demanding money with various degrees of menace. They weren't the biggest problem, however. There were at least three pubs to every parade of shops, and their pissed-up all-male client base made them a seething cauldron of hatred for the likes of us that was both violent and incomprehensible. Was it the cut of our clothes or our knockabout humour that so enraged them? In any case, that short stroll was an invitation to a thrashing.

There was aggression everywhere in Manchester, but I was used to that. It wasn't the kind of art centre it is today: it was a heavy-industrial town, and most working people got belligerent drunk of a weekend.

The aforementioned Jimmy Dynes had recently bought a Norton 650, swapped his drape coats and poo-mashers for winklepickers, a leather jacket, cheap T-shirt, and dirty jeans, and seamlessly morphed into a Greaser. As a Greaser you didn't really need an extensive wardrobe: maybe a Montague Burton suit for court appearances. Apart from that, everything you had would last you for the rest of your tragically foreshortened life (see 'Leader of the Pack' by The Shangri-Las).

Jimmy was a good-looking kid. He had brown hair, which he slathered in Brylcreem just to make it look black. I know I'm always comparing people to movie actors, but no doubt about it, he had the look of Mickey Rourke, hard as nails, with that dirty blond Eddie Cochran quiff, the tattooed knuckles and all that.

Jimmy went for a drink on his own one night and his pretty face went to hell when he was glassed by a gypsy. Later on, the scar only added to his bad-boy allure, but at first it was shocking to see him so disfigured. We thought he was finished, and women were heartbroken: *a handsome lad like that*. I ran into him a few months later and learned that he had recently exacted his bloody revenge.

Having tracked his attacker down, Jimmy gave him the kicking of a lifetime. Apparently Constable Truelove, usually his arch-enemy, had given him the nod and then looked the other way. In Jimmy's own words, 'God knows, me and Mr Truelove have had our differences, but he came good on that occasion.'

In my neighbourhood, gang- and/or alcohol-related violence was just one of any number of potential threats to life. The area seemed to house a disproportionately large number of the criminally insane. For a while, Jimmy and a couple of other Greasers hung out with a truly terrifying individual called Terry Elgin. Terry was a real embittered nutter, known to everyone as Lemonhead, although no one would have dared call him that to his face – it was 'Yes, Terry, no, Terry, three bags fucking full,

Terry.' Not only did he have alopecia, but because of a malformed palate or something (I'm not an expert) he also had a speech impediment which made him whistle whenever he pronounced the letter 'S'.

Lemonhead was such a psycho that even his own gang decided enough was enough and somehow extricated themselves from his company. I don't know how Jimmy shook him off, but after a very short time, if he was asked, 'Seen owt of Terry?' his reply was always the same: 'What? That lemon-headed psychopath cunt?' Followed by a look of panic, and the question, 'He's not around, is he?'

Lemonhead went completely rogue, and finished up on a piece of waste ground in Higher Broughton called the Cliff, where mining subsidence at Agecroft Colliery, together with the River Irwell, had eroded one side of the floodplain creating a landslide, hence its local name, the Lanny. The road had collapsed, leaving a one-sided parade of uncharacteristically middle-class semis perched perilously close to its vertiginous edge. You could still see the partially submerged tramlines, mangled, twisted, and knotted like steel spaghetti. Below was a pestilential tangle of semi-uprooted trees, out-of-control weeds, and poisonous foliage, girders, rubble, mudslides, and at the bottom, that 'melancholy stream', the River Irwell.

No other river made a greater contribution to the industrial strength of the nation than the Irwell, such was the concentration of industry along its banks. On a fifty-mile stretch, countless cotton mills, paper mills, coal mines, tanneries, slipper factories, bleach works, gas works, paint works, and dye works spewed a million gallons of grotesquely coloured effluent into its waters. There was Clayton Aniline, Tootal, Macphersons Paints in Bury, all pumping chemical-rich poison into the stream. Every day it was a different colour. Sometimes the rancid scum on its surface was so thick that birds could walk on it. God help you if you fell in – one mouthful and you would have been dead on arrival.

Horror stories understandably grew up around the Lanny. There were said to be venomous snakes, poisonous lizards, treacherous swamps, rank hazardous mires, quicksands even. Why, a bread van was reportedly pushed over the edge and to this day has never been found. There were super-piranhas that were immune to the industrial poisons of the foetid Irwell. All these hazards and more awaited the hapless saunterer. It was like going into the fucking Congo. Plus, there was the possibility of sliding to your death down some slimy, precipitous ravine.

Now, to make things worse, the ultra-alienated Lemonhead had got hold of a .22 rifle from somewhere and had taken to squatting in a particular tree in the Lanny, an unseen position from which to take potshots at any passing citizen, and in so doing attained the folk-devil status of the indiscriminate sniper. Although neither I nor any of my friends would have gone out without the requisite railroad knife, what good would that have been in these circumstances? The situation brings to mind the memorable pronouncement by Ramon in *A Fistful of Dollars*, 'When a man with a knife goes against a man with a rifle . . . then, the man with the knife is a dead man.'

Lemonhead was the worst, but there were other nutters who would invite themselves into our company and by virtue of their nuttiness were never gainsaid. We just had to put up with them. When Ernie Heaton was around, for example, there was always a genuine risk that we'd end up getting into trouble with the police.

Ernie had a glass eye; something to do with a pair of scissors and the scraping of gloss paint off a door, one of many chores undertaken for his mother. Poor Mrs Heaton, she probably blamed herself for her son's consequent insanity. He told us the story many times, with increasing relish. There he was scraping away, scrapity, scrapity, scrape, and then whammo, boing, schlurk!!! Right in the fucking eyeball. He was forever removing his prosthetic. Horrible.

1. Hilda and George Clarke, my mum and dad, in front of the half-timbered asbestos shed in next door's back yard.

2. The building I grew up in, its plywood windows indicating its imminent demolition.

3. The neighbourhood corner shop, Forshaws', where 'The Saint' used to buy his boiled ham.

4. Great Cheetham Street, Salford, round the back of our building.

5. The Rialto cinema. This must have been taken from our front door.

6. With my cousin Estelle in Rhyl, during the convalescent years.

7. Me, Michael Partington and – who was that masked man? – my cousin
Sid in the back yard. To the right is the asbestos shed, and behind us
is the scrubby shrub that formed the background to every photo
taken in our yard.

8. Me, aged about seven.
'Stick 'em up!'

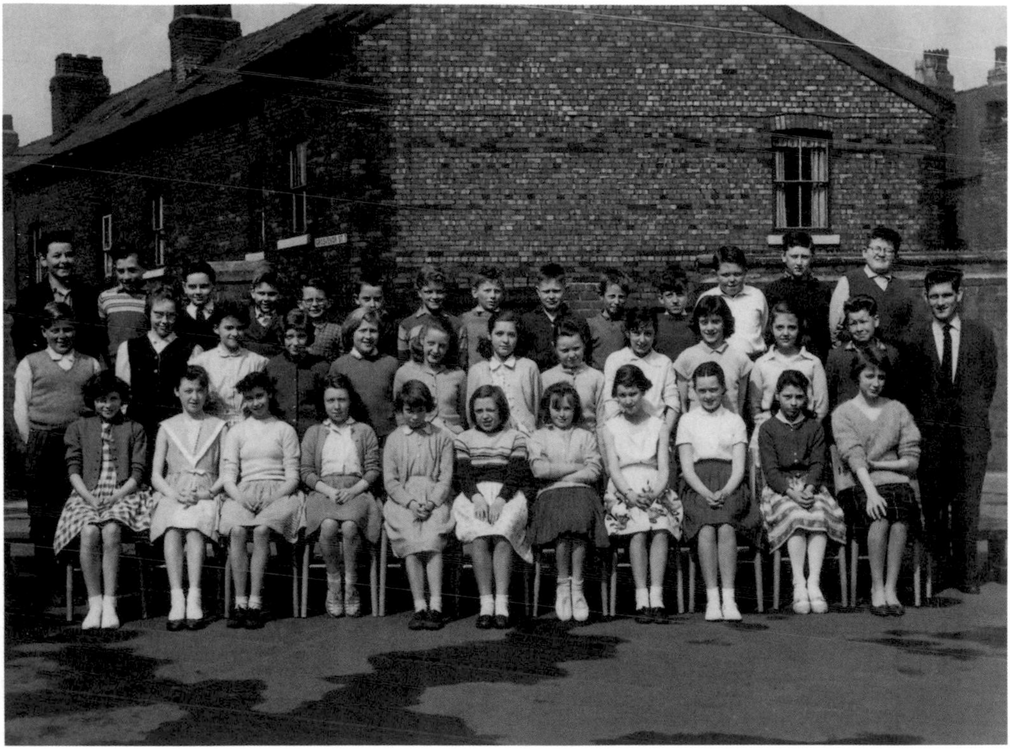

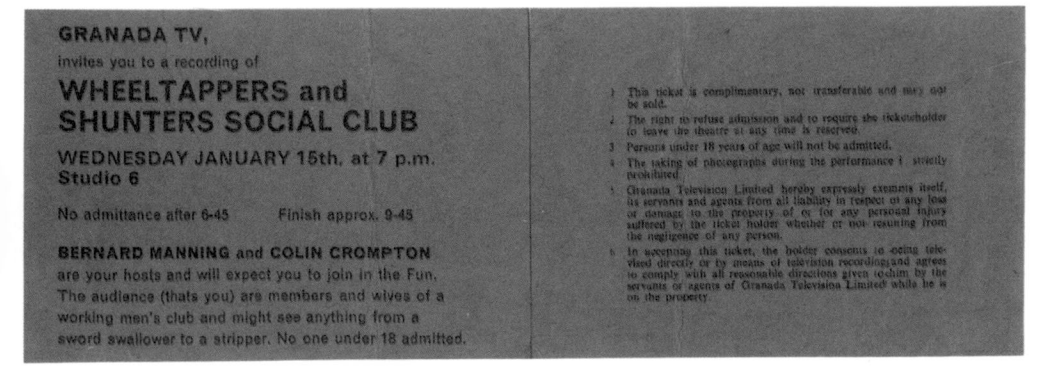

9. The traditional school photo: spot the poet (back row, second from right). Mr Malone is on the extreme right.

GRANADA TV,
invites you to a recording of
WHEELTAPPERS and
SHUNTERS SOCIAL CLUB
WEDNESDAY JANUARY 15th, at 7 p.m.
Studio 6

No admittance after 6-45 Finish approx. 9-45

BERNARD MANNING and COLIN CROMPTON
are your hosts and will expect you to join in the Fun.
The audience (thats you) are members and wives of a working men's club and might see anything from a sword swallower to a stripper. No one under 18 admitted.

1 This ticket is complimentary, not transferable and may not be sold.
2 The right to refuse admission and to require the ticketholder to leave the theatre at any time is reserved.
3 Persons under 18 years of age will not be admitted.
4 The taking of photographs during the performance i strictly prohibited.
5 Granada Television Limited hereby expressly exempts itself, its servants and agents from all liability in respect of any loss or damage to the property of or for any personal injury suffered by the ticket holder whether or not resulting from the negligence of any person.
6 In accepting this ticket, the holder consents to being televised directly or by means of television recording and agrees to comply with all reasonable directions given to him by the servants or agents of Granada Television Limited while he is on the property.

10. My dad was a regular at the Wheeltappers and Shunters.

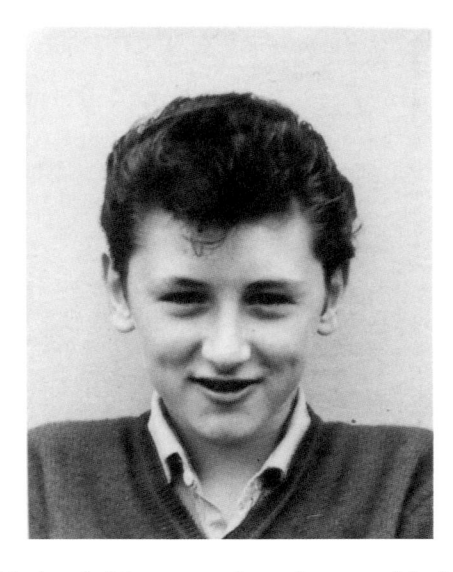

11. Aged thirteen or thereabouts, with the
soon-to-be obsolete Tony Curtis hairdo.

12. The Vendettas. L. to R.: Mike Cawley, Dennis Walkden (aka Woggy) and me.

13. Another picture for the fans, sitting on the bins in front of the asbestos shed: The Chaperones, L. to R., Me, aka Brett Vandergelt Junior, Mike Cawley and, newly recruited, cousin Sid, with his jumbo maracas.

14. In front of the foliage in the backyard, sporting an embryonic moustache.

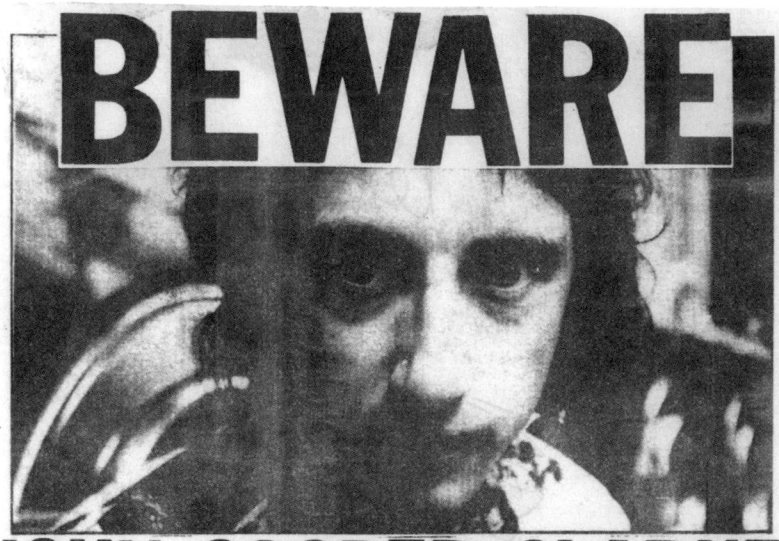

BEWARE

JOHN COOPER CLARKE

This man is preaching red dogma to your children, under the pretence of entertainment, is spreading the virulent and rabid ideoligies of so called "anarchism".

A so called poet his works are putrid gurgling of a decadent running sore on the clear skin of British morality.

Act now to staunch the flow of pus that is dripping from these sly and insinuating lips.

This man's obscene fat and sinister paymasters have fineangled him onto an innocent-looking tour — in sold out auditoria everywhere. He is at this moment preaching his filthy doctrines.

Not until the strong clear sounds of the marching bands ring out from over Europe from east to west will we be free from the pansy menace of these so-called artistes.

With his big nose and wretched effeminate hairstyle, he is using that most dark and sinister of forces — charm, to implant his amoral philosophies deep in the fertile mulch of impressionable young minds.

If you feel, as we do, that politics and filth have no place in entertainment complain to the press, hall manager, record label or the person next to you!

YOUR voice must be heard!

15. A moral–panic–style flyer, composed by Martin Hannett at Rabid Records.

'No, I don't want to see your empty eye socket! Put it back, you daft cunt,' I would have said if I'd had the nerve.

If Ernie caught you in the street it was advisable to avoid all eye contact (which was pretty difficult, considering he was in a position to actually sling one of them in your direction). He was dangerous, a real fucking head-the-ball, and violent with it. Nutter. And when I say nutter, I *mean* nutter.

He went for karate lessons three times a week, and would demonstrate his expertise by dropping the nut on lamp posts, brick walls, or any hard, fixed, inanimate target, including trees. 'Fucking impressive, Ernie. Fucking impressive!' You had to keep him sweet, that was the thing. Who would come off the better: Ernie or the tree? You could maybe nut a wall down, if it was badly maintained, but a tree is going nowhere, what with the extensive root system.

Another local psycho was David Vardin. I only met him once. He had ginger hair and impetigo – his face was a terrifying mask of freckles and gentian violet. He lived down Back Roman Road, a narrow dirt track that ran between Frank Wong's chip shop and the County cinema. Once, when I strayed into his manor, he relieved me of my movie money at the sharpened point of a ratchet screwdriver. Back Roman Road was a five-minute walk from our backyard, but with a busy main road in between, thankfully, it was easy to avoid.

What with him, Ernie 'The Nut' Heaton, Lemonhead, and the hazards of the Lanny, it's a wonder I lived beyond sixteen.

Chapter Eighteen

THE WORLD OF HENRY ORIENT AND THE PYJAMA PARTY

I turned fifteen in January 1964. My education was at an end and my future was closing in.

I had already determined that somehow I was going to be a professional poet. This ambition didn't cut it with the school employment officers, however. This was a secondary modern school after all, and some industrial position was the usual option. When it came to my turn, I don't know what I thought I was doing, but I must have said I liked cars, and that's how I ended up with a grease-monkey apprenticeship at a local garage called Kennings, starting that September.

It was my own fault: I should have said I was interested in cars, but that my curiosity was purely cosmetic. I was only really concerned with the styling and the colour schemes: I was a bit of a petrolhead in that way, and spent a lot of my schooldays designing muscle cars in my exercise books, but that was the extent of my engagement. I wasn't the slightest bit interested in learning about what went on under the bonnet.

That spring, my mum and dad announced that they were going to take my baby brother on a summer vacation to Southport. I had no interest in Southport, and anyway, I considered myself too old to go on holiday with my parents.

While the rest of the family were off sunning themselves, I would have the whole apartment to myself for a week. A plan immediately began to form. I figured that with its high ceilings, lavish fenestration, maximising the solar illumination of the workplace, a panoramic view, the place could pass as a kind of bachelor pad, ideal for a party. Me and my pals were always looking for an excuse to talk to girls: this was a once in a lifetime opportunity to engage them in a meaningful conversation.

My immediate friends had already left school and were working or at art college: Mike Cawley had just started a commercial art course at Salford Tech, where he had met Terry Irvine (of Bond Street collar fame), a handsome lad of English-Jamaican parentage and the best-dressed guy I had ever met at that point. Through Terry, we had become pals with his cousin Dave Redshaw, who was a trainee cutter at Quellrain, a weather-wear firm in Cheetham Hill. Later Dave moved jobs to work at Baracuta, manufacturers of the world-famous G9, the Harrington jacket to you.

Dave Redshaw was also known as Bullwinkle, or Bullwink, after a character in an American cartoon that we were all crazy about, *The Rocky and Bullwinkle Show*. Rocky was a flying squirrel and Bullwinkle was an absurd, anthropomorphised cartoon moose. When he was younger, Dave had a Teddy Boy haircut with three partings that for some reason was called the South Bank. It was the cut that Gene Vincent had going on at the time, involving quiffage like a bunch of greasy grapes with the sides scooped up and everything pushed forward to an absurd degree, a low parting on each side and one across the back of the head, culminating in a DA.

Dave's hair was fair, fine, and straight – quite enviable in a way, but utterly unsuited to his chosen 'do'. The side bits would separate in the middle and fall outwards into two horns (think Viking helmet). This lent Dave's head an unmistakable silhouette – hence the nickname, although by the time we were pals he had happily abandoned all attempts at this unattainable ideal in favour of a perfectly reasonable College Boy cut.

We were always following girls around. Everybody did it. Once in the cosy anonymity of the city centre, we had several shop doorways that we used to stand around in. There we would be, smoking cigs, swearing, engaging in projectile expectoration contests, telling filthy jokes, and trying, ineptly, to connect with girls.

Girls were a complete fucking mystery to us. We didn't even know where they went, so we actually used to follow them around town, at a distance, just to see where they were going. None of them, obviously, was remotely interested in us. We were invisible to them. There was an advert for Kia-Ora, the fruit drink sold in cinemas, with some chick shouting 'KIA-ORA!' in a very high register. For some reason, this became our battle cry, but it was all done a bit half-heartedly. Occasionally one of us would yelp out a suitably squeaky 'Kia-Ora!', and when a girl reacted, we would affect an innocent demeanour, like, you know, 'Don't blame us!' I don't know what victory would have looked like, but our efforts were usually countered by that most withering riposte: 'Grow up.'

They must have thought, what a bunch of idiots. Thankfully nobody ever called the police. We'd watch them meet their boyfriends, disappear down into cellar clubs and various places of entertainment, then we'd fuck off.

But now, my forthcoming party provided us with the oppor-tunity to engage with the ladies, a reason to actually talk to them. We'd tell them about this anticipated big event, and it would go on from there. Who knew what beautiful avenues this would lead to? That was the plan anyway.

Woggy, Terry, Dave, and Mike were all quite visual people. Like me, they were very interested in the way people dressed in the movies we admired. The detail of our party-plan, therefore, was inspired by Hollywood's idea of contemporary bohemianism, down to the drinks, the decor, the music, and the dress code. We'd all recently been to the Rialto to see *The World of Henry Orient*, starring Peter Sellers as this exotic boho pianist guy in Greenwich Village for whom two teenage girls have developed a fascination, to the extent that they have taken to stalking him. Henry Orient is having an affair with one of the girls' mums, and thinks the girls are detectives sent by the woman's husband. He's a real hepcat who schlepps around his house in an assortment of Oriental Dr Fu Manchu-type loungewear – Shantung leisure pyjamas and gold, pointy babouches, kimono-sleeve dressing gowns, and, for sleepy time, a black-velvet jet-set eye mask. I was deeply impressed. So that was it: this wasn't going to be just any plain old house party. And here's where the dress code came in: it was going to be a pyjama party. Nobody, but nobody, would be admitted without their night attire.

It was going to be great: chicks in nighties all over the gaff. Obviously, some of them were going to tell us to fuck off, but law of averages, and with weeks and weeks to talk it up, some success was expected. We told them straight: 'Bring your pals, but no guys. If you bring a guy you won't get in. Or if you're not dressed in your pyjamas, you won't get in.' As the big night drew nearer, realising that some of the girls' attendance would involve a bus ride, we relaxed this rule, with the proviso that they change into their nightwear immediately upon admittance.

Mike Cawley and Terry Irvine had access to printing media at college, so we had real cutting-edge modern-art tickets printed out: 'Pyjama Party: bring a pal. (NO BLOKES).'

We wanted to look good. We couldn't wear our normal candy-stripe flannelette pyjamas; we wanted to look like swinging cats, exotic even. It had been proven by that film that chicks go for guys in that sort of loungewear, so on the strength of that irrefutable evidence we got Dave Redshaw to knock up some Henry

Orient-style leisure pyjamas in which we could entertain an unlimited number of women.

Redshaw was good with a pattern, and had access to a load of satin coat linings in wild iridescent colours at his work. He persuaded one of the machinists to turn our self-designed pyjamas into a reality: Aladdin pants, flared sleeves, with a Nehru-meets-Emperor Ming stand-up collar that had to be stiffened with cardboard, the whole look completed with a contrasting night cravat. The five of us each chose different colours, mine being a shot-silk number in dark plum chameleoning into an attractive shade of burgundy. The others' were variously aquamarine, vermilion, magenta, and gold-oblique-electric blue.

Extreme.

We wanted to give the impression that we didn't live in our various homes with our parents, and it was just about feasible that five teenagers could be renting a converted Victorian apartment like mine. So as soon as my folks left on holiday, we did the place up and made it look like some kind of uber-hip beatnik salon. We rearranged all the furniture and managed to shift all my parents' stuff into a wardrobe: any ornaments that smacked of middle-aged taste were hidden away. We put red light bulbs in every available socket.

Action painting was a major concern of the demi-mondaine – we took the unpatterned side of old rolls of wallpaper, decommissioned bed sheets, and tablecloths, and hung them on a line in the yard to be Jackson Pollocked in splatter-coloured household emulsion. Abstract art. We did our best. When pinned to the wall, these action paintings obscured the crap mum and dad wallpaper.

Drinks-wise, given that we were expecting a mainly female crowd, we catered accordingly. It was shorts all the way: South African port (about five bob a pint), various bottles of VP, Emva Cream, QC sherry, a quantity of Israeli raisin wine, and a crate of Babycham. And for nibbles? No expense spared: a couple of platters of pork pies, the odd bagel, bowls of crisps, some Ritz crackers, and three cans of pineapple chunks.

On the night of the party, red lights glowing, records playing at top volume on the mono Dansette record player, and us in our slinky pyjamas, all we had to do was wait for the doorbell to ring and answer it with smiles on our faces.

Loads of chicks in nighties turned up. Some arrived in their nightclothes with an overcoat on top, others carried teddy bear pyjama cases. Some brought their favourite records with them. It was a great success in that respect.

On the downside, a lot of them brought their boyfriends. An unwelcome and unexpected presence, muscling in on our action. What with the booze and the average age, the party soon got out of hand. There was noise; people spilling out, shouting and screaming up the fire escape. I was getting antsy about stuff getting smashed, an anxiety which only further amounts of Babycham could address. Somebody complained about the music and the cops came round and told us to keep it down.

That, however, wasn't how my parents found out about the party. Somebody had posted a load of pork pies through Mr and Mrs Korn's letter box downstairs. These unrequested gifts would not have been ratified by the Beth Din, and proved very traumatic for my elderly neighbours. I didn't even know it had happened, but I got grassed up. Mrs Korn was extremely offended, and complained to the neighbours about this unwelcome avalanche of trayf. The whole street was on about it for a year afterwards.

It didn't take long until it got back to my mum, who paid a visit downstairs and managed to convince Mrs Korn that I had no part to play in the whole pork-pie unpleasantness. When she got back upstairs, however, I didn't get off so lightly, and a personal apology was called for.

Chapter Nineteen

A ROCK 'N' ROLL LIFE: IN THE MAFIA

Earlier that year, Mike Cawley, Woggy, Terry Irvine, and I had decided to form a pop combo.* We'd all seen the 1960 movie *Pay or Die* starring Ernest Borgnine as Lt Joseph Petrosino, the only honest Sicilian cop in Little Italy, up against the Black Hand and their empire of extortion. We had noted the prodigious elegance of the Mobster dress code; if this movie was anything to go by, those guys seemed to be getting it all. Our enthusiasm inspired our group name: The Mafia.

The Cawleys were a pretty musical family. There was Eddie, the youngest, Mike the middle one, and their older brother Pete, a really handsome bastard, who played the drums in a moderately successful local group. Mike had an electric guitar, a red and black Dallas, solid body, two pickups; you could get splinters off the fucker, but they weren't that common. To know anybody who possessed an electric guitar was quite something back then. It wasn't the ubiquitous chunk of furniture it is

---

* Why no Dave Redshaw, you may ask. Redshaw had no interest in being in this outfit. Even though he was the first guitar owner I had ever known, he had never got round to actually learning any chords. He would just wear it around the house and mime to Eddie Cochran records.

today. Mike was also, unfortunately for me, a dead ringer for George Harrison.*

When we formed The Mafia, apart from Mike none of us could play. As far as I was concerned, the main requirement in any musical career involved poncing about in a silk suit. The playing of chords called for a degree of manual contortion beyond my abilities. I therefore opted for the bass guitar. One string at a time. How difficult could it possibly be?

I bought a second-hand bass, a Framus Star, from Reno's, where they sold repossessed musical equipment at a knock-down rate. I got it for the prohibitive price of £38 and was paying for it on hire purchase. The Framus was a respectable instrument – Bill Wyman had one, albeit the larger model with two pickups, but I preferred my single pickup because it was dinky with a single cutaway design, redolent of a Gibson Les Paul. On the downside, it had a hollow body and was inclined to feed back. That didn't bother me; on the contrary, I was never confident about my abilities on any instrument and it gave me an excuse to turn it right down to an inaudible level.

Terry Irvine was going to be on second guitar. He'd recently acquired a Rosetti Lucky 7, also from Reno's. After the Vox Stroller, it was the second cheapest electric guitar you could get. It came in a black into turquoise sunburst finish, featuring a single pickup and scratchplate unit made out of plastic, dressed in that iridescent fake abalone pearlised stuff often found on fountain pens, flush door handles, drum kits, cufflinks, and most piano accordions.

I had also acquired a big battleship-grey Philips reel-to-reel tape recorder, the kind of thing you see in movies used by black-mailers, or kept men who want to have their wealthy wives

---

* Who hasn't got a fucking Strat today? I'll shake their hand personally. They've lost all cachet since fucking Tony Blair showed up.

committed to an insane asylum: '*I distinctly heard his voice.*' '*You're imagining it, darling.*' I don't know what my fucking plan was, but I thought a reel-to-reel would be a more versatile and fun vehicle for music than a mere record player. It also came with a micro-phone and had a three-inch plastic speaker in a plastic case so it doubled as an amplifier, although you couldn't plug a bass guitar into it or you'd have blown it to smithereens.

Woggy was the designated drummer, so at some point a kit was deemed necessary. Everything was on the drip, obviously: we didn't have the kind of kerplinky to go buying expensive drum kits. Even on hire purchase, our choice was limited by budgetary constraints. The cheapest kit he tried out was a Gigster, but that was more or less a toy: the cymbals were the size of a pan lid and the drums were like the bucket from a kid's beach bucket-and-spade set. Woggy looked like a giant on it. Given our serious ambitions for The Mafia, a more proportionate kit was necessary, and Woggy went for the second cheapest option: a 'marine pearl' Broadway drum set, yes, clad in that iridescent fake abalone stuff that flush door handles, fountain pens, cufflinks, and most piano accordions are often made out of.

Other than that, we didn't have any equipment at all. Rehearsals would take place at each other's houses in a vague rotary system. Mike would plug his Dallas guitar into my Philips reel-to-reel 'amplifier' and it was all systems go until somebody told us to shut up. When we were practising at our place, it would be the usual words of encouragement from my dad: 'Bloody awful, that!'

We only knew two riffs: the Bo Diddley 'Shave and a Haircut Ten Cents', and 'High Heel Sneakers' by Tommy Tucker, also used on 'Hurt by Love' by Charlie and Inez Foxx: bam bam bam bam bam bam bam bam. Oh, and 'Hoochie Coochie Man'.

Not long after the pyjama party, we somehow secured a booking for the Class of '64 Freshers' Ball at Salford Tech, where Mike and Terry were studying. Various groups were playing that night, carefully chosen to reflect the Mod/beatnik demographic predominant in every art college at that time. This was our big break. We were even on the posters, just below the bottom of the list.

Mike Cawley's brother Pete's group was called the Challengers. They were a little bit old-fashioned to our taste, like the Shadows: they all wore the same suits and had quiffs. Then they got this singer who could carry a tune, but his name was Stan something or other (back then, everyone was called Stan). The condition of his joining was that he changed it to something that would alliterate with the Challengers, anything starting with 'Ch-', like Chick:

'I'm not calling myself Chick; I'm not a woman.'

'Oh all right. Charlie then.'

'I'm not calling myself Charlie. They'll call me a right Charlie.'

The one that didn't seem to invite ridicule was Chet, and so it was that they became Chet and the Challengers, a very old-school sort of name to us. But they were really serious about making it, and got a lot of bookings, including at one of Manchester's largest and most prestigious venues, Belle Vue Gardens. Why? Because they could really play, and they obviously had proper equipment, including Selmer amps, which were second only to Vox AC30s.

We tried to blag some kit from them for our debut outing at the Tech in order to look like a proper outfit.

'Ask your kid, Mike.'

'I'm not asking him. He'll tell me to fuck off.'

'Put the mither on him, Mike. It's our only chance.'

Chet and the Challengers weren't very encouraging. The word 'punk' was even uttered in its pre-Seventies pejorative sense, but they grudgingly came across with two amplifiers and a Reslo microphone. No guitars.

You only get one chance to make a first impression. With this in mind, I decided that we should all go blond for the big occasion. We bought this stuff called Colaire, which came in a small plastic bottle along with an applicator the size of a mascara brush. The instructions read, 'Use Sparingly'. It should have been evident by the size of the brush that Colaire was for highlights only, whereas I wanted the full blond cover. Finding it just wasn't working fast enough, we wound up emptying a whole bottle each over our heads.

We looked all right in my bedroom, but when we got out the front door into the sunshine . . . It was a case of 'What the . . . ? Huh?!' It wasn't blond. It wasn't even golden blond. I've seen golden blond, and this was just *gold*. *Gold*, I tell you. Full-on metallic-Christmas-tree-decoration gold. We just gawped at each other.

'What the fuck are you going as?'

But we all looked the same. We were like Martians, visitors from a rock and roll planet beyond our galaxy. Terrible. And it was too late to do anything about it.

Top of the bill was a group called the Measles, a bunch of long-hairs modelled on the Stones. Their extremely charismatic frontman was the whippet-shaped Red Hoffman, name-checked on their only single, a moderately successful cover of 'Castin' My Spell', which had been a stateside hit for Marie Adams and the Johnny Otis Show in 1959.

The Measles wore those Madras cotton blazers with brass buttons beloved of Georgie Fame and the Blue Flames: muted candy stripes in mustard, maroon, and bottle-green. And centre stage on vocals, maracas, and gob-iron, Mr Hoffman in a different coloured jacket, of course.

But it was the second act that gripped our imagination: the Victor Brox Blues Train. They had a three-horn brass section, and Bruce Mitchell, the greatest drummer I've ever seen – and I don't usually notice drummers, to be honest. Victor himself, with his elegantly topiarised Vandyke and his snakeskin jacket, sang and played electric organ, violin, and pocket cornet.

We were on first. Thirty-watt amplifiers were a new sonic experience for us, and we'd never heard ourselves at full volume before. Now we were not only inept, we were also unignorable. What a thrill: we were giving them full voltage and there was nothing anybody could do about it. To this day, I don't know why the entire audience didn't head for the exits.

In a world where anything goes, it was enough that nobody else sounded like us; and nobody else sounded like us because they could play. We had invented a whole new sound, all right. The one that everybody had avoided up to that point. We were unquantifiably bad, but any criticism was met with scorn. To us, our primitive untutored approach was enviable, a badge of authenticity, a welcome breath of fresh air.

Obviously, we expected to get loads of bookings after the Freshers' Ball, but inexplicably, not a single offer ensued. This didn't make us question our performance, however: we convinced ourselves it was nothing to do with our lack of expertise. No, it was our unsympathetic nomenclature. *That* was the stumbling block.

Gangsters in general were getting a bad press because of *The Scarface Mob*, a movie starring Neville Brand as Al Capone and Robert Stack as his nemesis, Eliot Ness. A spin-off TV series, *The Untouchables*, soon followed, and all of a sudden nobody had a good word for La Cosa Nostra.

We changed our name to the Vendettas.

Chapter Twenty

THE WEEKEND STARTS HERE

I, meanwhile, had taken up the apprenticeship at Kennings. I knew already that it was a non-starter: I showed no aptitude for the work, and I didn't like getting dirty.

It was a job, nevertheless, which lent me a measure of independence and a modest sum of disposable cash (i.e. a fraction of my erstwhile milk-and-honey Black Magic days) with which to furnish my capsule wardrobe.

A weekly wage was also essential to fund my increasingly active social life. Woggy, Terry, Mike, Dave, and I had achieved membership of the various music clubs in Manchester. Like me, they were all totally Americanised: suckers for certain clothing brands and movies, sick humour and slang, cartoon characters, flamboyant criminals, and music, music, music.

Manchester had a culture of American black music way before London. All those soul records that hadn't enjoyed stateside hit status but were nevertheless fabulous, along with crates and crates of comics and the trash fiction that stuck like bubblegum to the teenage imagination, were all randomly slung into the ships' holds for ballast before the higher-ticket consumer goods bound for Manchester or the Western-facing ports of Liverpool, Glasgow, and Bristol. Like most things American, this stuff was considered cheap, tawdry, tinny, and morally vacuous. Dock workers used to just give it away . . . and then people started reading those comics and that trash fiction, and listening to those records, many of which were eventually covered by the Northern Beat groups* of the early Sixties.

The city-centre clubs were essentially extended coffee bars where you could go to hear records and live acts, hang out with other young people, meet girls, and drink Coca-Cola; their underage demographic precluded an alcohol licence. I wasn't fussed about alcohol – none of us drank much – although I was already into drugs. But occasionally someone would nip out to a nearby pub to blag a pint or a short. If you stuck to cider, or something like that, you could go in and nobody would call the cops. The worst that could happen was that the barman would question your age. That happened once or twice, but most of the time I got away with it because back then I was considered tall for my age,[†] and although Dave Redshaw was a bit older than me, he was slightly shorter and got asked his age much more often than I did, so I used to buy his drinks.

Each club had its own slightly tribal music policy. Some featured live acts, others were essentially discotheques with a resident DJ whose record collection dictated his level of success. Personality didn't come into it: they were only as good as the records they played. It was a highly competitive scene in that respect and utterly democratic.

The first club of which we were card-carrying members was the Oasis, a two-hundred-capacity basement venue that featured a live group every night: The Animals, The Who, Jimmy Powell and the Five Dimensions, The Stylos, Wayne Fontana and the

---

* Back then, it was always 'groups', never 'bands'. If you said you were in a band, the reaction would be, 'What do you play? Trombone?' Bands involved a multitude of musicians, none of whom played an electric guitar.
† I don't think people would describe me as being tall any more, but if you had to describe me back then you would have said 'tall and thin'. You don't really see as much stunted malnourishment nowadays.

Mindbenders, The Cymerons, and long ago, The Beatles. Yes, The Beatles! And from America, Bo Diddley, Charlie and Inez Foxx, 'Little' Stevie Wonder, Lee Dorsey, Doris Troy, the Sir Douglas Quintet . . . plus much more, and then some.

The Animals appeared at the Oasis weeks before their first hit, 'Baby Let Me Take You Home', but they already had quite a reputation, and were already big enough to have a group uniform: pale blue four-button suits with a dark grey silk edging.

I don't know where the dressing rooms were located but it was always necessary for the headline act to walk through the audience in order to gain access to the stage. When 'LITTLE' Stevie Wonder came through, he turned out to be seven feet tall, skinny as a rake, and wearing one of those evening suits with a Hispanic twist: a hip-length bolero-style jacket and a wide sash around his waist with a ruffled shirt. His hair looked like it was painted onto his scalp, as short as you could possibly get it, with a shaven-in side parting. He was an exceptionally good-looking kid; kind of otherworldly.

'Little' Stevie's band were a skeleton crew of top in-house Detroit musos from the Motown Corp, although as a multi-instrumentalist he made most of the running, alternating between a Vox Continental organ, a harmonica, of course, and the drums.

Thanks to the worldwide success of the Merseybeat craze, it wasn't long before we got a Manchester version of the Cavern. Aptly enough called the Cavern, it was a tiny venue in Cromford Court with a 150 capacity (if you broke the fire regulations). It was a real khazi of a building, frequented by what people called Dossers.

The Dossers always carried bedrolls wherever they went, even if it was just down to the Cavern, the subtext being that they were homeless, rambling beatniks. *Ain't got no home in this world any more* – you know, rebels against society, kids with long, unwashed hair who bought their entire wardrobe at the Army and Navy Surplus stores.

Of course, we shopped at the Army and Navy too, but while

we went for the more discerning Mod approach with the dandified chef-pants-and-Hospital-Blues ensemble, these Dossers stuck
to the brown-and-olive-drab-fatigue palette. Their uniform was
combat jackets with their favourite group's name roughly painted
on the back – a bit of a corny move, to our collective mind.
Meanwhile, the Dossers hated us because we were poncified.

There was a lot of crossover on the club scene – musically, at
least. We weren't *that* tribal: one minute we'd be saying, 'I wouldn't
be seen dead in that place', but if the right person or group was
playing there, you had to go. We went to see The Kinks at the
Cavern, for example, in the days when they were wearing the
whole strip with those hunting-pink frock coats.

The Cavern played host to many out-of-town combos both
well-known and obscure: The Cimarons; Rev Black and the
Rockin Vickers featuring the young Lemmy, later of Motörhead;
Sounds Incorporated; Four Plus One; the Myaks; the Groundhogs;
The Walker Brothers; Bo Diddley; Julie Driscoll, Brian Auger
and the Trinity; and any one of a thousand long-haired Rolling
Stones knock-offs who specialised in the kind of primitive, raucous
music so beloved of that snotty, malcontented tribe for whom
enthusiasm outweighed technical expertise.

The Dossers were at the obsessive centre of what became the
British blues boom, intensely loyal to any group whose repertoire
was dictated by Chicago's hyper-electrified version of the blues,
especially the output of Veejay and Chess Records. Ownership
of any of these records depended on a level of dedication which
only the Dossers could maintain. Songs by the likes of Willie
Dixon, Muddy Waters, John Lee Hooker, Jimmy Reed, and the
big two, Chuck Berry and Bo Diddley, would have provided
eighty per cent of any of the Dossers' required set list.

If the Dossers had a house band, however, it had to be The
Pretty Things, namely Phil May, Dick Taylor, John Stax, Brian
Pendleton, and Viv Prince, probably because they had the longest

hair in show business at that time; even longer than the Stones. That was what shot The Pretty Things to fame. Their name came from an old Bo Diddley tune, 'Pretty Thing', which was highly ironic because, Phil May aside, you wouldn't describe any of them as an oil painting, unless you factor in the late Hieronymus Bosch.

Another dosser hang-out was the Heaven and Hell, which was in an old office building in Sackville Street, a two-floor establishment, hence the name: hell was downstairs in the basement, upstairs it was heaven, the most squalid approximation of paradise imaginable. It was dark, hard, and pungent. If there were any soft furnishings, I didn't see them: everything seemed to be made out of masonry, corrugated metal, and filth. No wonder the Dossers were all on dope. If anyone had told me that people relieved themselves on the floor, I would have believed them.

Slightly upmarket from this was the Jungfrau, a 'Swiss Coffee Dance Club' just behind Manchester Cathedral. The Jungfrau, in a tiny basement done out to resemble a wooden Alpine ski lodge, had both live music and a DJ who played an interesting mix of stateside records: soul music, Tamla Motown, the Beach Boys, Dick Dale and the Deltones, Jan and Dean, Ronnie and the Daytonas, and the kind of outfits who would inspire the punk rockers of a later generation – Sam the Sham and the Pharaohs, ? (alias Rudy Martinez) and the Mysterians, Joe 'King' Carrasco and the Crowns, the Sir Douglas Quintet, and the Sonics.

Notable among the live acts at the Jungfrau were the Mockingbirds, a bunch of Jewish kids from my neighbourhood including Graham Gouldman, who went on to write songs for the Yardbirds and Herman's Hermits, and the Hollies' 'Bus Stop'. Graham Gouldman lived near Broughton Park, and I'd seen him around. Given his address, I'm convinced that the bus stop in question was just beneath our rain-spattered front window: the same bus stop where I stood waiting day after day for the bus that would take me to my place of work in the centre of Manchester. The exact location of the song. If ever there was a personal connection to the pop world, this was it.

On the other side of the musical coin was the Plaza in Oxford Street. It was a Mecca ballroom, slightly smaller than its sister venue, the Ritz: the same Ritz that has been immortalised by the poet John Cooper Clarke in his poem 'Salome'.

The Plaza was where you went for the slightly more cleaned-up, neater-haired and uniformed Manchester Beat combos, who were more Beatles than Stones. With its pre-war association with ballroom dancing, it had respectability written all over it, the guys all loitering nervously on one side and the chicks on the other, so you had to walk across a large sprung dance floor in order to be rejected by the girl you'd just plucked up the courage to ask to dance. This was a regular haunt of that dynamic duo, my fragrant cousin Mary and her hairdresser friend, the lovely Ruth Dudson. It was the kind of place that Auntie Marge might have approved of.

There were lots of groups on the Manchester scene: The Beatles weren't the first, they were just the best. Freddie and the Dreamers, for instance, were around for ages before The Beatles, then there were the Hollies, Herman and the Hermits, The Cymerons. It wasn't a requirement back then for a beat group to write their own material. They would perform competent covers of all the current Brill Building hits by songwriting teams such as Pomus and Shuman, Goffin and King, Mann and Weil, Bacharach and David, Sedaka and Greenfield, and of course Lieber and Stoller.

Herman and the Hermits were the resident band at the Plaza with a regular Friday and Saturday night slot, and they would do all the Drifters and Ben E. King numbers: 'Up on the Roof', 'Saturday Night at the Movies', 'Under the Boardwalk', 'Stand by Me', and 'Spanish Harlem'.

My favourite local group was Wayne Fontana and the Mindbenders – or Wayne Fontana and the Mindfucking Benders, as they were known – who featured a lot of what later became

Northern Soul classics: 'The Entertainer' by Tony Clarke, for instance, and their cover of 'Um, Um, Um, Um, Um, Um' by Major Lance, which was probably their biggest hit. But their version of 'Road Runner' was just sensational; it was psychedelic before the event. Extremely versatile, they even covered the impossible: 'Duke of Earl' by Gene Chandler.

Our chosen domain was the Twisted Wheel on Brazennose Street. It was open every night of the week, and also during the daytime as a caffeinated rendezvous for various beatnik art-school proto-Mod types. It started out on the site of a place called Amigos, changed its name to the Left Wing Coffee Bar, then morphed into a sort of modern jazz hang-out with yet another new name: the Twisted Wheel. The Wheel's DJ was the now legendary Roger Eagle, who was something of a musical pathfinder. Soon the music policy expanded to include rare and imported US blues, R&B and soul records by Ray Charles, Lou Rawls, Jimmy Smith, Jimmy McGriff, Cannonball Adderley, and then Motown, Booker T and the MGs featuring the Memphis Horns, and especially the hardest-working man in show business, the godfather of soul, soul brother number one, mister please please please, mister dynamite, the funky president, James Brown. I'll say it in one sentence. Wow.

They also introduced the odd bit of Blue Beat, later known as reggae.

Thanks to its unrivalled stateside playlist, the Twisted Wheel was rightly seen as disco-unero-numo, but it also hosted many live 'bands', as groups were beginning to be called, on account of their horn sections no doubt, among them Georgie Fame and the Blue Flames, The Graham Bond Organisation, Jimmy James and The Vagabonds, the Victor Brox Blues Train, Chris Farlowe and the Thunderbirds, Charlie and Inez Foxx, Sonny Boy Williamson, Ben E. King, and every Monday night, Alexis Korner's Blues Inc, free for girls. Alexis Korner was an exquisite representative of the metropolitan demi-monde, the first man I ever knew to a) wear a bandana and b) address another man as 'baby'.

Hitting on girls was not part of the agenda. You went to the clubs to listen to the music first, dancing second – solo dancing, at that, involving the most minimal moves. It wasn't like the later Northern Soul guys with the back flips and splits, there was never enough room on the dance floor. Someone would popularise an arm movement – pointing at the floor, say – that would somehow catch on, and suddenly everybody would be pointing at the floor. If any fool wasn't throwing the latest shape, their attitude was noted.

Before long, the Twisted Wheel enjoyed national notoriety. The main event was the Saturday all-nighter, which would draw punters from all over the country, especially off-duty GIs from the nearby Burtonwood military base in their sharp Continental threads. As a Salford Modernist in Greaser HQ, I naturally acquired the must-have accessory: the Pan-Am travel bag, a dual-purpose accoutrement that both carried the change of clothes to guarantee round-the-clock freshness for the all-nighters and, of course, reduced the chances of a pasting.

The GIs were a reliable source of pep pills, goofballs, and doobs, notably that military-strength pick-me-up, Drinamyl, aka Purple Hearts, available to all and free at the point of delivery until the resultant moral panic led to their criminalisation.

Drinamyl was an agreeable amphetamine preparation, with an added dash of barbiturate to alleviate the inevitable jitters. Also available were Durophet spansules, Black Bombers to you, and later Drinamyl spansules, alias Green and Clears.

Our leisure time was limited – some of us had jobs to go to – and every overstimulated moment of the weekend was amplified for all it was worth. Come six o'clock on Sunday morning, sedatives would be employed as part of the winding-down programme: Seconal, Nembutal, Mogadon, Tuinal, and even Mandrax would be on the breakfast menu.

Chapter Twenty-One

CARRY ON, LONDON

There was a popular Saturday night radio chat show that began with the line: 'Once more we stop the mighty roar of London's traffic to bring you, *In Town Tonight* . . .' After an hour of conversation with the likes of Errol Flynn, Jane Russell, Gary Cooper, or Doris Day, presenter Eric Maschwitz would conclude with the parting words: 'Carry on, London.'

Wow. Obviously, for the casual visitor nothing was too much trouble.

My knowledge of the capital, however, was pieced together from the Scotland Yard casebook of Edgar Lustgarten, and was thus limited to the West End, in particular Soho, that square mile of vice where some tweedy, chain-smoking flat-foot in a battered hat and a reliable raincoat engages in the relentless crusade against the sharp-dressed crooks, all silk-suited pussy magnets in suede shoes, leading idle, dissolute, sex-drenched lives.

One Friday in 1965, Mike Cawley and I took the all-night bus to London on a two-way ticket. Saturday morning, we opened our weary eyes: Victoria Bus Station, Buckingham Palace Road. Blimey! Door to door! Who knew our Queen would be so reachable?

There was a derogatory term for people like us: 'Weekend

Ravers', ergo arrivistes, provincial dilettantes, ersatz usurpers of the dropout creed; poseurs whose true commitment to a better future was always called into doubt. Nevertheless, we looked the part, each with our all-important doss bag casually hooked over one shoulder.

We trod those alien pavements, where a million visual treats await the casual saunterer, eventually arriving in the unpopulated early morning streets of Soho; *The Small World of Sammy Lee*, in colour.

Every publishing deal I'd ever read about happened at the Pollo restaurant in Old Compton Street. It was known for its generous servings of lovingly prepared Italian food, and for being cheap with it. Ten hours had passed since we'd eaten anything, so taking our seats in one of the oxblood booths we scanned the menu. There it was: that mysterious word I'd questioned my mother about for so many years.

Pizza.

Finally, I was in a position to order one up. On arrival it seemed to lack the circumference of the New York model, and it had a surprisingly minimal topping: just a schmear of tomato sauce and two black olives. Perfectamundo, and what with the olives I was the most sophisticated guy in town already.

For dessoit, we schmied a few doors down to the Amalfi, a terrific Neapolitan-style cake and cappuccino joint with mosaic tabletops on wrought-iron legs, plus moderne ceiling mouldings and evocative Sorrentine murals.

We'd heard of a few music venues where admission was cheap or even free. One of the latter was Bunjies, a tiny coffee bar and folk cellar in Litchfield Street, just off the Charing Cross Road, and that evening we tracked it down.

At street level, it was an Italian cafe, and downstairs it was an unventilated dive with candles in Chianti bottles and about seventy people, all of them smoking. People were continually going upstairs for a breath of comparatively fresh air, so the inevitable crowd around the entrance gave the impression that this was some kind of hotspot.

It had been a skiffle hang out in the Fifties, I imagine, and there were photographs all over the walls of people I'd never heard of, like Dave Van Ronk, 'Spider' John Koerner, and Tom Rush. Some subsequent superstars have name-checked the place, including Martin Carthy, Paul Simon, Peter Sarstedt, and yes, Bob Dylan.

The streets of London seemed to be crawling with doss-bag-toting youths, usually with guitar and harmonica at the ready to denote an enthusiasm for the blues. I myself carried a harmonica: if I'd carried a guitar, sooner or later somebody might have asked me to give them a tune, and I didn't want that to happen. Especially in Bunjies, where I might have been roughed up by aggrieved Dave Van Ronk fans.

At some point we needed a safe place to crash out. We didn't have a plan, but a couple of helpful dossers recommended Willesden railway sidings, where the idle carriages were left unlocked over-night. Taking advantage of this wasn't entirely approved of, or encouraged by the authorities, and it was necessary to climb over a few walls and negotiate several yards of barbed wire, but it was better than sleeping in some West End doorway. I wasn't bothered about being robbed — after all, I didn't have any money — but I was just sixteen, and if Edgar Lustgarten was anything to go by, it would have been asking for trouble.

We took the Bakerloo line from Oxford Circus, which back then cost a matter of pennies. When we got to Willesden Junction there were a few dossers already in place. They warned us that occasionally a guy came round with a flashlight, and we should keep our heads down to avoid eviction. We found a vacant carriage with soft bench seats. Luxury. Pure, unashamed luxury. Zzzzzzzz zzzzzzzzzzzzzzzzzzzzzzzzzzzzzzzzzzzzzzzzzzzzzz.

Chapter Twenty-Two

KARMA KARMA KARMA
KARMA KARMA, CAR MECHANIC

Longtemps, je me suis couché de bonne heure . . . said the late Marcel Proust. With me it was the other way round. Unlike that leisurely denizen of belle époque Paris, however, I was now expected to clock in at Kennings at 8am sharp. My night-time activities had to be curtailed; the Purple Hearts had to go.

Just like that, I knocked the amphetamines on the head. Enter peripheral hallucinations, mood swings, nameless loathings, and vague obsessions, all of which amounted to one thing in my self-diagnostic imagination: the much–anticipated nervous breakdown. I'd only been working for six weeks at the time.

I went to the doctor's and told him the symptoms – little animals running up and down my shirtsleeves; peripheral hallucinations of small furry or spiky creatures, e.g. hedgehogs, scuttling along the skirting board, which upon further inspection were not there at all.

I said, 'Give it to me straight, Doc. What's my problem?'

It didn't take him long to reach a diagnosis: 'You've been taking too many pep pills. You can't just suddenly quit like that.'

There was no suggestion of any character defect on my part – it was simply a question of avoiding the side effects of an abrupt cessation and ongoing quantity control. He suggested that I limit my intake to weekends and bank holidays. In the short term, he prescribed some downers along with a couple of weeks off work, for which he wrote out the all-important sick note: amphetamine psychosis.

The next day at Kennings, I gave it to the foreman, Mr Jeffries, who looked at it and said, 'The wife had that. She was real bad with it.' And he sent me home to rest up.

Amphetamine use continued to be regarded as a purely medical matter until the Sunday scandal rags whipped up a moral panic around the pepped-up delinquency of the new teenage generation. Suddenly we were implicated in the breakdown of society. These once freely available pharmaceutical products had become indispensable to the hyped-up schedules of our weekend routine, but now we found ourselves branded as outlaws by the citizenry at large. As I read those articles, it was difficult not to feel partly responsible.

The Mafia's special debut outing at the Salford Technical College Freshers' Ball had been a tantalising taster of the rock and roll life. Now, as the all-new Vendettas, we were hungry for more. We needed to crank things up a gear, and could no longer rely on Chet and the Challengers for amplifiers.

That's where Georgie Williams came in. I don't know how we ran into him, but as I said, Georgie lived in the brand-new Silk Street flats, the nearest thing to skyscrapers in Manchester. I was always interested in high-rise apartment blocks, so we arranged for him to audition at his gaff, and I finally got a look inside one. I was dead impressed.

More importantly, Georgie had some serious equipment. He had a Fenton Weill solid body guitar *and* a sky-blue and cream wedge-shaped Watkins Dominator amplifier. Not only that, *but also* an actual and totally state-of-the-art Watkins Copicat, the very first serious echo unit on the market.

There was just one stumbling block: Georgie's hair was all wrong. He was wedded to his Gene Vincent quiffage, and that mattered to us. It took us ages to talk him into it, but eventually he agreed to comb it forward. Once he'd done that, he looked all right, so he got in.

There was quite a scene, meanwhile, back at the Twisted Wheel. I had acquired a large circle of friends, including some really, really posh county chicks who started to invite me and my pals to parties in places like Altrincham, Nantwich, Wilmslow, Hale Barns, Lymm, and Bowdon; places where United football players had houses. They probably all live in Glossop now, but back then, the des reses of the nouveau riche were in Cheshire, which for a while was the most expensive place to live in the UK.

Somebody would always be on the rob at these Cheshire soirées. (I knew a few of the people involved in this thievery, I'm ashamed to say.) After a certain hour, the parties would usually degenerate because everyone was drinking, dancing, the Moss Side dudes smoking weed, whereas we would be totally on the case because we were amped up on the pep pills. While everyone else was reeling about and spilling drinks all over the Axminster, whoever had the wheels would be stationed out on the lawn, and somebody else would be going through the parents' wardrobes.

These were decidedly high-class dos, so there would be top-dollar schmutter: mink coats and suede and leather pieces. For a while, the most coveted item of clothing was a suede or leather – but preferably suede – three-quarter-length single-breasted overcoat, button-through with an optional tie belt, usually in a bottle-green or navy blue. If anybody owned what was an eminently desirable garment it was the Cheshire set. The thiever would select the choicest items and throw them out of the bedroom window for the guy down below in the garden to catch, then make an early exit from the party.

One of the very few licensed premises we used to hang out in was the Dive Bar in the newly built Hotel Piccadilly, which was the most modern place in Manchester at that time. For about half an hour around ten o'clock on a Saturday night, there would be a sale of these ill-gotten goods from the back of a van parked just outside the hotel. Shamefully, even though I'd seen the thieves at it and knew their MO, I did buy a fabulous jacket from them: double-breasted three-button in an inky-blue suede, like a pea coat – very similar to the one Bob Dylan's wearing on *Another Side of Bob Dylan*. I wish I still had it now.

There was a lot of thievery going on among our Twisted Wheel brigade, it can't be denied. That whole 'I dig labels, man' thing really applied to us. If you were a working-class lad and you had an office job, you wanted to be so smart as to make the boss look bad. You'd change your shirt three times a day. It was an obsessive-compulsive disorder. Amphetamines didn't help, they just exacerbated the situation; consequently shoplifting became a popular sport. I used to steal a lot of clothes. It was easy back then. The kids who worked in the shops would actually help you out.

Chapter Twenty-Three

DRUGSTORE BANDITS

Along with the posh party girls from Cheshire and the Cheetham Hill crowd, other recent acquaintances included a couple of Moss Side kids with whom I would swap goofballs for hashish, and two brothers from South Manchester called Angie and Marcel. They were thieves.

Marcel was a modern-day Robin Hood; he would rob from the rich because the poor have no money. He was in on the Wilmslow wardrobe capers.

Angie meanwhile specialised in regional pharmacies. He knew the business hours of every apothecarist north of Nuneaton. His only equipment was a suitcase full of bricks and a goose-neck wrecking bar. His MO was necessarily formulaic: he'd visit during opening hours, buy a packet of razors, and case the place in order to locate the dangerous drugs cabinet. Research completed, he would return after closing time, put a window in and yank the cabinet off the wall, throw it in the back of the car and make his getaway. Like a road-agent robbing a stagecoach, he'd make an inventory of what was in the strongbox later.

One night, I think we were at the end of an all-nighter or at one of the Cheshire parties, on impulse I asked Angie to take me with him on one of these expeditions. He was glad of the company.

'Grace . . . space . . . and pace' all in the Jaguar Mark VII, a full-size, four-door luxury saloon car with a running board and a top speed in excess of 100 mph. It was in just such a car that we travelled to the Peak District with a suitcase full of bricks. I don't think the Jag belonged to Angie.

We wound up in a choc-box village in Derbyshire on a sleepy Sunday afternoon, and pulled up outside a Victorian chemist with a beautiful front window. The uninterrupted acreage of ancient plate glass presented a seemingly fragile target, but you'd be surprised how hard it was, even with the strapped-up suitcase full of bricks. Time and time again our burglarious assault was denied. You could sort of see the glass bending, but it just went *BOING!* and the suitcase bounced off.

'You've got to get hit in the bottom left-hand corner,' advised Angie. It took about six more attempts, and then with a spectacular cascade of shards we were in, and scrunching over the splinters of broken glass to the back of the shop and the dangerous drugs cabinet. Angie quickly wrenched it from its moorings and into the Jaguar's boot. He drove off at a stately pace and we exited the village like gentlemen.

Apart from the window and the suitcase, it had been quite easy, but I tell you, after this glimpse into the world of the career thief, I wouldn't want to do it for a living. I mean, who doesn't have fantasies about pulling off the perfect heist? Who isn't on the side of Ocean's Eleven? But the price is too high. Blimey. I was on the verge of crapping my pants for the short ten minutes of the entire operation.

Once we reached an uninhabited tranche of the Peak District, Angie pulled over so we could inspect our ill-gotten pharmacopoeia. He was in this line of work mainly for the pep pills and barbiturates – anything else went over his left shoulder, until he came to a flagon the size of an aqualung made out of green glass bearing a yellowing label with a copperplate inscription that hadn't been read since the days of Samuel Taylor Coleridge: *Opium Suspended in Alcohol*. Give it a name, laudanum.

Angie wasn't interested. There was no call for that – his clients wanted to stay awake, and this wasn't going to help them: not the milk of paradise, not the Chinaman's nightcap, not this kind nepenthe. No, that's going to put you in a fucking coma. But being a poet, I was like, 'Fucking hell.'

Due to my tubercular childhood, I was familiar with opiates and their dreamy side effects, in particular the morphine-laden cough suppressants that had made my young life possible. And now, back home in the privacy of my bedroom, the inimitable bitterness of the first spoonful brought back that familiar state of inner cosiness. As far as I was concerned, it was me and my portable buffer zone from here on in.

I made that flagon last: I had it for years – I mean, years and years. It was a massive cache of the stuff, and I could only take a teaspoon at a time, plus I was always aware of driving up my tolerance level. The idea of running out was unconscionable, and when I finally reached the last few drops I started diluting it with Old Charlie, a brand of cheap dark rum available in miniatures.

It ran out eventually. The beckoning spectre of the Nervous Breakdown skulked in the shadows of my every waking hour. If ever there was a trigger, surely this was it.

Thank God for my Moss Side mates at the Wilmslow after-parties: it was hashish to the rescue.

Chapter Twenty-Four

THE SCHNORRER!
THE SCHNORRER!

After six months as an apprentice at Kennings, it became necessary to sign my indentures, whereby I couldn't leave without giving an agreed period of notice, nor could I be dismissed for anything other than a serious crime. Before I reached that milestone, Mr Jeffries and I had a serious talk about my aptitude for the job. It was he who kicked off my performance review.

'So, John, I don't think you're cut out for this kind of work, are you, sunshine?'

I had to agree. Then as now, I was the most hygienic guy alive, with a nancy-boy's aversion to filth, sweat, and physical exertion.

It was a mutually agreed parting of the ways. There were no hard feelings. In fact, Mr Jeffries wrote me a glowing reference: 'Gets on with people, blah, blah, blah. Seems like a decent sort and blah, blah, blah, etc.' So it was that, with a hint of mild regret, I bade farewell to the automotive industry.

I now entered a prolonged period of self-imposed unemployment. I hadn't worked long enough to get the required amount of National Insurance stamps, plus I was living at home, so I wasn't entitled to any government payouts. Staring abject penury full in the face, I had taken to cadging cigarettes from my parents.

Cigs were always a bone of contention in our house. Running out was simply not to be contemplated.

Some degree of financial independence, however, was achieved when my mother took a job as a part-time shop assistant at Paley's, a high-class tobacconist and confectioner's across the road from our place. The arrangement was that I would look after my three-year-old brother Paul in return for a modest fee. This suited all of us. Mum could leave the house and spend time with her old friend Irene Paley at the shop. And it gave me a raison d'être, while removing the taint of the schnorrer. I could buy my own cigarettes, and the odd bag of sweets for me and my baby bro.

A visit to Elsie and Charlie Forshaw's corner shop was a highlight of my day. The council had just built these apartment blocks and maisonettes in Higher Broughton, named after all the great racecourses: Ascot Court, Goodwood Court, Epsom Court, Aintree Court, Sandown Court. It was as good as council accommodation got back then, plus there was a super-luxury section with penthouses and swellegant shag pads on the upper floors. It soon became a showbiz enclave: it was a very short ride down to the Granada Studios from our neighbourhood, so the television company rented them en bloc for their top stars.

The Forshaws' shop was also an off-licence, as I've said, and stocked beer from the local Wilson's Brewery, so all the celebs used to shop there. Any time I went in, Mrs Forshaw would tell me who'd been in in the past twenty-four hours: Elsie Tanner, aka Pat Phoenix; Mike Baldwin, aka Johnny Briggs – they always got their nom de TV; I'm not sure if Mrs Forshaw even knew what their real names were. Also the late unlamented Jimmy Savile, who had a penthouse in one of the Courts.

One day I went in to buy a packet of cigs, and the first thing Mrs Forshaw said as I walked in was not 'Hello' or anything, but, 'You've just missed him.'

'Who?'

'The Saint,' she announced. Not 'Roger Moore'. Like, not 'The actor Roger Moore'. Not 'Roger "Star of TV's *The Saint*" Moore'. Just 'The Saint'.

'Really? Bloody hell! Excuse my French. What, Roger Moore? Roger Moore was here? What did he get?' I desperately wanted to know what he'd bought, to get a glimpse into his world, and Mrs Forshaw didn't disappoint: 'A quarter of boiled ham and a bottle of Wembley.'

'Any cigs?' I replied. She answered in the negative. I've never forgotten, because I could just imagine him saying it in that smooth voice of his: 'Good afternoon, madam. I'll have a quarter pound of boiled ham and a bottle of Wembley, please.'

Fantastic! Not only was I in the same manor as The Saint, but now I knew what he had for his dinner. It was like I knew him a little bit: we ate the same ham, me and the future James Bond!

That knowledge has enriched my life, no end.

I have always been pervious to public opinion, and for me the pain of disapproval militates against the possibility of any lasting happiness. While I continued to enjoy a certain amount of leisure time alongside my babysitting duties – idleness, after all, was the minimum requirement for the fulfilment of my literary ambitions – I couldn't help feeling that there was something a bit dishonourable about looking after my little brother so that my mum could go out to work.

There were millions of jobs, and any unoccupied able-bodied individual was immediately under neighbourhood suspicion. At first, passing enquiries carried a note of sympathetic concern.

'Not got a job yet, John?'

'No. Still looking around.'

'Good luck with that.'

As the weeks went by, however, the conversations took a more judgemental tone.

'*Still* not got a job, John?'. . .

I was skulking the streets in torment, draped in the robes of the social pariah.

My parents had been extremely understanding when I left the garage, and very generous with the cig money, but it was generally agreed that the best thing that could happen to some-body in my position and with my level of education was to 'get a trade'. I couldn't actually counter this attitude at the time. I didn't have a ready response, and even though deep down it was true – I actually was a lazy fucker who didn't really want to work – I was anxious not to be seen as some kind of freeloading schnorrer who could work, but chose not to. To that end, I set my sights on a trade. Not just any trade. One which was very well paid, highly skilled, *and* notoriously hard to get into: printing.

I started telling all and sundry that I was trying to get a printing apprenticeship, with the immediate result that, instead of being written off as a skiving lazy bastard, I was viewed as somebody with a high degree of ambition, a man who was determined to better himself. Now, rather than 'Still not got a job, John?' or, 'You lazy bastard, still living off yer mother?', the conversation might go like this:

'Still trying to get into printing, Johnnie?'

and,

'Blimey, you'll be lucky. It's not *what* you know, it's *who* you know,' etc., and,

'That kid's going places! Nice to see such ambition in one so young.'

Thanks to this deceptive device, opprobrium morphed into sympathy as I gained the incremental approval of the community.

In their eyes I had chosen the difficult route to success and I was soon regarded as tenacious rather than simply work-shy.

Things got out of hand, though, because in order to consolidate this whole facade I actually applied to take the three entrance exams necessary for the first step into the exclusive printing trade.

I passed the exams, and was invited for an interview at which I was reminded that, owing to the rarity of any vacancies, I should expect to wait for a very long time. This I already knew. The outcome was an all-round win-win situation. Years and years of mandatory idleness.

Result.

Public opinion, however, got to me long before even a year was up.

The Vendettas were in limbo land too. In spite of our change of name, the equipment upgrade, and Georgie Williams' new hairdo, bookings were still markedly on the slow side, although we did do one private appearance at a house party in Altrincham for a mate of ours. It was just enough to be able to credibly say that we were in the music industry, and then came a fresh set back.

Terry's parents had moved to Heaton Park, the Golders Green of Manchester, where he had fallen in with a good crowd. Sunday afternoons would find them at the Woodthorpe pub, once the home of the late Joseph Holt, hero of the Real Ale crowd.* That's where Terry met Johnny B and the Beat League.

Johnny B and the Beat League seemed to be going somewhere. They had really good equipment including two Vox AC30s and a Fender Stratocaster for a start. One of them even had a Gretsch Country Gentleman, a top-dollar instrument: put it this way, George

---

* The Woodthorpe is where the funeral reception for Mark E. Smith was held; it degenerated into mass violence.

Harrison had one. They had a group uniform and everything. Thanks to regular rehearsals and a work ethic that had somehow eluded the Vendettas, they had racked up a level of technical expertise beyond our capabilities. Their drummer, the utterly gifted Tony Kay, whose Semitic good looks and unlimited wardrobe proved to be an irresistible honeytrap, was their radiant passport to rock and roll immortality. Who could compete?

Terry was by now a competent guitar player. He was also a fabulously turned-out individual, and inevitably Johnny B and the Beat League recruited him as their bass player. He converted his Rosetti Lucky 7 into a bass by the simple expedient of buying four bass strings which he then affixed to its cheap plywood body. Terry's home-made bass brought down the tone all right, but not in a good way, so he quickly acquired a purpose-built model, also a Rosetti, but this time with a striking Jackson Pollock spray job. So there they were, Johnny B and the Beat League, available for birthdays, bar mitzvahs, weddings – not so much funerals, but you can't have everything – where would you put it?

No hard feelings. Business is business in the music business, especially when you mean business, although we obviously couldn't resist giving Terry a bit of grief. We all thought Johnny B and the Beat League was a real cornball name anyway, and reminded him of this almost constantly. 'Terry, you're in the know. Which one of you is Johnny B? Who is Johnny B? Can we meet Johnny B? What is the purpose of Johnny B? Are you paid as much as Johnny B?' And so on. 'That's probably enough now about Johnny B,' he'd protest, but would always be ignored. You couldn't blame us for being curious. An initial for a surname, that's always going to be enigmatic. Johnny B: genius or madman?

They eventually changed their name to The Good Guys, and I can't help feeling partly responsible. This brought some success, and unlike the Vendettas, they were always booked up for weeks in advance, which only intensified our collective spleen. We were always giving them the bad mouth. They threw our comparative ineptitude into stark relief, leaving us with the last riposte of the loser: 'Commercial rubbish'. We were punk rockers before that became a good thing.

Chapter Twenty-Five

BECOMING A POET

'It ain't what you say, it's the way that you say it' was a very early realisation for me. There was never a time when I wasn't convinced that the best way to receive and appreciate poetry was to hear it. I don't remember when I didn't feel that, because I came to poetry from hearing and reciting it at school, and listening to the radio.

Pre-literacy, the Great American Songbook was the soundtrack of my life, and where I first encountered the idea of rhyme and metre. Hour by hour, every conscious moment, the power of poetry was reiterated in songs such as 'Moonlight in Vermont', 'You Don't Know What Love Is', and especially, 'Stardust' by Hoagy Carmichael, in which I heard the word 'reverie' for the first time. Only a poet would utilise that word. At no time did I pay particular attention to the lyrics, which anyway concerned heartbreak, desire, loss, and the yearning melancholy of the adult world. And yet, I arrived at some kind of osmotic understanding.

At school, the mesmerising exactitude of Edgar Allan Poe's 'The Bells' had seized my attention, but it was because of a movie that I became properly fixated on discovering Poe's full body of work. I'd sneaked in to see the 1960 American International Pictures Roger Corman production of *The Fall of the House of*

Usher, shot in lurid-colour and starring Vincent Price as the very much anti-hero, Roderick Usher.

I was attracted to the hermetic world of Poe's heroes, who like Roderick were all bedevilled by a morbid acuity of the senses and often forced into a solitary quasi-monastic existence of their own design. At some point, as my flagon of laudanum dissipated to its last dregs, I knocked out a short piece entitled *The Wreck of the Prima Donna*, essentially *The Fall of the House of Usher*, but on a ship.

Adopting the point of view of Roderick's pedantic visitor, I wrote myself in as the hero of the piece, the ship's apothecary, who has been called to administer to the supremely unsuitable skipper, who had once more fallen victim to a sudden swoon, the like of which constantly bedevilled his pitiable precursor, Roderick Usher.

My preoccupation with Poe led me to Charles Baudelaire, who had been so taken with Poe's writing that he put his own work to one side to undertake the translation of his entire oeuvre into French.

Baudelaire was the citizen poet of modern Paris, a connoisseur of the street: his inspiration was the turbulence and intoxication of the metropolis, as opposed to the serenity of the countryside. Despite the fissiparous nature of the city, its capacity for decay and corruption remain constant. This eternal dichotomy was the very engine of his verse.

Gone were the footsore, rain-sodden floral tributes of William Wordsworth; as someone or other once said, 'It's a poor artist who only paints the picturesque'. The city demanded a new mode of representation, a new way to arrest that which is ephemeral and fleeting. Baudelaire called it *modernité*. There are flowers, and then there are flowers, and Baudelaire's *fleurs du mal* were slightly poisonous.

As a card-carrying nosey-parker and professional obsessive, I read up on the subject and learned that Baudelaire was a real pernickety dresser and a bit of a dude: this was my kind of guy. I too would be an Urban Poet.

Through Baudelaire I discovered his fellow-citizen Jean Nicolas Arthur Rimbaud. Rimbaud was a provincial, but again with an urban spirit. And then there was Jules Barbey d'Aurevilly, who made a virtue of the flash-in-the-pan fads and fashions of nineteenth-century Paris, and noted the influence of the English Regency dandy George 'Beau' Brummel on the post-Revolutionary urban French male wardrobe.

American pop art was another rich seam of enlightenment and inspiration. Andy Warhol, Claes Oldenburg, Roy Lichtenstein, James Rosenquist, etc. Here was a new *modernité*, an accurate, authentic kind of art celebrating America's great contributions to society.

Over here we had our own artistic rendering of the modern world, young British painters such as David Hockney, Peter Blake, Richard Hamilton, and in Salford, Harold Riley, a much younger, less depressing, and more poppy acolyte of L. S. Lowry, who put chip shops and pubs, advertising hoardings and electricity, even fat people into his paintings. All of them made a feature of the second-hand Americana that was creeping into British life.

As I've said, many of my friends were art students at Salford Tech, where all the lecturers were young go-ahead types au fait with all the latest 'happenings' in New York. Like every art student I knew, Mike and Terry weren't aspiring to be the next Rembrandt: they wanted to be 'commercial artists'. Art that makes money: how fabulous is that? The only art I'd ever heard of at school involved misery, struggle, and starvation, so the concept of a society in which an artist can get paid while he's still alive sounded like a dream ticket to me. When I finally twigged that this was actually art in the service of advertising,

I thought, 'Well, sure, why not?' 'Commercial Poet' sounded like a good job title to me.

After all, I was used to seeing poetry all the time on adverts: e.g. a cartoon guy is talking up dog food, holding a can of Kennomeat, and this beatnik dog comes up snapping its fingers, 'Open the can, man.'

I got into the work of an American commercial artist called Mel Ramos, a handsome young caballero with a very impressive moustache. Like his fellow pop art superstar Andy Warhol, Mel Ramos had begun his career in the service of industry, in his case producing artworks for clients such as Chiquita, involving topless pin-up girls emerging from bananas, and for Velveeta cheese spread, this time featuring a fully naked glamour model posing atop an oversized package of the product. His hyper-real creations also featured in campaigns for Lifesavers, 7-Up, Baby Ruth candy bars, and Doublemint gum. You might not approve of Mr Ramos's commercialisation of the male gaze, but you had to admit he was one hell of a smudger.

Television has not always been the public playground we know today. Far from it – it was once entirely possible to live a lifetime without clapping eyes on so much as a weather forecaster in the flesh. 'Hey, guess who I've just seen? That guy who does the weather!' No way would anybody ever believe you'd seen them in person. 'Did you fuck!' they'd say. 'You're kidding? Where would *you* run into the weather guy?' Undoubtedly, this exclusive and radiant medium would have been a natural home for the likes of Charles Baudelaire. In my teenage mind, if your poetry was popular enough you could crank it up a couple of gears and occupy the very airwaves. *If your poetry was popular enough.*

In this respect, the televisual debut of the Liverpool poets on Granada and the publication of their Penguin Modern Poets *The Mersey Sound* anthology later in 1967 gave me a measure of hope. I liked the way they included brand names even in their sensitive love odes. I thought it was better to write clever poetry about everyday shit than to feign an understanding of the entire world and beyond. There was undoubtedly a long tradition of casual product placement in popular lyrics, e.g. Slim Gaillard's 'Who put the Benzedrine in Mrs Murphy's Ovaltine?' – itself a rewrite of the old George L. Giefer Tin Pan Alley composition, 'Who put the powder in Mrs Murphy's chowder?'.

Tin Pan Alley, Poe, Baudelaire, Rimbaud, the Mersey Poets, Harold Riley and pop art, St Thomas Aquinas – these were the psychological avatars of my work in progress as The Urban Commercial Poet.

Reading about Shelley, Baudelaire, Rimbaud, and Byron, I found out that they held recitals of their work much as modern poets were now doing. Pre-mass literacy, however, professional success was largely a matter of hearsay and gossip in the fashionable salons of the day.

I had been sending my stuff off to various publications but never got any replies, good or ill. There was nothing else for it: I would have to take my poetry directly to the good people of Manchester.

Chapter Twenty-Six

IMPROVER CUTTER –
THE RAG TRADE

People think of the Mod scene in terms of certain visual signifiers: parkas bearing the ubiquitous target motif plus multi-directional arrows, the black-and-white checkerboard of Two-Tone, the bowling shoes, and, of course, the scooters. To quote those revisionist latter-day Mods, the Merton Parkas, 'You need wheels if you wanna make deals.'

But in my experience, it was two wheels OK, four wheels better. A scooter was just a way of getting about, no more no less; cleaner than a Greaser's bike and redolent of the stylish Italianate aesthetics of a Pifco hairdryer.

By 1965 at the Twisted Wheel nobody called themselves a Mod anyway. People in Burnley called themselves Mods, people with targets on their parkas. We called ourselves 'stylists' and for the stylist it was a car all the way.

I was very fussy. I read *Esquire*, *Nova*, *Town* and similar publications, so I was abreast of the latest London looks. One location on my radar was the Ivy Shop in Richmond, later called J Simon,* which seemed to be where all the modern jazz crowd in London got their stuff.

---

* John Simon still runs a shop, selling the same kind of stuff, in Chiltern Street in Marylebone. Worth a visit, it's like a museum of American clothing.

We had also finally got a contemporary male boutique in Manchester. It was in St Ann's Passage, a tiny glazed shopping arcade leading to King Street which housed an old-style Hyacinth Bucket-type tea room called Meng & Ecker, and two equally tiny shops, more like overstated glass cubicles – kiosks even.

The whole fantastical boutique consisted of a sleek, ultra-modern window display featuring a single outfit on a malnourished mannequin next to a Corinthian plinth bearing one shoe. It was all pared back to the extreme, beyond the Bauhaus, a form of entrapment with its tantalising glimpse of a better life. What other futuristic garments might be hidden in those Shaker-style cabinets within? They didn't even have price tags; that would have mucked up the space-age integrity. The name rendered in chrome lettering above the window was all in lower case: 'john michael' – way out and way out of my price range.

A change of john michael's window was a major event. On one occasion it featured a slash-neck hooped matelot top over a pair of cream hipster parallels, and on the plinth, a completely squared-off shoe, hyper-stylised with just one eyelet and a black shoelace. It was made out of a cream Italian glove leather with a coffee-coloured tuck-and-roll seam down the middle: soft as butter, it looked as if you could eat it. In no time at all there was a very well-known picture of Brian Jones wearing the entire strip.

Those shoes were an epiphany; they were the other side of the coin to the elastic-sided boot. If you were in St Trop, on a yacht, or down on the Boulevard de la Croisette in Cannes, they'd look right, unlike a big pair of shit-kicking boots with three-inch Cubans.

I'd been thinking about St Tropez a lot at that time, as I was borderline obsessional about the boyfriends of Brigitte Bardot. What common quality did they share? Mix me a person and I'll be that guy. To that end I would buy Continental magazines that featured Swedish films in which chicks got undressed, aimed at the art crowd. I bought them at the Cinephone box office, which killed two birds with one stone. I affected an interest in Continental cinema: 'Oh, I see Claude Chabrol is doing a searing indictment of the bourgeoisie again. What's more, Jean Seberg gets her tits out!'

Such was my preoccupation with Brigitte Bardot's love life that I started wearing my glasses because of Roger Vadim. After him came Serge Gainsbourg: she likes people in glasses and ugly boys with big noses. Double tick. Fantastic.

J. Simon, St Trop, fine knitwear, merino, cashmere, Sea Island cotton . . . the babysitting gig had been a sweet deal, but while I was waiting to get into printing, I needed more than cig money. Most of the layabouts I was getting to know in the bohemian world of literature and art were avoiding work. They were on the sausage,* but in order to get it, they had to be available for job interviews, praying for rejection each time. A normal job was anathema to these people, whereas I always needed money and didn't see any way of getting it other than some form of stop-gap employment.

Dave Redshaw was already working as a cutter at Quellrain, and he seemed to be doing OK. Why not me?

I was taken on as a starter cutter by Seidelbaum's, a clothing manufacturer that specialised in ladies' outerwear. It was what would be called a sweatshop today, except you didn't sweat if there was nothing to sweat over, and at least Seidelbaum's was in a purpose-built factory in the Swan Buildings in Ancoats, rather than the inadequate premises of a lot of the other companies, which were often just a couple of knocked-through terraced houses.

Apart from the machine room downstairs, which was all women, the workforce was almost entirely Jewish and male. The only

---

* Sausage roll = dole.

goyish exceptions were me, an ex-Ted called Albert, and the maintenance man, a hip Jamaican guy called Rupert, who wouldn't have looked out of place fronting a rock steady combo. He had the whole strip: one of those V-neck leatherette slipovers with a nylon polo neck underneath, and the popular high-crown stingy brim hat.

I was on the cutting-room floor: eight hours of non-stop hilarious cruelty and state-of-the-art piss-taking. Les the foreman ran a tight ship, but if you weren't busy, you didn't have to try to look busy. If there was nothing to do, you didn't do it, and a lot of the time we were just hanging around smoking cigs, drinking tea, betting on horses, and having a laugh. Ancoats was Manchester's Little Italy. Signor Vincenti's ice-cream van came round every afternoon and we took it in turns to get the orders in. It was a happy routine.

While we sweated in the comparative squalor of the shop floor, the business end took place front-of-house. Prospective customers were greeted in a swish showroom that looked like a Hollywood set with elaborate floral displays, fluted plinths, black marble feature panels, scalloped niches, and a raised catwalk along which sashayed Coral, Seidelbaum's very own glamorous Creole supermodel.

As a starter cutter and a complete novice, I was started off with the easy stuff, which was difficult to get wrong. I was cutting canvases, which were used as a stiffening agent between the fabric and the lining on certain stress points of a garment, thus imparting the correct structure and drape. My job was to mark off the pieces from a pattern and cut them out with a slot knife.

Uniquely, apprentices in the rag trade were free to renegotiate their terms of employment at various stages in their training. The next stage was 'improver cutter', so I was entitled to go to another shop and broker a pay rise. Business is business. But in my case, this was pre-empted by a generous wage increase: I was now on about £12 a week.

As an improver, I moved on to marking and cutting out the expensive satin linings by means of an Eastman, a powerful bladed machine that resembled the outboard motor of a speedboat. It was very precise work. I had to layer up multiple lengths of satin to a maximum thickness on the cutting table and firmly secure the fabric with several clips. I marked out the pattern on the top layer with tailor's chalk, then cut out all the layers rapidly in one go with the razor-sharp Eastman blade. It cut round corners like a dream, but it was a pretty lethal piece of kit. You had to pay attention, otherwise you could easily slice your hand off, or mis-cut a batch of linings that would have to be ditched. Seidelbaum's didn't like throwing valuable satin away. It was inevitable that there was some waste, but an important part of the gig was learning to mark up the fabric in such a way as to minimise scrappage.

As at my brief garage tenure, I never told any of my workmates at Seidelbaum's about my poetic ambitions. In the world of industry, the writing of verse was a filthy secret, even if in my social life I was an open book: I *always* told girls I was trying to impress that I was a poet. If fronted out with the correct degree of self-importance, one way or the other it always got a reaction. As a consequence, I was seen as part of the emergent beatnik craze, rather than the effeminate fantasist I would have been three years earlier.

While I might have denied being a Mod, I didn't mind people thinking I was a beatnik; indeed I cultivated my new-found bohemian reputation. In truth, I only knew about bohemians through reading some shock-horror magazine article or other, and I didn't truly have a clue about my fellow beatniks. (Back then, you couldn't just press a button and get all the dope on someone or something, you'd have to go to the library, actually read books and stuff to find things out.)

One cover of the ever-topical *Mad* magazine had featured Alfred E. Neuman sporting a chinstrap beard and a beret, but apart from that there was no visible evidence of the beatnik in my regular reading material, namely my mother's *Woman's Own*, cousin Mary's *Mirabelle*, and the *Daily Mirror*. The brief was simple: what is the look? And how do I get it? I'd seen Alfred E. Neuman, I'd read a couple of articles, bought a set of bongos, and I had a few ideas of my own.

The French version of beatnik involved existentialism. I imagined a dog-eared paperback copy of Jean-Paul Sartre's *La Nausée* sticking out of the back pocket of Brigitte Bardot's jeans. Sartre regularly haunted my beatnik musings. I pictured him as one of those tremendously tasty Continental types: offbeat, prodigiously elegant, socially mobile, drunkenly insouciant even in the daylight hours, handsome to a fault: somewhere between Charles Boyer and Alain Delon. Boy, did I talk him up in the playground of my imagination. Then, on the dust jacket of *Being and Nothingness*, the long-awaited photograph. What a fucking demmick. Bloody hell, *this* is Jean-Paul Sartre?

By contrast, Jack Kerouac I discovered was Hollywood handsome, but what with his dishevelled Tony Curtis haircut and his Brooks Brothers three-button sport coat, he didn't look like anyone's idea of the bearded outsider either. He seemed clean-cut, respectable, bookish.

The beatnik girls in the UK followed the sexy monochrome Juliette Gréco template. Their male consorts, however, seemed to be an Orwellian collection of fruit-juice-drinking, sex-maniacal, sandal-wearing, quack-diet enthusiasts; malcontents of every stripe. As the sworn enemies of America, they even invented the skiffle group as the antidote to Elvis. It didn't work.

As ever, the movies provided indispensable insights. As early as 1958 the mainstream studios had begun to feature beatniks as recognisable social stereotypes in movies such as *Two for the Seesaw*, starring Shirley MacLaine and Robert Mitchum and set in Greenwich Village; *The Subterraneans*, based on the novel by

Kerouac, starring Leslie Caron and George Peppard; and *The Sandpiper*, starring Elizabeth Taylor as a painter with a studio in Big Sur, California. This was beatnik with a Hollywood sheen: needless to say, *ça plane pour moi*.

Meanwhile, in other parts of the art world, the Vendettas were having an identity crisis.

After Terry defected to Johnny B and the Beat League, we drafted in my cousin Sid, who had got hold of one harmonica and two maracas, three of the essential components of any Bo Diddley tune. Bo Diddley, Tommy Tucker, and Chuck Berry were the VIPs as far as we were concerned.

Basically, we wanted to be The Rolling Stones.

As I've said, Terry's group were now renamed The Good Guys and they were doing all right. We held a group brainstorm meeting and decided that our gangster image had held us back for long enough. A complete break with the past was necessary, and we changed our name again, from the Vendettas to the Chaperones.

I fancied myself as the vocalist, but as I soon discovered, it was almost impossible for me to sing and play bass at the same time.* The only exception to this was 'Hoochie Coochie Man', or any other number in which I didn't have to multitask: in other words, when I could alternate the riff and my own unaccompanied voice: 'Bam bam bam bam bam . . . Gipsy woman told my mother . . . Bam bam bam bam bam . . . Before I was born . . . Bam bam bam bam bam . . .' Get the idea?

That was my one vocal contribution, because the rest of the time I had to concentrate hard on what my fucking fingers were up to. That's why I have a grudging respect for Sting; Macca

---

* It would take me twenty years to realise that this is because the bass is usually on the off-beat and goes contrapuntal to the actual melody.

doesn't seem to have a problem either. To me that's genius. And don't forget Mark 'Thunder Thumbs' King out of Level 42.

Our musical repertoire was still sorely limited. Three chords: OK. Two chords: better. One chord: fabulous. We had hitherto performed only covers, but I now became the Chaperones' self-appointed designated songwriter (publishing royalties), and knocked out a few gonzoid lyrics to fit the strict metrical requirements of the only two riffs we could ever pull off.

Gonzoid lyrics always had a place in the world of rhythm and blues: 'Transfusion' by Nervous Norvus; 'Choo Choo Ch' Boogie' by Louis Jordan; 'Alligator Wine' by Screamin' Jay Hawkins; 'Shombalor' by Sheriff and the Ravels; and such Leiber/ Stoller classics as 'I'm a Hog for you Baby', 'Charlie Brown', and 'Smokey Joe's Cafe', first popularised by The Coasters. Also the fabulously obscene 'Two-Time Slim' by the Johnny Otis Show under their X-certificate alias Snatch and the Poontangs. Profanity would later become an essential component of my own house style.

One of my first compositions employed the 'High Heel Sneakers' riff, and was called 'Mad Hat Madame'. I can only remember the first four lines:

Mad hat madame
Where d'ya get a hat that size?
I see where you're coming from
It keeps the sun right out your eyes

I was quite pleased with that. Put it this way: it had its own internal logic.

'Sick' was the hottest ticket in town, and found a place in the pop universe with a whole package of untimely death songs often involving high-performance motor vehicles: 'Leader of the Pack' by The Shangri-Las, 'Terry' by Lynn 'Twinkle' Ripley, 'Tell Laura

I Love Her' by Ricky Valance, and 'Johnny Remember Me' by John Leyton, featuring the ghostly voice of his dead girlfriend, and produced by the genuinely homicidal sonic-trailblazer Joe Meek.

Even the tweedy Downliners Sect released the *Sect Sings Sick Songs* EP (try saying that with a lisp), featuring numbers such as 'Now She's Dead' and 'Leader of the Sect'.

Inevitably, the popularity of this aberrant subgenre triggered a whole new moral panic about the miserable psyche of British youth. Like anyone of my age, I had a morbid streak a mile wide and I found this flash-in-the-pan craze to be a rich seam of inspiration. I would listen to these records and conclude that these people didn't know the meaning of heartbreak. Try 'Teenage Cremation' © John Cooper Clarke for size. I can't remember the lyrics, but the hook line went like this:

Teenage cremation,
Oh, how I cried when you died.

As I've said, when I started writing these songs the big three for the Chaperones were Bo Diddley, Tommy Tucker, and Chuck Berry. Uniquely, in the case of Chuck Berry the lyrics *are* the tune. As Mr Malone said, great poetry insists upon itself. Technically, Chuck crams in too many lyrics for the allotted tempo. Take this verse from 'Brown Eyed Handsome Man':

Way back in history, 3000 years
In fact, ever since the world began
There's been a whole lotta good women sheddin' tears
Over a brown-eyed handsome man
It's a lot of trouble for a brown-eyed handsome man

Those two words 'in fact' are entirely extraneous. A lesser songsmith would have left them out. The peerless Chuck Berry, however, adds them intentionally in order to deformalise the lyric, rendering it more conversational.

Chuck Berry's back catalogue was mercilessly plundered by every rock and roll outfit of the period, especially The Beatles and the Stones.

Beatles or Stones? It was always presented as a choice. Even now, usually at funerals, people of a certain age still argue about it. By 1965 the two groups seemed to be worlds apart. The Beatles had their precocious sophistication, while the comparatively primordial Rolling Stones traded in a kind of snotty allure which chimed with the Chaperones' corporate idea of ourselves. In our book, enthusiasm was the default setting of an idiot.

Our primitive approach was legitimised by the untutored likes of Jimmy Reed, T-Bone Walker, Buddy Guy, John Lee Hooker, Howlin' Wolf, Sugar Pie DeSanto, Sister Rosetta Tharpe, Koko Taylor, and Elmore James, in fact anyone who exemplified the souped-up electricity of the Chicago blues. These names had gained mass recognition thanks largely to The Rolling Stones, The Pretty Things, the early Kinks, and provincial fellow travellers like The Animals, Them, and The Spencer Davis Group.

The Manchester Free Trade Hall was the UK stop on the annual American Folk Blues Festival tour, leading to occasional appearances at the various basement venues while the legendary visiting musicians were in town. I attended most of these shows: there was a sense of urgency owing to the visitors' unhealthy lifestyles, plus their advancing years.

The 1965 package, for example, advertised Little Walter on harmonica. You may remember him from such tunes as 'Off the Wall' and 'Boom, Boom Out Goes the Lights'. On the night, however, he was replaced by Shakey Horton: Walter had been shot through the ankle in a recent gunfight in the South Side of Chicago.

Chapter Twenty-Seven

MY SUMMER OF LOVE

There's no two ways about it: all my friends were total pussy hounds. Don't get me wrong, I was as much up for the chase *in theory*, it's just that I was never very predatory *in practice*. Having been a tubercular kid with a malformed physique, I have a dread of any situation where the shedding of garments might be required. I can't even swim.

I don't know why, but art-school chicks always had it bad for me. It could have been the Picassoid ribcage, but paradoxically, I suspect that my reticence was the secret of my success.

When I was sixteen, I started going out with an older woman, an art student called Sheila. She was eighteen and had been at Salford Technical College for a while. She had her eye on a furnished flat on Camp Street, and even though it was a real khazi of a place, she couldn't afford the rent on her own. That's where I came in. My recent promotion at Seidelbaum's meant that I could go halves, so we put down two weeks' rent in advance and took residence in early summer 1965.

In spite of my self-censoring reticence in matters corporeal, if you're living with somebody you have to put it on a sexual level, and that was where I learned the facts of life, right there with Sheila. As the older woman, she seemed to know what she was about. It was a big event, obviously.

In those days, extramarital cohabitation, or living in sin, was the scandalous position of the irredeemable libertine. That was bad enough, but when my parents learned my address, their disapproval was palpable.

There were a lot of real kinky characters down on Camp Street. It was a street of once-grand decaying Victorian villas, shoddily converted into bedsits and apartments inhabited by students, prostitutes, rent boys, and all the usual denizens of a low-rent ghetto. They'd earned the area a louche reputation, but it wasn't really that bad. Halfway along at the intersection with Lower Broughton Road was the aforementioned Abe Sachs, tailor to the stars of *Coronation Street*, the Dougie Millings of Manchester, so it wasn't all hideous. Not entirely.

The flat itself was awful, just this side of squalid, full of heavy, dark, mismatched, horrible old granny furniture, a life-threateningly threadbare carpet that carried the popular multicoloured swirl motif, and discordant Regency-striped wallpaper marked by the outlines of several pictures, recently removed. On a pedestal with barley-sugar legs in one corner, an unhealthy spider plant cast out its sickly yellowing fronds. You only get one chance at a first impression, and this one depressed the fuck out of us.

We tidied the place up a bit and bought a goldfish. The front room had a massive bay window from the floor to the ceiling, so it was flooded with light until late evening. We rented a television. The freezing cold winters of Salford were far from our minds.

We had a two-ring Baby Belling with a grill so we could do toast. We had fish fingers a lot, alternating with Findus Crispy Pancakes and Chesswood canned mushrooms on toast. Most of our meals were on toast, plus we were between two equidistant chip shops. Throw in a set of bongos and we were quite the specimen freewheelin' beatnik couple.

A London band called Jimmy Powell and the Five Dimensions – who had earlier featured the young Rod Stewart on vocals and harmonica – had moved into the corner gaff next to Albert Park. I noticed their van parked on some waste ground off the street, so I assumed they were temporarily based in Manchester doing the Northern club thing. I can't prove it, but I'm sure I saw Rod walking around the neighbourhood. Either that or it's another product of my fevered imagination. One of the two.

At the beginning of September, we entered Manchester's rainy season. Almost immediately the apartment lost whatever charm we had forced upon it. The big bay window admitted only a chilling blast. It was gloomy and dank. We had an open fire, but couldn't afford coal deliveries. We kept the gas stove on constantly as we tried vainly to warm up the room. Everything felt damp. It wasn't healthy.

As the winter kicked in, we went hunting for wood. We were always on the lookout for the odd abandoned dining chair. I'd return home from work calling out, 'Hello, sweetheart, I brought a plank home.'

There were icicles *inside* the fucking place.

We were starting to get on each other's nerves and were cold and miserable all the time, living like savages. I thought I'd never survive such conditions.

We started paying regular visits to our respective parents, usually around teatime, until gradually we just couldn't face going back to Camp Street. One evening Sheila and I went to the Rialto to see *A Thousand Clowns* starring Jason Robards and Barbara Harris. That was the night we called it a day.

Chapter Twenty-Eight

CHRISTINE PEEL AND THE BEATNIKS

What's a town without coffee bars?

Without coffee bars we would have been condemned to walk the sodden streets in torment. The Prego, the Flamenco, the Expresso Bongo, the Offbeat, and of course the Mogambo run by Charlie Chan – not the well-known private eye played by J. Carrol Naish, but the dynastic founder of Manchester's famous China Town.

Then there was the Cona in Tib Lane, where the young Celia Birtwell met Ossie Clark. The Cona was next door to the CND offices, and featured folk recitals by Ewan MacColl et al. in the basement. The *dolce far niente* of its chrome-laden competitors was not in evidence here. Inside, a gloomy, serious ambience prevailed. The coffee had no froth, and tended to be black. Meaningful conversation took the place of a jukebox. Coca-Cola, as a symbol of American cultural hegemony, had been sacked in favour of V8. It was all angry young men and high-minded sex kittens. You weren't there to enjoy yourself.

Among the high-minded sex kittens was Christine Peel. Christine was the acceptable face of the Ban the Bomb movement, a textbook beatnik sort, straight out of *Mad* magazine.

She had shapeless long black hair and wore sunglasses inappropriately. She had a slinky black polo neck down to her knees and those Bri–Nylon ski-pants with stirrups (a bit *de trop*, even for me: they didn't crease round the back of the knee, which I always found a bit creepy.* When viewed as sports kit, I suppose, the ski-pant makes sense, but for some reason they never made it as 'athleisurewear'). All this was topped off with a long black cape – in all weathers. She was a lot like Morticia as played by the lovely Carolyn Jones in the popular *Addams Family* TV series.

She fancied herself as a bit of a troubadour, even to the point of penning her own ballads. To this end she carried a guitar at all times. Unfortunately, the heartfelt nature of her material was undermined by a Jonathan Ross-style inability to pronounce the letter 'R'. You just couldn't get past this.

Specimen dialogue: 'This is a pwotest song about the wacialist wegime in Whodesia.'

At that time I was a card carrier for the Young Communist League and thus not immune to her moral concerns in this matter. But what can I say? Kids can be cruel, and I couldn't help but battle to suppress my hysterical laughter, to the extent that snot would threaten to shoot out of both nostrils. Struggling to keep a straight face, I'd be all like: 'Go on Christine, do that one about Rhodesia. We love that one.' 'Yes, I think you're wight. I think I will. It's weally tewible; the more we wesponsible people wite songs about this atwocity, the sooner it will be wectified and wightfully welegated to the dustbin of histowy.'

Her life-threatening speech impediment was a big part of her allure, and surely the template for Candice Marie in the Mike Leigh masterpiece *Nuts in May*.

---

* The resultant look reminded me of Gort, the robot servant in *The Day the Earth Stood Still*, starring Michael Rennie and Patricia Neal. Gort looked great from the front, the ultimate art deco fascist robot with a death ray issuing from a slit where its eyes should have been. When you saw it from the back, however, you could clearly see that it was an actor wearing a pair of those stirrup ski-pants in some kind of metallic Crimplene.

Widicule aside, I was flattered by Christine's attentions. She was pwetty impwessive to look at actually, what with the cloak and the guitar, so in order to get inside her ski-pants it was necessary to consolidate my beatnik credentials. I told her that I too was a musician, *and* a poet. She called me out on it, and I produced a few sheets of obsolete Chaperones lyrics, riddled with slang, cartoon characters, brand names, buzz words, and the hyperbolic argot of Madison Avenue. O Lord, please let me be misunderstood, as Nina Simone almost said. That was my silent prayer, in the frail hope that Christine's silent incomprehension would work in my favour.

This was the early days of what came to be known as the underground press, and Christine was helping to launch a pacifist mag printed on a Gestetner in the CND basement offices next door. She was also involved in a forthcoming benefit concert to cover the production costs, and invited me to recite some of my poetry. She didn't have to beg. The way I had it figured, this could elevate me to the status of a king on earth.

I told my dad, who quizzed me about what kind of purse I might reasonably expect for this performance. I told him it was a benefit, all in a good cause, and that I wasn't the only one working for nothing. 'Nothing?' he replied. 'Anybody will employ you for nothing.' He was anxious that I shouldn't get mugged off at any point.

The event took place in the upper function rooms of the Castle, a pub in what is now Manchester's flourishing Northern Quarter. I declaimed a recent work entitled 'I Married a Monster from Outer Space', inspired by the 1958 movie, *I Married a Monster from Outer Space*.

I got the idea looking out the front room window of our apartment: there on the Rialto marquee was the longest movie title I had ever seen up to that point. It went right round the corner. It had copped the style of those sensationalist scandal-rag headlines, real grabbers that always demanded further investigation: it's one thing to be invaded by the ant men from another galaxy, but to marry one of them? What if?

Naturally, the ugly spectre of casual fascism entered my reverie, which included the lines,

Bad enough with another race,
But fuck me, a monster from outer space.

What had begun as a pop art cash-in had picked up a scintilla of social significance, and what with the 'fuck' word, bingo.

Chapter Twenty-Nine

THE PRINTER'S APPRENTICE

When I finally got the call-up to the printing apprenticeship, I didn't really want to leave Seidelbaum's, but having talked myself into the printing industry, that had to be that, and I handed in my notice.

Tears were avoided, but I like to think that everybody was real sorry to see me go. For Les the foreman, there seemed to be an upside. His parting words? 'I might be able to get a decent cup of bleedin' tea now!' How I would come to miss his cheery repartee.

I started as an apprentice compositor at Cheetham & Co. This entailed a significant pay-drop to £4 a week, about half of what I had earned as a schoolboy bookie's runner. Seventy-five per cent of that, what's more, went to my mother towards my upkeep, so now I was broke most of the time. Bloody hell! Seventeen years old and I'd known already the extremes of poverty and wealth.

Cheetham's was a small family firm in Ancoats run by a man called Charlie Hope with a small staff of six printers, including me. I was placed under Denis Jones and trained in old-school letterpress typography, which at that point hadn't changed for three hundred years. As an apprentice I attended night-school classes and was on one-day release, which meant that I spent a day at art college doing typographic design. The rest of the time I learned my trade working on the job.

Working conditions were Dickensian: a dismal, windowless basement room with a single strip light. Later we moved into the equally squalid Sedgwick Mill, a former cotton-spinning mill on Redhill Street right next to the Rochdale Canal, which housed hundreds of small firms of every description – die stampers, engravers, clothing manufacturers – all under the same roof.

Mr Hope was often out visiting clients, delivering orders, meeting suppliers, and so on. Back on the shop floor he operated the guillotine, neatening the edges of the finished print jobs.

Somehow, this tiny firm attracted a high volume of work. The bulk of the business was extremely tedious tabular jobs: the supply of sundry clerical items, most of which are now obsolete in the modern digital office – balance sheets and ledgers, invoices, receipt books, memorandum sheets, and circulation envelopes.

We printed a lot of event tickets, which we would tailor to typographically reflect somehow, in the broadest possible sense, the nature of the company hosting the function.

Considering the size of the composing room, we had a wide variety of fonts, many of which, although unfashionable, appeased the Victorian sensibilities of our older customers, a large number of whom were the relics of various drapery emporia: haberdashers who by virtue of their commercial efforts had become councillors, aldermen, ward officers, assemblymen, panjandrums, stipendiary magistrates, and Worshipful Brothers.

The Masonic lodges provided steady business. The annual round of ladies' evenings and charity functions required printed invitation cards, menus, orders of events, and minutes, all rendered in magenta ink, which had to be mixed by hand.

It would often fall to me to deliver printed matter to Cook and Watts, a textile importer trading in fine cottons from Madras,

Egypt, and the far reaches of the crumbling empire. Before Mr Watts amalgamated with Mr Cook in the early Sixties, it had been known for nearly a century as Watts' Warehouse, a five-storey emporium on Portland Street, designed after the fashion of a Venetian palazzo. There was a sweeping cantilever staircase and a balconied stairwell, roof pavilions lit by stained-glass Gothic wheel-windows, majestic mahogany display counters, marbled floors, and gleaming brass fixtures and fittings. This rococo wonderland still operated on the antediluvian Edwardian system where a counter assistant would place your order form in a copper conduit to be delivered by means of pneumatics to the dispatch offices upstairs.

In the Eighties, it was converted into the Britannia Hotel, the favoured accommodation of any visiting world-class celeb. Colourwise, the volume was turned up beyond eleven even, but the imperial splendour remained. Lately, it has been commonly perceived as a Class A gin joint with hot-sheet rooms. In short, a premiership shag palace.

Meanwhile, back in the Swinging Sixties, every so often some go-ahead new business required a more Bauhaus approach to typographic design. This involved sans serif typefaces, the creative use of white space, plus the abolition of capital letters and extraneous punctuation marks.

Cheetham's was the go-to printer for the vast Belle Vue Gardens entertainment complex, the Coney Island of the North, a stately pleasuredrome dedicated to overstimulation in every sensory department, home to the notorious Bobs, the biggest roller coaster in the nation outside of Blackpool. It was made out of wood!

There was a zoo with an aquarium, a hippopotamus pool, and performing sea lions, a poisonous snake pit, and a monkey house. There was a scenic railway, a boating lake, a flea circus, freak shows, and striptease. There was a purpose-built circus building, brass-band competitions, and business exhibition halls. There were casinos, hotels, and suites for rent, all named for some reason after anything vaguely to do with lakes: the Lake Hotel and the Windermere Suites, the Cumberland Suites and the Bavaria Suites.

There were boxing and wrestling arenas where World Championship title fights took place. There was a go-kart track, a stock-car track, a dog track, *and* a speedway circuit.

There was the grand New Elizabethan Ballroom, which hosted episodes of *Come Dancing*, and the Top Ten Club every Sunday hosted by – yes, it's that man again – Jimmy Savile. The fliers featured a photograph of him holding a (possibly traumatised) chimpanzee.

A couple of years into my apprenticeship, the Belle Vue company opened a club in Wythenshawe called the Golden Garter. Top of the bill on the opening night was Bruce Forsyth. There would follow many more megastars of the not-too-distant past, among them Matt Monro, Jack Jones, Kathy Kirby, Ken Dodd, Eartha Kitt, Roy Orbison, Frankie Vaughan, the Everly Brothers, Les Dawson, Cannon and Ball, Adam Faith, Helen Shapiro, Harry Webb, and the twin pillars of the MOR universe, Engelbert Humperdinck and Tom Jones. Maybe not entirely à la mode at the time, but in the words of my future mentor Bernard Manning, 'You can't knock success.' These acts were the foremost examples of the cabaret scene I would later wish to enter.

There were parts of Belle Vue I never even went to. It was a long way out of town and anything more than one bus ride seemed like a bit of a schlepp.

The Belle Vue concession had its upsides. Night school had provided me with a few modern ideas in typographic design, which could only be highlighted in certain display exercises: speedway posters, concert fliers, and dance tickets, for example, where some aesthetic judgement might be required.

The life of a printer's apprentice was hard. Gone were the happy-go-lucky days of ice cream and constant banter. In this world, for some reason, you had to look busy even when you weren't busy, which was harder work than actually working. Sorting shit out, reordering shit, cleaning shit up. In spite of the constant toil and the poor wages, however, some rewarding side action presented itself. Many apprentices supplemented their meagre stipend working Saturday nights for the Sunday nationals, humping papers onto the delivery vans and generally straining themselves. Although I was told that this was quite a lark, I wasn't too happy about sacrificing my weekends. Much better to sell a few hooky speedway tickets here and there, or blag into some company's annual dinner dance I wasn't invited to. Most lucrative of all was the ruse called 'doing a foreigner'.

Rather than a form of xenophobic assault, this meant using the firm's time and machinery for a bit of personal, off-the-books business. You could call it theft, I suppose, if you wanted to get shirty about it, but the extra revenue was always welcome on the shop floor, and I wasn't the only one at it.

One particular scam, or possibly scamola, was business cards. They were quick to do, and highlighted my design skills to great effect. I ran off a couple of hundred for The Con-Brios, a beat combo containing one of Dave Redshaw's cousins. They were really made up, to the tune of five pounds; the business card had given them that patina of class that no amount of bullshit could get. Others followed: The Abstracts, for instance, were rocketed to obscurity by way of my persuasive calling cards. I even ran off a few calling cards for myself – two colours, with 'JCC' in red, and my home address underneath, in whatever.

Thanks to these extras, I was saved from the misery of pecuniary embarrassment.

After I started working at the printers, I got seriously interested in the fortunes of the Belle Vue Aces, the resident speedway squad, which is still going strong years after Belle Vue's demolition. I'd pocket a few tickets and go with my pals, sometimes four nights a week. We'd stand in the dark watching the racers slide round the floodlit circular cinder track at great speed on those skinny dirt bikes, always at an angle to the ground. They had their foot right down, and their wheels threw up an almost invisible spray of cinder dust. The air would be thick with the ethereal miasma of methanol mingling with the hot dogs and onions.

I don't know whether I've made this up, or if it actually happened, but one day the Bobs went off the rails. Affixed to its wooden stanchions was a dramatic full-colour artist's impression of the speedway riders zooming around the bend, right at you, with speed stripes like in a comic book: *Pzzzzzwhit!* Anyway, in my memory I can see one of the roller-coaster carriages coming off its tracks and bursting right through this poster onto the main road, killing all of its occupants. I was sure that happened but, alas, have failed to find any record of this fatal accident. As I said, maybe it's from the fetid swamps of my overheated imagination. I often have to worry about this.

Some of the stars of the Belle Vue Aces would have their personal business cards printed at our place. That's where I came in with my newly acquired revolutionary Bauhaus take on typographic self-hype. My first speedway customer was the Aces' number-one rider, Ivan Mauger, pronounced Major. I'd found a 1920s printing block that was perfect: a stylised engraving of a guy on a speeding motorbike, vaguely art deco, complete with velocity stripes. Orders quickly followed from the rest of the squad.

Chapter Thirty

BEYOND THE BEATNIKS

At some point towards the late Sixties, things started to get a bit sloppy and facial hair was suddenly acceptable. As a bloke, I always figured that you had to know what you'd look like with the full beard. Me? I looked like the kind of cunt I'd been avoiding all of my life. Plus, it was uncomfortable, so in homage to Victor Brox I carved it down into a neat Vandyke number. Then I decided to get rid of the beard, leaving only the moustache and a triangular soul patch beneath my lower lip.

It was around then that I read an article in the *Daily Mirror* under the headline 'Beyond the Beatniks'. The piece described Andy Warhol's Factory scene in New York. I was already a big fan of his soup-can masterpieces, and although it would be a couple of years until I was able to actually see them, the notoriety of his recent cinematic output had not entirely passed me by: *Haircut No. 1, Blow Job, Batman Dracula, Chelsea Girls* featuring Nico, and the 1964 *Empire*, which involved a single fixed real-time camera shot of the Empire State Building sustained for eight hours and five minutes, the only movement provided by the passing clouds and the trajectory of the sun.

This Factory write-up was accompanied by a photograph of

Warhol's latest production, an art-rock beat combo called The Velvet Underground. Although they had long hair, they looked OK – sort of East Coast patrician, totally monochrome. Even their name was intriguing, like some secret society with a luxurious agenda. Unusually for a rock group, one of their number, John Cale, was playing an electrified viola. What's more, he sported a moustache – not a beard – a black moustache after the fashion of Don Diego de la Vega, alias Zorro.

Obviously, I immediately Feng Shui-ed the face furniture in the same fashion, and darkened it with eyebrow pencil. I wasn't entirely happy with the result. That's where Spanish Fred came in.

I had a couple of new pals from the printing game who were big into Trad jazz. I'd met Mike Newell at night school and he introduced me to his pal Al Tomlinson, who worked at the same firm as him. Mike was a trainee compositor like myself, and Tommo operated a Heidelberg press.

The appeal of Kenny Ball, Dick Charlesworth, Bob Wallis, Alex Welsh, and Mr Acker Bilk had hitherto eluded me, but now, here I was, hanging out in the jazz joints of the city: Club 43, the Black Lion, the Alma Lodge, and the MSG – no, not monosodium glutamate in this case, but the Manchester Sports Guild.

The MSG was very old-school, a worthy sort of place with quite a grown-up atmosphere, nothing to do with 'youth culture' about it at all. It was run by this guy called Jenks who was one of George Orwell's typical sandal-wearing-fruit-juice-drinker cranks. Downstairs, if anything, it was mainly people my dad's age, boozers watching fat guys with pints playing trombone. There was a bar in the middle, and upstairs was folk music where quite famous musicians like Martin Carthy, Alex Campbell, and Christy Moore used to play.

The MSG would also host some of the overseas acts appearing in those annual blues packages, so it was always worth keeping an eye on who was on. I saw Arthur 'Big Boy' Crudup there, for example: he's the guy who wrote 'That's All Right Mama', the first hit for Elvis Presley; obviously I was there like a shot. I mean, that ain't nothing!

The resident band at the Black Lion was the Zenith Six. Their number-one fan was a guy called Fred whose psychotic attention to detail made quite an impression on me. Dressed in a pinstripe suit and spats with a fuck-off diamond stick pin holding his necktie in place, Fred had jet-black wavy hair oiled back with Macassar and a matching coal-black slimline soup strainer on his upper lip, the ends of which were carefully waxed into rigid curls like some cartoon ice-cream vendor. They called him Spanish Fred. He was the obvious consultant.

'Fred,' I said, 'how *do* you do that with your moustache? Where do you get that sort of moustache-grooming aid?'

'Boots,' he replied without hesitation. 'It isn't on display, but they keep it in a drawer behind the counter in the gents' toiletries department.'

I duly invested in a tube of Ed Pinot Pomade Hongroise, a moustache wax available in a range of shades to suit every hair colour. I went for black, the better to achieve the desired Errol Flynn/Don Ameche/Douglas Fairbanks Jr. effect.

I was now way, way beyond the beatniks.

Tommo was neatly built and graceful in his movements; he was well-dressed, had a filthy sense of humour, and was a dedicated pussy hound. His swarthy good looks and his ardent pursuit of women had naturally led me to believe that he might be Spanish, but he later explained that he was in fact of Armenian descent. Anyway, the point is he could grow a beard in one afternoon.

Mike played a bit of clarinet and alto sax, but Tommo was a gifted trombone player, in thrall to the likes of Kid Ory, Chris

Barber, and, especially, the bludgeon-wielding sonic assaults of J. C. Higginbotham, the star trombonist of the Luis Russell Orchestra circa 1937.*

One night, sometime in early 1966, we went to the MSG to see the avant-garde sax maestro Archie Shepp. Tommo immediately started scoping the joint for female company. His relentless gaze fell upon two extremely attractive girls upon whom he put the moves before I'd even got the drinks in. In time-honoured fashion, he had gravitated towards the shorter of the two. Her name was Lynn. The choice had been made on my behalf. It should have been me. Boo hoo hoo.

A few months later we went to Club 43† to see Roland Kirk, a blind modern jazz genius who was famous for playing three saxophones at once. Tommo was already a devotee of Roland Kirk, but for me he was a recent discovery. I'd come across him courtesy of a contemporary art TV magazine programme called *Tempo* which went out on a Sunday afternoon and was watched by me, Al Tomlinson, and about seventeen other people.

It was at Club 43 that night that someone told us about a planned 'Happening' at Bolton Art School. They said they were looking for people to get involved.

It was early doors for Happenings. They were one of those things like Fluxus, the Situationists, and Harold Pinter in which I'd become an expert, thanks again to *Tempo*. If getting involved in the Happening meant taking part in something out-and-out weird, that was fine by us. We'd lately begun to smoke a lot of marijuana, so the biggest job would be keeping a straight face. Plus, Tommo had been reading about Happenings in *Playboy*

---

* See their release 'Jersey Lightning' of 1930.
† Club 43 was Manchester's most contemporary jazz club; its founder, Eric Scrivens, had been instrumental in bringing the American modern jazz greats to the city since 1940.

magazine, and how they sometimes involved female nudity. He was right up for that.

The Happening took place in a darkened lecture room illuminated by shifting globules of light projected onto the ceiling and the floor. It was like being inside one of those plasma lamps. The sound of the Charles Lloyd Quintet emanated from an unseen hi-fi system in the background, and in the middle of the space was a human sculpture, dressed like a secretary in a crisp skirt-and-blouse combo. The Charles Lloyd Quintet faded out, and there she was, sitting on her Corinthian plinth while a few nervous punters snipped at her garments with outsized pinking shears, as I, John Cooper Clarke, declaimed some narcoticised verse over the slide-trombone stylings of Mr Al Tomlinson, who was now sporting a Vandyke that he'd grown about three-quarters of an hour ago.

Don't get me wrong, I'm not the spontaneous participatory type at all. In fact, I find spontaneous people weird and terrifying. But this was all unfolding in such a cool space. Plus, the public were all on some kinda dope. People sat around thinking about shit, nodding and yadda yadda yadda, and all the while the human sculpture maintained her dispassionate demeanour even as the pinking shears closed in, finally leaving her inadequately draped in crinkle-cut shreds. That was the Happening. Structured, drowsy, and strange.

Unusually for the Casanova of the Northern Quarter, Tommo didn't cop off with anybody at the Bolton Art School Happening, but as I mentioned earlier, for some reason I was always being hit on by female art students, and that night was no exception. Enter Pauline, a budding sculptress with olive skin, a bubble perm, and a bubble mother. Double bubble!*

---

* Cockney rhyming slang again. Bubble and squeak = Greek.

One way or another, the Happening went in our favour. It gave me and Tommo a sheen of contemporary relevance, and now we were available for christenings, birthdays, weddings, bar mitzvahs . . . and Happenings.

Around this time, the 'As Seen on Granada Television' Mersey Poets held regular readings in O'Connor's Tavern, Liverpool 8, but there were no such venues in Manchester. There was, however, some kind of binary relationship between poetry and jazz.

Emboldened by our Happening success, Tommo and I pitched our double act at the bebop crowd. The modernists saw themselves as far more bookish and socially progressive than the Trad aficionados, and were keen to introduce a literary side to their little scene at Club 43 and the Alma Lodge.

Now we were performing for an audience who were attractive, well-dressed, and, yes, appreciative. We got to hear some great acts, including Marion Montgomery and the Laurie Holloway Trio, Elaine Delmar, hepcat songwriter Mark Murphy, and Champion Jack Dupree, a piano player and blues singer from New Orleans who had married a Yorkshire girl and settled down in Halifax. He'd been a prize-fighter, an errand boy for the local Mob, and very unusually at the time he had a diamond stud earring, a very exotic-looking guy.

Free drinks, a modest wage, and some important drug connections – it seemed like a sweet deal.

In Manchester, poetry-wise, there was one guy, and one guy only: John Cooper Clarke.

Chapter Thirty-One

THE *MONTHLY INDEX OF MEDICAL SPECIALITIES*

Around 1966, LSD started to crop up as the party drug of choice in leafy Altrincham. Everybody was at it before it was even illegal. Well not everybody, obviously. Hallucinogens were a bad idea for a control freak like me.

I was always very specific about my drug-taking: I wasn't one of those people who would 'try it and see'. I think that's why I'm still alive. I took a scholarly interest in the whole issue of drugs in general. Me and my pals had seen our lifestyle pathologised before our very eyes, and now Tombstones and Purple Hearts always arrived with a side order of shame. Yet, in the Mod era, it seemed to us like the contemporary thing to do; we had watched our dads pouring pint after pint down their throats night after night, so as far as we were concerned, taking a single pep pill was frankly the streamlined option.

The itinerant jazzbos of the recent past took heroin for similar reasons. Antisocial hours, often spent in dry towns – what's a young American going to do at 2am but create his own nocturnal social life? Often this involved narcotics, hookers, and dice games.

Such was my preoccupation with pharmacology that I got hold of a copy of *MIMS* from somewhere, I don't know how. A veritable bible, the *Monthly Index of Medical Specialities* was only available to the medical professions – you couldn't get it out of the library.

This fully illustrated pharmaceutical reference guide provided information on every drug in the British formulary – opiates, cannabis, uppers, downers, and psychotropics – medicaments photographed in every known format, with all their alternative names. It had to be updated regularly, like a phone book, as new and better drugs from Switzerland supplanted their predecessors.

Now I could look up all the foreign brand names for the drugs we liked, all the interactions and possible undesirable side effects. I got to the section on marijuana, and upon learning of its non-addictive properties, determined to smoke the shit for the rest of my life.

Soon after the Happening, I shot up for the first time. I was with an old acquaintance called Stan (what else?), the wayward son of one of my dad's mates who was a local chimney sweep.

Early in 1962, I used to go with my cousin Sid to the Friday night Jimmy Savile Disc Club held at the renamed River Boat Lounge opposite our place, now the Whisky-a-Go-Go, and Stan would often be there. He was always a guy to clock, because he was quite the mover and shaker: he wore his hair in that grown-out College Boy style, a style about to be universalised any minute by The Beatles.

Later on, Stan had somehow wangled an apprenticeship with Sid and Aubrey Silverstein. He was a bit older than me, but younger than anybody else at the barber's at the time, so while I was waiting for Aubrey to do the business, Stan and I would talk about books and movies and shit. Spookily enough, it was Stan who lent me Nelson Algren's *The Man with the Golden Arm*, for instance. We were interested in similar stuff: how things looked, social developments stateside, music, style. We were always discussing clothes and where to get them.

Then Stan didn't work at the barber's any more, and we didn't see each other again for ages, until I ran into him one night at His Excellency's, a club over Burton's on Broad Street, where The Abstracts were playing. Stan was a habitué of a kind of hepcat shebeen in Cheetham Hill called Banjo's, where he'd got hold of some cocaine from a bus driver. He invited me round to his sister's house the next day to try it out.

Cocaine was not the ubiquitous nose-candy one finds everywhere today. I'd never heard of anybody snorting anything, but I *had* read about shooting up. Naturally, I consulted my *MIMS* on the matter of administering cocaine. I hated needles, I hadn't even had a polio jab, but thanks to my non-existent diabetic sister I got hold of an outfit from a pharmacy on the other side of town, and went round to Stan's sister's place. We played a few records and worked out how to get with this hypo thing. We thought we were quite the chaps about town. Admirable.

That busted my taboo around syringes, although it would be some time before I would repeat the procedure.

Chapter Thirty-Two

THE LOVELY FLOWERS

December 1966, and the Mods were in retreat as their flagship show was working its notice. Characteristically, the penultimate *Ready Steady Go!* ushered in the next big thing: Jimi Hendrix.

I've never been a punter, as you know, but a month after his *RSG!* introduction, I was prepared to pay cash money to catch this guy. The Jimi Hendrix Experience were playing at the New Century Hall, a purpose-built venue constructed and run by the Co-operative Insurance Society.

It operated what was fast becoming an outmoded dress code, involving the compulsory necktie. After seeing Hendrix on telly, however, I didn't want to get fingered as some kind of anachronistic schmuck. I wasn't exactly a hippy, I just wanted to blend in, but there I was: the sole flouter of the hall's neckwear regulations. An example had to be made and I was refused admission.

I can't prove this, but I reckon Jimi would have done his nut.

By 1967, psychedelic pop had gone mainstream. For instance, The Paramounts, a jobbing beat group from Southend-on-Sea, rebranded themselves as Procol Harum to record 'A Whiter Shade of Pale'. This baroque sonic excursion, with its arcane lyrics and plaintive Hammond organ figure purloined from some classical piece or other, spent six weeks at number one, and is widely remembered as the international anthem of the psyche-delic age.

Then there was The Move, a bunch of Mods from Birmingham who were gradually orientalised as the Sixties progressed. 'Ace' Kefford, their bass player, was the first guy I ever saw wearing love beads on *Top of the Pops*, albeit underneath his neat thirty-eight-gram suit. Raiding the classical dressing-up box became quite a thing, and like Procol Harum, The Move co-opted one of the better-known classical riffs for their first hit, 'Night of Fear', in their case the *1812 Overture*. Their third hit, 'Flowers in the Rain', was the first chart single played by Tony Blackburn on the brand-new Radio 1.

The Move never adopted the full Eastern-esoteric look, but things did get a bit lairy — lustrous locks and walrus moustaches, seed-packet shirts, kick flares, exaggerated tailoring, the sudden appearance of the kipper tie, and what with the love beads, you know, here comes hippy. Their singer, Carl Wayne, however, didn't seem to be buying it. He alone persisted with the textbook Beatle cut, tuxedoed up with an oversized dickie bow. He looked like a cruise-ship performer surrounded by psyched-out hippies and gone-wrong Mods. As The Move began to introduce elements of auto-destructive theatre into their act, Carl, unsurprisingly, departed for the world of cabaret.

And what of Ace 'Love Beads' Kefford? I was recently in a position to quiz the band's lead guitarist Roy Wood on the subject.

'He left for health reasons, really,' replied the deadpan Brummie. 'Everyone wanted to kill him.'

Pretty soon, psychedelia infected everything as the style-conscious teeny-boppers blossomed into flower children.

The late-Sixties reinterpretation of the fin-de-siècle dandy was foppish, languid, and decadent, all about flamboyant orna-mentation, frills, ruffles, and chunky jewellery. The go-to boutique in London was Granny Takes a Trip on Chelsea's King's

Road, where Nigel Waymouth and hotshot schneider John Pearse specialised in fine tailoring using expensive and opulent fabrics: skinny crushed velvet or silk trousers; Liberty tana lawn and poplin shirts; neat-fitting lilac velvet suits; double-breasted jackets in floral William Morris prints. The likes of Anita Pallenberg, Julie Driscoll, Robert Fraser, the Stones, The Pretty Things, The Animals, and The Move were regular customers. Also the Jimi Hendrix Experience.

I was largely immune to these exotic trends – the way I dress has always been the same since 1965. My only nod to the whims of fashion was in the hair department.

As evidenced by The Move's new look, haircuts had started growing out a bit. We're not yet talking the full-on flowing mane of Phil May, but rock and roll hairstyles had evolved into a longer, layered sort of feather cut, usually with the ears sticking out, and spiked up at the crown. I would cite Steve Marriott of the Small Faces as the ideal. He had the perfect hair* as far as I was concerned.

I have to say it, though, the *gold standard* is Rod Stewart circa 1966, when he got a bit more messy, choppy, *coupe sauvage*. This was textbook Rod the Mod, and thanks to him, things started going my way in the hair department: my thick, rather coarse locks were a great boon in helping the barnet to stand up on top.

---

* There are only two acceptable rock and roll haircuts – the quiff, and the post-Beatles alternative that still pertains today: the one favoured by the Runaways, Chrissie Hynde, Jane Fonda in *Klute*, Ron Wood, Steve Marriott, most members of the K-pop corporation, Dr John Cooper Clarke, and especially Rod Stewart. Is it a mullet? I don't think so. For the mullet in all its horror I would refer you to Billy Ray Cyrus. (Now that I've mentioned his name, I defy you to expunge the infectious 'Achy Breaky Heart'. There are only three songs that will rid you of this earworm: the theme from *The Magic Roundabout*, 'The Macarena', and 'Never Gonna Give You Up' by Rick Astley.)

Maybe it was my Rod Stewart look, I don't know, but at some point around now I got it into my head that the Chaperones should try to cash in on the whole horticultural vibe, and I persuaded Mike and the remaining members to change our name to The Lovely Flowers.

Talk about one extreme to the other – The Mafia to The Lovely Flowers. You can see we were chasing success at all costs. What do you want? We'll be that thing. Why not? I had already adopted an ambidextrous take on commercialism: on the one hand applied to me, it was a good thing. In fact, it was the whole point. On the other hand, in anybody else, it was detestable.

The Lovely Flowers, alas, were disbanded before we even got going. Woggy took the Queen's shilling and joined the army. We begged him not to do it, but to no avail. He'd been bitten by the travel bug, and had always been impressed by soldiers and their swaggering airs.

I didn't really have a handle on that San Francisco thing anyway, so we were doing half-arsed covers, and as steady relationships and even marriage disrupted our collective ambition, we gradually wilted away. For the full story I would refer you to Gene Vincent's 1956 version of a song entitled 'That Old Gang of Mine':

Not a soul down on the corner
That's a mighty certain sign
That wedding bells are breaking up
That old gang o' mine
There goes Jack
There goes Jim
Walking down lovers' lane
Every now and again
We meet but then they don't seem the same
I get that lonesome feeling
When I hear those church bells chime

Now wedding bells are breaking up
That old gang o' mine

The Lovely Flowers. Great name. No band.

By the time Woggy left, we were like changed characters. Dave had got a car and become our designated driver. He was never much of a night owl, and probably got sick of us lot getting shit-faced while he had to ferry us about, so the minute he got a girlfriend our chauffeur went walkabout (or should that be 'drive-about'?). Consequently, we were always on the lookout for car-owners to take advantage of. For a while we latched onto this ginger fucker called Jeff. He was a bit of a cunt, but he had a banged-up Sunbeam Rapier.

Jeff turned out to be a fucking liability. He was a maniac behind the wheel. I was scared for my very life, but we couldn't shake the fucker off. Whenever we needed transport, he'd spookily materialise: 'In a hurry? Jump in!' It was Ernie 'The Head Butt' Heaton all over again.

There was this guy I got to know from the overspill corporation estate in Langley, Middleton. I can't even remember how I got involved, but it was the early days of the 'Clapton is God' period and he was a self-styled guitar hero; a fucking egomaniac cunt who'd seen the Jimi Hendrix Experience and thought 'me too'. He was looking for a couple of patsies who would obligingly fade into the background the minute his reputation went strato-spheric – that was his plan, anyway. He had a drummer, and he needed a bass player and a group name, both of which I was in a position to provide. I should mention here that at some point the band members had all adopted stage names, so now my busi-ness cards read: 'Brett Vandergelt Junior: Bass Player with The Lovely Flowers.'

Chapter Thirty-Three

THE EMBASSY CLUB

I felt trapped in my apprenticeship at the printers. If I'd been more mobile, I could somehow have put my plans of becoming a professional poet into operation, but what can you do when you have to make money?

Getting out of Manchester was the pull: I had London in my sights, obviously. I aspired to be part of that urban milieu, peopled with all those witty, urbane fringe characters I'd read about, like Ned Sherrin, Kenneth Tynan, and Peter Cook. I'd watch the likes of *That Was the Week That Was* and see provincial people making it in that world: David Frost, for example, a guy with a regional accent who was nevertheless a sharp disseminator of controversial opinion.

My parents, as I have explained, were not encouraging about my proposed career. At every turn I was advised against it by everyone, in the strongest possible terminology, and with very good reason. 'There have been plenty of poets,' went the argument, 'but show me *one* that earns a living at it.'

'Oh, you'd have to go back into history,' I'd say.

'All right, name somebody from history then,' came the retort.

For a while, I had laboured under the delusion that the life of the poet precluded any kind of day job. How wrong I was. Now I discovered that most modern poets had to work as teachers, bank clerks, insurance salesmen, doctors, diplomats, railroad workers, tax collectors, publishers, or postal clerks. Even England's 'other poet laureate', Philip Larkin, turned out to be a librarian by day. I couldn't point to any fucker who'd ever made a living out of it. But I figured there must be some way round this.

Long gone were the days of music hall and the likes of Gus Elen, Billy Merson, Harry Champion, and the monologue purveyors of yesteryear such as Phil Harris, Stanley Holloway, and that darling of the musical theatre, Rex Harrison. Even so, I was beginning to see myself as part of some sort of ill-defined tradition. I figured there had to be a place for my kind of poetry in the world of entertainment. Why wouldn't there be?

That's when I decided to go round to the Embassy Club, Bernard Manning's joint out in Harpurhey. It was shit or get off the pot. That's all there was to it.

If any gig would have impressed my dad it would have been there. To him, Bernard Manning was a reliable yardstick of local success.

I must have known instinctively that I'd have to start out the hard way. If I'd gone to an audition and told the booker that I'd done this benefit for a pacifist magazine run by a chick I was vaguely involved with, his reply would have been along the lines of, 'Yeah? Very interesting . . . Fuck off.'

Instead, I went to the other extreme. An appearance at the Embo could open a few doors.

I went to Rochdale Road and delivered my pitch to the head honcho himself. It didn't start well. 'Don't waste your time,' Bernard told me. 'They don't like poetry here, kid. Half of them can't fucking read. You want to try one of them colleges.'

He was trying to be helpful in his tin-pot way; he saw poetry as some kind of high-falutin' academic thing, but I corrected him on this. 'It's not like that, Mr Manning. It's "Albert and the Lion" sort of stuff.'

So he said, 'Give us a demo.' And that's when I hit him with 'Salome', a poem set in a world I knew he would be familiar with from his days on the Mecca ballroom circuit as a singer with the Oscar Rabin Band. The poem contains this couplet:

When the ambulances came she was lying on the deck
she fell off her stiletto heels and broke her fucking neck.

I thought he'd like that: I mean, it had 'fucking' in it, and people always laugh when somebody falls over. Every fucking time.

That clinched the deal. 'It's very good that, aye,' he said. 'That's the Ritz all over, that is. "Fell off her stiletto heels and broke her fucking neck." All right, go on then. Give it a go.' Cruelty pays: I learned that from my mentor, the late Bernard Manning, the first man to give me cash money for doing what I do.

I didn't tell anyone at Cheetham's about my Embassy debut. I never even let slip that I wrote poetry. It was like a double life: I couldn't have handled the inevitable piss-taking sessions every day of the working week. Or worse: Mr Hope turning up in the front row with his wife.

At that time Rochdale Road in Harpurhey, a couple of miles from the city centre, was one of the roughest and most deprived parts of Manchester. The Embassy was housed in a former Temperance Billiard Hall, which was actually just a glorified Nissen hut with a concrete art-deco-flavoured frontage, its features picked out in red light bulbs. Kind of low rent, but perfectly comfortable. The interior had a homely vibe, with those cut-out cardboard Day-Glo stars announcing forthcoming acts pinned to the back of the stage, knick-knacks here and about, and utilitarian furniture. World-famous class acts would come and go, but apart from Bernard there was just one permanent fixture, the Dave Green Trio.

Every evening would be quite considered, from a variety point

of view. It was filthy humour, but otherwise good clean fun. The
Embassy didn't feature strippers – Bernard had his whole family
working there: his wife was general manager, his mother was on
the till, and all these sweet old broads who should have been
working in a cake shop were serving behind the bar, seemingly
impervious to the obscene repartee. Not the place you'd go on
a first date.

The night would unfold with Bernard conducting the proceedings. He'd take to the stage, immediately establishing an atmosphere
of hilarious animosity. He'd tell a few gags between introducing
the acts, and would have a go at some of the people in the front
rows. 'Fucking hell! Who cut your hair? We'll get him for you.'
Or he'd pick on someone going to the bar: 'Either that suit's on
upside down or there *is* no law of gravity', or, 'What's your name,
kid? Any idea?'

For obvious reasons, nobody wanted to sit ringside, so there
was always a vacant buffer zone between Bernard and the audience,
which he would attempt to close up as a big part of his act. 'Bags
of room here, love. Move a couple of chairs in here.' Occasionally
a naive family group would take him up on it – 'A full table here.
Come on, down the front here, ladies and gents.' He would then
address the husband of the youngest woman in the party with the
words, 'Fucking hell. Is that her mother? I'm not being funny,
but that's what your missus is gonna look like in forty years.'
Comedy as a blood sport. You don't get entertainment like that
any more.

Bernard was a self-made hate figure who over time achieved the
status of folk devil. It was in his professional interest to keep it that
way. He was, however, capable of doing good by stealth, and there
are many stories of his personal generosity. Be that as it may, Mr
Manning is disapproved of by many, even beyond the grave.

At the Embassy, he booked all the big Northern cabaret acts
of the day, plus stars from all over the country. On any given

night you'd have a broad mix of stand-up comedy, oddball variety artists, magicians, and some of the great vocalists of the not too distant past. Bernard himself would also always knock out one or two songs – he was a very nuanced and versatile singer.

Gerry Dorsey, aka Engelbert Humperdinck, Freddie and the Dreamers, Cilla Black, singer, impressionist and comedian Freddie Starr, singer and impressionist Joe Longthorne, The Grumbleweeds, the yodelling country singer Frank Ifield, Cannon and Ball, who at that time were a singing act called the Harper Brothers, Lynne 'star of TV's *Coronation Street*' Perrie and ditto Liz Dawn. The Reg Coates Combo, the Four Statesmen, Second City Sounds. The young Paul Daniels worked there, as did impressionist Mike Yarwood. Syd and Eddie, later known as Little and Large, were a very popular act. Syd played a bit of guitar and, as a spectacles-wearer, was something of a Buddy Holly specialist, whilst Eddie was a gifted impersonator.

The comedians who played the Embassy were mostly, though not exclusively, from Manchester and Liverpool: George Roper, Stan Boardman, Mick Miller, Norman Collier (who was from Hull), who had the broken mic routine; Jim Bowen off *Bullseye*, Johnny Goon Tweed, Ken Goodwin, Jackie Carlton, and from Belfast, Frank Carson and Roy Walker, plus up from Hackney, Mike 'Frank Butcher' Reid. Then there was John Paul Joans, a left-field provocateur, not quite the sort you'd expect to find at the Embo.

When it was my turn, Bernard's introduction went something like this: 'Here he is, all the way from Higher Broughton. He's not my cup of tea but you might like him. Ladies and gentlemen, John Cooper Clarke.' Apart from the headliner, for whom he had to indicate a level of grudging respect, he was like that with everybody.

I don't remember being terrified, not even the first time; I think my ambition outweighed any terror. They say about people in show business, 'They ain't got something extra, they've got something missing.' And I think that something is any reticence about performing in front of people. You've got to think you're top dog or you wouldn't be doing it in the first place.

I think I threw in a few gags, just so the audience wouldn't think I was the self-improvement section of the show. I'm not saying that they paid any attention. Maybe the odd bit – I could hear people laughing, but I didn't know what at. There was always the omnipresent hum of conversation at the bar – ordering drinks and clinking glasses, barking out instructions to the staff. I got used to that, but if the noise spread to the room at conversational level, it was all over.

If you're reading poetry without any accompaniment your big enemy isn't hostility, it's high-volume indifference. That was the most likely reaction, actually. Shouting shit out, or heckling, was preferable: at least it was some kind of reaction. People remember if it goes off, and anyway, the performer has the advantage of a microphone and, hopefully, a large supply of counterclaims, e.g. 'Last time I saw a mouth like that it had a hook in it.' Or, 'Any more of this and I'll report you to your superiors. Find me anyone.' Or, 'I can't hear you, pal. Your mouth's full of shit.' Or, 'Go home, Dad!' Stuff like that. But against indifference, what can you do?

The main lesson I picked up from watching the other acts at the Embassy, especially the comedians, was this: if people aren't listening, never crank it up. *Au contraire*, drop the volume – if they can't hear you, there's just a chance they might stop talking amongst themselves.

I was getting about £15 a night out of Bernard, which was a lot of money. He wasn't one of those club owners who would put on a load of acts and pay them nothing. While he didn't pay upfront, you always got your money. He was good like that: a reputable businessman.

Speaking of which, I remember waiting outside his office at the end of the night in the cramped backstage area, now chock-a-block with cast-off costumes and various elaborate stage props. Through the door I could hear Bernard Manning chewing out one of the other acts. The conversation ended thus: 'When you said you were going to saw a woman in half, I'd *assumed* you were a fucking magician.'

Seriously, though, I might not have set the Embo on fire, but I had recited poetry at the most badass cabaret joint in town, and that ain't nothing.

Chapter Thirty-Four

THE PENNY UNIVERSITY

I had a couple of art student friends called Liz Sherwood and Patricia Ford, quite flamboyant characters: head-turners. Liz was half Italian and her hair was black and kinky like mine, so she had the haircut I wanted: the Julie Driscoll/Vidal Sassoon 'Greek Goddess', i.e. spiky on top, feathered and layered around the back and sides. Unisex slightly before the event.

According to Liz, the first time she saw me I was flying out of the door of the Good Food Inn on Deansgate, along with Tommo, Mike Newell, and our belligerent drunk troublemaking pal, the lovely Kenny Burgess Clark.

Back in the days when pubs closed at eleven, we used to go to the Good Food Inn, where if you bought a foot-long hot dog you were entitled to get a drink and hang around indefinitely. It was a way of extending the night while not being outdoors – there was nowhere to go, but you had to go somewhere. On the occasion in question, Kenny, for some reason, after consuming an entire cheeseburger, immediately complained about it and refused to pay. Kenny was always getting us into scrapes: he just wanted it to kick off, he wanted push to come to shove – some people are like that after a couple of sherbets. It wound up with all four of us being physically slung out of the place onto the street, and the block being put on all of us. After-hours hang-out joints were not that common, so consequently this put Kenny in the doghouse for quite some time, although, somehow, he continued to occupy the high moral ground on the subject.

That was Liz's first recollection of me; she'd spotted my moustache with the Pomade Hongroise and the antique three-piece suit I'd recently had modified at a tailor's, and which, unusually at the time, I wore with a watch and chain.

Liz and Pat had turned up one night at the MSG with a bunch of students from the art school that Liz hung out with. One of her lecturers at art college had talked them into it, and Tommo, Mike, and I somehow became part of that team.

Liz and I became really close. She was a good friend and an easy companion, very funny, with a distinctive giggle you could hear five miles away and a default facial expression of enthusiastic surprise. She was an immensely gifted painter, but like me she'd got the showbiz bug and her face was made for television.

She looked great, redolent of the young Amanda 'Carry On Cleo' Barrie. I don't quite know how to explain it: she wasn't conventional leading-lady beautiful, but she was very cute, kooky, with the fashionably angular Sixties physique, all of which I found very endearing.

She dressed very carefully, and always looked fabulous in the outfits she put together. Whatever it took to look right on the money at any time, Liz had it. She made it look easy; she was a great shoplifter – erm, I imagine.

Speaking of shoplifting, we spent a great deal of time in an up-market department store called Kendal Milne, the nearest thing Manchester had to Barkers. It was in a beautiful purpose-built art deco building (now House of Fraser) made out of Portland stone and glass bricks. In a certain light you can't quite tell what is transparent and what is opaque.

Kendal Milne had a furniture store on the opposite side of the road, which you could reach by way of an underpass, itself lined with little shops: a subterranean street, ingenious! We were mainly interested in The Way In, a trendy new women's boutique which occupied an entire floor of the building. The Way In was Manchester's equivalent of Biba, selling the latest fun fashions, shoes, and accessories. It also stocked Biba cosmetics. Liz loved that whole Barbara Hulanicki vibe – plum lipstick, fake eyelashes, statement sunglasses, oversized fedoras in amplified colours, and plastic jewellery. There were floral displays, potted palms, exotic plumes of all kinds, beanbags, scatter cushions, and gonks cast carelessly here and about.

Entire days would be squandered in this place, with Liz trying stuff on, and me helping myself to a free squirt of the latest fragrance from Paris, France. All the while in the background, on a seemingly endless loop, either 'I Can't Let Maggie Go' by Honeybus, 'Rainbow Valley' by Love Affair, or 'Excerpt from a Teenage Opera' by Keith West.*

If not The Way In, it would be C&A or Chelsea Girl, Marks & Spencer's ladies' department, Etam or Van Allen, the last two specialising in the skinny-rib crewneck sweaters I liked to wear. When it came to buying clothes, Liz was the perfect second opinion.

She and I were similar in many ways; I hate to say it, but we both had the same sense of entitlement. She never paid to get in anywhere either. We used to just sail in and out of clubs and gigs and parties and get invited to all sorts of shit. We were a kind of double act in that way – who did we think we were?

We were inseparable, but not actually an item: I never put the move on her. I didn't even put the mood on her. Liz was right up my street, but when it came to guys, I couldn't make her out.

---

* Show me the rest of the opera, Keith. Just saying!

She had all these boyfriends that I never approved of. I thought they weren't her type, that they didn't get it with her at all, that none of them were deserving of her special charms.

I can't remember her ever getting her heart broken by any of these unsuitable suitors; she always baled out before it got nutty. I never saw her exploited by anybody. She called the shots all the way. Whoever invented women's lib, it wasn't on her behalf.

Nobody had a phone, so we'd just run into each other at various haunts. In Cromford Court, the Cavern had become the Jigsaw, and now, in the Summer of Love, after a psychedelic paint job, under the stewardship of Roger Eagle it had been renamed the Magic Village. Liz used to hang out there with her mate Sue Richardson, so I made sporadic visits to the place. I didn't like it, but I never paid to get in anyway.

The Magic Village was just the same shithole as the Cavern had been, but with hippy self-expression splattered all over the walls, mattresses with Navajo rugs in lieu of seats, and the smell of putrefaction and poor water management now tempered by incense, hashish, and patchouli oil.

Roger Eagle was seeking refuge from the very thing he had pioneered, namely the music policy at the Twisted Wheel. He was now a soul fugitive, and with the exception of Jimi Hendrix, Richie Havens, and the Charles Lloyd Quartet, was playing the entirely white repertoire of the West Coast love crowd: *Twelve Dreams of Dr. Sardonicus* by Spirit, 'In-A-Gadda-Da-Vida' by Iron Butterfly, songs with guitar solos that went on and on and on for the rest of your life and beyond. Even so, there were a couple of tunes that I liked, namely 'On the Road Again' by Canned Heat featuring Al 'Blind Owl' Wilson on vocals and harmonica, and 'I Had Too Much to Dream (Last Night)' by The Electric Prunes.

Liz didn't care too much about the music one way or the other, but an outing to the Magic Village was an excuse to wear bandanas and tie-dyed stuff, plus these floaty garments that she and Sue

Richardson didn't usually have the opportunity to wear in Manchester. (What could be worse than wet chiffon? It just doesn't do that chiffon thing no more.)

Roger used to go round vox-popping the crowd about any future stateside acts he was about to book. How much they would pay to see Frank Zappa, for instance. He seemed inordinately desperate to hire Country Joe and the Fish, but these hippies were reluctant to cough up anything at all: believing money to be intrinsically evil, they expected musicians to travel from California and play for nothing.

When we weren't schmying around the city centre, Liz's main occupation was hanging about with Pat Ford in selected watering holes in order to schmooze with the media types who drank in them, with the hope of furthering their showbiz ambitions. I invited myself along for the same reason. They spent a lot of time in the Grapes, round the corner from Granada Studios, which was always full of TV personnel including Tommy Mann, who had left the grunt-'n'-groan world of Greco-Roman freestyle wrestling to become a fight arranger for Granada. He was also a stuntman and character actor who had played bit parts in *The Avengers*, *Softly, Softly*, and *Vendetta*. Another regular at the Grapes was Ian 'Star of TV's *Lovejoy*' McShane. I suspect the pub-grub menu was a big attraction. Unusually for a pub of that period, the Grapes served food, and when I say food, I obviously mean a Ploughman's. But not just any Ploughman's: this one featured Gorgonzola cheese!

Pat was a would-be socialite, a right climber, but she couldn't half drink. Pints and pints of beer. The thing about Pat was, she was always pushing people around – don't do that, do this. She couldn't help it – she had organisational skills. Impromptu soirées at somebody else's house were a speciality. If she decided you were having a party, that was all about it. She'd turn up with a shipload of sailors in tow: 'I'll show you a good time if it kills you.' She was very pretty, curvaceous even, and always travelled with a male entourage, an interchangeable chain of fools she led around by the nose, her slightest wish their command. A born leader of men. It didn't entirely work on me, what with my lack of team spirit, so it was a bit of a relief, frankly, when she got a part in the Glasgow Metropole production of *Hair*.

Pat organised an audition for Liz, who got a part in the chorus. According to Pat it was money for nothing, although she might be required to disrobe, but only if the vibe was right.

Ten months later, the run ended, and Liz and Pat were back in Manchester, any vestige of stage fright they might have possessed long ago ditched, along with their garments, on the stage of the Glasgow Metropole. We started hanging out in the Stables Theatre Club, a former hostelry for shire horses, now a social club after a billion-dollar makeover by Granada Studios.

The Stables was a louche late-night hang-out for the showbiz crowd: TV newsreaders, anchormen, weathermen, soap-opera personalities, sports reporters, producers, boxers, footballers, and gossip columnists. It stayed open all hours, occasionally featuring some rudimentary cabaret entertainment: someone on piano, a jazz trio, or one of the new breed of sensitive young singer-song-writers after the manner of Ralph McTell or Al Stewart.* The pre-*Taggart* Alex Norton, for instance, who was quite the handsome ragamuffin young balladeer back then − Aran sweater, finger in the ear, probably didn't shave on a daily basis, kind of Ewan McGregor before the event. He would do a set involving Woody Guthrie covers and one or two of his own songs, often rambunctious tales of drunken carousing in his native Glasgow.

There was a bit of a buzz going on around me doing poetry at Bernard Manning's Embassy Club, of all places. Poetry at the

---

* 'Year of the Cat'? What's all that about?

Embassy Club? Wow! That's a first! Pre-*The Comedians*, to these ponces at the Stables Theatre Club (with the honourable exception of Johnny Hamp, the Granada TV producer)* the Embassy was the other side of the universe.

The Stables was the perfect venue, so I started doing my thing there in return for free booze plus extravagant public displays of carefully considered adulation: a new experience for me. Most importantly, it helped me establish myself as a poet and professional raconteur in the comparatively new realm of endeavour, commercial television.

The first cab off the rank was 'Salome'. It had worked on Bernard, and I thought the TV crowd would also appreciate the compressed adjectival imagery. I pitched it just right: one early enthusiast was Ken Farrington, aka Billy Walker in *Coronation Street*. The show's creator Tony Warren was also a regular in the audience, as were, I imagine, the writer Jack Rosenthal and his future wife Maureen Lipman.

For good or ill, the thespian world runs on effusive language, and at this point it was running in my favour. One night, I was approached by Alex Norton and a friend of his, a photographer called Kevin Horgan, a man with the saturnine grace of the late Liberal dog-murderer Jeremy Thorpe. Alex explained that they had plans to open their own nightclub, which would become a magnet for Manchester's burgeoning young radical crowd. They were going to call it the Penny University. Apparently that's what coffee houses were called in the late seventeenth century, when they were perceived as the very percolator of caffeinated sedition.

---

* Johnny Hamp produced, among other things, *The Comedians* and later *Wheeltappers and Shunters Club*. He was also responsible for The Beatles' first TV exposure on *Scene at 6.30* and a series of television specials featuring blues-based American artists, notably *Whole Lotta Shakin' Goin' On* (1964), with Jerry Lee Lewis and Gene Vincent, and *It's Little Richard* (1963); then in 1964 *The Blues and Gospel Train* with Sister Rosetta Tharpe.

As I've said, at the time, most clubs had their own song. With that in mind, Alex had composed a Penny University anthem that needed lyrics. That was where I came in. He put a figure on it and played me the tune.

This was a big event: I was being paid to apply my artistic expertise to a project that wasn't my own. It was my first commission: ten pounds for the work of an afternoon. I was now a 'commercial' poet.

I still remember the tune, but I've forgotten the words. I'll have to ask Taggart: I wonder if he's got any recorded evidence? Surely there's a dossier somewhere in the files of Scotland Yard, or Strathclyde Police, or wherever he is. I haven't seen him since those days. He probably lives in a castle near Loch Lomond or something, probably got his own tartan.

Chapter Thirty-Five

KOMMUNES, KAFTANS, AND KATHMANDU

Towards the end of my apprenticeship at Cheetham's, Tommo, Mike Newell, and I went on holiday to St Ives for a week. We'd never been to Cornwall before, and it held the promise of eternal sunshine, that same eternal sunshine that had attracted artists and writers since year zero.

Obviously, the main objective of blokes in their early twenties on holiday is the acquisition of female companionship, and we were no exception. The other two got fixed up thanks to Tommo's expertise in these matters, while I, as usual, was hit on by an art student. Her name was Christine – from Stretford of all places: yes, the same Stretford that gives its name to the business end of Old Trafford.

Christine was a seriously pretty girl, a few years younger than me. She really reminded me of someone, but I wasn't sure who. We got chatting about Stretford, and before long Christine mentioned that I knew her sister. Then it hit me: she looked just like Lynn – yes, *that* Lynn, the same Lynn Tommo had copped off with at the MSG. Christine had visited her the previous week in Plymouth, where she now lived with her husband Brian, a splendid chap who worked as a teacher in the town.

I don't know how quickly this thought process formed, nor

do I understand how it persisted, but we got on reasonably OK, and I started thinking, 'Well, Lynn's out of the picture, but Christine looks exactly the same, so Christine it is.'

It turned out to be the holiday romance that got out of hand. After we got back to Manchester, Christine and I continued our relationship. We hadn't been seeing each other for more than a couple of months when my apprenticeship ended and I was free at last to look for work elsewhere. I found a job at Shaston Printers, a small firm in Shaftesbury, Dorset, and we decided to get married. Life in a choc-box country town had never been on my agenda, but now it had some kind of cornball attraction; plus, married status equalled a lower tax rate. It was a way out of Manchester for both of us. You don't need to be Claire Rayner to know that this was no solid basis for a lasting union.

We got married in Jackson's Row register office in the centre of Manchester, and went to Stretford for our honeymoon. A week later Cousin Sid hired a van and moved us and our meagre possessions – i.e. a few clothes and our respective record collections – to Shaftesbury.

Shaston Printers was pretty quaint. We lived above the shop, in a terrific apartment for a very reasonable rent. I'd just bought *Self Portrait*, a double album of mainly covers by Bob Dylan, while Christine's record collection largely featured artists who were unknown to me, and who I didn't like the look of. There were however two records I was grateful to be introduced to: *Astral Weeks* by Van Morrison and *Safe as Milk* by Captain Beefheart and the Magic Band. If I call our home life to mind, those records would be playing in the background until we got a telly.

My new boss Mr Mowbray had a physical resemblance to Rex Harrison, and was an amiable, easy-going sort of cove. At that point letterpress printing hadn't changed much since the days of the Gutenberg Bible, but the process had been speeded up with the introduction of electricity. I was working a massive Wharfedale

flatbed machine. It was heavy work. These were the days of Laura
Ashley and brown bread, and the latest metropolitan fad was a
move to the countryside, so we were printing a lot of gigantic
billboard property auction posters.

Other than smoking weed and having the odd drink, there
wasn't much to do in Shaftesbury, to be honest. Occasionally a
shipment of LSD might arrive, and Christine was quite the enthusiast, so that provided a step into another dimension for a while.
If you're going to take that shit, you're always better off in a place
of butterflies, birdsong, and bluebell woods.

We had made some good pals there, some of whom I still see
from time to time, but after a while the bucolic allure of Dorset
began to fade. 'The idiocy of rural life', a faintly remembered
phrase of the late Karl Marx, began to re-present itself in my idle
moments. Christine shared my growing malaise, and in one of
her regular letters from Lynn we learned of a vacant apartment
on Albert Road in Plymouth, and decided to take it.

It was an absolutely ghastly place, on the middle floor of a
very similar period house to the one I grew up in in Higher
Broughton. Downstairs was a violent drunken psychopath called
Kenny (aren't they all), who looked like one of Henry Cooper's
Neanderthal ancestors, and his long-suffering wife Joyce, who on
the two occasions I ever saw her, appeared to be the most oppressed
woman this side of Saudi Arabia.

I never met Kenny when he didn't have an axe in his hand.
Although he would try to be chirpy, everything he said to you
sounded like a threat, except once when I ran into him when he
had a smile on his face, an axe in his hand, and he declared that
he was 'pissed as a puddin'. To which I replied, 'Keep it up, son.'

You had to keep him sweet: I used to lie awake at night
thinking, any minute now that door's gonna go in and there'll be
claret all over the walls.

He had a drum kit in the cellar, and a mate called Harry who would occasionally come round and give it a bashing. Drums have never been my favourite instrument, but I didn't dare complain. Besides that, because they were both aggressive round-the-clock drunks, Kenny and Harry would have frequent punch-ups. One night, Kenny accused Harry of damaging the outer casing of his precious kit, which like many drum kits was dressed in that faux-abalone pearlised material often found on flush door handles, fountain pens, and most piano accordions. Kenny reckoned he'd knocked forty quid off the selling price, and Harry didn't agree. On another occasion it kicked off when Kenny accused Harry of putting the move on Joyce.

Upstairs was Mrs Bullmore, who was also hard as nails, and belligerent with it. She had a face like a bag of spanners, but had obviously once been married. Now she had entered the sex industry, with a regular pitch outside the gents' lavatories near the dockyard. She *was* the Plymouth Hoe. I was no stranger to hookers (I'd lived on Camp Street, don't forget), but Mrs Bullmore had a tattoo. It sounds odd now, but that was the most shocking thing about her: a tattooed lady was the stuff of sideshows and Groucho Marx lyrics.

Mrs Bullmore had lived in our apartment before she moved up to the top floor. It was awful: no carpet, a greasy linoleum floor, lilac curtains made of some fire-retardant material, wallpaper the colour of baby sick, and the whole place stank of her tom cat. We couldn't shift that foul reek, which took permanent residence in my olfactory epithelium even out of the house.

This vile creature had a bell round its neck, and it woke me up one Saturday morning running up and down the stairs jing-a-ling-a-linging all the way, until I got up, told it to fuck off, and threw a shoe at it. Unfortunately, Mrs Bullmore was lurking unseen on the landing upstairs and witnessed my outburst. She saw her arse about it, and you know what cat owners are like. I already dreaded leaving the apartment in case I bumped into Kenny the fucking psycho hatchet-man downstairs, but now it was agg from all sides.

I was looking for work in Plymouth. In the meantime, therefore, we had some cash-flow issues. I sold my only remaining decent garment, a made-to-measure three-piece suit, to a high-end second-hand shop for twenty quid. A week later we were broke again. I took stock of our scant possessions. I thought I'd done my bit. There was nothing for it: some of Christine's vinyl had to go. I knew she would never agree to it, but it wasn't up for discussion: while she was out, I gathered up all her Incredible String Band and Roy Harper albums and took them down to the shop where I'd sold my suit. I flogged the lot, killing two birds with one stone: we had money and I had rid myself of the stereo torture I'd had to endure on a daily basis. I don't think Christine ever forgave me for that.

I soon got a job as a fire-watcher at the Royal Naval Dockyard, the main employer in Plymouth. If anybody asked how many people worked there, the answer was always the same: about ten per cent.

Before I could start I had to fill in a questionnaire, one of the questions being 'Are you now, or have you ever been, a member of the Communist Party?' The full Joe McCarthy schtick. Given the fact that we don't have a Fifth Amendment in this country, I answered honestly. My patriotism was consequently called into question to the extent that I wasn't allowed anywhere near any nuclear subs, in case I was passing on military secrets to the Soviets. You can't be too careful.

It was close to the perfect job for me. I just had to turn up and keep an eye on things when a welder or a burner was in operation on HMS *Medusa* or whatever ship was in the dry dock. I had all the time in the world.

I joined the Transport and General Workers' Union, which was then the biggest and most powerful union in the country, run by the late Mr Jack Jones – no, not the 'Shadow of Your Smile' guy, but the veteran of the International Brigades back in the Spanish Civil War.

It was a good scene. My fellow workers were a chirpy lot, the 'working' conditions were great, and there were really good canteens. Every day it was a done deal: Cornish pasty. What else? They were gigantic, about a foot long, real proper stuff, chunks of potato and beef, lots of white pepper. There's good eatin', shipmates.

Emboldened and fortified, after lunch I would take a leisurely schmie around the docks, pumping certain people for information concerning any horses running that afternoon, and what have you. I'd go for an explore up on deck, and became quite the agile matelot, sliding down the ladders, shimmying up the rigging, darting up for'ard, back aft, and amidships, a-coiling in the ropes. All the more authentic being among these West Country yardies who all had the generic pirate accent. 'Aaarrr, back aft, up for'ard, up top, and down below,' 'Ahoy there,' and 'All right, my hand-some' – everybody called each other that. They'd even use the terminology when complaining of digestive upsets after a night on the piss: 'Spot of trouble amidships, my handsome.'

Eventually, I'd return to my watching station and settle in for the afternoon. I was a big fan of the French existentialists at that time, so I read the entire oeuvre of Albert Camus and Jean-Paul Sartre.

Most of the other guys were 'grabbers' – meaning they were available for any overtime that presented itself. They would fall out about it. What they liked about me was that I wasn't interested in working a minute longer than my eight to five. They couldn't understand why anybody would turn down the extra money, but I'd had enough, tired out from reading *Being and Nothingness* next to a welder all day.

Some people are always gonna take the piss. Nothing changes.

The best example I saw of this was when my colleagues were talking up the joys of working the night shift. 'You don't have to do anything at all,' they said. But I already didn't do anything at all. 'You don't even have to pretend to be doing anything.' But I already didn't pretend to be doing anything. The fact was, the night shift was the biggest skive available. Apparently, nobody checked up on you, you simply clocked in and clocked out. You just had to be there. As if that wasn't cushy enough, they had to push the envelope a bit further. They started showing up with flannelette pyjamas and alarm clocks, so they could actually go to work, go to bed at work, and set an alarm clock to wake them up in time to go home from work. Then they were bringing in blow-up mattresses, duck-down pillows, reading lamps, hot-water bottles. They had it real sweet until, predictably, they got rumbled. The superintendent did a spot check one night, and there they all were, Zzzzzzzzzzzzzzzz. Each one of them was rapidly re-acquainted with his P45.

Being the main employer in town, the Royal Naval Dockyard had an obligation to employ a certain amount of certified nutters – people who, while not insane enough to be in a secure insti-tution, had no future in the world of public relations. Thousands of people worked there, and most days you would find yourself with a different gang, so one daily entertainment was 'Spot the Nutter'. Some of them were perfectly plausible, and thus hard to identify. Occasionally, unbelievably, I myself fell under suspicion.

I had a particular workmate called Roger Spettigew: unusual name, top bloke. He was about my age, and had started the same day I did. We'd meet every day over pasties and chips and go for the odd drink after our shift; he had a good sense of humour, so we became an island of sanity for each other.

One of our daily rounds involved a visit to the guys who worked in a hut on the side of one of the dry docks. I don't know what their specific occupation was supposed to be, but I never saw them doing anything. The only man there who seemed engaged in any work at all was an elderly tea boy, a man with a chronic nervous condition, which meant he couldn't operate any machinery other than an electric kettle. Even that proved hazardous – his jittery demeanour was such that you'd only ever get half a cup of tea. I don't know if it was a symptom of his condition or what, I'm not a neurologist, but his reactions were slowed to the point that I once watched somebody come up behind him and tap him on the shoulder while he had a full mug in each hand, and a minute later he was still standing as if in freeze-frame, his face a mask of shock and anxiety. I knew what would happen, I had plenty of time to warn the other guy, but I didn't. I just watched it unfold: it took him a full minute to react, throwing each mug of tea simultaneously over his shoulders, the scalding contents splashing into the face of his unwitting co-worker.

I became quite pally with a bloke in the hut called Ray Kortz, who had a bit of a sideline in wet fish. He'd stick his line out of one of the windows, and the nervous wreck took the orders. They did quite a brisk trade in whatever fish presented themselves, usually mackerel, which they wrapped in sheets of *Daily Mirror*. It was all very fresh, that much I knew, but everyone involved had to be careful. Fishing was prohibited from Her Majesty's naval waters. If you didn't have written permission from the Queen's Harbour Master, it was instant dismissal.

At home, I lived in dread of Mrs Bullmore and Kenny, and didn't want to alienate them in any way. For this reason, I obviously didn't want to use the communal bathroom. Luckily there was Agnes Weston's Sailors' Rest between our gaff and the dock-yard, a seamen's hostel with bathing facilities that were open to the public for a small price. They were ship-shape, as you might expect, very well maintained, spotless and disinfected, so that became part of my routine. I especially liked to have a bath on a Friday evening, when I could also gain access to the Sailors'

Rest's full-size snooker tables. Friday night bath and a game of snooker was something to look forward to all week.

When I couldn't stand it in our awful accommodation any longer, we found a new apartment further up on the same side of Albert Road, but the other side of the universe. This one was quite well maintained, with a handsome yucca plant by the entranceway. The girl who'd lived there previously was a descendant of the late great Maréchal Ney, a man who fought a hundred campaigns on behalf of Napoleon, so the interior had been agreeably and fashionably Frenchified. Every room was painted in Adam cream, and there were floor-to-ceiling windows with louvred shutters giving out onto a generous front garden, home of the afore-referenced yucca.

Christine was the last of the official flower children. She was into all that floaty stuff: floral-print chiffon maxi-dresses, tie-dyed kaftans, and cheesecloth tops worn with tatty jeans. All her Plymouth friends were also keen practitioners of the hippy lifestyle, and in the main they were pretty ghastly.

I didn't like the clothes, the music, the attitude, the lifestyle advice, and especially the food (think Weetabix). Their politics were wilfully ignorant and proud of it. Everything that they wanted to achieve, I wanted to stop happening. There were more fucking rules in their fucking godless pagan fucking arcadia than in any of the Abrahamic faiths. I remember saying to one of them, 'Fuck me, you guys are hard work. We've only got ten commandments.'

Their mantra of communal harmony was so divisive it would have sent any right-minded person running for the exit.

The guys were all sticking it to the man in some way or another: selling dope, signing on, living off the earth.

The girls were like the Stepford wives. Cat maniacs who didn't believe in doctors.

It was as if they'd all watched the wrong bit of *Easy Rider*, where the agrarian hippy commune of dungaree-wearing shit-kickers get serviced by this gaggle of earth mothers who wait on them hand and fucking foot. That sort of promiscuous idyll offered women nothing except having more kids than they would prefer to have, while at the same time leading an over-analysed life: every move they made was subject to scrutiny. Three years of all that free-love crap and it's no wonder Germaine Greer took off.

Invariably, these people were the disgruntled offspring of the bourgeoisie, irreparably traumatised by their luxurious childhoods. Back then I was quite the little class warrior. I was simply too chippy for hippy.*

The application of a class analysis to any topical situation was met with disapproval, usually expressed in a disappointed tone of voice, as if they had expected better of me, followed by a reminder that the class system was all in my head. When it came to semantics, I always seemed to carry the burden of proof. I was once accused of being a capitalist for drawing a weekly wage. I tried to explain that the capitalist is the person who *pays* the wages, although in my case this didn't apply because my boss was the Ministry of Defence, a fact that surprisingly didn't seem to trouble them.

Christine's love crowd didn't like my poetry at all. Not only were they not encouraging, they were positively hostile. They thought any poetry that didn't speed the progress of their arcadian vision was worthless. Especially mine: it was too cynical, urban and harsh, devoid of medievalism, dryads, or rainbows, or whatever these morons were interested in. In short, I was wasting my time. I hadn't dropped enough acid. I hadn't listened to enough Roy Harper to see the world as it could be.

These herberts were always putting the hurt on me one way

---

* This didn't stand in the way of me liking posh chicks – in fact, I went seeking them out. Let's face it; they were more likely to be sympathetic to my choice of career.

or another. Their favourite threat involved someone called Gareth, whose imminent return from Kathmandu* I was encouraged to regard with mounting dread, e.g. 'Oh, yeah, Gareth. He's a real customer, he is. I'll tell you what,' they'd say, pointing at me, 'he'll suss you out for a start.'

The only thing I knew about Kathmandu was written by J. Milton Hayes sixty years previously. Here's an excerpt:

> There's a one-eyed yellow idol to the north of Khatmandu,
> There's a little marble cross below the town;
> There's a broken-hearted woman tends the grave of Mad
>   Carew,
> And the Yellow God forever gazes down.

The return of Gareth from Kathmandu was a constant menace. How best could I avoid this Damoclean blade? Obviously, I'm being sarcastic. What was there about me to suss out? It wasn't like I had a hidden agenda or something. As you can see, my life's an open book.

I never did get to meet Gareth. Upon his return he was immediately admitted to Freedom Fields Hospital, where he was treated for serum hepatitis with gastro-intestinal complications. Let's just say there's a guy who'll never shit right again, and draw a discreet veil over the subject.

* Or Tangiers, or some other hippy destination, but usually Kathmandu.

Chapter Thirty-Six

THE DOG THAT ATE MY DOLE CHEQUE

I've only ever drawn unemployment benefit for a total of two weeks in my entire life, and for those two weeks I was under investigation for benefit fraud.

After we left Plymouth, Christine and I wanted to see the world and everything, so we took a holiday in Holland for two weeks, staying with a young married couple we'd met who lived just outside Amsterdam in a place called Amstelveen.

When we got back, we moved to Yeovil in Somerset. Some friends we knew from Shaftesbury had recently married and moved to the town, and the idea was to stay at their house, sign on the sausage for a couple of weeks, then move back to Manchester.

I'd never been inside a fucking DHSS office in my life before that, and I had to jump through fucking hoops of fire to get about twenty-five fucking quid; I should expect it in the post any day soon.

The Yeovil couple had this pea-brained collie that used to eat anything that came through the letter box. They gave me fair warning of this, and I was advised to get up early, because Rupert would eat my giro cheque if I didn't get there first. These were the days when the mail arrived at 6am sharp. Fuck that, I thought, I'm not getting up at that time. They were exaggerating, surely:

the dog might chew the envelope up a bit maybe, but it couldn't eat it.

Yes it could, and did.

I had to go back to the DHSS office with that old fucking chestnut: the dog ate my giro. The oldest fucking excuse in the book. They said, 'Oh yeah? Wait in there.' I was under a cloud of fucking suspicion, all right. They left me to sit in this tiny office stewing in my own juices for two hours before the interrogation.

'Are you trying to pull a fast one, sunshine?'

Didn't they keep records? If they checked, surely they'd see that the giro hadn't been cashed. But no. In those days, it wouldn't have become evident until the end of the financial year, so I was under investigation. Remember Habeas Corpus? Did she die in vain?

Twice a week, for fourteen days, two detectives came round the house with the trench coats, the trilbies, and the whole Scotland Yard fucking schmear, firing questions at me – the only thing missing was the fucking light shining in my eyes and the shoulder holsters. '*Come on, Johnny. Spill the beans. The whole thing's a fucking scam. Or possibly scamola. Admit it, punk.*'

I didn't actually get slapped around, but it was fucking miserable.

Eventually, they dropped the case and issued another giro. After that I had to get up earlier than any working man I ever knew, just to make sure the lousy dog didn't eat the motherfucker.

That was my life as a claimant. Since then, I ain't asked them for dollar one. It was more fucking hard work than having a fucking job. These so-called scroungers – I admire their stamina.

So I got a job. We were in a pretty rainy period, and I'd heard that in labouring work on a building site, if you got rained off you just sat in a corrugated hut all day reading the *Daily Mirror* and smoking cigs, all the while racking up the pay. I consequently went out of my way to get such a position, digging foundations for a set of purpose-built garages.

The minute I got there, the rain clouds vanished and the sun came out and baked the ground rock hard. I was involved with laying concrete in the trenches, which necessitated a walk along this narrow plank with a wheelbarrow full of wet cement over a fucking ten-foot drop. It was a terrifying prospect, but as I discovered, it's amazing how a wheelbarrow aids your balance: like that pole tightrope-walkers use, the barrow pushes all the pressure into the exact centre of gravity. As long as the front wheel is on the fucking plank, you're sorted.

Even so, Michael Stipe had a point: everybody hurts sometimes. This was serious agony. It kept me awake at night. Muscles I didn't know I possessed completely seized up. My sinews were knotted and cramped, to an excruciating degree. Every ligament stretched to its tensile limit. A world of pain; my heart goes out to anybody in the construction industry.

It nearly fucking killed me.

Chapter Thirty-Seven

MONKEY BUSINESS

When Christine and I got back to Manchester, one of the first people I met up with was Liz Sherwood, who fixed us up with stop-gap accommodation in a dreadful house in Lower Broughton with a bunch of students.

It was a sweltering hot summer's day when we moved in with our meagre possessions, and I was horrified to see one of the students, Archie, sitting next to the waste pipe in the backyard reading the *Guardian*. Next thing a torrent of human sewage came splashing out of the drain, splattering onto the flags. It must have been a riveting article, because Archie just sat there impervious to the poisonous stench.

I couldn't live with that, and said we had to get the health people in, but Archie wasn't keen on rocking the boat: they had understandably been withholding their rent. I said it was a threat to the fucking neighbourhood. We couldn't have excrement just floating about in our backyard, and something had to be done about it, rent or no rent. It was a public health hazard. These people had been living like that for fucking months. It was fucking rank. Unspeakable.

They were begging me not to go to the council, and anyway I'm not very good at that sort of thing. Thank God for Liz, who loved hassling people. I volunteered to accompany her as far as the pub round the corner, and before I'd finished my rum and Coke, she'd talked them into coming round and fixing the sewage pipe that same day.

It was bloody awful there, and thankfully we managed to fuck off out of it before not very long, because then we got this fabulous place on Bury New Road, befitting the style I was used to: its vast Palladian windows, Regency plasterwork, high ceilings, generously proportioned rooms. We had this spacious apartment all to ourselves, so Liz moved in and shared the expenses with me and my now increasingly alienated wife.

The landlords were a team of local Hasidim and we had a pretty sweet deal there, but Liz and I heard about people who had successfully contested their tenancy at the rent tribunal. I felt terrible about it, really, and it was a risk: they might put the rent up, rather than reducing it. But they found in our favour: a reduction *and* security of tenure.

Liz's brother moved in, and then he and Christine got to know each other – in the biblical sense. There was no coming back from that, and after three years it was all over. We'd been married in a register office, so our union was never sanctified, and more importantly, was without issue. A no-fault divorce eventually ensued. I was hoping for a charge of mental cruelty, or emotional fascism, or something flash like that, but no: 'Irretrievable Breakdown' it had to be.

I fell into the arms of Liz, who provided the odd sympathy fuck before my rapid departure. Given the aberrant circumstances, things didn't get out of hand and Liz and I maintained our long friendship, a rare situation we had in common with Jerry Seinfeld and Elaine in the popular TV series.

I moved into a room above the neighbourhood hippy shop run by the wife of a friend of mine. It sold handmade stuff on a sale or return basis: alpaca knitwear with pictures of cottages and rainbows on it, love beads, dream-catchers, spice racks, mug trees, macramé plant-holders, totemic home decorations, ponchos, Navajo rugs, Hindu prayer mats. And that's not all – they also sold handmade clogs all the way from Hebden Bridge.

Newly single, I hooked up again with an old pal, an art student and cool cat character called Steve Maguire, a working-class kid from Barrow-in-Furness who was bursting with ideas and the skills to back them up. Before my marriage I used to see a lot of Steve, because he sold weed to supplement his meagre student grant, and that's when I had come across his fantastic, unforgettable paintings. He used to knock about with a girl called Stella Campion who had a platinum bubble perm and made her own clobber, including a striped boiler suit that made her look like Andy Pandy. At some indeterminate point when I was married and living in Plymouth, Steve had met Helen, got married, and moved to a house in Sedgley Park.

I would still occasionally do business with Steve, preferably at teatime. Helen was (and still is) a cordon-bleu cook, so there was always a chance of a high-end snack, and I started seeing them more often. They were lovely people.

I was smoking a lot of weed then, and was inevitably bothered by paranoia. I always thought I was going to get arrested and slapped about. It was a very real fear then: people's lives were ruined for possession of the smallest crumb.

My ex-brother-in-law Brian had been in touch since my marital breakdown. We exchanged a few letters and I learned that one of his hippy mates was living in Amsterdam, where he had a marijuana retail operation. He was planning a trip east on the Magic Bus, possibly Kathmandu. The only thing holding him back was Charlie, his live-in monkey. He also had a couple of valued customers: once or twice a week somebody would come and drop something off, and somebody else would come and pick it up. That's where I came in; Brian said I just had to *be* there.

Manchester was now a place of heartbreak and marital collapse, and a couple of weeks in Amsterdam might be just the ticket. Also, Holland had decriminalised cannabis. Wow. Paranoia-free marijuana use: that would be a whole new experience.

I had the use of the guy's apartment right in the middle of Amsterdam, just off the Leidseplein and all that that entails. After my brief stay in Amstelveen with the ex-wife I knew my way around the city and its delights, so for a few weeks I was free to mooch about the art galleries and bars at my leisure, all alone, just me and this monkey.

Charlie was no trouble at all. He wasn't a big monkey, but a fine little fellow – delicately featured black face, deft long, elegant fingers, silky silver fur – the sort of monkey you'd find with an Italian organ-grinder or perched atop a street photographer's shoulder. In Charlie's case, however, minus the Ruritanian bellhop uniform and magenta pillbox hat.

I would buy him all sorts of exotic fruit and nuts from the markets: rambutans and lychees were a particular success, because they occupied him in the peeling process, soft-shelled nuts likewise. In the main, however, Charlie just seemed to want a share of whatever I was having for my tea, which at the time was mostly chips. He'd sit beside me as I dined, closely observing every chip I shoved into my mouth, then he'd reach out and tentatively yet precisely select a single, choice chip from the paper bag. He would thoroughly examine his chosen morsel prior to its ingestion, affecting a snootily raised pinkie finger as he did so. Exemplary; what a fabulous creature. You could take him anywhere.

Not only did Charlie have impeccable table manners, he was perfectly house-trained too and would retire discreetly to a sort of sand pan in a corner of the apartment. As you'd expect, I had to muck it out every so often, but even this was not a terribly onerous task. Given Charlie's mainly fruitarian diet, with the odd chip here and there, it wasn't the putrid emergency which daily confronts the cat owner. Also, he was very good like that: he preferred to conduct his ablutions outdoors, and made this preference known. He used to mither to go out, pulling at my clothes and looking in the direction of the door.

It was summer in Amsterdam, so I would take him to the park. It was a bit of an ordeal, as people would stare, but I just had to get used to it. I had one of those extendable dog leads, and I'd let it out to the max and let Charlie scamper ahead to explore. His adventures tended to the vertical – he'd disappear into the upper foliage of the first tree he encountered and I'd be standing there for ages, holding one end of this leash with my arm stretched up above my head, while he scampered about doing whatever monkeys do up a tree. As I said, people tended to stare.

Once a day, in the apartment, he would have a shrieking moment with no visible motive – like a baby tantrum – running up and down the curtains screeching, and that was as unbearable as it got, in truth. Other than that, he was no trouble at all: about as much trouble as a kid, maybe not even as much. I didn't have to change his nappies for a start, and he never got bored or moaned about having nothing to do. If ever he incurred my displeasure, I would just point at the naughty corner, which he would grudgingly occupy in silence.

He was living the life of Riley, frankly, sitting about awaiting his daily delivery of ever more exotic fruits. The most mundane object could occupy his rapt attention for hours on end. Occasionally he would root about in my hair and I'm happy to report that his searches proved fruitless. He watched telly. He particularly liked cartoons. I guess he couldn't work out exactly what they were, but they made me laugh, which seemed to fascinate him, so he'd watch me and them in silence. He was semi-human, no doubt about it. We were a happy pair.

Meanwhile, I had made a life-changing discovery. During my forays into Amsterdam's bustling marketplaces, I had been availing myself of the diverse offerings in any number of the city's coffee houses. As I said, this had been a major factor in my accepting the monkey-sitting job. As I also explained, I thought my paranoia back home was bound up with the shit's illegality and the threat of arrest. But sitting by a canal, I was suddenly gripped by the Big Fear, proving conclusively that this was an intrinsic side effect of marijuana. I had been confusing weed-induced paranoia with legitimate anxiety.

When my stay was over and it was time to bid farewell to Charlie, it was a hell of a wrench. Heartbreaking. Having grown accustomed to the routine of living in accordance with the needs of a monkey, you know, I felt strangely at a loose end.

Chapter Thirty-Eight

MOTORBIKE ACCIDENT

Over the years, I have often been compared to Bob Dylan; e.g., 'Compared to Bob Dylan, you're not very good!' But seriously, there is one experience we have in common: a motorcycle accident.

. Back home in Manchester, this mate of mine called Clifford had just got a BSA Bantam with a two-tone tank – a lightweight 175cc conveyance – and as a would-be Belle Vue Ace, I was itching to have a ride.

As a learner, Clifford was forbidden to carry a pillion passenger, so it seemed to me the most legal move was for me to ride it myself. This I was perfectly entitled to do as long as an L-plate was visible – but not really, on account of I wasn't insured.

I say 'entitled', but there was the little matter of the owner's consent. Cliff wasn't too keen at first, pointing out quite accurately that I didn't know how to ride a motorcycle, had never had any lessons, it was a brand-new bike, and so on. But up until then, with the exception of Jimmy Dynes, everyone I knew with a motorbike had been a moron so, like, how difficult could it possibly be?

It took twenty minutes of turbo-charged mithering until Clifford finally caved in.

Soon I was crouched in the saddle, hurtling into the prevailing drizzle along a straight stretch of road, not on the face of it a dangerous spot, when BLAPPP!!!!! I'd been broadsided stage left. Some hotshot with his girlfriend in a convertible, quite the muscle car, had come shooting out from a side street. One minute I was enjoying the scenery, the next I was part of it. All I knew was that I seemed to be airborne for ages, and then I was skidding along the enslickened tarmac for even longer.

As I was lying in the road a priest came out of the nearby Catholic church with a chair. I thought, 'Oy gevalt! Extreme unction already. It's worse than I thought.' Also I'd just got this new suit.

In such traumatic, shock-laden situations as road accidents and punch-ups, the last guest to arrive is actual physical pain. I was, however, aware that certain injuries may have been sustained. Upon inspection, I noticed that the left trouser leg of my new suit was in tatters and my leg was sliced up real good, to the point that amidst all the claret my shin bone was visible. That's when I went a bit fucking flaky, falling into a sudden swoon.

The priest must have noticed my slack neck, or maybe it was the bilious shade of my complexion. Whatever the reason, he plunged my head between my knees, which returned me to my senses. Meanwhile, the driver and his girlfriend had come running from the car. They were visibly shaken, and commendably concerned for my wellbeing.

The driver was anxious to settle out of court, which was music to my ears because I wasn't even supposed to be on the motherfucker motorbike in the first place, and what with the lack of insurance I wouldn't have had a leg to stand on. (No joke intended.) I still had my head between my knees, but was vaguely compos mentis as all the financial stuff got negotiated. Thank God the priest had brought me a chair and I didn't have to think on my feet. The driver offered up a couple of grand, which at the time was twice the top prize on ITV's popular quiz show *Double Your*

Money. After paying Clifford the cost of repairing the damage to his bike, I was left with quite a chunk.

The subsequent visit to the hospital was hilarious. They had me in stitches. Seriously, though, I was in and out in no time: they didn't even check me for concussion. Lasting brain damage? You tell me.

I lost my appetite for motorbikes after that. On the other hand, the money was a godsend because it allowed me to get out of Manchester.

Now I had these disposables, I had some options. Liz had got a place at Manchester University as a mature student doing philosophy. That was her MO – generous grant, mature student, blah blah blah. I quite fancied doing that too, sitting around talking about shit, drinking coffee, smoking French cigs, *and* the government gives you money, so I applied. Then I found out that studying for a philosophy degree wasn't like that at all and I went off the boil. It was like I had a blank with the Classical world. As soon as I heard a Greek name I fucking turned off.*

I planned instead to go and live in Barcelona for as long as possible, or at least until the money ran out. Liz quickly got in on the deal. She had a few weeks before her term started, and we decided to hitchhike through France. Hitchhiking was one beatnik activity I had previously given the swerve. What changed my mind was *The Picasso Summer*, a 1969 film directed by Serge Bourguignon (no relation to Boeuf), starring the lovely Yvette Mimieux and fellow Salford lad Albert Finney as a young couple on a similar route.

It was the full-immersion Francophile course. We smoked French cigarettes, ate our own body weight of baguettes and tomatoes, and drank a lot of cheap red gut rot which went by the name of

---

* That's why I'm not allowed to practise medicine: a mere formality like my non-familiarity with Greek and Latin.

vin ordinaire: the worst stuff you could possibly buy at the time, but wine was wine to me, and if those French people were drinking it, well, they ought to know.

In retrospect, it was terrific, although in fact, the whole journey turned into a bit of an epic ordeal. Lifts were few and far between – we would sometimes be standing in the same spot for eight hours straight. We got so sick of looking at our surroundings that we didn't care where the next lift was headed, as long as it wasn't back to Paris. The first obliging truck took us to Limoges, and after that we embarked on a somewhat zigzag route via Orléans, Lyons, Toulouse, Avignon, all over Provence to the Côte d'Azur, all around Bordeaux, Béziers, Narbonnes, Nice, and Nîmes.

It took us a whole week to get across France, so Liz would only have a few days in Barcelona before she had to get back to college.

As I had quite a lot of dosh, and fancied staying there as long as possible, we went to Tourist Information to find some cheap accommodation. They gave us the address of a *pensión* just off Las Ramblas, Barcelona's lively main drag. When we rang the bell the door was opened by a handsome seven-foot-tall black gentleman in a white suit. His name was Miguel. He came from Brazil and spoke only Portuguese, but he welcomed us in and showed us up to a spacious, high-ceilinged room on an upper floor. It was cool and shady, with a flagstone floor and French windows with louvred shutters giving out onto a balcony over-looking the hustle and bustle of Las Ramblas.

It turned out that the owner of the *pensión* was in the Lebanon for some reason, and had left Miguel in charge. Miguel was the manager of a Brazilian dance troupe which was resident for the duration of an artistic event organised by the Spanish government, which was still under the autocratic control of Generalissimo Franco.

The owner evidently had a very loose arrangement with Miguel, whose dancers occupied the other floors. When I asked about

payment, he just shook his head. Because of the language barrier
we couldn't really hold a businesslike conversation, but from what
I gathered, nobody was paying any rent. It was a sweet deal: I
had the best room in the joint, and my only contribution was to
buy groceries from time to time.

Back then, you were advised not to drink the tap water in
Spain, so you had to buy great big plastic canisters of Font Vella
agua minerale. But Miguel had no truck with all that mineral water
palaver. Ushering me into the kitchen area, he said, 'You pay for
water? I purify it.'

He then demonstrated his method, which involved filling a
container with water from the tap and putting it in the fridge
overnight. How do you communicate with two degrees of sep-
aration that Louis Pasteur might not have approved of this purification process? I didn't want to follow Gareth into the serum
hepatitis ward, so thenceforth I made sure I had my own supply
of store-bought water.

After Liz went home, Miguel and I became quite chummy due
to our mutual interest in football, which seemed to be on telly all
the time. I also discovered that he had a lucrative part-time evening
job as a professional dream date for any rich American widows on
vacation in the city. His work involved nights out at the theatre,
the opera, fancy dinner dances, and late-night cocktails. Give it a
name: gigolo.

I fell into the Spanish lifestyle like a native. I've never been
one for the afternoon nap, so at first it was a real culture blow,
but I have to say I got into the whole siesta routine. I'd drop off
around 2pm in my shaded room, then a couple of hours later I'd
be awoken by the clatter of shutters and the rattle of awnings as
Barcelona was, for the second time on any given day, open for
business, heralding my pre-teatime livener in one of the many
local bars.

I lived like a king. Gambas straight out of the Med, heaps of olives from the fantastic food market, and this sensational Iberian ham called *pata negra*, which is almost black and melts in the mouth. Like the Irish, the Spanish are very good with a pig.

It was very free and easy in Barcelona, but being of a naturally nervous disposition and never having lived under a fascist regime, I was extremely paranoid. I suspected that I was being constantly watched. On one of the streets near the *pensión*, I was surprised to find a socialist bookshop with a window display featuring pictures of Leon Trotsky and shit like that. I figured this must be some kind of set-up in order to entrap any citizen of a left-wing persuasion, and with that in mind I went right out of my way to avoid the place.

Just a couple of stops along the railway line I discovered a small fishing village called Torredembarra. It was the best-kept secret in northern Spain. There was a nice quiet stretch of beach with a bar where you could get a sandwich and two-day-old English newspapers. It was run by a German guy called Fritz (I've no idea what his real name was) who wore a Zapata moustache and was learning English, hence the newspapers. He was keen to practise his conversational skills, and was glad of my company, so it became a daily routine. Thanks to Fritz's aptitude for abstract discourse, the hours would fly by: no pressure, a jar of sangria, the odd snack, a two-day-old copy of *The Times*, and my pal Fritz discussing the recent-ish events back in Britain.

At night, I'd go out and read a book in a bar. One particular night I went out on Las Ramblas, which at 11pm was always quite lively. As I was sitting minding my own business, this gypsy came up to me clutching a flouncy bright red, blue, and yellow floral gypsy dress, a proper flamenco frock like you might be able to buy in Andalusia. He was waving this dress and muttering something indecipherable at high speed in Spanish. I asked him to slow down, but he just kept warbling on and gesticulating with the dress. Maybe he was trying to sell it for booze money, I don't know, but I could tell he was making some kind of pitch or other.

I appealed to *los borrachones* at the neighbouring tables to help interpret, but they were lost in the inky depths of their Rioja. Suddenly the gypsy threw the dress around my neck as if it were a scarf and caught hold of the other end. Right away, I thought, 'This fucker's going to strangle me.' I panicked and pushed at his shoulders with the flat of both hands. It was the full saloon-bar punch-up: the impact sent him stumbling and reeling backwards, arse over bollocks across a table full of drinks, sending glasses and bottles smashing in all directions.

Naturally, the people at the table weren't happy about their spilt drinks, so now, along with the gypsy, the entire establishment was out for my blood. I didn't hang around. I threw some change on the table and it was hasta la vista, baby.

I kept running down the Ramblas until I thought I'd lost my pursuers, then nipped down a narrow side street in search of another bar. Just as I turned the corner, this guy appeared out of nowhere right in front of me, saying, '*Chocolada? Chocolada?*' I didn't know what he was going on about; I was paranoid as fuck after the incident with the gypsy dress, and I thought this might be some kind of obscene sex pitch, so again, I fucking shoved him out the way and ran. In my mind, everybody in Barcelona had a grudge against me, and I now had a whole posse on my ass.

I didn't care to look back. I ducked into a bar down another narrow alleyway and ordered a drink from this really horny-looking chick who was eating sunflower seeds and spitting out the husks.

People kept coming in and disappearing through a door behind the bar, so I figured I must have walked into some quick turn-around, cheap in-out fuck factory. My theory was reinforced when a guy came shooting out over the counter, a perfect white foot-print on the arse of his pants. Next thing, he was being chased, and it all went off again.

I managed to sneak out in the midst of this latest outbreak, but was scared to go home because that would involve a walk past the first bar where it had all started with the gypsy dress guy. I finally found a trouble-free bar where I could sit and wait it out until the heat died down.

All this probably took place in the space of about an hour, but I remember it as an entire night of solo adventure and anxiety that I didn't care to repeat. I think that's why I started spending more time in Torredembarra. I later found out from Fritz that 'chocolada' was actually the Spanish term for Moroccan hashish.

There was one girl with Miguel and the dance troupe who caught my eye: the spitting image of Sophia Loren circa *The Millionairess*, dressed ambiguously in a pair of St Tropez hipster clam-diggers and a foreshortened Breton top revealing an acreage of sun-kissed midriff, admittedly flat-chested, but so were a lot of girls in that era. She had her hair bobbed in a loose bouffant with forward side flicks, a style popularised by all the early Sixties screen sirens.

When I say 'she', I mean 'he'. It turned out that the object of my misguided attentions was a bloke. It was Miguel who broke the news, somehow making it known that an erroneous gender assignation had taken place. Thank God my infatuation went no further and didn't proceed to the distressing denouement, other-wise I could have been writing this book in a lunatic asylum, irretrievably traumatised.

So that was three close shaves: typhoid, a brush with murder, and, even worse, accidental gay sex.

Chapter Thirty-Nine

IS THIS THE WAY TO AMARILLO?

Back in Manchester, at the age of twenty-six, I got a job as a lab technician at Salford Technical College. It was not unlike being on the docks; in other words, I didn't do anything. I checked out power tools to joinery students; that took five minutes, and apart from that all I had to do was wear a white coat and not get in anybody's way.

You'll notice a pattern emerging here. I would always seek out jobs where the pay was OK and the workload negligible, if not entirely absent. Fire-watcher, lab technician, resident caretaker.* For seven months I was employed as a nightwatchman at a cranberry silo.

It was very pleasant working at Salford Tech. Our foreman was a guy called Desmond, who seemed old to me, but was probably about fifty-five and nowhere near retirement. Then there was Malcolm, who'd just moved up from somewhere in the Home Counties, and a kid called Steve, a hilarious speed-freak who was

---

* I'm not going to include monkey-minder here: Charlie may have been pretty well brought up, but the goofy little bastard did make demands.

a regular at the Wigan Casino, of which I had previously been ignorant.

Thanks to Desmond, we used to eat at one of the three available tables in the catering department's showcase restaurant, where the students were put through their paces in the preparation and presentation of high-end cuisine. Everybody else in Salford Tech had to put their name down on a waiting list, but Desmond had some kind of arrangement whereby the joinery department had a table reservation on a daily basis.

This did not go unnoticed by the rest of the college staff. Questions were raised concerning our privileged monopoly in this matter. Questions that never got answered. Senior lecturers, heads of faculty, bursars, rectors, even the chancellor himself had to make do with the lumpen foodstuffs in the regular canteen, while we gorged on gourmet delicacies and fine wines. Luxury, pure unashamed luxury.

The endless idle working hours produced reams of fresh verse, and my thoughts now returned to my neglected vocation as the Urban Poet. Another benefit came up, this time in aid of some local ultra-left-wing scandal rag. It was hosted at Mr Smiths, a city-centre cabaret club in Brazil Place. The bill comprised Heads, Hands and Feet, a band featuring Chas Hodges on guitar (not piano) and Albert Lee, before they were both justifiably famous,* plus the Richard Kent Style, the Victor Brox Blues Train, and me – basically people who would play for very little money. I still had that lesson ringing in my ears from the last benefit, so this time I told them I had overheads, transport and shit. They coughed up some expenses.

I wouldn't have frequented cabaret clubs for entertainment

---

* Chas Hodges as one half of Chas and Dave, and Albert 'Mr Telecaster' Lee as a guitar legend, playing alongside the likes of Clapton, Emmylou Harris, and the Everly Brothers.

myself, but performing at Mr Smiths revived my previous ideas of dragging my poetry into the world of show business. Ambitions I had postponed for the duration of my short marriage.

There were hundreds of clubs in Manchester at that time. The deluxe city centre venues like Foo Foo's Palace, Sinatras, Jerry Harris's Piccadilly Club, Fagins, and Mr Smiths were concentrated in a small area bounded by Oxford Road, Portland Street, and Piccadilly. This was Manchester's equivalent of the West End, and these were the kind of places I aspired to.

The city centre joints provided a venue for all those top-flight recording artistes of yesteryear, fading megastars of the recent past who, having fallen foul of the fickle nature of pop success, were no longer getting the hits, and were now plying their trade on the Northern circuit to the accompaniment of the resident combo. Nevertheless, they weren't completely tarnished; they retained a patina of residual magic, and had enough of what it takes to be instantly recognisable, albeit without the showroom finish of yesteryear. This world of cabaret had the kitsch melancholy allure of an off-season holiday resort. It's been proven time and again that melancholy is the most enjoyable mood a person can indulge in, and I guess that's what made the idea so poetic.

I went round to Mr Smiths with my pitch. Happily, it turned out that I wasn't an entirely unknown quantity to the bookers, because they'd caught my set at the aforementioned benefit. It was a whole new kind of gig for a joint like that, and my input must have made some impression: I managed to secure a Sunday night residency.

In Manchester, Mr Smiths was as top-notch as it got. It was a Talk of the Town kinda place: cabaret, casino, cocktails, and a sophisticated dinner menu. It catered for young married couples on a big night out, a chance to catch the crooners who had provided the romantic soundtrack to the days of their courtship. Next door was the Drokiweeny, Mr Smiths' discotheque, where the DJ sat on a revolving stage in the form of a giant disc, flanked by Goldilocks and Suzi Creamcheese, the scantily clad resident go-go dancers.

I was booked as the compère for the weekly 'Sunday Smiths' cabaret night. They were obviously going for a younger crowd and had a bit more of an edgy line-up than on the other evenings: I guess that's how I got the job.

As the resident MC, I had twenty minutes for my own material. Although I wasn't even credited on the bill most of the time, it was a platform for me to work up the odd routine – a few gags, a couple of poems, and then, 'Ladies and gentlemen, Whoever.'

This was the gig that cranked things up a bit. I was getting £30 for just twenty minutes at Mr Smiths, which impressed the fuck out of my dad. That was a good wage then, more than I earned in a whole week for doing nothing at Salford Tech.

I started to make inroads into the rich and diverse entertainment world that prevailed in Manchester at that time. I got gigs at the rival Piccadilly Club – the 'Rendezvous of the Stars' – which was run by Jerry Harris, 'the only comedian to play Hamlet . . . and lose'.

Here drinks were served by the Piccadilly Poppets, a glamorous battalion of waitresses decked out in black leotards and fishnet tights. Acts included the likes of the Bonzo Dog Doo-Dah Band, the Bob Gillespie Trio, and the Maori Castaways. It was the favoured hang-out of the city's football stars and visiting celebs, from the former world heavyweight champ Joe Louis to the then trendy chat-show host Simon Dee; also A-list media couples like Barbara Kelly and Bernard Braden, Tony Hatch and Jackie Trent, and for all I know, Pearl Carr and Teddy Johnson.

Foo Foo's Palace in Dale Street was another premier entertainment nightspot to provide me with work. Foo Foo's was very popular with hen parties and stag nights for its fine dining and full cabaret nights, but the main attraction was the caustic wit and raucous repartee of the stocky perma-tanned dame Frank 'Foo Foo' Lamarr himself.

Resplendent in frothy bouffant syrups, exquisite gowns dripping with sparklers, and six-inch killer heels, Foo Foo was swank incarnate: Shirley Bassey's 'My Life' punctuated by pure unadulterated filth and, like Mr Manning, the ritual slaughter of individual members of the audience.

Then there was Fagins* in Oxford Street, which often featured the Dougie James Soul Train.

If I could be said to have any 'chops', that's where I earned them. I had quite a lot of material in my back pocket then, and there was no pressure to keep coming up with fresh stuff: my chances of meeting the same audience twice in any one year were very slight. I'd already written 'Salome', 'I Married a Monster from Outer Space', 'The Day my Pad went Mad', 'The Day the World Stood Still', and 'I Walked with a Zombie', poems mainly inspired by movie titles or TV commercials, also some topical location-specific numbers that I've long since lost. I was quite responsive to social developments back then, and if I could get a funny angle on a newsworthy event in the Manchester area, that always went down well.

This was really the origins of what became my act, and the public face of the very person you have come to know, and hopefully dredge up some measure of grudging affection for.

I based my club persona on Anthony Newley's character in the aforementioned *The Small World of Sammy Lee*, a proto-Mod Jewish kid who's moved out of Whitechapel and now has this exciting Soho existence, working every night, double-booked as a wise-cracking spieler. This was the world of vice and glamour I aspired to move into: I styled myself as the alluring silk-suited entertainer, slicker than snot on a doorknob, using poetry as my ticket to the Big Life.

* Later on, post-Sex Pistols, Thursday night at Fagins became Punk Night.

I was modelling myself on a personality that was ten years out of date, but in my line of work it felt like modernisation. No one would have expected to find a poet in a cabaret club like this: just like Mr Manning said, half of them can't read, but there I was, knocking 'em bandy.

It was a fascinating time in the clubs. I remembered a lot of the other acts who had been real big hitters in their day and still enjoyed a high TV profile: people like Shirley Bassey, Anita Harris, Lena Martell, Shani Wallis who played the part of Nancy in the Oscar-winning film of *Oliver!*, and Joan Rhodes, a strongwoman in a cocktail frock who ripped telephone directories in half.

They'd even have the occasional top-flight American acts that many people won't have heard of now, such as Jo Stafford, Vikki Carr, Guy Mitchell, Jane Morgan, plus P.J. Proby, Gene Pitney, and DEL SHANNON!!!! Also be bop vocalists like Buddy Greco, Mark Murphy, and Johnny De Little, who exemplified a certain type of singer who specialised in the methodical deconstruction of the Great American Songbook: the liberties they took with the phrasing of these already familiar numbers were a great inspiration to me; the use of enjambement, for instance, the best example of which occurs in the song 'Mountain Greenery' by Mel 'The Velvet Fog' Tormé, in which he entices a woman with the prospect of an alfresco dinner date:

Beans could get no keener re-
ception in a beanery
God bless our mountain greenery
Home

I don't care how low-rent Jerry Harris's Piccadilly Club was, or that the people who went there were twice my age: if it was good enough for the Brown Bomber, it was good enough for me.

In my capacity as MC, the biggest star I ever introduced was 'the Man who made Elvis Possible', 'the Cry Guy', 'the Prince of Wails', 'the Nabob of Sob', 'the Atomic Ray', 'Mr Emotion', 'the Little White Cloud that Cried', 'the Million Dollar Teardrop' himself: Johnnie Ray.

Wow! Johnnie Ray at the Piccadilly Club!

The Nabob had a flamboyant way with a song, involving a degree of lachrymal overdrive that bordered on a complete emotional collapse. This inevitably endeared him to women. He didn't need any sound effects: he supplied his own, what with the histrionic sobs and his signature heart-wrenching vocal catch. Although Elvis had been a big fan and had co-opted some of his mannerisms, most guys didn't care for this effeminate approach. I think my dad spoke for most of mankind when he said, 'Call that entertainment? Bloody awful.'

Johnnie Ray was deaf in one ear, so his vulnerable appeal was greatly abetted by the unavoidable presence of one of those cream Bakelite hearing aids, the ones with the three-inch flex, as later affected by Morrissey in the early days of the Smiths. Ray already looked nervous and malnourished, but the lughole-furniture was the icing on the cake.

Although his four-night run at the Piccadilly Club was very late on in his career, he had retained his raw-boned good looks, and the shows did great business. It was a blast to be on the same stage as one of the true engineers of pop. Plus, his audience was majority female.

Chapter Forty

STRIPPER, FILTHY COMEDIAN, STRIPPER, FILTHY COMEDIAN, STRIPPER, VENTRILOQUIST, STRIPPER

The rougher end of the entertainment industry was catered for by less reputable venues like the New Luxor Club, the College Theatre Club, and Bunny Lewis's in the old Marsland Hotel. These clubs were slightly out of town in pre-demolition Moss Side, Gorton, and Hulme, which was then in the throes of transformation into the neo–Brutalist utopia we know today.

These establishments featured strippers and filthy comedians, many of whom were refugees from late-period music hall and the world of variety. They were largely men-only venues, specialising in out–of–order stag nights, pissed–up works parties, and intoxicated troublemakers on a boys' night out. Any minute the joint might be raided by the cops for offences under the Disorderly Houses Act 1751, so anybody semi–respectable was always ready to scarper, their identity enshrouded by a raincoat. Talk about sleaze.

The College Theatre Club in Coupland Street – 'the best cabaret in the North, at least sixteen acts on stage every night!'

– also boasted roulette tables, and the 'Sunday Special': wrestling featuring the likes of 'Butcher' George Base, Lord Percy of Oregon, and Wild Man Campbell. The club was run by Les Lawrence and Cecil Watch, and back in the Sixties it had attracted some of the big stars, from Bobby Day to the talented jazz trumpeter and mellophonist Nat Gonella. By the time I played there, however, it was teetering on the edge of demolition, standing alone in an ocean of rubble, as row after row of brick terraces were razed to make way for one of the largest public housing estates in Europe.

Bunny Lewis's joint was on the corner of Dorset Street in West Gorton. Bunny used to work in drag with Jackie Carlton, Eric Leroy, Diamond Lil, and Billy Dennis.

The New Luxor Club, a former cinema in Erskine Street, had gained local notoriety due to the regularity with which it was busted by the cops. On one celebrated occasion, six comedians and six striptease artists were charged with aiding and abetting the club owner Vincent 'Ginger' Chilton in keeping a 'bawdy-house'. There they were, all in the dock at Manchester Crown Court, as a police officer took the stand to read out a selection of the offending material for the benefit of the judge and jury, e.g. this gag, attributed to George Roper:

> 'A policewoman and a policeman were walking home from the station one night with one of the sniffer dogs. "Oh," she said, "I've left my knickers back at the station." "Don't worry," said the policeman. "Hitch up yer skirt, let the dog have a sniff." Half an hour later, the police dog comes back with the sergeant's balls in its mouth . . .'

The other five comics got fined, but George Roper got off with it, claiming he'd never heard that joke before. The next day, people were queueing round the block to buy the *Manchester Evening News* in order to read the court report.

When I worked there in the early Seventies, evenings at the New Luxor Club were presided over by Jackie Carlton, whose viperish repartee held dominion over this most disorderly of crowds. Jackie wore his hair in a bottle-blond College Boy. His Continental suits, I suspect, were the work of the aforementioned Abe Sachs. Jackie was a bit of a tough guy. He'd rip the piss out of the waiters and things like that. One of them, who looked like Cyrano de Bergerac, would be serving drinks, and Jackie added insult to injury: 'He's a bit pissed off tonight. He was going to get a nose job but Taylor Woodrow refused to do the scaffolding.' The same schtick, night in, night out, and all the funnier for it.

Jackie was also a well-known drag act, and appeared as such at every other club in town, often as one half of a successful double act with Bunny Lewis.

The New Luxor was a tough one for me. Like the College Theatre Club, it had seen better days. In the Sixties, the likes of Gene Vincent backed by Sounds Incorporated and even Chubby Checker, allegedly, had occupied its stage, but now it was mainly endless exotic dancers and stand-ups such as Al 'Not Guilty' Showman, who earned his moniker due to the number of disorderly house prosecutions he'd been involved in. Other popular gagsters included Jack Diamond, George Roper, and Stan Boardman, all of whom later found fame on Granada Television's *The Comedians*. There were a couple of maverick acts like Johnny 'Goon' Tweed, and Nick London, although he wasn't on too often, probably because his gimmick involved the avoidance of any profane language, even in the filthiest material. This earned him a reputation as something of an intellectual on the circuit. Imagine that: my poetical egghead cachet usurped by Nick London! It never stops hurting.

I'd get myself ready at home before I went over to the Luxor. In any club, space equals money, so although these venues did have dressing rooms they were very frugal and cramped, especially those places that heavily featured strippers. Every night, about thirty girls would be on in about four hours, so there wasn't too much tease. It was just a case of get 'em off and thank you very much and 'Next!'

Stripper, filthy comedian, stripper, filthy comedian, stripper, ventriloquist, stripper, then there would be a break in the proceedings for a bit of scran to soak up the beer. But don't go away, the star of the show is coming up. Never a dull moment.

Most of the clubs had a resident trio, piano, bass, and drums, but gradually the piano was being ousted in favour of the new compact Vox Continental or Farfisa electric organ – they had a more cheesy, loungey, sleazy wah-wah muzak sound which especially suited the strip acts.

I got to know a few of the striptease girls, and they were often working four or five shows a night at top-dollar rate in different clubs. Nowhere was very far away, and they'd have a driver to take them from one place to another. After their five minutes on stage at the New Luxor they'd head straight over to the College Theatre Club or one of the other joints, where under a different name they would strip out of a different exotic outfit: the Lovely Bonita in her grass skirt would become the Lovely Brigitte with a beret and a string of onions, or the Lovely Benazir, complete with nipple tassels and seven veils. One of them, under the name of the Lovely Morag, rocked a kind of truncated Caledonian look involving a claymore, a dagger, and a mini-kilt.

There were women of varying ages and shapes. They each had their own style, so there was something for everybody. They were doing very well, probably saving up to buy a house: they had good cars straight out of the showroom, that's all I knew.

Competition for punters was tough at places like the New Luxor and the College, so the marketing guys came up with lots of exciting offers, e.g. cheap beer until 9pm PLUS a free meal upon production of an entry ticket.

It was an unwritten rule in those days that clubs never sold full-strength ale – that was a recipe for trouble. It was piss weak, but who's going to complain at half price? Drinking all that cheap beer would make you hungry, so at ten o'clock, just at the right time, someone would bang a gong, and a guy with a ladle would dole out the dish of the day. It was too far to go to the chip shop, so everybody would form an orderly queue with their meal ticket, and there it was: big pot of steaming-hot grub, help yourself to a couple of slices of white bread and butter.

The 'menu' at the New Luxor changed every week: one week it would be 'Traditional Hot Pot Supper', the next it would be 'Hungarian Goulash'. It was exactly the same basic stuff – meatballs, potatoes, carrots, and onions in some kind of thin gravy arrangement, but this week with a bit of paprika thrown in. The next week, 'Brazilian Hot Pot', and again, exactly the same stuff but served with a garnish of banana. One week it was 'Paradise Stew', which proved a great hit as it included a lot of the very popular curry powder, and a handful of sultanas. Blimey.

I was in my element in these joints. I watched every visiting comedian. Occasionally there would be some class-A real old-timers. I remember introducing Jimmy Wheeler at the New Luxor Club. One of the greats, he went back to the final days of the music hall as Lucky Jim, a stage name supplied by George Formby senior. I knew him from radio programmes like *Midday Music Hall* and *Workers' Playtime*.

In the manner of Arthur English, he modelled himself on the Cockney spiv with a pencil moustache and a fiddle, performing humorous brief versions of well-known operas, which he entitled 'Hopra for the Higgerant'. His catchphrase at the end of the night was, 'Oi, oi, that's your lot.'

Sample routine:

'This tramp came round my house. He says, "Here guvnor, can you help out? I haven't eaten for three days." I says,

"You should force yourself." He says, "Nah nah, can you help out? I'm bleedin hungry." So I says, "Here, do you like cold rice pudding?" He says, "Yes." I says, "Well, come back tomorrow: it's hot at the moment." '

And:

'Manchester, what a town this is. This hooker just came up to me. I took her up on it. I gave her a sixpenny piece. She says, "That won't cover it." I says, "Here's another shilling. Go and buy yourself a barm cake." '

Or how about this one:

'I was walking past this shopfront and there was a sign on the window. "Cheese sandwich: ten bob. Hand relief: £1."
   I went in. There was a woman in an apron.
   I says, "Are you the woman who takes care of the hand relief?" She says, "Yer."
   I says, "Here's half a quid. Go and wash your hands and get me a cheese sandwich."'

That was the level of humour at the New Luxor.
   My friend Stan Gorton and I actually saved Mr Wheeler's life. The New Luxor Club wasn't the kind of place Stan would normally go, but he'd come to see my act for some reason. I'd known him back at the garage where I'd had my first legal job. Then he'd been a semi-dosser/early Mod type, always getting grief on account of his long hair.
   As we were leaving at the end of the night, we found Jimmy floundering about, effing and blinding, slumped up against his Austin Death-trap, which was parked outside the club. He couldn't even find the keyhole to get into the motherfucker. We begged

him not to drive: 'Jimmy, just go back in there. We'll ring you a cab. Please. Jimmy, don't drive. You're a treasure of British comedy. The world needs laughter,' that kind of thing. We had to crawl up his ass in our attempts to dissuade him from this suicidal act, but he was having none of it, and just told us to fuck off.

'Please, Jimmy. Don't do it. What about John Law? They've got breathalysers now,' we pleaded.

I can't remember quite how we got him into a cab, but we finally succeeded. Jimmy Wheeler, another age, another universe.

All the stand-ups had their own area of specialism. As a Mickey Mouser,* George Roper's jokes mainly involved Wellington boots, the building trade, and stereotypical 'thick Paddys'. A great favourite of mine was another Merseyside comic called Stan Boardman, for whom the Germans were still the legitimate victims of his humour. He didn't like the Irish much either, and the Spaniardos also came in for a good kicking. His material reflected the long-held belief in the superiority of the Latin lover. It was the heyday of the Spanish package holiday, so that was a great vehicle for gags, like this one, for instance, which neatly combines two of his three specialist subjects:

'So, there's this Irish fellow, quite a handsome chap but not very bright. He's unattached, he's made a packet on the sites, so now he has disposable walking about money. He gets off to Alicante. Why not? He's heard it's rich pickings for a hotshot like him. So, he's on the beach in his best candy-stripe Bermuda shorts, [possibly from Vince, we don't know], and he's lounging under this parasol, but he's not getting any action. All the girls are walking straight past him and putting it out to this Spaniardo further up the beach.

* Mickey Mouser = Scouser.

He's a good-looking fellow and he's a bit miffed by this state of affairs, so at the end of the day he goes up to his competitor, and says, "Excuse me there, you seem to be very successful with the ladies. I wonder if you could give me a few pointers. What's the secret of your success?" So the Spaniardo says to him, "Every morning I get up very early, and I go down to the fruit and vegetable market. I select the largest potato that I can find and stick it down my bathing trunks. It's always worked for me." So the Mick he says, "Sure, I'll give it a go tomorrow now."

The next day he's on the beach having taken a lesson from his Spanish friend, but now the chicks are not just walking past him, they're taking evasive action – they're not going *anywhere* near the guy. So he goes up to the Spanish gentleman who is in his usual spot, and says, "I did everything you advised me to do here, and sure now the chicks are fecking avoiding me altogether. Tell me, fella. Where am I going wrong? "

And the Spanish guy replies, "Tomorrow, put the potato down the *front* of your shorts." '

These were my contemporaries – and there were venues way down market from this.

Chapter Forty-One

HERO STEW

One night in early 1975, Steve Maguire turned up at my place above the hippy shop. Here was a guy with a broken heart: apparently he and Helen had broken up. It was her idea.

Helen and Steve had always seemed to me like the perfect couple. I naturally tried to reassure the kid: you're just going through a bad patch; maybe she just needs her own space for a while; she'll be back — all of that noise. But he was inconsolable. Who wouldn't be?

He invited me to move into their apartment in Sedgley Park near Prestwich. It occupied the entire first floor of a large Victorian villa, and I think he needed someone to help out with the rent and we were pals. I was working at Salford Tech and trying to hack it in the clubs, so I had a bit of disposable, which was just as well because Steve's cash-flow was always erratic.

Steve was still a student at the Manchester School of Art, but he was always under the cosh there. The way he saw it, he was the lone practitioner of representational art in an increasingly abstracted city, and those deconstructionist motherfuckers were always trying to kick his ass the fuck out. He was only hanging on in there by virtue of several psychiatric reports and a couple of high-profile character references. One of them was from his

favourite tutor, Ted Roocroft, a Cheshire pig farmer turned painter
and sculptor, a fellow realist, later to be justifiably acclaimed as
'the Michelangelo of wood'.

Steve's backstory involved pep pills and marijuana. He had no
significant history with booze. His chosen tipple up to this point
was the snowball, a lady's drink, the main ingredients of which
were Babycham and advocaat. But now he had turned into an
out-and-out beer monster for the best reasons known to man, as
most records by George Jones would attest. Although he didn't
fit the Dylan Thomas definition of an alcoholic, 'Somebody you
don't like who drinks as much as you do', if anybody could be
said to be one it was Steve. It was glug glug glug: I don't know
where it all went because he somehow maintained his feather-
weight status through all the years I knew him.

Public houses didn't chime with my idea of myself. By the
time I was eleven, I was familiar with most of the pub interiors
of my immediate neighbourhood, and had haughtily decided they
were strictly for schlubs. Even so, I wasn't much help keeping
Steve out of licensed premises. I'd accompany him on his increasingly frequent outings to his local – the George on Bury New
Road – but I couldn't keep up with him. I've always had a problem
with beer; it's largely anatomical, in that I lack the physical capacity
for the volume necessary to alter my mood. One pint and I'd
have to go for a piss and a nap immediately.

I wasn't seeing so much of Liz at this point. We hadn't fallen
out, but she'd acquired a bunch of snooty philosophy student pals
who were busy exploring the real meaning of a cupboard. Also,
she and Steve never got on. Neither of them would really discuss
the other. Basically, Steve thought Liz was a bit of a ponce and
Liz thought Steve was a snob, and I couldn't argue with either
of them.

Steve was a real kvetcher, but funny with it; his hilarious character assassinations of people he had never even spoken to were

priceless, and in spite of this misanthropic streak, he was a sweet-heart. We had some right fucking laughs. The mere memory of his sense of humour still cracks me up.

We had a good thing going, making out like bandits. We were living on what Steve euphemistically referred to as 'Hero Stew' – a big pot of some sort of meat with onions, cooked in a gravy that would thicken with the passage of time. That, and Spam fritters.

Me and Maguire were the only people with short hair in the entire Western hemisphere at that time. We were still looking good. Steve had been a peripheral hippy; he was too curmudg-eonly to go the whole love and peace hog, but he took the drugs and listened to the music.

He had obtained a quantity of the best acid available to mankind, without any money changing hands. A few years earlier, a friend of his had been to the Bickershaw Festival organised by Jeremy Beadle. Bickershaw is near Wigan, so naturally it pissed down the whole weekend. The Grateful Dead took the stage with the advice: 'Don't buy any acid.' It became apparent that this wasn't some out-of-character moral crusade on their part, because their road crew immediately began to throw cans of 'Budweiser' into the shivering, mud-bespattered crowd. Everybody was dodging at first – after all, a full can of lager would cause quite a bit of damage if you caught one in the face. But they were in fact light as a feather, crammed full of microdots, little pieces of blotting paper soaked in LSD straight out of the stateside laboratory of Dr Owsley* himself. One single tab would put you out of the game for ten hours.

One of these notorious cans found its way into Steve's posses-sion: enough acid to turn the entire North-West of England Day-Glo paisley.

As a gifted artist, colour was very important to Steve, so

---

* Owsley Stanley III, aka Bear, was a Berkeley-dropout-turned-LSD-chemist who became a financial and pharmaceutical supplier to the Grateful Dead.

naturally very early on he had acquired a colour TV set, the only one in the neighbourhood. Whenever there was a nature programme on the BBC, especially one of those Jacques Cousteau films featuring underwater marine life, we used to invite friends around to watch Cousteau and his crew on the *Calypso*, on condition that all guests must be tripped out. The programme would only last an hour, but the visitors would still be there the following morning, staring at the multicoloured interference on the blank screen. I'm not a great fan of the Grateful Dead, but credit where it's due.

That was the nearest I've ever come to what I call 'recreational drug use': apart from that brief period it's always been a necessity rather than a leisure activity with me.

As a loving husband on a budget, I had put opiates on the shove, but I was smoking a lot of weed. In the months living above the hippy shop as an embittered divorcee, however, I had reacquainted myself with the old Chinaman's nightcap and now I was always scoping around for it.

At that point there was no drug culture as we now understand it. At first, my only contacts in Manchester were the elderly recidivist addicts in Banjo's – old jazzers who played for Dougie James and Victor Brox, and dance-band musicians moonlighting in little quartets. A lot of those modern jazz people went out of their way to get a habit just because their heroes were all junkies. For them it was the keys to the highway. The lively Dixieland world of Kenny Ball, fuelled by copious amounts of ale, was anathema to them. They preferred opioids, heroin, cocaine, maybe marijuana, so theirs was a more narcoticised, drowsy strand of jazz: the sleepy approach of Chet Baker; the hipster meditations of John Coltrane; the improvisations of Sonny Rollins and Charlie Parker; the social perspectives of Ornette Coleman and Charles Mingus.

Before the methadone regime took hold, a few of the Banjo's crowd were still getting heroin off the NHS on a daily basis in the form of Jacks: tiny pills the size of a Splenda sweetener containing pure Swiss-manufactured BP diamorphine. Jacks were purpose-made for shooting up, and would instantly dissolve in a spoonful of cold water. No filter, no citric, no nothing: simply suck it up and crank it.

These guys always had more Jacks than they actually needed, but they weren't interested in selling it and at first they were also protective. But I told them that I already had a habit and just blagged it out of them in the end. Also, occasionally I would come into some cocaine, which would sweeten the deal no end.

There was no aggressive heroin market in Manchester at that time, but I always managed to get it from somewhere – that shit will turn anybody into a detective. A detective *and* a secret agent. My lack of contacts dictated that my narcotic usage, at first, remained sporadic and, I think, relatively undetectable. I never discussed it with anyone, not even Steve, such was the level of understandable opprobrium around this issue. He had no fucking interest at all in that world, and to be honest, it would have really upset him.

At some indeterminate point, however, heroin somehow made itself indispensable. It's very hard to be detailed about it, I wish I could, but sometimes I'd get some real good shit which would lead me to nod out for a little while; literally fall asleep on my feet. That's the attraction of it, I guess; you're looking for that kind of reverie for the rest of your life. But that reverie is short-lived. In no time at all, shooting up heroin becomes that thing you do like eating food, a way to get through the day, to get through life, and there's no way you can look for the tell-tale signs, because when you get them, it's too late.

Steve and I had fucking had it with rock. We used to go to shebeens like the Nile, the Reno, and the West Indian Centre, but especially Don Tonay's Russell Club, aka The PSV (Public

Service Vehicles) Club in Hulme, a facility built for the bus drivers'
union near Moss Side which put on rocksteady and reggae nights
featuring great singers like Roy Shirley, Dennis Alcapone, Winston
Groovy, Desmond Dekker and the Aces, Cheryl Garrett, Susan
Cadogan, and Audrey Hall. We got right into urban-
Jamaican gonzoid-Rasta heavy dub very early on: 'Train to
Rhodesia' by Big Youth; 'Hit the Road Jack' by Big Youth;
'Screamin' Target' by Big Youth . . . You see where I'm going
with this. Big Youth was my favourite exponent of the genre, but
we listened to all those toasters like U-Roy, I-Roy, King Stitt,
King Tubby, Prince Far I, Dr Alimantado, Ranking Toyan, Tapper
Zukie.

This was the main event pre-punk, as far as we were concerned,
space-age fucking heavy bass sounds: the only ticket in town.

We also used to go down to see loads of exhibitions in London.
The Sunday supplements provided a weekly glimpse of the metropolitan art world, and whenever there was a show worth a trip
south we would make a weekend of it, staying with a mutual
friend and former art student, Bernie Davis, or the Reverend
Bernie Davis as we called him, after the Reverend Gary Davis,
the blues-singing one-man band. The fact that Bernie had been
an altar boy until his early teens only consolidated his ecclesiastical
qualifications. What did Bernie do? He had two jobs – this and
that. Seriously though, he pursued his musical ambitions financed
by his sideline as a painter and decorator.

Bernie was the first of our little salon to make the move to
the capital. Well, Streatham actually. He was a virtuoso plank-
spanker and a composer of countless remarkable songs. He still
is. A regular Cole Porter for the rock age, he could utilise any
pop idiom of the twentieth century. His first job down there was
playing guitar in a revised iteration of Love Affair – you may
remember them from such hit records as 'Rainbow Valley' and a
creditable version of Robert Knight's hit 'Everlasting Love' – but

this time without their gifted vocalist Steve Ellis. In fact, the only original member was the drummer Maurice Bacon. (What kind of name is this for a nice Jewish boy?)

Later, Bernie would go on the road with The Houseshakers, who were part of the pre-punk rockabilly resurgence exemplified by the revived careers of Hank Mizell and Ray Campi. Malcolm McLaren and Vivienne Westwood's first shop, Let it Rock/Too Fast to Live, Too Young to Die, also plugged into this retro vogue, selling drape coats, poo-mashers, bolo ties, drainpipe trousers, and Day-Glo socks.

At some point another pal of Steve's from art school, a very good painter called John Wragg, also moved down there. It was via Johnny Ragged, as we called him, that we got the four-minute warning of punk rock. I don't know exactly what he did with them, but Johnny was part of the tour crew with Roxy Music, who were very much on the punk radar. Bryan Ferry seemed to be interested in all the things I approved of: clean lines, louche attitudes, smooth production values, retro sci-fi schlock, and the kitsch antiques of tomorrow, all reversing into the Hollywood future.

Ragged was ahead of the game fashion-wise, and a reliable arbiter of taste. He'd been to Malcolm and Vivienne's shop, now renamed Sex, and began to delineate the savage aesthetics of this new look, with its cheap bondage and fetish wear plus the equally cheap graphic sensationalism of its iconography.

One of Steve's hidden talents was as a pretty good guitar player. He played in a band called the Ferrets with Rick Goldstraw, a kid called Julian, and another called Sean on the drums. The Ferrets had a weekly gig at the Dog and Partridge, which was United's Stretford End pub: *the* guvnor fucking United Pub. The Ferrets had a real sweet number there: they were allowed to rehearse in one of the unused upstairs rooms whenever they liked on the condition that they played a set of covers on match days for the United crowd on their way to the game. Fuck, what a dream job: playing the Dog and Partridge to the Manchester United firm, the die-hard commando Stretford Enders. Wow, if only. Punk rock before the event.

The Ferrets would do covers of tunes I was also in favour of, such as 'First I Look at the Purse' by the Contours, which had always been on the Chaperones' playlist. I was always trying to blag in. But I never became a fully recognised member. I wasn't good enough.

Happily, within a matter of weeks after Helen and Steve's break-up, she came back. Thank God for that. And what's more, she and Steve were kind enough not to kick me out. I couldn't believe my luck: we were right back on the five-star cuisine. Helen's culinary skills elevated us to the status of Kings on Earth.

My gigs had started to pick up momentum. I was always multitasking: I had my residency at Mr Smiths and was doing both the cabaret joints and various modern jazz clubs all over town, notably the recently reopened Band on the Wall on the corner of Swan Street, just across the road from Seidelbaum's and Swan Buildings. Originally built as a landmark pub in the nineteenth century called the George and Dragon, it had been a popular music spot since the late Thirties when its owner had built a stage in a niche set into the back wall, hence its current name. The Band on the Wall had had a bit of a refurb and was now under new management, run by a jazzer called Steve Morris, a clarinet player who was also head of the Manchester branch of the Musicians' Union. He had a very enlightened and eclectic booking policy, and under his stewardship it became, and still is, one of the premiere venues of Manchester.

He must have seen my act at Club 43 or one of the other jazz joints I occasionally did; in any case, he liked my stuff, stuck his neck out, and gave me twenty-five minutes before the main acts. The Band on the Wall was a very cool, cerebral hang-out, just what I was looking for. It had a be-bop, modern jazz vibe to it: I guess it was like the Ronnie Scott's of Manchester. It had some quite big acts, George Melly, for example, who was having a moment at the time and seemed to be on a permanent tour with John Chilton's Feetwarmers. People like Victor Brox would get a scratch band together, usually featuring Bruce Mitchell, a guitar player called Norman Beaker, and occasionally Dave Tomlinson, aka Dave Formula (you may remember him as the keyboard operator on such smash hits as 'Fade to Grey' by Visage, 'Vienna' by Ultravox, and 'Girl', a Lennon and McCartney cover by the Saint Louis Union). Quite the little hit-maker. He later became the keyboard player for Magazine fronted by Howard Devoto after he left the Buzzcocks.

The Band on the Wall had a late licence and kept club hours, so usually I had a midnight slot. If you wanted to take the pulse of Manchester you could have done worse than go and hang out there late at night. It was never too particular about throwing-out time, consequently a lot of acts and musicians from the clubs where I had previously worked would drop in for a nightcap, along with policemen, printers from the *Daily Express*, reporters from the *Daily Express*, and workers at the nearby GPO and the meat market, all of whom worked erratic hours and would congregate there at the end of their shift.

Its proximity to the Cotton Club on Stevenson Square, hang-out of the so-called Quality Street Gang, along with my brother Paul and his mate Gaz, meant that denizens of Manchester's criminal fraternity would also gravitate towards this convenient nightspot.

Being so well-known and such a late-night place, with a crowd including people from the entertainment world and punters of all ages, it proved to be the ideal showcase for me and my poetry. Plus, it was a comparatively good purse.

I was also getting some work outside of Manchester to an extent, in places in Cheshire like Cheadle Hulme, Heaton Moor, Bowden, Hale Barns, and Altrincham, at jazz joints like the Warren Buckley, Bredbury Hall, and the Bleeding Wolf, with people from the Syd Lawrence Orchestra and the Northern Dance Orchestra dropping in to do a bit of improv in their recreational time, and where I could declaim my more beatnik material. I still performed at the Alma Lodge, and now also worked at a cabaret joint called Dante's in Stockport, which was quite a long way for me, seeing as I wasn't allowed to drive.

Steve Maguire was extremely encouraging. He was my number-one fan, so at the end of that year when Pam Ayres won the ITV talent show *Opportunity Knocks*, he was outraged. 'Call that poetry?' he railed, before turning to me and pointing out that she was taking food out of my mouth. The chippy communist brat inside me agreed with this evaluation, what with Pam's strong country burr and what I perceived to be her bourgeois demeanour, sitting there in her Laura Ashley floral maxi-dress.

My irritation, however, was tempered by her engaging personality, and her continued success on the show was a great inspiration to me. Now I could point to Pam Ayres as an example of a poet making a living. How could I kvetch? She wrote from her life, I wrote from mine. At last here was a successful contemporary.

Chapter Forty-Two

ROOM FOR ONE MORE ON THIS HIGH-SPEED BANDWAGON

One forgets the ugliness of the Seventies – the rotten food; the awful brutalist architecture (I quite like that now); the crimplene flared trousers and polyester shirts, and how everything and everybody stank.

The only acceptable contemporary clothes belonged to the London Rat Pack of the day. They were known as the Mayfair Orphans, notably Roger Moore, Terence Stamp, and Michael Caine. The Orphans got their suits not from the traditional outfitters of Savile Row, but from Dougie Hayward and Cyril Castle, who operated in the heart of that illustrious neighbourhood within walking distance of the Playboy Club Casino and their high-rolling chum Omar Sharif.

At the extreme end of men's tailoring was the aptly named Tommy Nutter. Everything from the house of Nutter was on a BIG scale: big fat aerodynamic lapels, capacious patch pockets with monster flaps, buttons the size of dinner plates, upholstered shoulders and deep, deep side vents, all cut from what looked like some windowpane-check tablecloth material.

I was a huge fan of the Northern Soul phenomenon – after all, me and my pals had invented it ten years earlier in the cramped basements of central Manchester – but now there was Wigan

Casino, which had all the required space to bust those famous moves. What a terrific scene. It was only the dress codes that kept me out: horrible skimpy short-sleeved leisure shirts with a sort of fake collar and a scoop neck, or wife-beater vests worn with high-waisted Oxford bags with turn-ups, multiple pleats and weird pocket placements, usually made from some fire-retardant fabric, and coupled with dreadful Corfam platform shoes. If any of those people had complimented me on my appearance, I would have wondered where I'd gone wrong.

Trying to look normal came at a terrible price: it invited the unfavourable judgement of less discerning fellow citizens. People looking like clowns in gor-blimey parallels and godawful flares would take the mickey out of *me* for wearing tapered Levi's, or 'Shite Catchers' as they were known in Salford.

The music of the era was mostly as bad as the clothes. There were some exceptions, from the likes of Bryan Ferry, Harold Melvin and the Blue Notes, the Stylistics, Ken Boothe, The Jimmy Castor Bunch, maybe James Brown, JJ Cale, and, as I've said, a whole lot of real good reggae: I went to see the Wailers, Toots and the Maytals, and The Heptones inside one month. Then there was The Velvet Underground, the Stooges, The Ramones, and the New York Dolls. But Genesis, Pink Floyd, Jon Hiseman's Colosseum, The Bloody Mues: forget it. I'd seen the cream of American rock and roll for nothing, so I wasn't about to shell out cash money to watch some wanker playing a forty-five-minute guitar solo.

Before The Sex Pistols' first appearance at St Martin's Art College in November 1975, I'd seen this very attractive girl called Linder Sterling on the same bus every weekday morning and occasionally around town in the evenings. She had a brand-new look factoring in the pre-Technicolor screen goddess and the kinky pin-up. I thought, 'Memo to Self: someday all women will look like this.' In her white Leichner foundation, heavy mascara, and semi-matte jet-black Biba lipstick, coupled with a tight black-leatherette shift, she was all sharp angles and shiny synthetics: a sneak preview of all tomorrow's people.

The first time I ever saw the term 'punk rock' in print would have been around this time too, in a review of The Ramones. If there was any understanding of the word 'punk' at that time it had to do with urban-American teenage delinquency: unsuccessful criminals, socially inept fuck-ups of every stripe. Put it this way, it was never a term of endearment.

With the rapid acquisition of their first album I discovered that The Ramones were a welcome return to the core values of rock and roll. They seemed to embody the harmonic sensibility of the Beach Boys, the production values of Phil Spector, and the social concerns of those girl groups who had inspired the New York Dolls, e.g. The Jaynetts, The Shirelles, The Shangri-Las, and, of course, The Ronettes. Their timeless appeal has been best summed up by none other than me in this piece I wrote for the fanzine *Sniffin' Glue*:

I love Bob Dylan but I hold him responsible for two bad ideas: a) the extended running time of the popular song and b) the lyric sheet. Both fine for Bob who usually occupied the extra time in agreeably entertaining ways. The rot, however, set in between 1968 and 1975 when the airwaves were clogged by over-manned combos of cheesecloth-shirted bozos, with names like Jon Hiseman's Colosseum, Supertramp, Barclay James Harvest, Yes, Genesis, Emerson Huntley and Palmer, Foghat . . . the end is listless. Not that I have ever listened to any of the above. Why would I? I hate them.

In late 1975, I read an article on The Ramones, a four-man gang from Queens. Much was made of their snotty asocial stage manner and the speed and brevity of their songs. The black and white photograph shot by the unimpeachable Roberta Bayley – surely the uncrowned queen of American punk iconography – showed them to be four terrific blokes.

I bought the LP: 'Blitzkrieg Bop', 'Pinhead', 'Judy is a Headbanger', 'Havana Affair', 'Now I Wanna Sniff Some Glue', 'Stormtrooper', 'I don't wanna go down to the Basement' 'Loudmouth'. The Ramones were and are, an enthusiasm of mine. They understood that it was better to have clever lyrics about moronic subjects than the other way round.

Any interest I had in punk came on the back of The Ramones, who seemed to be untainted by the sun-sedated sounds of psyche-delia with its nebulous dogma of free expression and universal 'love'.

It wasn't until I read the write-up in the back pages of the *NME* of The Sex Pistols' appearance at the Marquee Club in February 1976 that the word 'punk' appeared again.* The piece carried a tiny mugshot of the group's singer in action: at first I thought it was Johnnie Ray making an unlikely comeback, his paranoid face frozen in a mask of fugitive anxiety, eyes like saucers, his hair a multi-directional mess of greasy spikes, gaunt sunken cheeks, and the complexion of a compulsive blood donor. Actually, it wasn't the Nabob. It was Johnny Rotten. Wow! Is that his real name? Fancy looking like that!

Then I read the review, which reported renditions of lesser-known Dave Berry songs and the Monkees' B-sides, cavortings with scantily clad birds, furniture getting thrown around, and some French bloke shouting out, 'You can't play!' to which Steve Jones replies, 'So what?' You can't argue with that – what a fucking rotter!

* 'Don't Look Over Your Shoulder, but the Sex Pistols Are Coming', by Neil Spencer, *NME*, 21 February 1976.

By the time I blagged my way into the Lesser Free Trade Hall with my then girlfriend Trish, it was The Sex Pistols' second visit to Manchester, this time supported by Slaughter and the Dogs and the debut appearance by the newly formed Buzzcocks. After the reviews, I was expecting a level of ineptitude that never materialised. All concerned seemed reasonably proficient in their respective capacities. Steve Jones often credits the Pistols' recorded guitar work to Chris Spedding, even claiming that he was playing behind a curtain at their earlier gigs. Surely a piece of mischievous myth-making. The Steve Jones I heard was a one-man orchestra, a high-voltage practitioner with no visible equal. In fact, the sonic overload had me scoping around for the other nine hundred and ninety-nine guys.

This gig couldn't have been a better introduction to the punk phenomenon. In contrast to the ponderous aural sludge of the time, all three bands kept their songs fast and short, but that's where the similarities between them ended. Punk hadn't happened yet in Manchester – most of the kids in the audience were in flares and tie-dyed tops – but the line-up itself perfectly encapsulated three very different interpretations of punk fashion as we now know it.

The Sex Pistols were all in variations of the whole new look created by Vivienne Westwood and Malcolm McLaren. This involved visual elements of every youth tribe since the Second World War blended in a thoughtful, attractive, and artistic way: a three-button blazer, a ripped-up pullover, a leather jacket or a Teddy Boy drape worn with peg pants or bondage trousers along with shit-kickers, Day-Glo socks, and a homemade, slashed-up haircut.

Then you had the Buzzcocks, who looked like throwback ultra-Mods minus the designer labels; very striking in an odd, indefinable sort of way. Pete Shelley was in pink jeans and cheap Woolworth's gym shoes, and he'd got this crap catalogue cheapo guitar that he'd sawn the top off. Howard Devoto wore one of those French garbage men's chore jackets, buttoned up to the top like a shirt.

Slaughter and the Dogs, from Wythenshawe, were definitely going down the David Bowie glam route. Their singer Wayne Barrett wore a bottle-green silk pyjama suit with matching hair. This he would generously douse in talcum powder before taking the stage, then at the beginning of their set he would shake his head vigorously and his whole face would disappear in a white cloud. It was *better* than dry ice.

Even though the punk-rock look was a stylistic mélange, there was a right way and a wrong way. It was a matter of judgement; you knew it when you saw it.

Manchester caught on to the punk-rock vibe right away. Months before their infamous encounter with Bill Grundy on Thames TV's *Today* programme, The Sex Pistols made their first ever TV appearance in August '76 on Tony Wilson's Granada TV music show *So It Goes*, with a live performance of 'Anarchy in the UK'. So you know, credit where it's due. In the same episode, Clive James had done a studio interview with Peter Cook and later wrote about it in the *Observer*. He wasn't a Pistols fan apparently, describing Johnny Rotten as 'a foul-mouthed ball of acne calling himself something like Kenny Frightful'.

Very quickly the city provided a number of punk venues. Under Steve Morris's broadminded and go-ahead management, the Band on the Wall was an early platform for Manchester's burgeoning punk groups. To Steve, business was business: liquor sales came before any serious music policy. Aesthetically he may not have cared for the punks' music, but one thing about them was that they drank a lot, and if you were dragging in the punters, you were Steve Morris's pal.

Not long after The Sex Pistols event, I was doing my thing at the Band on the Wall and in the crowd was Pete Shelley along with Howard and Linder, who were now an item. It was delightful to meet them so soon after their performance. Now that I saw Linder in context, her look immediately made sense. Give it a name: punk.

Linder had graduated from Manchester School of Art, and was now responsible for the in-house graphics at New Hormones, the Buzzcocks' independent record label. Her monochrome Fluxus-style cut-ups and collages seemed to be more considered than the soon-to-be ubiquitous ransom-note graphics of Jamie Reid at Glitterbest.

In my club entertainer uniform of neat suit and wide-awake demeanour, I was the antithesis of what had been going down pre-punk, which was really default hippy. Even people's dads were growing their hair over their ears, sporting elaborate face furniture, and wearing flared trousers with seed-packet shirts, while I favoured a degree of restraint with my monochrome-block colour scheme and sharp silhouette.

Fortunately, in so doing I had unwittingly obeyed the only three rules of punk rock: narrow lapels, no flares, no beards. You could be as punk as you liked, you could sound like The Ramones, but if you looked anything like a hippy, you weren't allowed in.

Howard Devoto had an apartment in Lower Broughton and I started to see a lot of the Buzzcocks, Linder, and the band's manager Richard Boon (not to be confused with the screen actor of the same-sounding name who played Paladin in *Have Gun – Will Travel*). Howard was quite the aesthete, a bookish type whose literary enthusiasms seemed similar to mine: he was very keen on the work of Samuel Beckett, then as now a blind spot with me, but we were both fans of Albert Camus.

Howard was very supportive, and because of the way I looked, which was anachronistic enough to qualify as punk, he thought I should be working in that area. According to him, punk rock was really taking off, and now had international status: the Buzzcocks were going to fucking Paris the next week, and shit like that. He said I would fit right in. I didn't look like anybody else; I *looked* like a punk.

At that point, my plans in this regard were further emboldened by the runaway success of the American punk poet Patti Smith. I started to frequent the various punk-rock venues around town. As well as the Band on the Wall, there were Thursday nights at the aforementioned Fagins cabaret joint and disco in the town centre; Rafters, ditto, but a different night; the Ranch Bar next door to Foo Foo's Palace, an under-age drinking den done up like a Wild West saloon complete with oil lamps, cow horns, swing doors, and saddles in lieu of bar stools; the Squat, a disused Victorian school hall off Oxford Road; and the Electric Circus, which opened at the end of October 1976.

The Electric Circus was the club that punk built. Right from the start, it was A-Number One. A condemned movie theatre not far from the Embassy Club, it was a health and safety black hole. The demolition orders were already pasted on the wall outside so it always had that fin de siècle 'get it while it's here' kind of vibe. All of the big names appeared at the Electric: The Sex Pistols, The Ramones, Talking Heads, The Stranglers, The Damned, Warsaw, Buzzcocks, The Slits, Siouxsie and the Banshees, The Fall, The Drones, Johnny Thunders and the Heartbreakers, The Clash, and me.

There were lots of other bands as well, some of whom were unjustly overlooked: Terry and the Idiots, Eater, and The Drones, to name only three.

The Drones – M.J. Drone, Gus Gangrene, Steve 'Wispa' Cundall, and Pete Purfect (they later all adopted the surname Drone, presumably in homage to The Ramones) – were originally a Salford pub-rock combo. They had reinvented themselves as punk rockers with Paul Morley – yes, Paul Morley – as their manager, and were now signed to Valer Records.

Valer was a plastics firm like Ronco or K-tel, responsible for those multipurpose kitchen gadgets, As Seen on TV: one bit dices potatoes, another chops onions, another slices carrots, and all with a cheese grater fitted as standard. Valer had no reputation in the music business, but it did have a lot of plastic at its disposal; someone there had obviously seen an overcrowded marketplace and thought: 'me too'.

Don't go mistaking the Manchester punk rock scene for some whole other body: there was nothing cooperative about it. Quite the contrary. They all hated each other; 'everybody sucks but us' was the prevalent attitude. Equipment theft, sabotage, and casual violence were always in attendance. With characteristic wry humour, Pete Shelley would regale The Drones with the following catch line: 'Chop, Core, Slice, Dice!'

I love The Drones actually, and, more recently, often played them on my BBC Radio 6 show. They brought out a picture disc called 'Bone Idol' featuring a monochrome snapshot of the lads in some Salford front parlour. There they are, surrounded by mum and dad furniture, prostrating themselves in front of a life-size skeleton from a medical supply shop perched imperiously on a G-plan throne. Bone Idol. Geddit? It was so fucking corny you had to love it.

When I had the chance, I made sure to go and see some of my other punk enthusiasms when they came to town. I saw Patti Smith, with The Stranglers as support, at the Free Trade Hall in October '76. For ages I thought The Stranglers were an American band; I'd been reading about the CBGB axis, so I just assumed they were part of that New York scene. The name sounded American, they didn't sing in Cockney accents, they didn't sing about council estates or being on the dole, plus they had that Nuggets-y sort of sound, with the Hammond organ. I was a fan from that very first sighting, so to do a record with Hugh Cornwell later was quite a thing. The Stranglers were unique in many ways. They didn't obey any of the rules.

For a start, they were much older than any of the other punk bands, and they transgressed the facial dress codes: Dave Greenfield had a handlebar cookie duster, while Jet Black sported the full-face beard. Lastly, they had a level of musical expertise that allowed a degree of emotional nuance.

In December, The Electric hosted The Sex Pistols, The Clash, the Buzzcocks, and Johnny Thunders and the Heartbreakers on the Anarchy tour. Later, I would play with The Sex Pistols, but not as much as I would have liked. Not only because I didn't drive, but because a couple of gigs were arranged but never happened, which was obviously no fun.

Sometimes if trouble was expected, fanzines like *Sniffing Glue*, for example, which were only available to the cognoscenti at a small number of punk venues, would disseminate information about forthcoming Sex Pistols gigs under various aliases: the Swankers, the Flowers of Romance, to name but two. Even then, it was no guarantee that the gig would go ahead. Don't forget, this was before mobile phones; other than stopping at a service station along the motorway, there was no way of finding out if in the interim period the venue had been forced to call the whole thing off: hence the picture of the Pistols' tour bus, with the destination above the front window showing 'Nowhere'. It said it all. In many cases, that was true in a way; yes, they were going somewhere, but for no reason.

Eight out of ten of their early shows got cancelled by the local council at a moment's notice. What a unique rock and roll experience. I don't know anybody else that ever happened to, so for that reason I was quite judicious about going miles away on a train and stumping up for somewhere to sleep for nothing. That's when you start to question your chosen career: when it starts to cost *you* money.

Chapter Forty-Three

SELF-PROCLAIMED EMPEROR OF PUNK

The revisionist version of punk has been over-politicised, in my view. The sanctification of victimhood and the celebration of all that was negative were simply generally regarded as quite stylish.

By the time punk rock impinged on the provinces, though, it was generally perceived as an ugly, brutish new teen movement more invidious than any that had come before – worse than Teddy Boys, Greasers, Mods and Rockers, worse even than skinheads.

Since my initial appearance at the Embassy Club, I had tried to make the incongruity of the venue work in my favour. Poetry is usually seen as a silent, contemplative, even pastoral interest: punk rock and Bernard Manning helped me disabuse the public of that notion. I was either dismissed as a foul-mouthed malcontent with big ideas, or largely ignored. My outsider status was all very topical; as I've said, my aspirations had to do with sick American comics like Mort Sahl and Lenny Bruce, whose verbal routines could wind people up enough for them to be banned from an entire country – that was the kind of cachet I was after. My man Baudelaire was, after all, a poet who had been prosecuted on a morality rap.

At twenty-seven, I was too old to be a punk, really. As it turns out, I was one of the few who didn't lie about my age. You find out how old people actually are when they die. What a chump I was: if only I'd lied like everybody else, I might still be alive today.

Independent record labels had started sprouting up in the provinces, especially in Manchester, but I had London in mind. I was old-school enough to be desirous of a metropolitan profile in common with every previous pop star, and I included The Beatles. In the words of Frank Sinatra, 'If I can make it there, I'll make it anywhere . . .' The alternative was to be written off as a local eccentric. How ghastly would that be?

Performing alongside punk acts, I realised, was my ticket to the capital and beyond. Hitching my steed to the punk-rock bandwagon, however, was a calculated gamble. Punk wasn't the mass sensation that people now make it out to be; there were only ever about seventy people really involved in it, although the amount of publicity it attracted was disproportionate. Most cities were openly hostile to it, and in those where it did thrive it was borderline niche. At first most of the punk venues I worked in, therefore, were shitty little underground clubs, and grotty discos like Nikkers in Keighley.

Soon after they formed, I did a lot of shows with The Fall. These took place largely in municipal-facility-type venues in places like Kirby, Skelmersdale, and St Helens – yeah, yeah, overspill estates.

Their singer, Mark E. Smith, was about eight years my junior, so I first knew him as a schoolboy. His mother worked at the post office in Sedgley Park where all my artist mates cashed their giros. As was often the case in those days, the post office doubled as a newsagents and stationers, so I used to drop in at least once a week to look through the music papers in case I'd been mentioned in dispatches. For a liberty taker on a budget, Mrs Smith's post office quickly morphed into my own personal reading room; all the music press, of course, but also *Yacht Monthly*, *World of Golf*, *Practical Zombie*, the *Jewish Chronicle*, and the entire Mills and Boon back catalogue. It's amazing how much you don't know you're interested in. Every so often Smithy would make an appearance in his school gaberdine, hitting his mum up for chip money, etc.

Before long, I would spot him and his mates in the George during my compulsory visits with Steve. The George was frequented by cadets from the police training centre up the road and a lot of trainee teachers from the College of the Faithful Companions of Jesus, a pedagogical order of nuns. We knew Marky and his pals weren't yet of legal drinking age, and remember, the place was teaming with embryonic fuzz, so this turned me into some kind of unofficial uncle to him, you know, the type of uncle who doesn't give a fuck what you get up to. Maybe that's why I was never subjected to any of his famous explosions.

One afternoon as I was speed-reading *Automart* in the post office, Mrs Smith volunteered the following information, 'Our Mark's in one of those punk-rock groups.' What the . . .? Huh? In my eyes, Mark was just a kid, so I thought, 'What, *him*? This I've gotta see.'

Of course he was sensational, transformative, right from the start. Smithy reinvented himself on stage, and that's what rock and roll is there for. He achieved this without actually doing very much. He had a kind of glamour that was invisible in everyday life, but take him out of the crowd and stick him in front of a microphone and hey presto – Captain Charisma.

I've worked with the best of them, but The Fall I would watch night in, night out; each performance seemed unique. Like many young bands, they did a lot of covers; the usual punk choices of The Standells, The Stooges, The Seeds etc., but also 'Race with the Devil' by Gene Vincent, 'I Can Hear the Grass Grow' by The Move, 'White Lightning' by George Jones, 'There's a Ghost in My House' by R. Dean Taylor, 'Victoria' by The Kinks, and 'Mr Pharmacist' by the Other Half. There were others; it's an intriguing catalogue in itself.

I remember going on a mini-tour with them, and most nights it was punch-up city. Smithy was no help in that regard — if anything he fucking encouraged it, even though he never came off best. He'd mouth off, get involved, hitting people with chairs and throwing things around, and then, inevitably, he'd get pasted. He was irritable.

In my medical opinion, he was hopped up on goofballs.

I was working my ass off, doing as many club nights as I could, but actually getting any money out of people was a big problem. I didn't have any kind of management: I was a one-man band and had to deal with all that unpleasantness myself. I was always trying to get paid on arrival, before I did my set. I'd read about how Chuck Berry wouldn't put a foot on stage until there was a bag of sand* in his back pocket; any encores were a hundred bucks per number.

I was barely earning three figures for these gigs, but all the awful dives were run by gangsters, and as I was a nine-stone weakling, my Chuck Berry-style negotiations got me nowhere. I'd always find myself in a back room at the end of the night, haggling with some hard-nut surrounded by gorillas. In Birmingham there were Don, Chris, and Eddie Fewtrell, who ran several venues, including the Cedars Ballroom and Barbarella's. To me, the Fewtrell Brothers were like the Kray Twins of Birmingham, so I'd be shitting it by the time it came to collect my wages. Their schtick was to withhold payments with menaces. Threats were muttered within earshot and questions raised regarding the money, e.g. 'Ah, yes. The money. My brothers have been most vocal upon the subject of the money. "Who wants

* Bag of sand = grand.

this money? Why should he get the money? How much money?"'
And so on. Never once did my fee go uncontested. When I
eventually got my money, I always had the impression that it
could be snatched back at any moment, so I'd effect a rapid exit
before I got coshed.

I'd schlepp to some gigs in towns where nobody was interested
in The Sex Pistols or punk rock. Their posturing ineptitude cut
no ice in the industrial towns of the north. In places like Barrow-
in-Furness, for instance, a blue-collar town where the shipyards
were still in full swing, audiences wanted value for money, for the
very good reason that their money was hard-won. Many of them
were fans of heavy metal, where musical proficiency was respected.
Bands who had learned to play, paid their dues, done their apprenticeship. A welder in the shipyards could relate to the idea that
hard work, dedication, and craftsmanship will get you rewards.
They thought punk rockers were taking the piss.

Even in Birmingham, the second largest city in the country,
none of the punk clubs had more than a two-hundred capacity,
and even then they weren't always full. Birmingham had to wait
for the New Romantics and Duran Duran to make an impact at
the Rum Runner, run by the Berrow family, another Birmingham
clubland dynasty.

At Mr Smiths I had only twenty minutes to get the audience
on my side, so I went straight in for the laughs with my area-
specific poems and gags. I couldn't take that routine south of
Macclesfield, however, so I raided my notebooks for old Chaperones
lyrics that could be tarted up and punkified.

Down in Plymouth in the early Seventies, I had bought the
contemporary myth that there was no place for rhyme in modern
poetry, and like everybody else I was writing blank verse, for
example 'Eat Lead Clown', 'Psycle Sluts Part One', and 'The
Marginal Pre-Dawn Schedules Present . . .' Fortuitously, this
'Plymouth period' stuff tapped into the punk ethos: snapshot lyrics,

cheapo graphics, sick humour, schlock TV and shock-horror movies, commercials, cartoons, comic books, and Kojak reruns: all the messed-up glamour of a previous age.

Poems about passing fads and flash-in-the-pan gimmicks also proved popular. I was the first cab off the rank when it came to the Kung Fu craze. I had written 'Kung Fu International', having been an avid fan of the TV series also known as *Kung Fu*, starring David Carradine as Kwai Chang Caine. All the punk ingredients of the day were eloquently conveyed therein: gratuitous violence, filth, bad language, alienation. The title I swiped from a Roy Alton song featured on the album *Twenty Reggae Disco Hits*.

Any swearing always went down well; 'Twat' in particular, which I performed at maximum speed, thus perfecting the 'machine-gun' delivery for which I am justifiably famous. I'd always been fast, but thanks to the high-energy ethics of punk, it was now cranked up to the max.

Chapter Forty-Four

SUMMER OF '77

God Save the Queen and all that, but Steve Maguire and I were dogging out for fucking Jubilee parties, which were supposed to be happening in every street across the nation. The previous evening Granada teatime news had been full of it. We were promised snacks, jazz bands, bouncy castles, and booze.

We called up our pal Al Robinson, a professional thief-turned-milkman-turned-VHS-dealer, now a reformed character and utterly terrific bloke. Robbie obligingly came round in his Ford Granada and drove us around all four corners of the city, including the outer suburbs, but *haciendo nada*. Not so much as a fucking balloon, never mind the Union flag. As we turned each corner, we were greeted only by the old muted trumpet of disappointment: 'Whaap. Whaaap whaaaap whaaaaaaaaaa . . .'*

On the career front, however, by the summer of '77 things were happening for me. I'd done a couple of low-profile cameo appearances in London at the Nashville Rooms, an old gin palace on the Cromwell Road, and also at the Hope and Anchor in Islington, but the opening night of the Vortex in Wardour Street was a high-profile event by punk standards.

---

* To the tune of the National Anthem.

I'm not sure why, but I don't remember it as an entirely encouraging experience. I'd travelled down from Manchester in the same van as The Fall, the Buzzcocks, and a guy from a fanzine called *Ripped and Torn*. We had to get there in the afternoon, so we were up really early, plus there was some kind of mini-heatwave going on, so we were all under-slept, cantankerous, and sweaty by the time we got there. There was also the problem of where to shoot up.

At that point, neither I nor The Fall had any sort of a name in London, so I went on first. It was terrible. I was all over the place. Nobody paid any attention.

The Fall didn't fare any better. The onlookers really didn't cotton on to their chain-store clothes and their homegrown hair-cuts. The Fall always dressed like that, in fact Man at C&A was Mark's nickname at the *NME* for a while. But the audience were more interested in each other than anything that took place on-stage that night.

At some point Johnny Thunders and the Heartbreakers turned up unannounced – they were about to be deported or something – and did a couple of numbers after the Buzzcocks had finished their set. For me that was an unexpected bonus, but it went down badly with Garth, the Buzzcocks' new bass player, a titanic presence from somewhere near Wigan. He was getting all snarky about Johnny and the Heartbreakers, calling them gate crashers and worse; all this anti-American shit, and on the 4th of July already! It all kicked off. The only credible drug around this time was amphetamine sulphate powder. Cocaine was vociferously dismissed by the punk coterie as a symbol of the bloated excess of the fuckwit stadium rockers. It was like a point of honour, but there was loads of fucking Peruvian flake around: *everybody* was banging it up their fucking schnozz on the sly.

Not that night at the Vortex. The amphetamine sulphate powder stank like a tom cat, but like the pep pills of old, it was an ideal alertness aid. Speed: the clue is in the name. Possible side effects included weight loss, insomnia, irritability, and psychosis. Amphetamines; once in their clutches, a man is doomed. *Doomed*, I tell you.

Garth went mad, throwing stuff around and generally coming the cunt. He was a big guy, and people got scared. I was offering to kill him, but the bouncers kicked him out. Meanwhile, Eric Ramsden, the Buzzcocks' roadie, was so pissed off he'd nailed Johnny Thunders' leather jacket to the dressing-room floor.

On the upside, Richard Boon had really taken care of business on the logistics front. That's when I got the bug for staying in hotels. Richard had block-booked an entire floor at the Strand Palace Hotel, which still had its art deco entrance made out of frosted glass, the colour of which I can only describe as 'peach'. The following morning we went down to the full English served by liveried waiters: bone china, Sheffield cutlery, tablecloths, napery, the lot. The Strand Palace Hotel: luxury, pure unashamed luxury.

People always ask me if those early punk shows were nerve-wracking. Well, yes, but it wasn't anything I couldn't handle. As I've said, indifference is the worst enemy of any performer, so after the Embassy, these vicious, drunken, delinquent, blocked-up punks held no terrors for me. Admittedly, the airborne bottles were surplus to requirements, but the worst offender was gobbing.

Punk subverted all the aesthetic ideals: everything ugly was beautiful. By this logic, some idiot put it about that ergo spitting was a mark of respect, and for a while it really caught on. It was awful: you never knew what kind of bacilli were flourishing in this hail of saliva. I couldn't afford to buy a new fucking suit every week, so I ended up spending a fortune at the dry cleaner's. Unsurprisingly, the projectile expectoration didn't play well with the visiting CBGBs contingent. They didn't like it – as far as they were concerned, if somebody spat in their direction, they were a-hankering for a spankering. So, yes; those gigs could be unpleasant and dangerous, but at least there was no place for indifference.

In August, I got involved in a TV series called *Granada Roadshow*, a late-night niche programme featuring folk singers filmed in various towns within the Granada region: Ramsbottom, Liverpool, Kirkby Lonsdale, Hebden Bridge, those kinds of places. I was still an unknown quantity then, and obviously I wasn't allowed to do my more outré stuff, but they paid triple figures. The show went out after the pubs closed, and telly exposure like this didn't happen every day.

One day they were filming the Liverpool Scene, involving quite a few of the Mersey Poets and local folk singers, at Kirklands, a beautiful former Victorian bakery turned wine bar on Hardman Street. With the help of a tame motorist I showed up for this all-day event featuring Adrian Mitchell, Carol Ann Duffy, Roger McGough, Adrian Henri, Stanley Reynolds, and the presenter Trevor Hyett, who was the sports reporter on Granada teatime news. He also had a folk-singing sideline with his then girlfriend, Anna Ford.

This was the first time I'd ever met any successful poets. There were loads of residual nutters swarming about: there were actors from the Everyman Theatre on LSD, a couple of bored policemen had their noses stuck up against the vast plate-glass windows, nosy layabouts and half-pissed students kept bumbling in and interrupting the proceedings. The Liverpool poets were getting antsy. Everyone was overheated, sweating, quite possibly dehydrated, and kvetching about the incompetence of the TV crew. Then, one by one, the bulbs in the studio lights started to detonate, showering the already frazzled audience with tiny shards of glass.

The programme was supposed to go out after the *News at Ten*, but on the night there was a last-minute change to the advertised programme. Apparently I had uttered some profanity or other. I can't remember what it was, but it was enough to get the whole thing spiked, and it was never spoken of again. After all that earache, Roger and his Mickey Mouse mates must have done their collective nuts.

To this day, I can't help feeling partly responsible.

Chapter Forty-Five

INNOCENTS

From early 1977, Monday night at the Band on the Wall was Rock Club night in collaboration with the *New Manchester Review*, a leftist events magazine. On the Grand Opening Night of March 7th, I apparently performed alongside a country-rock combo called Pete Cowap and Country Rebel, along with the Poynton Jemmers, an all-woman clog band. Me neither!

As a platform for the various wannabes on the Manchester music scene, Rock Club became a truly diverse and happening event. Depending on the headliners, it might be a completely different type of crowd every time, and it became the magnet for any finger-on-the-pulse media hotshot: connections were made and deals went down. It was the ideal outlet for my poetry.

Word gets around, and I quickly built up my own little coterie of recognisable fans. I went from being a nobody compere at Mr Smiths to a major attraction at the Band on the Wall.

Eventually, I had to stop doing the cabaret joints. The two things seemed incompatible. It was a trade-off because I started to get noticed and reviewed. I made good copy, I suppose; New York had that CBGB punk–poetry interface of Lou Reed, Patti Smith, and Richard Hell, but here in the UK, I held the monopoly. In spite of my irrepressible self-belief, I never really imagined that my career would go beyond the shores of the United Kingdom: I was expecting trouble in the Scottish Highlands and parts of Wales even then. Now I was getting name-checked in any international dialogue regarding the current UK scene.

Naturally, this had an impact on my material. I was very interested in the punk-rock house style, which had its own very poetic qualities in a way. People think of it as a visceral and quite thuggish movement, but the punks were interested in lyrics. If you look at the songs of Johnny Rotten, Joe Strummer, and Mick Jones, the lyrics often have a social significance beyond the usual concerns of pop.

It must have been at the Band on the Wall that I first met Martin Hannett. Alongside Tosh Ryan and the aforementioned Bruce Mitchell, Martin had co-formed Music Force, a sort of radical hippy musicians' collective committed to 'Keeping Music Live'. Music Force made studios available to some of the young punk rockers of Manchester, booked and promoted gigs, arranged PA and van hire, etc. It was largely kept afloat by a lucrative fly-posting business.

Martin had a finger in many pies. He was around my age, and had a chemistry degree from the University of Manchester Institute of Science and Technology. A clever and funny writer, he edited and wrote for Music Force's own fanzine *Hot Flash* and for the *New Manchester Review*. In the meantime, he was known as Martin Zero, record producer.

At Music Force, Martin had booked the Buzzcocks for a couple of shows, and had subsequently produced *Spiral Scratch*, their 1977 debut EP. He had always wanted his own recording studio, and when the Music Force office moved to new premises, he could finally fulfil that ambition. In 1977 Rabid Records was formed with Hannett as its mad-professor-style in-house maestro.

Rabid's small roster included Slaughter and the Dogs, Ed Banger and the Nosebleeds, The Primetime Suckers, and later 'Jilted

John', who had a massive number-one hit of the same name. Also, 'Gordon the Moron', Giro, Chris Sievey, later known as Frank Sidebottom, and me.

Before I met Martin, I hadn't even thought about making a record. I wasn't convinced that I wanted to put poetry on an album, but Rabid seemed to think a quick exploitation release was a good idea, and we made the *Innocents* EP, which was released in November 1977.

I'm a total perfectionist; a refiner of language. My poems are never finished – only abandoned. Once they're published in a book or released on vinyl, however, that's it: they're nailed – I can no longer do the annual autopsy upon them. So, I'm doomed to be forever haunted by my own mistakes.

It was never really my idea to put music to the poems. At the time, though, I was publicity hungry, and couldn't come up with an argument against it. After all, who plays a record without music on it? We put a one-off backing band together – which we called The Curious Yellows, after a Swedish erotic art movie currently running at the Cinephone – and went into the studio with Martin to record three tracks: on the A-side, 'Suspended Sentence' and 'Innocents', with 'Psycle Sluts, Parts One and Two' on the B-side.

I didn't really enjoy the recording process, and the results were mixed. Occasionally, it somehow hung together by accident, and I was pleasantly surprised, but generally I could only hear the mistakes. It is what it is, as they annoyingly say, but I'm glad somebody bought it.

That's when I discovered that the studio is an unnatural environment for a congenital control freak like me. I don't like it. I like to be able to claim full responsibility and blame for anything you think about what I do. I don't want to have to credit some cunt on a guitar as having anything to do with it. It's borderline hostility: I like guitar players but not in my studio.

My poetry has its own kind of organic momentum: it speeds

up, then slows down, then speeds up double, then slows down again, etc., etc., etc. . . . What I do depends a lot on varied speed; I leave people with the impression that it's really fast, but it isn't always. That's the knack. Put me working with expert musicians and it's like nailing my foot to the floor. I listen to my stuff with music and it's like I've been grounded. There are moments when I come on like a broken arm, an injured gazelle, a bird in a gilded cage: and who breaks a butterfly on a wheel?

Plus, whatever you do, when you play anything back in a top-dollar sound studio, it's going to sound fucking great. Those seductive Sensurround chords, the fathomless reverb, an entire eternity of echoes: the full Phil Spector. Wow. These aural gardens of delight are all very well, but what's it going to sound like on a car radio?

In that way I'm quite minimalist. There were people doing what I do a thousand years ago, and there will be people doing it in a thousand years' time. There could be a worldwide power cut tomorrow which could last forever, but it's not going to end my career. Wherever people gather for amusement, that's where I'll be, like the wandering balladeer of old.

Don't get me wrong, every day I pray to God thanking Him for the gift of electricity. I never take it for granted. Nobody appreciates electricity more than I do. But having said that, what couldn't I do with just a quill and a roll of parchment? You'd have to pay me to stop. I'd take a stick and scribble in the dirt if I had to.

Chapter Forty-Six

CONFESSIONS OF A PUNK PERFORMER

Less than a year after it opened, the Electric Circus was under fire from the authorities for various Health and Safety infractions. Apparently it failed to meet the legal requirement that each person should have eight and a half feet within which to pogo, so it was closed down. Over the first weekend of October 1977, the Electric opened for two final nights in aid of the Pat Seed Scanner fund, the big Manchester cause célèbre at the time.* On the Sunday, I appeared alongside various Manchester bands – Warsaw, The Fall, the Buzzcocks, Magazine, Rip Off, John the Postman, The Prefects, The Worst, and Manicured Noise.†

---

* In 1976 Pat Seed was admitted as a cancer patient of Christie Hospital, Manchester. Specialists considered she would only live a few more months – she was to prove them wrong. While Pat was a patient she heard of a new technology, Computerised Axial Tomography (CAT) scanners. Hospitals at the time were unable to launch fund-raising appeals. With the help of North Fylde MP Sir Walter Clegg and the Minister for Health, Roland Moyle, Pat succeeded in lobbying for an amendment made to the 1948 Health Act and she helped to raise £1.75 million for the hospital. The campaign turned Pat into a national celebrity, meeting royalty, and she was even the subject of a *This is Your Life* TV profile.

† The whole thing was filmed and recorded, and later released on vinyl as *Short Circuit: Live at the Electric Circus*.

It was all in a good cause, but the cheque for £750 apparently bounced.

Later that month, I was at Liverpool Tech, in between the New Hearts and the Buzzcocks. A local fanzine write-up read (bafflingly) thus: 'Special Offer: Salford Tech tool hander outers accent not supplied [sic]. However a 2 ½ hour course is available at a minimum cost. Full 39-year courses do come slightly dearer. Applicants will also recieve [sic] a full-colour photo of Margret [sic] Thatchers [sic] nipples, sent in a plain brown envelope.' Apparently, my performance was the best bit of entertainment this reviewer had seen since a bloke fell off the loading bay at his workplace, and I had to do several encores before the crowd would let me leave the building.

It got to the point where my shows at the Band on the Wall were advertised in advance. As a result I reached the radar of Tony Wilson, who gave me a ten-minute slot on *So It Goes*, his weekly music show on Granada TV.

Much to the excitement of my family, the Maguires, and my work mates, Tony Wilson brought a film crew down to interview me at Salford Tech, plus they filmed some out-and-about stuff in clubs around Manchester. Say what you want about him, but he gave The Sex Pistols their first live TV appearance, and he also featured many of the new punk acts over from America: Television, Blondie, Iggy Pop, Patti Smith, The Heartbreakers, all of whom were really niche at that time. There's a guy who stuck his neck out.

In those days nobody knew anybody who had been on TV. It's hard to imagine now, but before videos, DVDs, Netflix, and watch-on-demand, you had three channels and when they closed down, usually around midnight, there was no more: you'd have to wait for *Pebble Mill at One* or the horseracing the following afternoon. Airtime was limited and to be on telly was a real big deal.

If somebody was doing a vox pop for the local news in the middle of town and they asked your opinion on, say, the revised bus schedules or something, you'd be straight home getting the telly warmed up. Neighbours would inform their friends and relatives, 'Bloody hell, that John Clarke's on telly in five minutes. Hurry up. Switch it on.' The whole street would be watching, hanging on your every word, all five seconds' worth – 'I think it's terrible,' or 'Not before time. These bus-timetable revisions are well overdue in my opinion.' So to be on Granada TV for a *whole ten minutes*, as John Cooper Clarke reading his poetry – I mean, for fuck's sake. That was a big, big step; to get on the telly had always been part of the Urban Poet's masterplan, and Tony Wilson was instrumental in making it happen.

Now I was 'As Seen on TV', with all the added work that brought with it. I was getting booked four or five nights a week in all kinds of out-of-town joints – places like Eric's in Liverpool, the Limit in Sheffield, Nikkers in Keighley, Barbarella's and the Cedar Ballroom in Birmingham, and a real good one for me, the Rock Garden in Middlesbrough, next door but one to Club Marimba.

So now, like my pal the Reverend Bernie Davis, I had two jobs: this and that. Often I wouldn't arrive home until around 4am. I was still clocking in at Salford Tech, but luckily I had an agreement of sorts with Desmond, the foreman. As long as I kept him amused with salacious accounts of my nocturnal activities, I was on flexitime. The dirtier the excuse the better, as far as Desmond was concerned: he was clearly getting great vicarious kicks from these tales of my unlikely escapades.

The details came straight out of *Confessions of a Pop Performer* and the *Carry On* franchise. You know, stories about pretending to be a vacuum-cleaner salesman, hiding in the wardrobe, shimmying down a drainpipe on her husband's untimely return, and all of that junk.

Those Robin Askwith *Confessions of . . .* movies caused quite a stir. They said romance was dead, but those films' popularity proved otherwise. Robin Askwith's arse double – wasn't that every young man's ideal job? You'd get to bounce up and down on Jill Gascoine, Maggie Wright, Suzette St Clair, Linda Wright, aka Brenda Climax, and Sheila White, aka Rosie Noggett, *and* get paid for it. Anyway, I had what felt like a lifetime's material to draw on, and Desmond was happy. It was like he felt he had some kind of agency in this seedy double life he thought I was leading; it was our filthy secret, and you can't buy that level of second-hand glamour.

A week or two before its official release in November, John Peel played a couple of tracks from my debut EP, two nights running. This was another major first: I'd never heard myself on the radio before, never mind twice in a fucking week.

John Peel had defined himself in opposition, playing the kind of music most people wouldn't like. Certain acts, including The Fall, Captain Beefheart, and myself, undoubtedly benefited from this policy. He did me a solid favour, because thanks to this preview, the EP went straight into the punk-rock hit parade.

On 4 December I was back on *So It Goes*, this time co-presented by Tony Wilson with the assistance of Sooty and Sweep, featuring a film of me performing 'Kung Fu International' at the Elizabethan Ballroom in Belle Vue Gardens.

Prime-time TV; radio airplay; three-figure fees; I'd exhausted almost all the early Seventies soft-porn canon – it was time to ditch the day job, and just in time for Christmas. Desmond organised a farewell booze-up in the Flemish Weaver, and we all stifled a manly tear.

On 27 December 'Suspended Sentence' came in at number five in John Peel's annual Festive Fifty. The toppermost of the poppermost.

Chapter Forty-Seven

A PROFESSIONAL POET (ON TOUR WITH BE-BOP DELUXE)

After all those years of doing this and that, now I was just doing this: I was a professional poet, performing most nights of the week.

I didn't have a Malcolm McLaren to look after my wellbeing, but I did have representation, of sorts, through Rabid Records – as much as anybody else in the world of punk anyway. At the very least, I could now refer people to 'the office' for bookings, plus Rabid had the promotional facilities.

Rabid may have been going to be my management, but they were very indistinct about their role in that. I didn't really know what they were supposed to do either. Perhaps I was expecting more help than was reasonable, or maybe I just wasn't that manage-able. The habit was beginning to impinge. I was off the case, permanently distracted by the acquisition of narcotics, or the acquisition of the money to get the narcotics. It was a millstone around my neck, but it was also the engine room: to spend a lot of money, I had to make a lot of money. I thought this worked in everyone's favour. If anything, it made me *more* reliable; when it came to money or dope, the catchphrase was always the same: 'I need it, man.' That being the case I was always available for work. Even so, I acquired a reputation around Rabid Records for being both feckless and difficult. When in doubt, blame the junkie.

In January 1978, I went down to London with the Rabid posse – Tosh Ryan, Laurence Beadle, Martin Hannett, and their lawyer – for meetings at all the big record companies with a view to signing me with a major label. We saw all the head honchos, including Chris Blackwell at Island, but I seemed to hit it off best with Maurice Oberstein, head of CBS UK, so the Rabid cohort and CBS's lawyers proceeded with the necessary negotiations.

While I was down there, I did my first interview with Steve Clarke (no relation) for the *NME*. Because of my high-velocity house style and my crisp silhouette, along with my constant gum-chewing plus various nervous affectations, which were probably the product of stage fright and general existential angst, the press tended to mark me down erroneously as some kind of pathological speed fiend. I didn't complain; in a way, this distracted from the fact that I was actually a fucking heroin addict. They could say what they liked, it's a free country, but as far as I was concerned, it was 'No Comment' every time. Whatever your drug of choice, you kept it between you and your supplier. There was no mileage in any kind of reputation, and who needs a visit from John Law.

In those days I used to score at a place in Sussex Gardens where I'd run into another *NME* journalist called Nick Kent, one-time paramour of the pre-Pretenders Chrissie Hynde. Nick lived in a series of boarding houses all over London, fucking flophouses frankly, with his intriguing Parisian girlfriend Hermine. Hermine was quite high-profile, very chic, a dancer and a professional high-wire walker. She had been a mentor to that guy who walked between the Twin Towers on a tightrope.

Nick was extraordinary-looking, way more exotic than any of the people he ever interviewed. He would have made anyone look like a schlub. Honest to God, he was like some tropical bird of paradise, usually dressed in a Lewis Leathers biker jacket, leather jeans, top-dollar leather motorbike boots with buckles, a ruffled blouse, and the full mascara. If you saw him across the road you'd go, 'WOW!' A fantastic rock and roll apparition, but when you got up close you'd notice the patina of grime. It was like he slept in his clothes all the time, or perhaps never even went to bed. Occasionally, he'd go to Boots in order to douse himself in perfume. What they call 'a whore's bath'.

His legs were the same length as my entire body. To witness him approaching was like watching a giraffe's slow-motion gait. He wrote a song for Marianne Faithful called 'My Flamingo'. He was quite the exquisite, and had a mythological band, The Vicarians.

Nick was also a fan of the Buzzcocks, The Fall, and The Only Ones, so I bumped into him all the time at various gigs and out and about in the West End. He would go around the major record companies in Soho blagging 'white labels' – pre-release copies of albums sent out to reviewers, that didn't have any information printed on the label at all. Anorak collectors would pay top dollar for them, so Nick would be round CBS in Soho Square ripping off the mega-star end of the market with white labels from Bruce Springsteen, Johnny Cash, Teddy Pendergrass, Charlie Daniels, The Clash, ABBA, whatever. He used to flog them to a shop in nearby Hanway Street, one of those obsessives' record outlets as portrayed in Nick Hornby's *High Fidelity*. One of the sales assistants had a sideline in drug distribution, so any money Nick made on the white labels was probably spent in-house in one smooth transaction.

In February 1978 I embarked on my first major UK tour of large halls, with a group from Wakefield called Be-Bop Deluxe. This seemed counterintuitive, given that Be-Bop Deluxe had nothing to do with punk. What they had, however, was a high mainstream profile: they'd been on *The Old Grey Whistle Test*, and were popular with erm . . . Music Lovers. The punk scene revolved around small clubs, and this was my way into the larger venues.

Be-Bop Deluxe were a little bit prog rock, a little bit new wave and electronic experimental, with a touch of David Bowie modern glam – not entirely my cup of tea, but I could see it had some kind of value. Their music was very much predicated upon the extreme technical proficiency of Bill Nelson, their virtuoso guitar player, but they didn't do concept albums, all-night solos, or anything self-indulgent like that. Plus, they looked good in their own way: nice clothes, space-age equipment, short hair, apart from Charlie Tumahai, their Maori bass player, who affected the 'fro.

Given that recent guests on their tours had included proper musos like Steve Gibbons and the Doctors of Madness, you might well ask why Be-Bop Deluxe thought it a good idea to have John Cooper Clarke as their support act. After all, in 1978 the only poets most people were aware of were Pam Ayres and Cyril Fletcher out of *That's Life*. Perhaps they felt slightly out of date and were anxious to be seen as up to the minute. Having a punk poet as the support act would give them a credible modern edge, whereas the snotty approach and youthful energy of, say, The Drones, Eater, or Terry and the Idiots might have made them look a bit last week. I couldn't do that – no poet could upstage a band; you can't compete with music. It was *me* who was taking the risk.

The Drastic Plastic tour was as big as it gets: we were playing in venues like the Hammersmith Odeon, the Manchester Apollo, the Grand Theatre in Leeds, places of that magnitude. I had to crank everything up a bit in order to meet the requirements of a seated crowd in a large theatre.

Be-Bop Deluxe travelled in a tour bus. Martin Hannett, my producer at Rabid, now doubled as my driver, and would ferry me back and forth in a top-of-the-range Volvo on lease-hire. At this point Martin had tragically acquired a habit, although frankly I soon saw the upside. We pooled our resources. He had connections I didn't know about, I had connections he didn't know about, and between the two of us, we were always sorted for dope. It was as smooth as it gets, but there are always dramas around that shit. Even with the best plans in the world, things get nutty. Whatever – deal or no deal – showtime was 8.30pm on the nose.

Some of the shows were quite encouraging, but Be-Bop Deluxe's people were not necessarily my people. They were a weird cross-over mixed bag: young married couples, prog-rockers, David Bowie types, some kind of borderline hippys, air-guitarists, one or two head-bangers, maybe the odd foreign student – but no visible evidence of the New Wave. Unlike a lot of people in his corner of the rock biz, Bill Nelson was quite amenable to the more imaginative elements of punk rock; he liked The Clash and The Sex Pistols. The Bopsters, however, didn't always agree with him on this, and saw people like me as an unwelcome intrusion. Some nights, they would even scream curses and blame me for the ills of society.

The Be-Bop road crew, however, liked my act because of the jokes and the filthy language. They were fond of a bit of banter, and liked to wind me up. After those shows when the audience had been less than enthusiastic, they would say something encouraging like, 'Think that's bad? Bloody hell, wait till you get to Glasgow!' 'What about Glasgow?' I'd ask. There would be a lot of muttering, darkly veiled hints of what might be in store, the general gist of which, 'They're gonna fucking kill ya! Them porridge wogs don't take no prisoners.'

It was the first time I'd performed in Scotland, plus it was at the Glasgow Apollo, a four-thousand-seat former movie theatre that had been known as Green's Playhouse, a massive place with two balconies. The original carpet was still intact – indeed, an offcut now covers the floor of Rod Stewart's LA games room. Anybody who is anybody in the Sassenach world of showbiz has died there at one time or another, so if I could nail it there, I'd make it anywhere. I was shitting myself for the entire two weeks, or however long it was, before we got there.

I lasted four minutes. Instant outpourings of pure hate. Jeering. Thousands of Sweaties* proactively withholding their love. I just stood there for the entire four minutes, with no indication that the hostility would ever abate. You can't fight that level of animosity, so as soon as the volume dropped a fraction, I just said, 'Let's call it a draw.' Even in a situation like that, I had to have the last word.

After that night, had it not been for Elvis Costello, I might never have gone back to Glasgow again.

The Be-Bop Deluxe tour taught me how to roll with the punches. Like all artists, I have a delicate ego, and what I require from an audience is a unanimous display of carefully considered adulation. In Glasgow, this was not forthcoming, but you know, put it into perspective: nobody died.

* Sweaty socks = Jocks.

Chapter Forty-Eight

DISGUISE IN LOVE

By this point my sole contact at Rabid, really, was Martin Hannett. He was a bit of a flake, and always at loggerheads with the office. Martin and I were confederates, I suppose, but as I've said, we weren't good for each other. We were up and about at all hours in order to keep well. The fact that I was being driven around by a man who was sedated by opiates, and also distracted, didn't bother me. In fact, the safety aspects of this arrangement never even entered my head. It was a solution rather than a problem.

I consider my hours spent in the passenger seat of an automobile to be golden. That Iggy Pop tune is a page out of my life: the rolling scenery, the controllable heat, the wraparound sound system. Nice. Martin would often be in the throes of production, so he'd always have a stash of cassettes featuring some work in progress. In this way I became familiar with the sublime bass-heavy melancholia of Joy Division's *Unknown Pleasures*, centuries before its eventual release.

Once we drove from London to Edinburgh without a break. Then as now, Scotland was awash with heroin, but not on this occasion. We were going to be working up there for at least a week, and I wasn't due on stage until the next evening, so I thought, fuck that, went straight over to Waverley Station and caught the sleeper back to King's Cross and my usual suppliers. I was there and back within fourteen hours. That was nothing; you'd do anything for that shit. If you don't have it, you can't take care of anything else.

In April 1978, I played at the Roundhouse in Camden. Top of the bill were the excellent Steel Pulse (the Handsworth Revolutionaries), I was third after Wreckless Eric, and opening the show way down the bill were The Police. Every punk rocker hated The Police and thought they were really corny, which wasn't surprising, really: they were attractive to women.

The deal with Maurice Oberstein at CBS had gone through, and I was signed up in a five-figure recording contract. Was it a good deal? Was it a bad deal? Then as now, I have no idea, although, in retrospect, even I should have seen that signing over the copyright in my poems to a record company wasn't the smartest business move anybody ever made on my behalf.

CBS's UK HQ was in Soho Square, in the same building as the Fender Soundhouse, which stocked all the latest limited-edition custom Fender guitars. CBS gave me a Fender grey sunburst Telecaster custom as a bit of sweetener. It was a top-dollar guitar at the time, with a toggle switch so you could get the thin treble-y delicate Telecaster sound; with the flip of the same switch you could employ this diMarzio pickup and turn it into a Les Paul with that big fat fuzz sound. Two years later I would sell it for a song at Macari's on Charing Cross Road in order to buy gear; there was no good haggling about the price, I just needed a quick sale, as unfortunately, it was no good trying to offer a guitar to a dealer by way of collateral. I tried it once: he opened a door and there was a whole fucking front room full of big-ticket musical instruments. He didn't want another fucking electric guitar. Anyway, you'd just about get a quarter of a gram for a Fender, so if you were going to go down that road, it was always better to sell it at a reputable second-hand outlet and buy a decent amount of gear for whatever you got for it. That was what I thought, and I didn't play it much anyway. I sold it for £150, which bought me an amount of heroin that was completely used up and forgotten about within about a week, and there I was with the same problem all over again. If you want a picture of moral relativism in all of its ugly fucking detail, look no further than the universe of the addict, whose every move, no matter how heinous, is informed by the phrase, 'Who wouldn't?' It's the death of the soul.

My first album for CBS, *Disguise in Love*, was once again produced by Martin Hannett, along with a summer single release, 'Post-War Glamour Girl', with a live a-capella rendition of 'Kung Fu International' on the B-side.

We recorded the album at a studio in Deansgate, with two tracks from a live show at the Ritz Ballroom in Manchester. Martin put together a bespoke backing band called The Invisible Girls with guest musicians like Pete Shelley, Stephen Morris, Karl Burns, Paul Burgess, and my new pal Bill Nelson. The one-note guitar solo on 'Post-War Glamour Girl' took eight hours to record!

In advance of my CBS debut, Rabid had crashed out *Où est la maison de fromage?*, a shamelessly cheap, probably illegal move by a bunch of no-mark chisellers, secretly recorded and marketed without any input or consent from me. Naturally, I only want to present the polished end-product of my labours, therefore its very existence is a continuing thorn in my side. It never stops hurting. If you love me, throw it away.

In the end, Martin Hannett and I were cut adrift by Rabid; everything went wrong. The whole Rabid axis – Tosh Ryan,

Laurence Beadle, all of those people – I thought I knew some of them. It turned out I didn't know any of them at all.

Their offices were on the other side of town, and I didn't have a car. Actually I did have a car, but I wasn't allowed to drive it. Whatever, I was always in the dark business-wise. Whatever they proposed, I went along with, within reason, as long as it didn't directly impinge upon my personal happiness. Whenever I was presented with a bunch of figures looking for an argument, I let it ride. I'm not one for confrontation.

In August, Slobby Rabid Opportunists (their words, not mine) had me headlining at a series of gigs in Manchester and Liverpool to promote their roster. On Friday the 18th, I performed at the Factory at the Russell, supported by Giro, Ed Banger with guest appearances from Prime Time Suckers, and 'Gordon the Moron' of 'Jilted John' fame. Most of the time the Russell would have bingo and domino nights, or appearances by various reggae artists. From 1978, after the demise of the Electric, it was requisitioned for two nights a week by Alan Erasmus and Tony Wilson as the Factory. Alan Wise (of whom more later) was the promoter, and somehow managed to book some real top-flight acts.

I was still living at Steve's, and he and I had become a bit of a double act. It was a cross-inspirational thing: his pictures would induce a train of poetic ideas or would call forth a snappy title. For a self-portrait in front of a marine horizon, for example, I suggested 'Back to the Sea', a John Masefield reference which I would revisit for the poem 'I Mustn't Go Down to the Sea Again'. Steve, likewise, would occasionally illustrate my poems.

He was always mithering me to take my poetry to the publishing world. By this time, I had enough material to make up a collection, so now that I no longer had a job to go to, when I wasn't out doing gigs he and I did the very unpunk thing of putting together a book with actual artwork. It would be entitled *Ten Years in an Open Necked Shirt*, the title of one of Steve's earlier works.

Steve's illustrations were meticulously gradated pencil drawings with extraordinarily fine cross-hatch detailing, each of which took weeks and weeks to complete to his satisfaction. Pencil is the slowest, dirtiest medium; you just had to breathe on one of the drawings and it was smudged.

None of my management at this time, nor anyone at the new record company – *no one* – was remotely interested in this joint project. What Steve did was amazing, but it wasn't *punk*. 'Fuck that,' they all said. 'Just stick in a bunch of photographs.' I was in it with Steve for the long haul, though, and adamant that his craftsmanship would turn the book into something special.

It was down to me, therefore, to get a publishing deal on my own. Steve always had more than one painting on the go, which was his legitimate excuse for not getting involved in the business end. So there I was, pounding the unfamiliar pavements of Bloomsbury, knocking on the doors of that indifferent neighbourhood.

I offered our work to small publishers at first. I got a lot of knock-backs, but Jay Landesman was enthusiastic enough to meet me at his recently formed Polytantric Press. He was having success with Heathcote Williams's *Hancock's Last Half Hour* and his reissue of *By Grand Central Station I Sat Down and Wept* by Elizabeth Smart. Jay was a hipster in the original sense of the word, but he wasn't interested in 'art' books.

That was also the message from most of the bigger publishing houses. What seemed to be required was a quick scissors-and-paste exploitation job with the usual punk graphics – sliced-up photographs featuring tower blocks, barbed wire, and flyovers, with the odd mugshot of the author here and about. Although Steve's illustrations were often admired, the feedback was always the same, 'Maybe later.'

★   ★   ★

Disguise in Love came out in the autumn, with sleeve art featuring one of Steve's existing works,* a bas relief in the manner of René Magritte on a conveniently square piece of chipboard, lending itself perfectly to the album-sleeve format. Paul Morley in the *NME* gave the album a hefty thumbs up: 'The problems of how to handle Cooper Clarke on record, away from the advantageous atmosphere of a live recital, have been handled triumphantly. [. . .] The music is cute and all integrity is retained.'

CBS/Epic had a red-hot publicist called Judy Totton who worked with some really big-name acts, including ABBA, the Jacksons, The Vibrators, and The Only Ones, who had signed to CBS the same week as me. They were pals of mine, and I did a hell of a lot of shows with them.

Judy was a real professional, brilliant at her job, a real trouper and sweet with it. Before I had a place in London, she let me stay at her flat in Chepstow Road, just behind what was then the Odeon on Westbourne Grove. At that time, before it had been gentrified by the post-Richard Curtis intake, Ladbroke Grove and Notting Hill were a sort of low-rent hippy ghetto, still populated by people who had been living there since the days of the notorious Peter Rachman, with a new intake of bohemian types, jazz musicians, painters, the crowd that started *Oz* magazine, and other denizens of alternative culture. All that made it a really easy place to buy drugs, especially marijuana. Judy put up with a lot, especially as I was shooting up shit in her house, and she was from the other side of the world in that regard.

It was a really happening manor. Stiff Records, indeed all the punk-rock business, seemed to be based nearby, so I would run into all sorts of people: Billy Idol, Ian Dury, Declan MacManus aka Elvis Costello, Declan's manager and Stiff founder Jake Riviera,

---

* CBS insisted on the addition of the eyes behind the joke glasses, which I think was a mistake.

poet and nominal Stiff publicist Jock Scot, The Clash, even Lemmy of Motörhead fame, on occasion. But my most useful contact at the time, for obvious reasons, was Peter Perrett of The Only Ones.

The Clash were all proper West London types, QPR supporters. Mick Jones lived just round the corner in a flat in Chepstow Place, and later moved to the slightly plummier Pembridge Villas just off Portobello Road, with Tony James of Generation X. We started to see each other quite a lot. It must be around this time that I first met my gentleman driver and dear friend, Johnny Green, who in those days was the road manager for The Clash. Johnny was originally from Gillingham in Kent, but he always lived around Notting Hill and Camden, where he had a cold-water apartment at the Rehearsal Rehearsals studios just inside the gates of a former British Rail goods yard on Chalk Farm Road. It was within walking distance of Dingwalls and the Roundhouse, so I'd be running into him all the time, and not just in London, but when I was on tour at the same time as the band.

When *Disguise in Love* was released, we needed to whip up some interest in the capital, so Judy organised a publicity stunt at Speakers' Corner in Hyde Park on October 22nd.

At Speakers' Corner you can say anything you like as long as it isn't amplified. With that in mind, Judy got hold of a bullhorn in the full knowledge that its use was illegal and that the fuzz would step in, providing the perfect paparazzi shots of me and the law in an adversarial position.

The whole thing worked like a charm – Elvis Costello even turned up under heavy disguise along with Bebe Buell, his extra-marital inamorata of the time, which caused a bit of a showbiz frisson. But what was more, later that night the *Evening Standard* carried the money shot – me, head to head with John Law, like some kind of victimised 'public enemy number one' type. The accompanying caption went so far as to suggest that I had narrowly missed a sleepover in the Scrubs.

Judy was really good at this kind of scam, or possibly scamola. She would also plant stories and rumours in the press that I would be called upon to vehemently deny. E.g. I didn't have my sunglasses glued to my temples. You read it here first. It never happened.

At some point later that year, I fell into a brief liaison with Bebe. She had a colourful romantic history; for several years she'd been in a relationship with the hotshot LA singer, song-writer, multi-instrumentalist, and producer Todd Rundgren. She made a particular point of dating rock stars, and had been linked variously with David Johansen of the New York Dolls, Mick Jagger, Rod Stewart, Jimmy Page, and Steve Tyler. At the time, though, I didn't know much about her backstory, just that she was in London, on the rebound from Elvis Costello and at a loose end, so I did the gentlemanly thing and ushered her out a few times. It was her idea; I was always prey to vampish women. Bebe was in charge all the way – she could organise your entire life.

Bebe was the original rock-chick babe: everybody knew who she was. She wasn't just some anonymous groupie or something. She was one of the beautiful people, a real IT girl. I wasn't deluded: I knew I wasn't going to make it in the world of hunks and Hollywood buff tings, but I figured with my kind of looks, I could cut it in the punk world. There were uglier and more drug-dependent people than me at CBGB after all, and they seemed to be doing all right. I wanted my slice of that slutty, messed-up glamorous pie. As for Bebe, she put it best herself: 'I was a young girl and had brilliant suitors. I sort of had that fantasy of being one of the muses of Paris and hanging out with Toulouse Lautrec and Picasso. I just followed my heart, you know? I was a free agent. And I was a very independent, successful girl. I did my own thing, I made my own money, I bought my own airline tickets. I'm also one of those people that even when I have a backstage pass, I like being in the pit.'

The publicity Judy generated to promote *Disguise in Love* was phenomenal. At the end of October I recorded a session for John Peel featuring tracks from the album, and into November did various shows with Joy Division, The Fall, the Drones, and the Buzzcocks. I seemed to be appearing at Eric's in Liverpool on a weekly basis. Roger Eagle who was a long-time friend of both Tosh Ryan and Alan Wise had long since vacated the Magic Village and was now running this place. I also appeared on *The Old Grey Whistle Test* presented by Annie Nightingale performing 'Readers' Wives' and 'Kung Fu International' with The Invisible Girls. The shows were filmed at Radio Manchester Studios on Oxford Road, and were recorded live: you only got one chance to get it right. At the time the broadcasting industry was highly unionised, and you weren't even allowed to turn your own amplifier up. If you wanted to pull one plug out and plug another one in, you had to get a technician to do it for you. The anxiety was palpable.

I got a lot of gigs on the strength of *Disguise in Love*. This created difficulties at first, because I was now known through the medium of the album, on which I'd been accompanied by all these top of the range session guys from the Dougie James Soul Train plus various celebrity cameos. I was perceived to be the front man of this 'supergroup', and my appearance on *The Old Grey Whistle Test* only confirmed that belief.

I wasn't very happy with this turn of events. I had long ago been convinced by my erstwhile teachers that I had no team spirit, and every school report confirmed it. I like pottering around in a car. Just me and the driver, not a fucking Wallace Arnold coach party.

For almost a year after the album came out, I was really swimming against the tide in that respect. I'd turn up at the venue without a band, and as you can imagine they'd be both puzzled and annoyed, especially abroad. Every time I'd have to reveal that there *was* no band, there never was a band, I couldn't afford a band, I didn't need a band, and anyway, The Invisible Girls were purely a studio phenomenon. What I do is poetry. Just me, the PA, and the public.

Chapter Forty-Nine

ARMED FORCES

Nobody can handle fame. It just ain't right. You'd actually have to be some kind of a monster, a *sociopath*, for it not to devastate your personality. So at the first glimpse of celebrity, like anybody in their right mind I was immediately fucked up. Immediately.

The only time I've ever been a persistent sex offender was after I'd been on prime-time television. As I've said, owing to the perilous post-tubercular state of my physique, promiscuity had never been one of my vices, but after my five minutes on teatime telly, I was suddenly introduced to the life of the libertine and the horrors of the corporeal world.

Where I come from, if you'd been on telly for any reason other than multiple rape or murder you were an instant VIP. I mean, I dined out for fucking months on seeing Nobby Stiles at the Whitsun Walks. I was in town with my dad watching the Italian parades around Ancoats and Stephenson Square. It was a prestige event – you know, life-size Madonnas bedecked with jewellery carried by hefty men, people sticking money on the statuary, a proper Italian Catholic spectacle, on top of which there was Norbert Stiles with his kid. The old man spotted him first, otherwise even he wouldn't have believed it.

Any time I appeared on TV there was a spike in the number

of female sex pests, so as you can imagine, after my appearance on BBC 2's *The Old Grey Whistle Test*, I went from being a total Poindexter, a bookish niche act at best, to Casanova already.

After a while it seemed churlish to resist – then I was putty in their hands. Naturally, in no time at all I contracted a gonorrhoeal infection, with all the social leprosy that involves. Not only that, but I passed it on to my girlfriend at the time, who as a ballerina had muscles in her piss. I shouldn't have wound her up. She pasted the fuck out of me. She was a bit mercurial like that, but you know, venereal disease . . . Nevertheless, we somehow patched things up, but then she got evicted from her flat, and still feeling somewhat on the back foot what with the gonorrhoea unpleasantness, I invited her to move in with me at Steve and Helen's, temporarily of course. I don't know what fucking possessed me to do that – it wasn't my house; I was a fucking lodger. But I had no moral defence: it was my way of making it up to her, I guess.

It was terrible. She moved in with this cat that she was a bit nutty about. Steve fucking hated cats, but at least she only had one. It was me who couldn't handle it. The thing was walking all over Steve's artwork for the book and shit; I thought somebody was going to die. Anyway, all the unhappy consequences put the whole promiscuity thing into perspective, and never again did I embrace the life of the voluptuary.

At some point in the midst of this whole sorry episode, I got a call from Elvis Costello, who offered me a guest spot on his forthcoming Armed Forces tour, alongside the excellent Richard Hell and the Voidoids. It was going to be a massive twenty-five-city junket playing large halls, starting in December with seven nights at London's prestigious Dominion Theatre, and continuing into January '79, spanning the UK from Bristol to Aberdeen, taking in every major town en route.

I'd just bought Elvis Costello's, debut album, *My Aim is True*, and thought it was fabulous – it wasn't formulaic punk, more a very cerebral sort of high-end pop, plus I was already a big fan of Richard Hell and the Voidoids. Given the strain of the domestic situation in Sedgley Park, I didn't take much persuading: when I saw that the Glasgow Apollo was on the date sheet, I was in. My Glasgow fiasco with Be-Bop Deluxe was still a source of much mental grief, and getting on board with Elvis Costello plus Richard Hell and the Voidoids was a golden opportunity to get right back in that saddle. I figured that anybody writing it up would give me some credit for having the cheek to come back within a year for the re-match.

Mid-December I was back in London for the first leg of the tour. Richard Hell was housed aboard Jake Riviera's houseboat in Chelsea Harbour while I'd been accommodated amid the belle époque splendour of the Russell Hotel in Bloomsbury. It would later go down the nick for a bit and lose some of its magic (Evie and I stayed there recently, and the windows were really draughty. We also had issues around the inadequate water management; I mean, if you're only there for one night you don't really want to be spending it with the plumber), but back then it was a terrific joint; no two rooms were the same shape. I had all sorts of people coming in and out, delivering narcotics at all hours of the fucking day and night. I think that's when I first made contact with Jackie Genova in Stoke Newington, who would later become my driver-cum-supplier. Jackie Genova was this Italian Cockney kid; great-looking but tiny, tiny. He looked like a miniature Keith Richards. He had a fucking huge Harley-Davidson, so there was tiny Jackie Genova riding around on this massive bike. He had loads of customers and all sorts of rock and roll connections, so I probably got his number via Eddie Chin of The Tourists, the first band to feature Annie Lennox, later of Eurythmics. Jackie Genova had known Eddie for ages.

Punk was taken extremely seriously at the time, and Declan's lyrics were very arcane and carried certain literary reference points. There was room for reflection in his particular style. Unusually, he dealt with adult themes; he was after all married with a child and a job at Elizabeth Arden in North Acton when he wrote 'Alison', an intimate song tinged with a level of regret unavailable to most teenagers. To me, it really stood out because most other punk rockers were eighteen and didn't know anybody who 'had a husband now'.

Richard Hell also enjoyed a degree of literary gravitas. Before his recent reinvention and the adoption of his new surname (inspired by Arthur Rimbaud) he had co-founded Television with his pal Tom Miller (now Tom Verlaine). The seventeen-year-old Richard Lester Meyers had dropped out of school in Virginia and moved to New York to realise his literary ambitions. He had co-created and published a literary magazine, set up his own publishing venture, worked as a packer at Strand Books and Cinemabilia, and been published in various magazines from *Rolling Stone* to the New Directions *Annuals* – all before he was twenty-one already. He and Tom Verlaine also invented an alter ego, a non-existent poet called Theresa Stern, and published a slim volume of poetry by her under the title *Wanna Go Out*. They told everyone that the reason Ms Stern never showed up to any public readings was because she kept having abortions. If you want to know more, read Richard's brilliant autobiography *I Dreamed I Was a Very Clean Tramp*.

Sandwiched between such lyrical giants, I didn't want to be perceived as some kind of light-relief niche act. Generally, I liked it to be known that humour was a major part of my routine, but this was my one chance to get, well, not serious exactly, but, you know . . .

As the opening act, usually taking the stage at 8.30pm, I had thirty-five minutes, which was a long set on a tour like that – enough time to hit the audience with my best shots. It was a chance to hone and develop my performance, and make it a real act. That's when I wrote 'Beasley Street', 'Thirty-Six Hours', and 'Chickentown'. These were proper punk poems, light on their feet with a sort of social edge, not necessarily funny, and without any specific geographical reference points. The template for 'Beasley Street', for example, was Camp Street in Salford, but anyone could identify with the imagery and atmosphere because every town has that sort of area.

Sometimes you get hit with an idea out of left field, and a lot of times I get the last line of a poem first. That's what happened with 'Beasley Street'. The inspiration came from the titular song of the 1933 Busby Berkeley musical *42nd Street*, starring Ruby Keeler and Dick Powell, which finishes off with the lines:

Naughty, bawdy
Gaudy, sporty
Forty-second Street

Big clunky rhymes building up to the big production finish. So I thought, what's the reverse of that? How best to convey the opulent squalor of my erstwhile neighbourhood? If I'd called the poem 'Camp Street', however, it might have been misinterpreted, so I needed a credible street name. Streets are normally named after illustrious citizens, and that's where the jockey Scobie Breasley came in. I took his surname, knocked off the 'R', the better to obviate any potential litigation, and then, working backwards, the poem seemed to write itself. This is the prosaic machinery that hopefully gives rise to the poetical masterpiece. That's the plan, anyway. It's all about getting an angle.

We did seven nights on the trot at the Dominion, including Christmas Eve. I copped three and a half grams of Chinese rocks on Christmas Day, the better to avoid a cold-turkey dinner, and the tour resumed after Boxing Day, with shows in Brighton,

Portsmouth, Bath, and Canterbury before the New Year. It was relentless. Jake Riviera worked us hard, and inevitably tempers occasionally got frayed. That said, I always got on great with Declan and his band, the Attractions, namely Bruce Thomas, Steve 'Nieve' Nason, and Pete Thomas. Bruce, their terrific bass player, and I got along particularly well, bonding over any mutual obsessions.

What Declan and I had in common was the presupposition of mass literacy. Generally, people who liked me liked him and vice versa, and we would go on to work a lot with each other. As his lyrics would suggest, he was quite intense, intelligent, and thoughtful, but like so many people of that nature, he also had a great sense of humour and was very easy company; he wasn't always *on*. His net has always been wide – you know, eclectic. He and I shared an interest in books, movies, comedians, and, unusually for the time and our punk milieu, the Great American Songbook.

Of course, he had the advantage of his musical background: like Bernard Manning with the Oscar Rabin Band, Declan's dad Ross MacManus sang with the Joe Loss Orchestra as part of a close-harmony pop vocal trio with Larry Gretton and Rose Brennan. Ross was the balladeer. Declan had grown up in that world, so he had an intrinsic understanding of every corner of American musical history: country, showtunes, the blues, the crooners, soul, and of course, rock and roll. He would sing 'My Funny Valentine' at the sound check, and would often throw one of his old favourites into the main act, such as 'I Stand Accused', a hit for The Merseybeats in 1965. Plus, let's not forget that Elvis Costello was the last person to feature Chet Baker on vinyl, playing the trumpet solo on 'Shipbuilding'. Richard Hell and the Voidoids were the icing on the cake. I was obviously in awe of the whole CBGB axis, and fascinated by that world inhabited by these people who were friends of Patti Smith, The Ramones, and the remnants of the New York Dolls. These people were on actual speaking terms with Lou Reed – the Voidoids' lead guitarist Bob Quine had even played on one of his records.

Along with Tom Verlaine, Richard was a founder member of Television, the first group on the New York scene to play at CBGB. He had then been employed by Johnny Thunders in an early incarnation of the Heartbreakers. Richard was the guy who created that whole carefully constructed razor blades, ripped-up clothes, and safety pins look with the *coupe sauvage* hairstyle: apparently Malcolm McLaren copped the entire punk-rock aesthetic from him when he'd been over in New York trying to manage the New York Dolls.

Most of that tour we were all travelling on the same bus. For me, it was the full immersion course: the sexed-up, drugged-up, rockin' rollin' roadshow – which wasn't always as fabulous as I'm making it sound. For a start, when I say drugged up, I mean within reason. Elvis Costello and The Attractions were basically booze hounds: juice heads with a side order of speed and/or cocaine. Richard Hell and I, on the other hand, being bounden slaves in the trammels of opium, had to keep quiet about it. Jake and the Stiff Records people were mainly ex-hippy types, so if there'd been the slightest suggestion of heroin we would have been instantly sacked. Richard had only got the gig after he convinced Jake that he'd cleaned up, so even though we were icky sick with the agonising pangs of frustrated drug hunger, no matter how bad it got we just had to suck it up. As I've said, back then you could be banged up for possession of the smallest amount – Hugh Cornwell from The Stranglers went inside for just a ten-quid bag. He was sentenced to eight weeks in Pentonville; they let him out after five, but even so, who needs it?

I didn't want Jake to know I was using. I figured nobody knew – I was smiling through the tears and doing a very good job of covering it up – but of course they did. Perhaps it was the frequent visits to the chemists to buy up their entire stocks of codeine linctus and Stadol, and glug glug, that gave the game away. Richard and I were permanently full of all sorts of shit we didn't usually take, which just about kept the edge off. This, coupled with copious amounts of amphetamines, was the only way we could keep well enough to do our thing on a nightly basis.

It wasn't all horrible, though. In fact, a lot of the time it was pretty funny. It was always a pleasure to watch the Voidoids' set, for example, because they got a worse time than I did. They were used to it, though, because about fourteen months previously they'd been on tour in the UK with The Clash in their 'I'm so Bored with the USA' period. As a New York band, the Voidoids had been hired knowingly, a nuance entirely wasted on the more meathead section of the crowds. They swore they'd never be back, especially after the spitting, so Jake Riviera had done well to persuade them. There was a little bit of residual hostility from some audiences, but if anything, it only spurred them on. They seemed to thrive on animosity, that was one of their great strengths.

The tour bus was state of the art, all mod cons. It even had a video player with a big screen. VHS was very new, and hardly anybody had a player at home, so to have that kind of entertainment system at our fingertips was just *wow!* We'd sit on the bus and watch old episodes of *Kojak*, which at the time were not that old, actually.

Richard Hell had brought a VHS of *T.A.M.I. Show* from the States. We knew about it, of course, but I'd never had the chance to watch it in its entirety. It was a 1964 film of a concert held over two days at the Santa Monica Civic Auditorium featuring performances by a list of transatlantic rock and roll and R&B greats. As far as pop music on film goes, *T.A.M.I. Show* has no equal. It's just so great on so many levels, everybody live on stage at the time they were at their absolutely fabulous best, all in front of a multi-ethnic American teenage audience got up in the Mary Quant look, jiving away with their five-point dos, and featuring go-go dancers in white-leather kinky boots. It just nails the period.

Anybody and everybody you can think of is there: the Byrds, The Beach Boys, Chuck Berry, Gerry and the Pacemakers, Lesley Gore, The Barbarians, Billy J. Kramer and The Dakotas, (Smokey Robinson and) The Miracles, The Supremes, Jan and Dean, The Stones doing 'Time is on My Side', and the Ronettes in those gorgeous stylised Mao Tse-Tung pantsuits with mandarin collars and a little kick flare at the hems. Scintillating. Everybody is hitting you with their best shots, and then right at the end of the show, what could possibly top all that? James Brown and the Famous Flames, that's who. After a line-up like that, there he is: James Brown in his finest hour doing 'Please, Please, Please'. He's wearing a black and white houndstooth jacket-and-waistcoat combo, with black slacks and flamenco boots, falling into the splits and immediately springing right back up, snapping his high heels together: death-defying, yet he makes it look like nothing. Then into that ermine-cloak-imperial-crown-elastic-band-encore routine with the cardiac specialist (white coat, stethoscope) begging him to desist for the sake of his health. You know, a man can only give so much before it becomes medically inadvisable.

There were loads of stories on the road, mainly because of Richard Hell. There was a strict 'No Chicks on the Bus' rule, which even Declan had to obey. Obviously, if they'd let Mrs MacManus on the bus everybody else would want their wife and/or girlfriend on it too, so it was right across the board. Everyone toed the line, except Richard – though to be fair, it wasn't his fault. He attracted stowaways; chicks were desperate to get next to the guy. He was the pin-up boy of punk, a professional dreamboat, pussy magnet to the stars, so naturally we were always finding women hiding in the luggage racks. He got the hard word from Jake on account of all this: 'Oi, Richard, you've got to do something about these boilers on the bus. You shouldn't encourage it.' That was unjust: on the contrary, Richard had that sexiest of qualities, utter indifference, and as a result there were females up and down the country getting into actual cat fights over the dude.

He had that New Yoick street-punk way of speaking, and would lay on the accent real thick with the ladies. But he actually grew up in Lexington, Kentucky, the 'Athens of the West', the 'horse capital of the world', and when he wasn't at work he'd lapse into this bluegrass cowboy drawl that made him even sexier offstage than on. Fucking Hell.

Richard and the other Voidoids – guitarists Robert Quine and Ivan Julian, plus drummer Frank Mauro – were bookish, cerebral, delinquent. They had some sort of Brainiac credibility that the West Coast sun-worshipping drug-downing hippy wasters simply couldn't compete with.

Richard was a fellow poet, as I've said. Ivan Julian had studied music theory and was a fellow Edgar Allan Poe fanatic. At the age of seventeen, he'd toured with The Foundations – you may remember them from such top ten hits as 'Baby Now That I've Found You' and 'Build Me Up Buttercup'.

Robert Quine, in particular, was a great source of fascination, above and beyond his undoubted genius as a guitar player. For a start, there was the male-pattern baldness that established the Voidoids' position as an ongoing adult concern. Bob was a virtuoso musician who later played on a few Lou Reed singles, including 'I Love You, Suzanne'. He was an intriguing character with an incredibly diverse range of reference. He had earned a law degree from Earlham College 'out of inertia' and wrote tax-law textbooks, for example. He had great taste in music, and cited many people as influences; he was very interested in his contemporaries and people who had led him to take up the guitar in the first place. He dropped all the great names: James Burton, Lonnie Mack,

Link Wray, Steve Cropper, and, especially, Mickey 'Guitar' Baker, the Mickey half of Mickey and Sylvia, responsible for the 1956 classic 'Love is Strange'.

In show business, male-pattern baldness has always been an unmitigated tragedy, something to 'come to terms with', or 'dealt with' by way of prosthetics, weaves, toupees, beanie hats, and finally, the barcode comb over. Given the care and loving attention I squander on my own thatch, what with the unguents and pomades, I suppose this affliction has always held some terror for me, thus anyone who manages to pull off the naked skull with some degree of elan can only be admired. That said, there has never been a better time for a guy to go bald than now, thanks largely to the social heavy-lifting undertaken by the late Robert Quine and other notable slaphead heroes like Yul Brynner, Telly 'Star of TV's *Kojak*' Savalas, and Cyril Jordan from the Flamin' Groovies. Oh, and don't forget Mark Strong, Stanley Tucci, Billy Zane, and Michael Stipe. Thanks to these people, baldness today is a legitimate lifestyle option.

Bob Quine used to kvetch about the Voidoids and how they banned the preppy clothes he loved to wear; his Brooks Brothers button-down Oxfords and the Florsheim loafers ran counter to the Voidoid position as feral undernourished urban saboteurs. They were always trying to get him into a leather jacket, but be reasonable. They finally agreed on a clingy black turtleneck, black tapered trousers, and a blazer made out of black alpaca. Exquisite, but it made Bob look kind of beat, with or without his Ray-Ban Wayfarers. Still, you wouldn't really have called him a punk because he was a little bit too old. Nevertheless, now all in black, with his baldness and general air of jittery urban paranoia, he added a welcome sinister edge to the proceedings.

Nobody took liberties with Robert Quine. He had an unabashed misanthropic aura that I found enviable; if approached by a mendicant, you could see him looking for somewhere to run. I'm from the inner city myself, and I've never seen this antisocial quality worn with such easy grace.

It was when we got to Edinburgh, however, that we found out who he *really* was. Up until that point, he'd been Mr Sanguine. The minute he got across Waverley Bridge, he turned into the archetypal American tourist abroad. He put on his beloved powder-blue Brooks Brothers Oxford button-down shirt and suede sport coat, a pair of stout walking brogues, and his Burberry mackintosh, and went striding up the Royal Mile, a state-of-the-art camera draped about his neck, looking for his family tartan, giving it the full haggis supper: 'Say, I'm a quarter Scottish myself!'

I went with him. He signed us up for the full guided tour of the Castle, and he fucking loved it. I don't normally go for that sort of thing; I've seen *The Black Shield of Falworth* starring Tony Curtis and that'll do me, but it was good to see him genuinely charged with enthusiasm for once. He'd got some energy from somewhere, and was darting around taking photographs of Lochaber axes, Highland broadswords and Mons Meg. You know what Americans can be like about that sort of shit: 'Hey, Johnny, would you look at that suit of armour!'

Meanwhile, Richard had his own agenda. He'd come out to eat with us and so on, but he'd often go off on his own to an art gallery or something. Or as it was Edinburgh, maybe he was hoping for some kind of dope connection, as was I.

Before I knew it, it was the Glasgow Apollo and the return of the comeback kid. Emboldened by a fast connection in nearby Cardonald, I wasn't taking 'Fuck off!' for an answer, and my diffident charm paid off good style. It could have been like *Groundhog* déjà vu all over again, you know, a bit samey, but thank God, thank God, thank God Almighty, crikey, I slew those mother-fuckers to death.

I was so glad I was able to return to Glasgow so quickly and nail the Apollo, rather than having it hanging over my head as the playhouse of the damned. That's a real big place to go under, so the redemption of that night was priceless. Ever since then, my Glasgow audiences have been some of the wildest in the world. It's a wonderful city full of beautiful people.

Looking back on it now, I can see that although I like to think I've led a charmed life, I never took the safe route. I always thought, it might not be good right now, but it's going to pay off later; this gets me that. And every time, I've been proven right in the fullness of time.

Chapter Fifty

THE RUSSELL HOTEL

January 30, 1979 and we were back in London for the closing night of the Armed Forces tour at the Hammersmith Odeon. Having been on the road for most of the previous year without a break, Elvis Costello and The Attractions were plum tuckered out. For me, on the other hand, it was an invigorating finale to what had turned out to be an important point in my career – the tour that introduced me to ever greater numbers of the Great British public. As *NME* reviewer Charles Shaar Murray put it, 'Showing no strain and feeling no pain, he bounded out on stage in his red tux to motormouth the audience [. . .] and grabbed his moment with the zeal and alacrity of a man at the peak of his powers.'

Later there was the traditional end-of-tour party, a chance to let our hair down and also to say our goodbyes to the American contingent, who would soon be flying back to New York. It would be sad to see them go, but I had other things on my mind.

As the party was just getting started, Richard and I were standing opposite each other, me saying, 'Well, I'd love to stay, but I've got to go.' Richard likewise seemed to have ants in his pants, 'No, sorry Johnny, sorry about the abrupt departure but I gotta go too.' And that was that; we went our separate ways.

Forty minutes later, however, when I arrived to cop off at Jackie Genova's, who should appear from behind a door but Richard. He'd beaten me to it, and we could have shared a cab.

Now that the tour was over, I had no pressing need to get back to Manchester. Or rather, I would have found any excuse *not* to go back to Manchester, because that would mean a reunion with the ballerina, who by now would have her dancing feet firmly under the Maguire table.

Our relationship had got a bit slack long before I'd left for London, what with the VD unpleasantness, but now there was an added complication: I'd since got involved with a young trainee journalist called Iris (or she got involved with me, as she would probably tell it) whom I'd met when I appeared at the Africa Centre in Covent Garden just before the Dominion shows with Elvis Costello in December, and we were now an item. I was going to have to come clean and break up with my then girlfriend, and I couldn't face it. Plus there was the fact that the minute we were no longer involved romantically, she would be out of the Maguires' place on her ear. I just couldn't go home to that, so I moved into the Russell Hotel with Iris, abandoning the ex and her cat to their fate. I resolved to make everything OK at some indeterminate date in the hopefully not too distant future.

I was exhausted from the rigours of the road and the enforced withdrawals, so when I finally copped a quarter-ounce of Chinese White off Jackie Genova, I didn't have the energy or the inclination to look for somewhere permanent to live. Iris and I spent my entire wages from the tour shacked up in the Russell Hotel, living like royalty, dining on room service and ordering in the other necessities. Every few nights, when the mood took me, I'd ask reception to move us into another room with another view. I think that's when I got the bug for staying in posh hotels. I got quite used to the lifestyle – and the staff got used to having me around, and to all these sinister Turks coming in at all hours of the night and leaving envelopes in my pigeon hole. Luxury; pure unashamed luxury.

Reluctantly, I had to leave the hotel every now and again to fulfil my business engagements. After the tour I was in demand; the venues and gigs got bigger, there were more of them, and now I was headlining. I also started to get reviews and press attention outside the UK, and because my Armed Forces appearances had gone so well, Jake Riviera and Elvis Costello invited me along on the Scandinavian leg of their European tour in late summer.

In early February I appeared at the South London Polytechnic with Joy Division as support, and at the end of the month I headlined at the Nottingham Playhouse, again with Joy Division. Unfortunately, however, they were late, so I opened for them. It was a freezing cold night, and by the time they finally arrived, I'd barely managed to warm up the audience. They went straight on and played a short set, including 'Transmission', 'She's Lost Control', and 'New Dawn Fades'. The sound was bad, so nobody listened. Joy Division, all in black and white and totally stationary, remained anonymous for the entire set: no introductions, no chat between numbers. I then came back on and did my main act. We later found out that when I'd introduced the band, it had been generally misheard as 'Geordie Vision', thus bringing about the mass indifference one might expect.

The band's bassist Peter Hook later clarified the reason for their late arrival: Chas Banks, their road guy and Hookie's cousin, had borrowed a PA from Sad Café only to have it written off in a highway pile-up on the way to collect the guys. Chas had finally arrived covered in cuts and bruises after crawling from the wreckage.

At some point soon thereafter, I went to Ireland on a seven-date tour with Dr Feelgood minus Wilko Johnson. On about the second night, in Cork or somewhere, I was coming off a stage for which a rickety chair stood in for a set of steps. This was pre-health and safety. It was dark. The chair wasn't secure and I fell, fracturing my wrist. I had to go straight from the venue to the nearest nursing convent, where one of the sisters plastered me up. She asked, 'What is it you do?' I said, 'Well, I'm a poet, sister.' She replied: 'Oh, you are. Would you be after reciting some of it?' 'You wouldn't approve of my poetry, sister,' I told her. 'It's very rude, and I wouldn't want to befoul your ears.' I think they appreciated my reticence in this regard.

The sister did a perfectly good job, but she was anxious that I get an X-ray, so I told her I would be in Belfast the next day. 'Oh, you'll be all right there,' she said. 'They've the best doctors in the world.' For obvious reasons. This was at the height of the Troubles. The next day I was in the outpatients' department in the Royal Victoria Hospital, expecting some guy to come in any minute looking to get his face stitched back on.

We were staying at the Europa Hotel in Belfast city centre, famously the most bombed hotel in Europe at that time. The Feelgood gang were all proper round-the-clock schickers, whereas I was a fucked-up druggy. I was informed one too many times by the late Mr Lee Brilleaux of the hotel's bomb-scare policy. Apparently, if you had to vacate the building due to one of the all-too frequent terror alerts, it was free champagne all the way.

I'm no detective, well, again, not unless you count that thirty years I spent working for the Scotland Yard Forensic Division, but I could see where this was fucking going. One of these cunts was sure to ring up hotel security with a bogus threat, so I didn't bother getting into my pyjamas, but just waited for the inevitable alarm to go off. Sure enough, I wasn't disappointed. Lee Brilleaux, Gypie Mayo, and the Wedding Guests from Hell didn't seem inordinately upset about this chain of potentially life-threatening events. Put it this way, they hadn't changed into their pyjamas either. While everybody else at the muster station was inadequately draped in their night attire, shivering their bollocks off in the freezing Belfast drizzle, we were in our Crombies and scarves, impatiently waiting for the all-clear, and the promised tidal wave of shampoo.

The part of CBS I was signed to had now changed their name to Epic, and wanting to cash in on my recently heightened profile, decided to put out a live album in the summer. Having just returned from Ireland, I named it after Charles Haughey's 'Walking Back to Happiness' campaign – a fitness drive initiated by the future prime minister. It had also been the title of a Helen Shapiro hit in the early Sixties.

Walking Back to Happiness was recorded live at the Marquee in Wardour Street, and featured numbers including 'Gabardine Angus', 'Majorca', and 'Twat'. A lot of people think the final track is called 'Gimmix Play Loud', but actually it's just 'Gimmix'. The 'play loud' was simply a recommendation added at my insistence – as was often the case with Martin Hannett's records, I thought it was too quiet, thus the user instructions to crank up the volume. Anyway, whatever my thoughts on the production values, the pre-release of 'Gimmix' as an orange, triangular 10-inch single was a UK top forty hit in March.

Delightful as it was to have some chart success, I was more concerned about getting a publishing deal for *Ten Years in an Open Necked Shirt*. Epic were only interested, like everyone else, in putting a scissors-and-paste job together, and fine, fair enough, anything they said went. In any case, they weren't interested in books: they were a record company. That's where the John Cooper Clarke *Directory* came in: a rough 48pp tongue-in-cheek paperback in the style of a Thomson's local telephone book, deliberately defaced and featuring a very few of my best-known numbers, including 'I Married a Monster from Outer Space', 'Post War Glamour Girls', and 'Psycle Sluts'.

It was a quick exploitation pamphlet really, rather than a full-on poetry collection, but that said, it was a good thing, because it was put together by a terrific graphic artist, the late Barney Bubbles, a fabulous vinyl album cover designer,* and was copiously illustrated in black and white throughout, with photographs by Kevin Cummins, Tom Sheehan, and Paul Slattery.

It was originally released by the CBS/Epic publishing arm Omnibus Press, and then, as a sweetener, it was given away free with every copy of my third album, *Snap, Crackle & Bop*. Now it's a rare collectors' item, and goes for three figures on eBay. If I were you, I'd snap 'em all up. In a thousand years you could be a millionaire.

Good as this post-punk graphic-design marvel was, *Directory* was not the volume of poetry I wanted to be remembered for, so the pursuit of a publisher was another good reason to stay in London.

After a couple of blissful months in the Russell Hotel, however, my money eventually ran out and I went back to couch-surfing, at Bernie Davis's in Streatham or, more often than not, chez Judy Totton near Westbourne Grove. Judy had left CBS to form her own PR company, taking The Only Ones and me with her, and very quickly attracting high-earning clients like Status Quo, Toyah Wilcox, and, for a while, The Clash. Later on, she was hired by some of the big rock acts including Kiss, INXS, The Kinks, and Rory Gallagher. I was fortunate to be with her, because she had great contacts and we were all in it together; Judy could use her big-name clients as leverage, but more importantly she was a class act and a real mensch to put up with me as a semi-permanent house guest.

The Only Ones were and are one of my favourite English beat combos. We did quite a few shows together. I spent a lot of time at the Perretts' place in Forest Hill: not only did we have a publicity

---

* For further examples of the great Barney Bubbles's work, I can highly recommend *Reasons to be Cheerful: The Life and Work of Barney Bubbles* by Paul Gorman: the definitive publication.

agent in common, we also had a mutual interest in pooling our resources in order to procure increasing amounts of dope for smaller amounts of money. I had my own connections, of course. I had contacts all over town, in Kent even: distance no object.

So now I'm eating out all the time and going to all sorts of shows with Judy, but after a while, I figured that I couldn't impose on her indefinitely; we got on great, I was doing my bit, and she never made me feel unwelcome, but having me staying at her house must have been like taking her work home. Iris was living with her dad's ex-wife in a house in Pimlico, which had a basement apartment with a nice skylight onto the street. She suggested I move in. I agreed.

In June, I went on a mini-tour to coincide with the release of *Walking Back to Happiness* along with two support bands, Fashion and Joy Division. We played gigs at Eric's, Liverpool, the Royalty Theatre in London, and the Nuffield Theatre at the University of Lancaster, ending up at the Free Trade Hall in Manchester.

As a trainee journalist assigned to the Westminster Press, Iris was obliged to work for whichever of their roster of regional newspapers she was assigned to. One of their regions was Bermuda. It was either the *Bermuda Star* or the *Stevenage Gazette*. At first I was, '*Bermuda Star*! *Bermuda Star*!' There was, however, the matter of the non-existent dope connection, so Stevenage it had to be. That's when I finally got a glimpse of the Shredded Wheat factory with its profusion of windows maximising the solar illumination of the workplace, and the grain silos.

We lived in Stevenage for a couple of years. It was leafy, close to London, and quite revolutionary in that it didn't have any traffic lights, just loads of roundabouts, underpasses, and flyovers. I immediately recognised the centre of the New Town as the setting for *Here We Go Round the Mulberry Bush*, the charming Swinging Sixties comedy starring Barry Evans, Judy Geeson, and Adrienne Posta.

Soon after we got there, one of Iris's early assignments was covering the Knebworth Festival for the *Gazette*. Knebworth was a big deal, at least as big as Reading is now, and only about ten minutes from our house in a taxi. The main attraction that year was Led Zeppelin, but I was more interested in the New Barbarians featuring Keith Richards and his mate, the pre-Stones Ronnie Wood. This guaranteed the attendance of Nick Kent, so I thought we might be able to cop without having to go all the way into Central London for once.

Nick was a mad Stones fan. Pre-punk, the *NME* had paid for him to go on the road with them. He had a major man-crush on Keith, who once threw up over Nick's leather jacket, and he'd never washed it since. To this day, his leathers carry the micro-remnants of Keith's second-hand shepherd's pie.

Anyway, we went to Knebworth and it was great, for one reason and one reason only: yes, Nick Kent was there, and yes we scored, but the thing that really blew me away was Chas and Dave. It was the first time I'd seen them live. I thought, 'Fucking hell. I pity the fools who have to follow this!' It was 'see you later' as I left Iris and Nick to deal with the New Barbarians: I had the dope, so I bought a bag of doughnuts and went home.

Mid-August, I was off on a whistle-stop tour of Holland, Norway, Denmark, and Sweden, opening for Elvis Costello and The Attractions. It was my first visit to Scandinavia, and my abiding memory of this excursion was that after a short walk through the freezing Nordic streets, a man gets kind of hungry. I was informed by the promoters that a great feast had been prepared in honour of our arrival, and sure enough there was a table about a mile long, groaning with comestibles. I walked the length of that table, looking for something hot, sustaining, and preferably delicious, but on that whole mile-long table not only was there nothing hot, everything on offer was actively cold: platters of raw fish on a bed of ice. What the fuck? Imagine coming home from a hard day at the fjords only to be offered raw fish, pickled this, frozen that, marinated the other, *nothing* cooked. Not even a potato. It was unbelievable. Plus, the only liquid refreshment was a choice of iced water or bottles of chilled Jolly Cola.

Like every self-deprecating Englishman, I had always thought that the food of foreign lands was infinitely more flavoursome than our own. This may be true of the Mediterranean, and the far reaches of the crumbling empire, but the food of Northern Europe, with its Calvinist aversion to flavour, made even British institutional cuisine seem positively sumptuous. Holland: cheese for breakfast? Now that ain't right. Germany: the invention of vegetarianism and the outdoor life. No thanks. Then there's Sweden. My one visit to Ikea left only the olfactory memory of the meatballs. It's school dinners, really; they're not even particularly spicy. Meanwhile in Denmark, Plumrose chopped ham with pork. Norway, sild. Almost, but not quite, sardines. You see where I'm going with this?

Dope wasn't going to be a problem, however. Just before I left England, I had got hold of a load of DF118s from a dentist. (DF118s, aka dihydrocodeine – opioid painkillers available only on prescription.) I'd got them on account of a tooth abscess, along with a medical cover-note saying I was entitled to have them in my possession. I had enough to exceed the stated dose – one always overstated the case, and thus got more than one needed. I probably also told the doctor I was going to be in Scandinavia for seven months or something. So as long as I didn't operate any machinery, everything would be fine.

I was sorted, but the rest of the guys couldn't even get a drink. I don't know what it's like now, but back then Scandinavia seemed to have stringent measures in place which obviated any chance of casual drunkenness. A family wedding would involve an application three months in advance to a government official, in triplicate, just to get a single case of champagne. Other than that, forget about it. Off-licences didn't seem to exist.

Maybe it was their enforced sobriety, but the others in our party were beginning to lose their temper. The only booze available in Copenhagen was at the pre-show dinner in the hotel restaurant. It was like a baronial castle with flag floors, vaulted ceilings, chandeliers, a walk-in fireplace, and extensive wine cellars. We dined in the library. We had a whole pigeon each, and for the first time, for me anyway, a bottle of wine that cost three figures.

Jake Riviera was quite the oenophile, a gentleman connoisseur with a flourishing cellar of his own. Scandinavia is not known as a centre of viniculture, but Jake was in possession of a case of green wine that he'd got from somewhere or other. He obviously foresaw some desperate measures from the forcibly ensobered band members, so the safekeeping of the wine became my responsibility — as a drug addict, I was considered a safe pair of hands in that regard. As he hid the booze under my bed, I was sworn to secrecy and told that it wouldn't be ready to drink for another five years — not only would it not taste very nice, but its ingestion could have violent gastro-intestinal consequences. If I knew anything about addiction, though, if those guys couldn't get a drink after the show, they'd be necking the Aqua Velva aftershave or whatever the fuck. Sure enough, Bruce and Pete Thomas came a-knocking around 3am. 'Where is it?' they demanded. I denied all knowledge. They bribed me with cocaine, but that not being particularly my drug of choice, I stood firm. They nevertheless went about searching the room for somewhere to chop out some lines. Every surface in this castle was rough-hewn, hammered, pitted, textured, or covered in elk fur, even in the bathrooms. In desperation, they must have looked under my bed, where of course they unearthed Jake's precious vino stash, some of which they instantly absorbed. Thus emboldened, the subject of the nose powder re-presented itself.

To that end, I removed a massive glass-covered painting from the wall above my bed. Ever the hygiene freak, I insisted that the glass be washed clean and rendered germ-free before any lines were hacked out. Barely had we started the sterilisation process, however, than there was a great big crack and the glass shattered. We managed to get a couple of lines chopped out on a flat, undamaged area, and then looked upon the inadvertently vandalised artwork. Concerned about the welfare of the cleaning staff, we decided to deglaze the picture before putting it back on the wall. It had to be rendered safe: after all, I had to sleep underneath it.

There were splinters. Blood was shed. Then there was the matter of what to do with the bits and pieces. Finally, we agreed to wrap them all up in two bath robes and a bed sheet and put them out on the balcony, to the point where only an idiot could injure themselves. Even so, we thought we'd better put a warning notice on it. After much deliberation on the appropriate wording, I wrote on the sheet in felt tip: 'Beware: Shards.'

Next morning at breakfast, the physical condition of Bruce and Pete told Jake all there was to know. He wasn't happy. 'I don't mind a laugh,' he kept telling me, 'and it isn't just the money. But the thing is, it wasn't ready for drinking. Now they're going to get sick, and it's all *your* fault.'

Chapter Fifty-One

NEW YORK, NEW YORK

New York City, gateway to the Americas. And yes, a wonderful town. In late August, within days of getting back from Scandinavia, I was packing my bags again for my first trip to the Big Apple. Again, I had Jake Riviera to thank for this. He had organised a guest appearance at the New York Palladium with Rockpile and the David Johansen Group.

I was staying at the Gramercy Park Hotel, but after an eight-hour flight, my first priority on arrival had to do with the attainment of heroin, or its closest relative. I was fortunate in that everybody I knew in New York was a junkie. Armed with only Richard Hell's address, I took a cab to the Lower East Side and showed up at his place.

Richard was on some kind of drying-out regime, and understandably didn't want to get involved in any dope deals. I put out some feelers, and of course everybody was anxious to help, but these people all had one thing in common: they were junkies. Hand them any money and I'd never see them again. Not this trip, anyway. Give anybody an inch and they'll take a fucking mile; that went double for junkies, perhaps the most liberty-taking demographic of them all. There was nothing for it but to make the short excursion to Avenue A and get it myself.

In the early Eighties, before Rudy Giuliani cleaned it all up, the whole of New York was deemed extremely dangerous. At the time, I think it had the worst violent fatality rate of any city in the world. The subway was full of murderous junkies with guns and was patrolled by a self-appointed paramilitary vigilante gang called the Guardian Angels, to whom everybody was extremely grateful. Alphabet City, indeed much of the Lower East Side, was a no-go area, with garbage piling up in the streets, potholes five feet deep, burning cars in the middle of the road. Only an idiot would have gone anywhere near Avenue A, but a junkie's gotta do what a junkie's gotta do.

I was advised that it would be madness to enter into this without some form of protection and to that end, Roberta Bayley, a neighbour of Richard's who had seamlessly morphed into my girlfriend, put me in touch with this rich chick called Audrey. Roberta was and is a hot-shot photographer, the premier chronicler of punk, responsible for all The Ramones album covers and, along with 'Legs' McNeil, the incomparable *Punk* magazine.

Her pal Audrey was in possession of a Sears & Roebuck fucking Harrington & Richardson .22 special revolver. I put down a $300 deposit on the revolver, returnable only when I handed it back – undischarged: 'If this gets fired,' said Audrey, 'I don't want it back. You get rid of it, and I keep the three hundred dollars.' Forget about it – I didn't want to use it. It was a deterrent, and in order to deter people they had to see it, so I was advised to carry it in my hand at all times. That way I was less likely to panic and murder somebody. Nobody wants to die, not even for dope. But you know, at the same time, do you want the gear or not? The idea of *not* having anything was inconceivable. I'm no tough guy, quite the reverse, but what is more dangerous than a hot-headed coward with a gun?

You bought the gear in dime bags, which weren't a dime, but ten dollars. Everybody I knew, even people with flourishing rock careers, would make the trip every day, just for twenty dollars' worth; they would never buy a bulk quantity. I didn't fancy having to repeat this routine any more than was strictly essential, so I took a hundred dollars with me, which is a lot of money for a junkie.

Richard gave me the address, and I took a cab and arrived at this tall foreboding tenement building; the cabbie knowingly asked if he should wait for me. My connection was on the seventh floor and there were no elevators, just a seemingly endless dank, unlit staircase. On every landing a clutch of impoverished sick local junkies were skulking around, just waiting for somebody like me to show up. They were either going to get my money on the way up, or my newly acquired dope on the way down.

Gun or no gun, I was shitting my pants every step of the way. After all, it was death or Rikers Island. I finally made it up to the seventh floor without incident, and knocked on a door with a sliding hatch. On the other side of the door was a thirteen-year-old Puerto Rican kid with a bucket full of wraps. I handed over the century, received ten bags in return, made a rapid descent, and then, thank God, thank God, thank God Almighty, stepped out into the dazzling afternoon sunlight and into the idling yellow cab, pocketing the gun as I did so.

Fucking hell. That wasn't terrifying or anything!

I was in the Gramercy Park Hotel for about three weeks. I also spent one night in the Chelsea Hotel – this being widely recognised as part of the Manhattan total immersion experience – but it was all scuttling cockroaches, clanking pipes, and shuddering radiators on account of somebody three floors up taking a shower in the middle of the night. I preferred it at the more upmarket Gramercy Park, a great hotel in every respect, even though it was also riddled with supersize roaches. Roberta had taught me how to deal with them, though – every time I went back to the room, I switched on the light and threw one of my boots into the middle of the floor. You could see them scuttling for the skirting boards, each one the size of a tortoise.

Before the Palladium date on the Monday evening, I had the weekend to discover the city of the Bowery Boys and *West Side Story* at my leisure. The Gramercy was a short walk from Richard Hell's apartment. Richard was as arty and effete a young New Yorker as you could get, and typically had been first in line for cable TV, so what with the resultant infinite channel list *and* his unparalleled VHS collection, this was home entertainment heaven.

Me, Roberta, and a bunch of Richard's pals gathered one night to watch *Force of Evil*, directed by Abraham Polonsky, starring John Garfield. During the course of the evening Richard asked me a surprising question: 'Hey, Johnny, you watch a lot of English television, right? Did you ever hear of a guy called Benny Hill?' – you know, like he was introducing me to some iconoclastic underground cult figure or something. Whatever you think of Benny Hill, there's no American equivalent, and the New York intelligentsia were crazy about the guy. Who knew he had this international reach? You wouldn't expect his British seaside post-card humour to travel that well, but actually he was no mere smut-peddler. He was a gifted impressionist (by which I don't mean Pierre-Auguste Renoir was losing any business; I obviously mean in the Bobby Davro sense of the term), and also a terrific song writer. You may remember him from such hits as 'Harvest of Love', 'Transistor Radio', and, of course, the haunting 'Ernie (The Fastest Milkman in the West)'. On his home turf, however, his career would soon be cruelly shattered by the likes of Ben Elton and Co.

The Palladium wasn't the best show I'd ever done: quite the reverse. I was muttering into a void. It was horrible, but hardly surprising really – they were a rock and roll crowd, that's all there was to it. Nick Lowe and Rockpile were one of Jake's acts who had followed him to Radar Records. They were a fabulous retro-rockabilly outfit, every one of them a star musician and every song a hit record. And I was already a big fan of the David Johansen Group, who I'd recently seen at the Russell Club in Manchester after buying his first album on Blue Sky Records. The gig may not have been my finest half-hour, but it paid for the trip and my accommodation, plus I'd wangled a couple of shows on the West Coast on the back of it.

Right after the show, David Johansen, who is a very erudite, poetry-loving gentleman, said to me, 'Hey, John, you're good, kid. But they don't know who you are.' He then took it upon himself to become my personal MC and helped me to sort out some club dates in Philadelphia and New York, notably at the Mudd Club, Hoorahs, and CBGB. Thankfully, these gigs went really well, owing to the fact that David gave me the big build-up. I can't thank him enough for that: if I had come back from New York with only failure to report, it would have broken my heart a lot more than Glasgow ever could.

The Mudd Club in TriBeCa was the ultra-poseurs' place with a seriously exclusive door policy. The dress code was ruthless, and people would hang around outside all night, begging the proprietors to let them in.

Hoorahs was a discotheque frequented by the more poppy end of American punk, and people like Willy DeVille, Kim Fowley, and Leee Black Childers were in my audience. It was a great night, not least because that's when I first met Ronnie Spector. She won't remember it, and I doubt I'd get a name-check in *her* memoirs, but, well, amazing. I hadn't seen even a photograph of her for years and years, and there she was at *my* gig. Then as now, she looked sensational.

If that wasn't exciting enough, next up was the legendary CBGB. The whole rock and roll scene there had long called to me. Ever since I'd first discovered The Ramones, it had been an ambition to visit the place, so to have ex-New York Doll David Johansen himself introducing my set was beyond fabulous. Everybody I was into was in the joint: Debbie Harry and Clem Burke out of Blondie, David Byrne, Johnny Thunders, Jerry Nolan, Richard's pal Tom Verlaine, 'Legs' McNeil, Steve Maas, Stiv Bators, and several members of the Dictators, to name but a few, and Roberta was there to rigidly police the prevalent door policy. I don't think they made a special point of it just because I was on, it was simply *their* scene. I was in love with those people already, so to have them in my audience was just sensational to the point where the Palladium could kiss my ass.

CBGB made much of being an utter khazi situated in the worst part of the impoverished New York of the day – the Bowery, synonymous with skid row, bums, losers. The male dress code was a mix of that Ramones leather jacket/blue jeans/juvenile delinquent gang uniform and the kind of menswear that ceased to be generally available circa 1967. The women were like The Shangri-Las revisited in a George A. Romero feature. Everybody was trying to look like some kind of messed-up cartoon character. After that first New York trip, for a while I started to look a bit more textbook punk. That was the nearest I've got to reinventing my look: I kept the slimline silhouette, but my hair got more fucked up and I got myself a leather biker jacket. It was a cast-off from Jackie Genova, so it fitted me perfectly. Call me Mr Neat and Tidy, but this was a real step in another dimension. It made sense, though: utilising hotel valet services every night in a touring situation was a luxury I couldn't keep up. The leather jacket was a tough, low-maintenance garment: a couple of drops of Dettol and simply wipe with a damp cloth.

In New York, I was constantly being mistaken for Stiv Bators. Stiv was the singer with the Dead Boys. Even his friends thought I was him. I didn't mind: the Dead Boys may have been arrivistes in the CBGB milieu, but so was I. If Stiv got on the bandwagon just to get money for junk, who didn't?

Speaking of which, those ten dime bags didn't hold me for more than a week. All that action in the Lower East Side and all for what? I had to be banging it up every five fucking minutes just to get straight, and now what was I going to do? I couldn't quit. I'd given Audrey her gun back. I didn't want to go through all that again.

Roberta came up with a stop-gap supply of peach-coloured Palfium tablets, synthetic opioids way stronger than the anaemic Avenue A shit. Admittedly, crushing them up and making them shoot-up-able was a bit of a performance, but it was worth the trouble: better than any heroin you'll ever fucking buy. I've been looking for it ever since.

After a week, however, even that was running out – and it was Roberta, once more, to the rescue: a few days later, she landed me a chunk of all-organic opium about the size of my fucking fist. If you're going to go the junkie route, it's the farm shop equivalent: opium with nowt taken out. After that, all the pressure was off and it was *Confessions of an English Opium-Eater*.

I even went to Canada for one night. It was a late addition, but it was a good purse for just one performance in Toronto, and then I was back in New York the following day. I took a trans-portable portion of the opium with me, and when I got into the queue for the passport check, I stashed it in my mouth. What I hadn't reckoned on, though, was the extremely volatile nature of opium in its pure form. It's not like any other substance you've ever seen, and is pervious to the slightest application of heat: hold it in your hand and it's like a lump of glass turning to liquid in less than a minute, leaving a sticky puddle like molten caramel. The moment I put it in my mouth it started to melt, and was all running down the back of my throat at a rate that meant I wouldn't have any left by the time I made it to the front of the line.

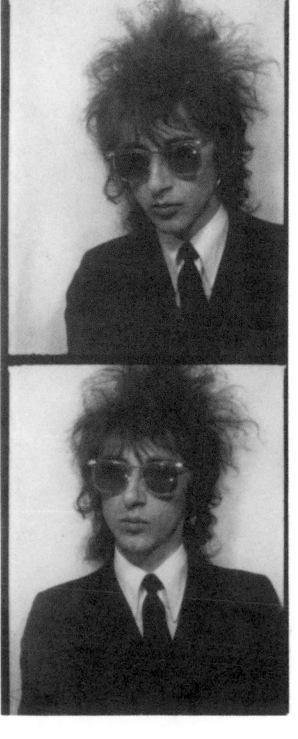

16 and 17. Photobooth specials: you can pose as much as you like without having some guy behind a camera thinking you're a cunt.

18. A publicity shot for the 1982 Arts Council film, *Ten Years in an Open Necked Shirt*. Stained-glass necktie courtesy of the late Jock Scott.

19. Hold it right there, who's shooting who? Australia, 1985.

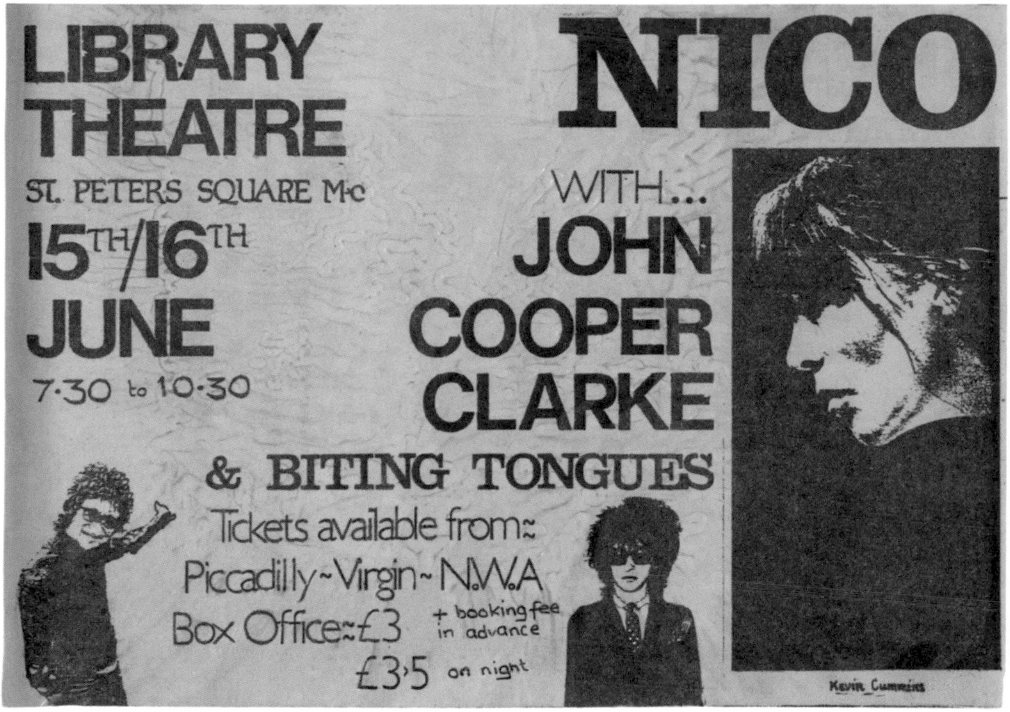

LIBRARY THEATRE

ST. PETERS SQUARE M·c

15TH/**16**TH **JUNE**

7·30 to 10·30

NICO

WITH...

JOHN COOPER CLARKE

& BITING TONGUES

Tickets available from:-
Piccadilly ~ Virgin ~ N.W.A
Box Office:- £3 + booking fee in advance
£3·5 on night

Kevin Cummins

20. Appearing with Nico at Manchester Library Theatre in 1983.

MUSIC & POETRY

Saturday Sept 28th:

* **JOHN COOPER CLARKE with support HA!**

A return visit by this leading charismatic contemporary poet whose frequent TV and radio appearance have gained him a large following.

Last year we sold out, so book early!

21. Headlining with support from Ha! in 2013.

22. Pages from my scrapbooks: random souvenirs I haven't yet managed to lose.

23. Note the fading picture of my grandfather in the top left-hand corner.

24. Me and Evie in our courting years, at my mum's apartment.

25. Me and Evie on our second visit to the Salvador Dali Museum in Figueres, the eighth wonder of the world.

26. My brother Paul, his wife Wendy and
me, in Manchester.

27. Me and Evie in Manchester, taken by Stella.

28. With Stella at a family wedding in France.

29. Stella, me and Evie on a boat trip down the Loire,
with a couple of interlopers in the background.

30. Spot the poet.

Chapter Fifty-Two

PERSIAN BROWN

I had survived my first outing stateside and made it back more or less unscathed to the relative calm of Stevenage. Iris and I had moved to a place in the old town, and other than the regular commute to London for supplies, plus the occasional show or strictly necessary promotional obligation, I hardly ever left the house. There's only one thing worse than agoraphobia: going out.

After 1979, heroin was stupidly easy to obtain. The fall of the Shah and the subsequent theocratic regime had resulted in a mass exodus of Iran's moneyed class, many of whom converted their assets into easily exportable narcotics – the consequences if you were caught trying to leave the country with heroin were far less harsh than if you tried to take your money with you. The Ayatollah didn't give a monkey's how many fucking Westerners got strung out, so now London was awash with barely refined brown heroin.

The big difference with this Persian heroin was that you didn't have to go anywhere near a hypodermic. You could snort it, put it in a joint, or smoke it on a piece of tinfoil, making it the instantly attractive, user-friendly drug of choice for a whole generation of young people in London who up until then wouldn't have been interested; now syringo-phobia was no excuse. For once, I became the voice of moral panic, believing that this dragon-chasing epidemic could only lead to the suspension of all civilised values.

As I've said, I've always had a medical side to my personality. Right back to when I got hold of that *MIMS*, I've always been extremely fastidious about every drug I've ever taken. With heroin, however, I took things to scientific extremes: I was clinical about every aspect of the content and administration. I mean, there's obviously a limit to how much you can take in one day, therefore a rigid routine must be established. There's no mileage in over-doing it: it's either going to push up your tolerance levels or kill you. Having said that, of course, each new shipment carries a certain risk – it could be three times the strength of the last stuff you got. If you snort or smoke it, you can stop when you think you might have had enough, but when you whack something right into your bloodstream, you can't get it out again. By neces-sity, therefore, the life of the junkie is very ritualistic. If everything goes to plan, every day is exactly like the one before, and will continue to be so until such time as you're shown the old red card.

I've got to admit, to my way of thinking, an elegant syringe was an essential gentleman's accoutrement, something I imagined Sherlock Holmes would secrete along with his glove stretchers, ivory paper-knife, and tortoiseshell comb in his crocodile-skin dressing case. I had therefore acquired an actual glass and steel Everett hypodermic syringe from the surgical suppliers in Welbeck Street, which I would boil up and assiduously sterilise prior to each injection. It was part of the fun. But eventually my Everett went missing – I think somebody pinched it – so when I was in Amsterdam at the One World Poetry Festival in autumn '79, I bought a Rand Rocket from an apotheek. This was an upgrade. Streamlined and stylish, the sports car of the syringe world.

I was used to Chinese White, thus my first port of call was still Jackie Genova. Like me, he was a needle enthusiast, and as such was still getting his stock from a dude on Gerrard Street in Chinatown. Jackie Genova was very reliable, but thanks to popular demand the clean Chinese White dried, and the filthy brown stuff was the only dope in town.

The whole rigmarole of rendering Persian heroin into a shoot-up-able form was bothersome – you had to break it down, mix it in a spoon with a drop of water and some ascorbic or citric acid powder, or failing that a squirt of Jif lemon juice, and bubble it all up. Even then you couldn't just suck it up into a syringe, what with all the molecular filth and subatomic debris that's unavailable to the human eye. No – it had to be filtered through a ball of cotton wool. What you don't want is a dirty hit.

Occasionally though, no matter how careful you were with the purification process you'd get an invisible flake of something you're not meant to get in your veins. It's not usually life-threatening: weird cramps, hyper-active lachrymal ducts, raging shakes, muscle spasms, uncontrollable grinding of the teeth, and feeling feverish and freezing at the same time. Not quite the screaming ab-dabs, but close enough. Sometimes it would pass in three-quarters of an hour, sometimes it could last all day. Rotten. You just had to wait for it to wear off.

My entire life was more or less taken up with the junkie routine. I would shoot up three times a day, which would enable me to live the life of a normal citizen: I was a so-called 'functioning addict', or I thought I was. It didn't impinge on my work, really, although actually it did: I didn't write so much.

Thus 1979 rolled peaceably to its end. In September I was part of the line-up at the inaugural Hammersmith Poetry Festival, along with some big-name contemporary poets including Linton Kwesi Johnson, Brian Patten, and George MacBeth. My first wife's favourite artist was also on the bill. Yes, the dreaded Roy Harper. On a slightly more illustrious note, in October I was invited to the star-studded One World Poetry Festival in Amsterdam, where I met with Kathy Acker, Heathcote Williams, Jim Carroll, author of *The Basketball Diaries*, and the late, great Rotterdam poet Jules Deelder. Gregory Corso was also involved and we quickly became junco partners. He would be in and out of my life until his death in 2001.

Jules Deelder also became a good friend, and I have to say, one of the very few Dutch people it was possible to have a meaningful conversation with. Perhaps this was due to the fact that he was from Rotterdam, a blue-collar chip-on-the-shoulder kinda town, and not Amsterdam with its flaky anything-goes ethos. His sense of humour was sharp and slightly sick, and his dress code obsessively late Forties. He wore these zoot-flavoured gangster suits in some kind of rotatory system. When I went round to his place, there were always at least eight of them on show – same style, different fabric – each draped on a tailor's dummy adjusted to his particular chest size, and each topped off with a coordinated fedora, plus necktie and pocket square. His physique was slender to the point of emaciation; his hair was a jet-black patent-leather widow's peak – he looked like Count Dracula's better-looking kid brother, tasty bastard.

In November, I ventured over to the University of East Anglia campus in Norwich for a Manchester package-type show. I was supported by The Out, featuring the million-dollar smile of 'Guitar' George Borovski, and The Freshies with their composer and front-man Chris Sievey aka Frank Sidebottom. The Freshies were Manchester's contribution to the short-lived Power Pop craze, best personified by Squeeze with their bouncy rhythms, strong melodies, and lyrics that told a story, but there were others, like The Pleasers, who were obviously in thrall to The Beatles. Stateside there were the Flamin' Groovies and the Cars.

It even developed a psychedelic side with bands like London's Mood Six.*

Chris Sievey's sole semi-smash with The Freshies, 'I'm In Love with The Girl On A Certain Manchester Megastore Checkout Desk', originally released as 'I'm In Love With The Girl On the Manchester Virgin Megastore Checkout Desk',† would later get to number 54 in the charts in February 1981. Like me with 'Postwar Glamour Girl', they were lined up for a *Top of the Pops* appearance, but our ambitions in this regard were stymied by industrial action.

Then it was Christmas. That year I went with Iris to her parents' house in Kent, but not before I'd copped a load of stuff from Jackie Genova. It was the one and only time I've ever spent Christmas at somebody else's house. Why? Because there are two ways of doing Christmas: the way your mum did it, and the wrong way. It's got to be exactly the same every year. I'm quite rigid about this. I mean, where is the place for boredom in any annual event? 'Not bloody turkey and roast potatoes *again*? We had that last year!' When have you ever heard that as a Christmas dinner-table complaint? And yet, now they try to sell Christmas with novelty in mind. You know, 'Try something different this year.' Why? Why? Didn't you like it last year? Was there something wrong with it last year? You seemed to enjoy it.

To us at home, Christmas dinner was just like a Sunday dinner, pimped up to the *n*th degree of deliciousness. We didn't really do turkey because there were only three of us, and by the time my brother was on solids, I'd practically moved out. Instead, we used

* If you're interested, check out their compilation release, *Songs from the Lost Boutique*. I wouldn't be surprised if they weren't highly influenced by Fairfield Parlour and their should-have-been-a-hit single, 'Bordeaux Rosé'.
† Changed following objections raised by the BBC about using the Virgin brand name.

to have chicken, which in itself was quite a treat. Blimey, back then *any* species of poultry was a special occasion: for Christmas or Easter only. The Christmas dinner of my childhood, therefore, was chicken, Paxo stuffing, two types of potato, roasted and boiled, sprouts, carrots, gravy, and for afters, Christmas pudding with custard. No trimmings to speak of: no pigs in blankets, no cranberry sauce, maybe mustard, at a pinch, probably powdered. No mince pies, and none of that brandy butter. I used to read about things like that but they were never on our menu.

One year my mum and dad announced that they thought we'd have a change, so they'd ordered a leg of pork. As a conservative child, this disrupted my mental universe. Already I thought my Christmas was buggered. Ruined, I tell you! 'Are you mad? It's Christmas. I'm not having pork, not at Christmas!' I wailed. 'It's chicken at Christmas! It's traditional!'

They stuck to their guns and had their pork, but these oven-ready capons (which, it turned out, were pumped full of oestrogen) had just been made available, so I got one of those. It was like a very fat neutralised chicken, really plump and succulent, and I had the whole fucking bird to myself. Blimey.

I'd just seen *The Private Life of Henry VIII* on the telly, where Old Coppernose is ripping birds apart with his hands and eating them, so there I was like Charlie Laughton, tearing into this juicy little bird with my bare hands, gobbling it up, gravy running down my neck; if only we'd had a dog, I would have thrown the bones over my shoulder to the slavering hound. So it turned out it was the best Christmas ever. Fucking terrific, baronial already. Still, why change an annual event is my point.

It reminds me of the story about a silent order of monks. They're allowed to take it in turns to utter one sentence per year on Christmas Day. It's Brother Francis's turn, and he stands up and says, 'The porridge is too thin.' The following year Brother Benedict comes in with, 'The porridge is never hot enough.' A year later Brother Ignatius pipes up, 'The porridge is always lumpy.' Then the next year Brother Dominic stands up and announces, 'I wish to leave the order,' causing the Abbot to break his silence, the better to ascertain the reason for Brother Dominic's momentous decision. His reply: 'I'm fed up with this constant carping about the porridge.'

Charming and welcoming though Iris's family were, as I said, that Christmas in Kent was a one-off. It was the first time I'd ever seen bread sauce. Someone passed me a jug of this white gack. I was fucking horrified. 'What the hell is that?' I asked. 'Bread sauce,' they said. 'Don't you have bread sauce?' 'No, certainly not,' I replied. We never had it at our house. Three kinds of fucking potatoes on my plate. I mean, you don't need the extra carbs. Leave some room for the meat and two veg.

Chapter Fifty-Three

SNAP, CRACKLE & BOP:
THE END OF PUNK ROCK AS
WE KNEW IT

There's a saying in the Rooms: 'If you hang around a barber shop long enough, sooner or later you're going to get a haircut.'*

Iris was a London girl. She was a bit of a coke head when we'd first started going out but, within a year of meeting me, she had acquired a habit. I'd gone to great lengths to discourage her curiosity about heroin. I figured I wasn't a particularly good advert for that lifestyle anyway, what with its myriad inconveniences and countless daily punishments, but once when I wasn't looking she fucking got a noseful of it, and sure enough, her world turned fabulous.

As I've said, everybody cracks up as soon as they get recognisably famous. You think you know what it is — after all, that's what you wanted — but even imaginative people *can't* know what it is or what it does to you. Nobody has any idea. You don't even know what it's doing to you *while* it's doing it to you — and once you turn it on, you can't turn it off.

* The Rooms, aka AA meetings.

That's the thing: even with the minuscule amount of fame that I've had, it's against nature to be recognised wherever you go. If you're a normal person, at the first glimpse of fame your personality begins to disintegrate, in one way or another: some people get suicidal, some have a nervous breakdown, while others become addicted to booze or some kind of dope.

I was not equipped psychologically to deal with any of this new reality, and very quickly things got nutty. I had become what I always wanted to be: a professional poet. It wasn't a hobby any more: the idea of the poet waiting for the muse to present itself went out the window. Inspiration is for amateurs. Idleness has always been my natural default setting, and since my main imperative was now the acquisition of ever-increasing amounts of heroin, there was always something better to do than write poetry.

Now that I was shopping for two, I had to commute from Stevenage to London two or three times a week. On one occasion early in 1980, I made the train journey in a particularly bad state. I was well overdue and icky sick, so I kept dropping off, as you do, but only for about a minute at a time. At some indeterminate point, I woke up with a jolt to find the train wasn't moving. I leapt up in a panic, believing it had arrived at King's Cross. Thinking I'd better disembark before it started on its return journey, I opened the carriage door and stepped out into thin air, dropping like a stone onto the tracks three feet below. Fuck me, it might as well have been fifteen feet. I went down like a sack of shit, and shattered my ankle. Only then did I realise that the train had made an unscheduled stop at Wood Green, overshooting the platform as it did so.

Somehow, I scrambled back up into the carriage, and as the train eventually trundled towards King's Cross I watched my ankle swell up under my Converse high top sneakers. I knew it was broken, but I thought I'd better get some stuff before I went to the hospital: I wasn't registered as an addict yet, and I was very anxious not to be known as a heroin user. That presented a dilemma, and between Wood Green and King's Cross I thought about it a lot. I don't know how I managed it, but I got into a cab and sorted myself out at Jackie Genova's before heading to the Royal Free in order to get plastered up. Paula Yates somehow found out about my eventful trip and gave it a mention in 'Natural Blonde', her weekly pop gossip column in the *Record Mirror*. As she said in the piece, my mind was on a higher, nobler plane than the other commuters.

Apart from such occasional occupational hazards, life was sweet. The new album, *Snap, Crackle & Bop*, had been in the throes of production with Martin Hannett and The Invisible Girls on and off for over a year. We couldn't always get studio time, so we were tweaking it right up to the wire.

In March I made another *Old Grey Whistle Test* appearance, and in May, *Snap, Crackle & Bop* came out. As part of the publicity drive orchestrated by Judy, I guess, I presented a half-hour Granada TV *Celebration* programme featuring me, me, me, and back to ME.

I was invited to perform the opening event of the first Oxford Poetry Festival, held in the Oxford Union theatre. The organisers were thrilled because my gig was a sell-out, and the resultant purse went towards the travel expenses of the other participating poets (as I've said, I am a river to my people), in particular those of the founder of the International Concrete Poetry Archive, the Polish 'domesticated mystic', Zbigniew Herbert.

'In effect John is paying Zbigniew Herbert's fare across from Berlin,' the festival director had told Iris. The way I heard it was The Big New Herbert.

Snap, Crackle & Bop was probably the most commercially successful of my albums: it was my highest charting, at least – reaching number 26 in the UK hit parade, it just managed to squeeze into the *NME*'s 1980 Top 40 Albums of the Year at number 39.

To a team-spirit-averse person like me, making records with other people was the least enjoyable part of what I was doing then. But that said, I think *Snap, Crackle & Bop* is also my most aesthetically successful album. I never listen to my records, but if anything works with music, that's the one. If I hadn't been in a studio with some tracks to fill up, I wouldn't have written 'A Distant Relation', for example. The music came first: that time-honoured C, A-Minor, F and G pop sequence, very Smiths-y arpeggiated chords in a lovely jingle-jangle treble thanks to Vincent Reilly of Durutti Column fame, who at that time was playing with Ed Banger and the Nosebleeds, another Rabid act. I can dig that. I got the feel of the chords and the pace of it, and I just wrote the words to this quite poignant, rather ethereal little number, which is almost a song. Funny, isn't it – nobody would ever cite it as their favourite track, but it's the one I like, so it wasn't all doom and gloom.

The album cover was designed by award-winning award-winner and winner of several awards Peter Saville, in-house graphic guru of Factory Records: a photograph of a jacket with a built-in faux breast pocket in order to house a slightly re-designed edition of Barney Bubbles's *Directory*, now available only as part of the package with the first pressing of the LP – an early example of a BOGOF.

In June, Epic released 'It Man' and 'Thirty-Six Hours' on a seven-inch single to mostly pretty good reviews. To cite Deanne Pearson in *Smash Hits*: 'The maniacal Mancunian continues his series of Hints on Hilarity. He spouts crazy but intelligent (if you get the drift) words to a musical backdrop which has just the right balance: interesting, easy listening that does not intrude on the star's glory and yet also manages to stay above wallpaper schmaltz.' *Punky Gibbon*'s reviewer wasn't so impressed: 'Does this count as another gimmick? Two songs from *Snap, Crackle & Bop* and not even the decency to provide a picture sleeve.'

The cheapskates at Epic had evidently blown the budget on the album design.

In June I turned up at the Beat the Blues Festival at Alexandra Palace, where I performed in the pouring rain alongside The Slits, The Pop Group, and, aptly enough, The Raincoats. I read from a recently composed fake autobiography (later printed as 'Ten Years in an Open Necked Shirt', the titular piece of my debut poetry collection). As I was heading into my finale, 'Kung Fu International', a punk rocker with a bleeding head wound lurched onto the stage, followed by several belligerent-looking meatheads. I helped the casualty over to the attendant medical personnel and concluded my set without missing a beat, my Tonik™ two-piece bespattered with gore.

By this time, punk rock had got hijacked by politicos. I think that's what killed it. Before then it had just been a genuine explosion of naive rebellion, a means for the young to express themselves in whatever way they imagined within the punk-rock guidelines. In that sense, punk was the last real youth tribe, but as soon as it got tied up with the propaganda, narrow politics, and sloganeering of activists, all the fun and imagination was kicked out of it.

Punk rock was no exercise in socialism, I know that for a fact. Most of the punks weren't at all political: even the swastika stuff was only there to wind people up. The political brigade didn't understand rock and roll, or really know anything about it: for them, the entertainment was secondary to the propaganda. They didn't subscribe to the star system which rock and roll thrives on, but they knew a big name when they saw it. The memorable April 1978 Rock Against Racism concert in Victoria Park in East London, for instance, was due to be headlined by the Tom Robinson Band, but the late addition of The Clash rather usurped their status as top of the bill. A world-class act, just back from the States, they were keen to lend their name to a noble cause. As guest vocalist on 'White Riot', the event also provided Sham

69's Jimmy Pursey with the opportunity to cast off the taint of fascism he had so unjustly acquired.

I was very anxious not to be seen as a part of any narrow political agenda, but there was always a danger of that happening in a small place like England. I never wanted to be seen as being in anybody's pocket. If you're an avowedly political artist you're a sloganeer, and that's the end of it: a base hireling who propagates the ideas of others. The record companies only want your money, but those other people want your heart. To know any artist's political worldview is unhelpful. It's unhelpful for the artist, and especially unhelpful to an appreciation of their artistic products. That's particularly true of actors.

In the autumn, I embarked on my first and last tour with a backing band. The full coach party, involving Pauline Murray and The Invisible Girls, took to the open road, stopping at the Manchester Apollo, the Leeds Apollo, the Birmingham Odeon, Newcastle City Hall, the London Lyceum, and the Brighton Top Rank, ending up at the Friars Club in Aylesbury, which was quite a big venue for a certain level of act.

For this outing The Invisible Girls comprised Martin Hannett, Steve Hopkins, Vini Reilly, Paul Burgess on drums, and honorary IG Robert Blamire, the guitar player from Penetration, Pauline Murray's previous band. Martin hated appearing on stage. He was never entirely comfortable in front of an actual real-life audience, and would only agree to performing on my sets. Just as I had struggled to play bass and sing at the same time, Martin found simply standing up while playing a bit of an ordeal, preferring to perform sitting down. He cut an odd figure, as a *Sounds* reviewer present at the Newcastle show observed: 'Zero was seemingly making up guitar fills on the spot like a degenerate, seated, chain-smoking Segovia.' Bloody hell.

By November I was back to what I do best and went on a little solo tourette of the Emerald Isle, first stop Queen's University

Students' Union, Belfast. This was the height of the Troubles, when you could have got shot through the fucking throat if you took a wrong turn down the Falls Road. Everybody had warned me about going over there on my own, and as I've mentioned, I'm normally risk-averse in any war-zone situation. But this time I was fearless in the face of the forebodings of my familiars. 'Don't be silly!' I reassured a tearful Iris. 'I mean, on the one night I'm in Belfast, what are the chances of me being anywhere near a bomb?'

I was staying in a hotel somewhere near the Botanic Gardens. When I rolled up there after a very successful show, the whole place was locked up and the fucking night porter had nodded off. I could see him through the glass doors in a deep and stupid slumber, his head on the reception desk. I was standing in the street in just my burgundy-to-purple Tonik™ suit, freezing my bollocks off in a fucking gale, ringing away at the bell that's supposed to call the staff up, banging on the fucking glass: nothing. It wasn't even outrageously late – all right about 2am, but this was a hotel for fuck's sake. There was nobody around at all, and there were hardly any street lights so it was extremely dark, and after about half an hour I was starting to get a bit spooked, never mind the hypothermia already. The only thing I could think of was to leg it to the nearest telephone box, get the number of the hotel from directory inquiries and ring this fucker up. I got the operator on the phone, and just as I was in the middle of explaining the situation, there was this deafening *KABOOM!* A fucking unmistakable incendiary going off in the near distance. What the . . .? Huh? Then the operator's voice started to crack with fear: the bomb had been right beside the telephone exchange, so I figured that meant it must be close to where I was because I'd heard it loud and clear as well.

Even the operator, herself a Belfast girl, was shitting herself. That was when the panic kicked in. I asked for the address of the telephone exchange and a couple of cab numbers, but we got cut off.

I tried to reason with myself. 'What are the chances? You're only here for a night; pull yourself together man,' you know, the internal dialogue of the hero. On a practical level, however, the cowardly option began to present itself: a taxi to the nearest police station, and then an armed escort to my hotel. Or at least an urgent wake-up call from the police to the night porter. The snag with this plan, however, was that I had loads of shit on me: a quantity of dope, a packet of ascorbic acid, a syringe, even down to a stolen dessert spoon and a couple of alcohol swabs, plus the gigantic room key I had foolishly forgotten to hand in earlier that evening – all clanking about in my pockets. So there I was on the street in the middle of Belfast, bombs exploding all around me, pockets awash with narcotics and the paraphernalia thereof. Still, as the complainant, I figured that the Royal Ulster Constabulary weren't likely to give me the once over, so I rang 999 and asked for the address of the nearest police station to the hotel. I was well and truly shitting myself by now, but they said it was literally three minutes' walk, so I fucking bottled it out.

The police station really was just around the corner, and easy to spot because it was behind a barricade of sandbags and barbed wire. Very welcoming. I went up to the desk sergeant and told him the whole sorry tale: how I could hear the bombs in the middle distance etc. etc., and how I'd thought I'd better get under some kind of shelter, thus my calling by at this inhospitable hour. Would he mind, I asked, A) putting me up for the night in one of their more comfortable cells? Or B) allowing me to hang out there until he got in touch with the hotel's night porter? And C) in that event, could I get a lift back to the hotel, preferably in an armoured vehicle? Two out of the three requests were met with a negative response, but he did finally manage to get through to the night porter and he also called me a cab. Even for that short distance, I'd had enough exercise for one night.

The next morning, I got a train down to Dublin. As I was sitting reading my paper I was approached by two unlikely looking companions: one looked like a chief librarian, the other had the fugitive look of a recently released H–Block resident.

Mr Bookish had steel spectacles, a neat ginger beard, and wore a Dunn & Co. tweed sport coat, Viyella shirt, brown corduroys, and stout polished walking brogues. His sidekick was a real shifty-looking fucker in one of those awful greasy quilted blue-nylon anoraks with a bit of fake fur round the hood. He was squeezing the last drags from the stub of a microscopic roll-up. He even smelled like jail: that lethal olfactory cocktail of institutional cabbage, Old Holborn, and TCP.

'Anyone sitting here?' inquired the librarian. 'Be my guest,' I replied.

Obviously, I figured this fugitive-type didn't know who I was. Why would he? He'd been in jail for the last five years, so it had been a while since he'd read the *NME* and the punk-rock phenomenon had passed him by. The bookworm guy, on the other hand, was properly clued up, because the next thing he came out with was: 'You're something of an anti-establishment figure yourself, Mr Clarke.' I was very much perceived like that, unjustly, in my view.

Pulling a sheaf of weird-smelling paper from his pocket, the fugitive announced, 'I'm a writer myself, Mr Clarke.' He said he'd composed some memoirs while he was in the Maze, and showed me sheets and sheets of Izal strong medicated lavatory paper, on both sides of which he'd recorded his life story in microfilm-sized handwriting: I couldn't read it even with my glasses on. He told me he'd written it with the inside of a Bic ballpoint pen, and had kept the paper rolled up in its plastic outer casing. This he had stuffed up his jacksie to keep it hidden from the prison guards.

'We're trying to get it printed in one of the papers in the Republic,' said Mr Bookish. Could I put in a word for them with the *Irish Times*?

To this day, I swear it was Gerry Adams. After all, it was his business as the Sinn Féin media spokesperson to keep up with events over in England. Back then Mr Adams was not the household name he is today: he was just a shadowy figure, the respectable face of terrorism who occasionally showed up on the teatime news looking like a fucking geography teacher. You wouldn't catch him in a balaclava.

Long story short, we exchanged false addresses and went our separate ways.

Chapter Fifty-Four

ME AND MY BIG MOUTH

1980 ended with the *NME* printing a couple of new poems describing two fictional days in the life of yours truly, 'The Day my Pad Went Mad' and 'The Day the World Stood Still'.

As a poet, in some ways, I guess, I was better able than most to ride out the ebbing tide of punkdom. After all, what was I going to do? Split up owing to artistic differences with myself? I was still on the up, getting headliner shows as well as national airtime and other media attention.

The many years spent schlepping around the streets of Bloomsbury in search of a publisher for *Ten Years in an Open Necked Shirt* were finally paying off too, thanks to James Ware at Arena, an imprint of Hutchinson whose offices were in Fitzroy Square, although he wasn't any more sold on Steve's drawings than the rest of the publishing world had been. His reasonable assumption was that I was the known quantity here: people weren't going to buy this collection on the strength of its artwork. However, I talked him into it on the condition that I paid Steve's fee out of my end, and we agreed a contract.

Was it a good deal? Was it a bad deal? Once again, then as now, I have no idea. At the time, though, the main thing was that *Ten Years in An Open Necked Shirt* finally had a publisher.

At some point soon thereafter, I also found a professional manager. Although I still relied on Martin Hannett to drive me to and from gigs, any meaningful relationship with Rabid management was by now non-existent. On the recommendation of Judy Totton and Martin, therefore, I placed my affairs in the hands of a fellow called John Arnison.

John Arnison had worked with Status Quo, Rory Gallagher, Aswad, and Penetration featuring Pauline Murray: a mixed bag that seemed to favour the heavier side of rock. Indeed, when I met him he was managing a heavy metal group from Barnsley called Saxon. Back in Manchester I had often clocked their double-crown Day-Glo posters advertising gigs in the largest halls available, and this impressed the fuck out of me. Heavy metal was never my cup of tea but it wasn't going to go away – you can't knock success. Generically, it is beyond fashion. Since its invention at the end of the late-Sixties British blues boom it's had millions of fans worldwide, and each generation adds to their legions. I figured, if John Arnison was dealing with the hyper-hyped affairs of the mainstream rockers, well, I'll have some of that. After all, punk took its time to reach even the provinces in the UK, never mind the States.

Thanks to my new management, I now had a wider circle of muso acquaintances including the likes of Micky Moody and Bernie Marsden and ex-Deep Purple singer David Coverdale. I'm not really an expert on this, but I believe they had recently formed Whitesnake. In the flesh, with his perfectly streaked and blow-dried leonine mane, Coverdale actually looked like he himself had been air-brushed. He radiated a kind of stain-resistant sun-dried patina.

Along with these people came an ever-changing retinue of cartoon sex-pots – pneumatic rock-chick stadium groupies who had somehow latched on to my entourage. One of them had landed a cameo in the Bond film *For Your Eyes Only*. I told her

I'd once almost met her romantic lead, in fact he had been a close neighbour of mine. Obviously, I asked her what he was like, and was happy to learn that Roger Moore was amusing, extravagantly generous, and generally a class act all the way. She was constantly putting the move on me, but having previously met her fiancé, a hard-nut Glasgow squaddie, I found her advances easy to resist.

Meanwhile, back in Manchester, Steve Maguire was also having a heavy metal moment. Ozzy Osbourne, who had recently been sacked from Black Sabbath for drug- and alcohol-related reasons and gone solo, was so taken with Steve's cover artwork on my first album that he invited him to visit his mansion in the rural Midlands to discuss a possible collaboration. Ozzy wanted to commission Steve to provide an illustration for the sleeve of *Crazy Train*, a single taken from his debut solo album *Blizzard of Ozz*. Whenever I ran into Steve, he'd regale me with the horrors of his and Ozzy's last meeting. On one occasion Ozzy had ushered him into the basement, where he produced a plastic shopping bag full of high-grade cocaine, Steve's favourite drug, and instructed him to feign ownership in the event of his wife Sharon asking any questions. As if Sharon was likely to fall for that. Like Steve, your archetypal impoverished artist, his famished frame clad in a frayed shirt, patched-up jeans, and a threadbare donkey jacket, was going to be in charge of three million quid's worth of sniff.

On another occasion, after hoovering up about five grand's worth of the stuff and gargling with a full bottle of Napoleon brandy, Ozzy suggested a séance. Steve declined – he wasn't superstitious, but when faced with nonsense such as this his default position was extreme paranoia. Instead, Ozzy produced a couple of shotguns and took Steve out on a moonlit rabbit hunt in his Land Rover. Steve was quite sentimental about rabbits: he had one for a pet, Mr Natural, who lived like a cat in the apartment. After that, for one reason or another, the collaboration went off the boil, and Steve's meticulous artwork remained unused.

John Arnison was a nice guy, a safe pair of hands: I had a lot of confidence in him, and although I imagine I came close to giving him the dreaded nervous breakdown, he did the business, keeping the ship on course, and me in useful employment.

In early January 1981 I took part in a weekly BBC 2 series called *16 Up*, an early, somewhat earnest glimpse of 'yoof programming' before the lovely Magenta Devine spiced that field up a bit. This was more like the teenagers' answer to *You and Yours* or *That's Life*. The format was roughly this: a short documentary film on a hot topic, a song, followed by a heated debate, interrupted by me declaiming some verse that seemed roughly appropriate. One week, for example, it was 'Drugs – A Different View: If your doctor prescribes drugs for you, that's okay. If you take them for fun, you could be in trouble.' (I would have put it this way: 'If your doctor prescribes drugs for you, you could be in trouble. If you take them for fun, that's OK.' Spot the 'different'?)

The filming took place in Manchester, so I was back at Steve's briefly – a chance to take stock of progress on the illustrations for our book. While I was there, Alan Wise booked me for a show at Rafters with the Blue Orchids featuring Martin Bramah and Una Baines, along with a couple of other former members of The Fall.

In May *Me and My Big Mouth*, a sort of 'best of' album, was released with little fanfare from Epic, and I went on the road for a one-off appearance with The Invisible Girls which saw us back at the Friars Club in Aylesbury, this time supported by Caledonian rockers The Scars, Way of The West, Art Nouveau, and a local third-generation prog-rock group called Marillion – nice lads, terrible music. They were what I imagined Genesis were like, although how would I know anything about Genesis? A band so awful that I made it a point of honour to remain ignorant of their oeuvre, a state of affairs that prevails to this day.

In June, I made my third *Old Grey Whistle Test* appearance, and performed at the Project Art Centre in Dublin along with a ragamuffin young arriviste by the name of Michael D. Higgins. The next time I ran into him, he was the President of Ireland. This brings to mind the introductory opening to the seventies Japanese TV series *The Water Margin*, voiced by my late friend Burt Kwouk: 'Do not despise the serpent for having no horns, for who is to say he will not one day become a dragon.'

At the end of that month I did Glastonbury for the first time, taking to the newly built Pyramid stage on the Saturday evening along with Aswad, New Order, and finally the headliners, Hawkwind. There is footage of me somewhere doing 'Night People' with backing tapes. Back then Glastonbury was a much smaller affair: a hot-dog vendor and a couple of ice-cream vans. There was only one stage, so everybody's experience of the event was virtually identical. Same went for the acts, who would all congregate underneath the stage, that whole area serving as the communal green room.

That August, on the say-so of Judy Totton, I did the Cambridge Folk Festival. Judy used to talk me into doing all sorts of shit I wished I hadn't done, so at first I was 'Bloody hell, Jude! What now?' I told her that as a punk rocker, the Cambridge Folk Festival was the last place I wanted to be spotted, and that I didn't even like folk music. But she knew the business better than I did. She'd been at CBS for five years before I'd even got started, after all, so I took a lot of notice of what she said, and she was insistent about this one. She told me it was going to be a big event that year – they had Dave Van Ronk *and* John Sebastian on. I quite liked the Lovin' Spoonful but what clinched it for me was Donovan. I was always a big fan. I don't know what it was about that dishevelled young warbler, but I liked his voice and his songs were wistful, spooky, and maniacal by turn.

This was way before the internet, and Cambridge was miles from anywhere: I thought I could do it in secret, so I said, 'I'll do it for Donovan, but for fuck's sake, Judy, don't go telling anybody that I've done anything with the word "folk" in it.'

Anyway, we drove up there and the whole car journey I was on at Judy, all anxious: 'I hope nobody sees me at this here folk festival. I feel like ridiculous, or something.' When I got out of the car, right away I could smell weed. I followed my nose, and it led me to a car containing Joe Strummer and Don Letts. They were also there for Donovan and, as such, were in this as deep as I was.

We never spoke of it again.

My set went down really well with the folk contingent, it has to be said, and I gained some fans that I otherwise might not have. As ever, Judy was right.

I made my second trip to America for some headlining club dates in New York, Philadelphia, and San Francisco at the end of September. I was interested in San Fran and Big Sur, because of their mythological status among the beatnik crowd via the City Lights bookshop run by Lawrence Monsanto Ferlinghetti. I had a gig lined up at a small club called the I-Beam which had featured shows by, among others, The Fall, Faith No More, Motörhead, and Screamin' Jay Hawkins. What got me there was the erroneous idea that it had been one of Lenny Bruce's regular gigs: I'd mistaken it for the famous 'hungry i' club, which had closed its doors in 1970. That naked ninth letter of the alphabet had tricked me into this misapprehension.

While I was in New York, I ended up playing two extra unscheduled nights at the Ritz as a last-minute replacement for the Pretenders, who had been forced to foreshorten their US tour after their drummer Martin Chambers had punched a lamp in his Philadelphia hotel room, severing a tendon in his hand. The Pretenders were justifiably quite big in the States, so there must have been a level of disappointment in the crowd. Who wouldn't be disappointed? I myself was disappointed on their behalf. I loved the Pretenders.

The rest of the band wound up in New York with time on their hands and I hooked up with their bass guitarist Pete Farndon, and also Keith Levene from PIL, who was in town. We were looking to cop somehow and wound up at the home of Allen Lanier, erstwhile boyfriend of Patti Smith and member of the Blue Öyster Cult. You may remember them from such tunes as 'Stairway to the Stars' and '(Don't Fear) The Reaper'.

It wasn't my idea to go round there. What did I know from Allen Lanier or the likelihood of him being in possession of any opiates? But either Pete or Keith seemed reassuringly certain, and I just knew I didn't want a repeat of the Avenue A routine. Mr Lanier wasn't very forthcoming in this regard, and feigned sickness himself. The unspoken MO was to wait the motherfucker out and just hang around his place until the inevitable time when he would need a hit and then get out the old mooching sack. To our collective mind, this superstar hippy bastard was sitting on a junk pile.

During the course of our prolonged visit, I clocked what I thought was a guitar in a corner of the room. It caught my attention due to its striking candy-apple red, mock-croc finish. Closer inspection revealed sympathetic strings running diagonally across the body of the instrument. Also, certain frets were scooped out, the better to achieve that Asian twang. What we had here was an electric sitar. I picked it up and gave it a bit of a seeing to, and even in my inexpert hands, it reminded me of the sitar riff featured on 'Cry like a Baby' by the Box Tops featuring Alex Chilton. I conveyed this to its owner, to which he replied, 'This is that very instrument.'

What the . . .? Huh? 'Fuck me! Wow,' I said. 'That's gotta be worth a million clams. Let's go cash the motherfucker in and get some dope!' My usual courteous demeanour was showing signs of strain. That never happened, and we all went somewhere else.

Chapter Fifty-Five

PUT YOUR TROUSERS ON – YOU'RE NICKED

Not long after my return from the States, in November 1981, I was busted and charged with possession of marijuana – the irony was that it wasn't even mine.

I'd been in London to do my bit for Britain at the second Poetry Olympics held at the Young Vic. At the previous year's inaugural Olympiad at the Poets' Corner in Westminster Abbey, I'd been lined up with, among others, Gregory Corso (USA), Stephen Spender (GBR), Derek Walcott (LCA), and Edward Limonov (URS). This time I was pitted against fellow countrymen Linton Kwesi Johnson, my old Kirklands pal Roger McGough, Heathcote Williams, R. D. Laing, and James Berry; newcomers Seething Wells, Attila the Stockbroker, and pop wordsmith Paul Weller. From Russia came the poet Andrei Voznesensky, and representing the US of A, Elizabeth Smart and Fran Landesman.

I can't remember how I got back home to our apartment in Stevenage, but it was really late. Iris was away at her parents' in Kent for some reason, and I must have just stumbled in and gone straight to bed without even closing the front door, because the next thing I knew I was being shaken awake by a couple of plain-clothes officers from Stevenage police station. What the . . . ?

Huh? Someone had apparently spotted the wide-open front door and called the cops.

Detectives can be nosy parkers, it's a well-known fact. As I was fumbling for my specs, the detectives had clearly been scoping our sleeping quarters, and stepping over to the dressing table, one of them, picked up a small piece of hashish and asked me what it was. I had no idea what he was going on about; what with the habit, I never touched the shit. But, yeah, there it was: this micro-scopic amount of Moroccan.

I was right on the back foot there, but I suppose some crackpot code of chivalry must have kicked in, because rather than say, 'It must be my girlfriend's. I'll give you her parents' number and you can ring her up and charge her,' I took responsibility. Anyway, obviously there was much worse than that on the premises, so I certainly wasn't going to make life difficult for myself by kicking off about it. The Peelers were always going to have the last word.

For some reason, the senior detective lacked the usual note of belligerence I associated with his profession, and they only half-heartedly semi-ransacked the joint – opened a few drawers, chucked a couple of shirts around – just enough to make it a bit unpleasant. Then I was duly arrested, escorted over to the station, and charged with possession.

I don't know what it was about the Stevenage Constabulary, but it was like *Carry On up the Police Station* in there that night, with all these really hot blonde-bombshell police-officer chicks all over the custody suite. I'm not even kidding, loads of them, all in these saucy, truncated mini-uniforms (or is that a product of my fevered imagination?). I thought, I'll fucking get the last word in here. As I was taking my leave of the arresting officers, I turned round and said to the desk sergeant, 'These two guys have made a right mess of my apartment, sarge. All in the line of duty, of course, but would it kill you to send a couple of these young ladies round to tidy up a bit?' He was all like, 'You wanna watch it, sunshine,' but I was playing to the gallery there. Even the arresting officers laughed: male banter, canteen culture, institutional chauvinism, what can I tell you?

Seriously though, I didn't think anything of it just then, but I was pretty annoyed when it dawned on me that in the event of a conviction, I could kiss America goodbye. And it took me thirty-five years of begging to get back into the States, just for that little bit of marijuana. No negotiation. I ran into the arresting officer a few days later. He was all smiles, very friendly indeed, and introduced himself as Doug. He said he was glad he'd run into me, because he wanted to ask me if there were any apartments going in our block, and could I put a word in with the landlord for him? 'Aye aye,' I thought. '*The Sweeney* all over, this one. Fucking classic policeman's wife syndrome.'

He was that kind of sclerotic Jack Regan type: a bad liver and a broken heart. His marriage has irretrievably broken down, he's been denied access to his kids, and he and his wife have split the house – he must have got the outside, because now he's asking me if there are any vacancies in my building. Some people, eh? Unbelievable. Anyway, we parted on good terms. 'I'll see what I can do, Dougie,' I said, 'but obviously I, as a tenant, can't make you any promises.' First-name terms now; he'd shown me his vulnerable side and you'd have to have a heart of gold not to burst into tears.

I appeared in front of the Stevenage magistrates in early 1982, pleaded guilty, and was ordered to pay a fine.

Now with a criminal record, and my debt to society outstanding, I went on a thirteen-city tour with Linton Kwesi Johnson. Poetrywise, we were the hottest ticket in town, selling out big-capacity venues wherever we went. I'd run into Linton at the Poetry Olympics just a few months earlier, but I first met him in February 1979 at a show with the very newly formed Public Image Ltd. at the King's Hall, Belle Vue Gardens, Manchester.

The Belle Vue complex was in its dying days, its once ground-breaking attractions supplanted by state-of-the-art theme parks like Alton Towers. The King's Hall, the cavernous home of the Belle Vue circus, was now standing next to the abandoned zoo in a half-dismantled fairground, the once-famous Bobs rollercoaster sold for scrap. The draughty old circus building still retained the smell of straw and sawdust, and miscellaneous animal ordure, which to me at least was part of its charm although I'm not sure it helped any with what must have been an uncomfortable night out for our audience. The heating was barely functioning, and did little to counter the chill of a Manchester gale that came blasting through the aisles. There wasn't even a bar in the place, so it was stone-cold sober, literally.

I was already aware of Linton's status as the John Cooper Clarke of the Jamaican community. There was this measured pulse to his poetry that was informed, obviously, by reggae and by a vastly different historical perspective from mine. He was the exemplar of an oral tradition, that same oral tradition that had informed the likes of I-Roy, U-Roy, Prince Far I, King Stitt, Big Youth, and all of those aforementioned top toasters.

Linton and I both had our own style. For stage wear, he had a vast selection of collarless silk shirts in various showbiz shades: fuchsia, heliotrope, crushed raspberry, lilac, and mauve. These he purchased from Camberwell outfitter the Baron. Off-stage, he studiously avoided that trad Rasta ragamuffin look, favouring instead the kind of clothes you might find on sale at Dunn & Co., which specialised in those garments worn by retired military types: cavalry twill trousers, Byford knitwear, Viyella shirts, maybe the odd corduroy item, all in some variation of buff, maybe with a splash of stone, beige, camel, caramel, oatmeal, taupe, umber, lovat, khaki, possibly even bottle-green, plus the usual array of checks: puppy tooth, houndstooth, dog tooth, Prince of Wales, Tattersall, and windowpane.

Linton loved all that. He was also big on herringbone, his various ensembles all topped off with one of Dunn & Co.'s signature stingy-brim trilby hats in a flecky salt-and-pepper Donegal tweed.

Around the time I finished the tour with Linton, Iris's stint at the *Stevenage Gazette* came to an end and we moved back to London. We went to live with her sister in Hammersmith for a while, then John Arnison very kindly got us a really good apartment on Redcliffe Road, on the edge of Fulham and Chelsea. In the upstairs apartment was one of his other charges, blues guitar player Rory Gallagher, and his brother. I wasn't automatically impressed. After all, in Salford I had counted Roger Moore as one of my close neighbours.

We got this cleaning woman round every week to give the flat the once-over, but she was a right old gasbag. She used to tell us about all the other places she cleaned. You should have heard her on the subject of Rory Gallagher's flat: 'They smashed the place up last night. Gawd, I tell you, Guinness bottles all over the show! Bloody hell, they can't half drink, them lot.'

We had to spend ages tidying up and hiding all the fucking paraphernalia before she arrived, because I knew for a fact that in no time she'd be telling everyone in Chelsea that we were junkies. Anyway, the old bird was more trouble than she was worth, and in the end I had to pay her not to come.

In May, *Zip Style Method*, the long-awaited follow-up album to *Snap, Crackle & Bop*, was released. My writing had taken a darker, more introverted turn, taking me into more existential and surrealist territory. The new album material had no jokes, fewer puns, no hook lines; there were even a couple of love songs. It also had the best cover art of all my records, with fantastic photographs by Niall Doull-Connolly and designed by Rosław Szaybo, the chief artistic director at CBS/Epic. You could see it from a mile away, but it didn't help shift copies: in spite of some critical acclaim, the sales were meagre, and this would be my last album before I was dropped from the label.

Nevertheless, as ever, the tireless Judy Totton wizarded up the usual round of impressive PR opportunities, including an appearance on BBC's prime-time Saturday night *Pop Quiz*, with fellow panellists Jools Holland, Depeche Mode frontman Dave Gahan, Paul Jones, and Sal Solo of Classix Nouveaux.

In June, I did a string of one-off gigs to promote the album, with dates at the Hacienda in Manchester, Factory's high-tech disco which had only opened a few weeks before. The building had once been a yacht showroom, and, now reimagined by Factory's Ben Kelly, it featured all his signature architectural flourishes: the avoidance of all soft furnishings, and the industrial safety infographics and gaffer tape playing up the brutal recent industrial past of the city and making a virtue of it. There was hardly any ventilation, so it always smelled like a chip shop; all hard surfaces and no cushions, industrial slip-proof stainless-steel flooring, staircases like fire escapes, everything made out of concrete and iron with sharp corners. That's why people were always dancing: there was nowhere comfortable to sit. Yet like iron filings to a magnet, they came there from all over the world. It was an artistic situationist statement all the way; that was the point of the place.

On the night of the launch, local legend Bernard Manning made a guest appearance, quipping, 'I've played some shit-holes during my time, but this is really something.' Unfortunately, the Hacienda crowd didn't get Bernard's jokes and he returned his fee.

I didn't go out much to clubs by this time, and I never went to the Hacienda, other than to do the odd show now and again, but to me the acoustics didn't do the musicians any favours. Any groups that played there must have had a hell of a job getting a sound. I did one all-day show there early doors with Nico and The Fall, and what with it being a bit reverby, only Nico made any sense. Nico was not a person who went in for a great many lyrics: it was just her voice and harmonium. On the albums she brought out after The Velvet Underground, *The Marble Index* and *Desertshore*, her songs relied more on the sort of trancified sound of a lot of long-held notes, which conveyed an aura of oriental mystique. I always put it down to the Turkish side of her family. That was all part of her appeal: full of Eastern promise. So, whereas everybody else fell on their arse, Nico came out of that Hacienda show looking good.

Next up was the Dalymount Dublin open-air festival, with the bizarre line-up of me in a Meat Loaf and Shakatak sandwich, closely followed by a trip down the M4 in a torrential midsummer downpour to the Glastonbury CND Festival. The weather was horrific, so it was a case of the now legendary field of thick wet mud. Thank God I was just in and out of the car and on stage on the Friday after Black Uhuru and just before the Polecats, a rockabilly outfit whose one notable hit, 'Rockabilly Guy', went something like this: 'A rocka rocka rocka rocka rockabilly guy. I'm a rockabilly guy, ain't never going to change my style.' It's a good number. I'm not doing it justice.

In October I flew to Amsterdam for a show with Nico at either the Paradiso or the Melkweg, I don't exactly recall – but one of the two – and at which we shared a band – well, a couple of scratch musicians anyway. I'd known Nico from before in Manchester, probably because of connections involving gear, plus she lived near Sedgley Park, so when I moved to London I'd always get news of her from Steve, who used to run into her a lot.

Amsterdam was the one place where a junkie was free to do any sort of business they liked, so top of the list was getting that sorted before we went over to do the gig. When we arrived at our hotel Nico said to those concerned, 'If anybody wants to score, give me your money. I know a really good guy. We won't have to wait for him. He'll be waiting for us.' That never happened, like it says in the Velvet song that Nico sang every fucking night, 'He's never early, he's always late, First thing you learn is that you always gotta wait.' But she was insistent that this time her guy would be waiting for us in the green room at the venue. I was giving it the argument, pointing out that I had connections of my own. Who hasn't in Amsterdam: 'Why don't we go to my guy Simon? He's really cheap.' But she said, 'No no, he's my friend, I've known him for years. He will be waiting for us.' Then again it made sense, because rather than us all doing our separate deals, as I've said, the more you spent at the same place the more you got, and cheaper too. That's what swung it, so we all coughed up and let her do the sorting out with her friend. It wasn't like she could pull a fast one. How far was she going to get anyway? We were due on the same stage in four hours and we lived in the same fucking neighbourhood, so she was just about the only junkie I could possibly trust.

At the appointed time we all filed into the green room, looking around this empty room for the likely suspect and, sure enough – nada, niente, niemand. We were on her like white on rice: 'All right, where is he?', 'You said . . .', 'Where is he, Nico?', 'Give me my money. I'll just go to Simon. You've wasted enough of my time, I'm off.' But Nico simply shrugged, seemingly unperturbed. 'Honestly,' she said, looking round the door. 'He's a good friend of mine. Very reliable. He will be here any minute.' Then, next second, 'Uh oh,' and scooted off down the corridor.

She returned with this shambolic skinny guy looking like Geronimo's ugly kid brother: shuffling gait, long greasy hair, and a bandana, unshaven, no teeth at the front. He looked American, so I thought he was one of the many draft-dodgers in Amsterdam who 'weren't there, man', but nevertheless got a dope habit and stuck around. The place was full of them. Anyway, Nico turned to me and said, 'It's the guy,' and introduced us. Her guy was standing there looking at his handful of various-sized wraps, and he lifted his head up, looked at me straight in the face and in a barely audible semi-whisper said, 'Hi.'

So, knock me down with a feather when twenty years later Evie and I were watching the movie *Let's Get Lost* directed by the photographer Bruce Weber and boom, it hit me: 'There – that guy there, in the bandana and no teeth, I bought heroin off him. I swear that's "the guy".' I mean, Nico knew everybody – Federico Fellini, Jean-Paul Belmondo, Alain Delon, Serge Gainsbourg, Brian Jones, Bob Dylan, Jim Morrison, you name it, so of course she knew Chet. She knew that he lived there, she knew he spoke English, she knew he shot up dope, and she figured quite rightly he'd have things sorted out. And not ever did Nico say, 'That was Chet Baker, you know.' She just took it for granted. So, when I finally put two and two together, I wasn't that surprised. But, at the time, it didn't even cross my mind. I mean, I was a massive fan: I should have known it was him just by the way he said 'Hi', because he talked exactly the way he sang. But my memory of Chet was as the kid with the golden cheekbones, the James Dean of blue-eyed jazz, the unbelievably handsome fucker who modelled Arrow shirts for *Esquire* magazine, fucking pussy magnet number one, so no wonder I didn't recognise him. Not even when I heard his voice. And to think I could have been dining out on that for twenty years. The lesson here is that I'm not the star-fucking name-dropping cunt I thought I was.

Chapter Fifty-Six

DOWN UNDER WITH NEW ORDER

I tend to write the Eighties off as my wilderness years, but now that I come to put it down on record it doesn't seem all bad — the first half at least. Iris and I were quite the little jetsetters, in fact.

In November 1982 we packed our bags for a tour of Australia and New Zealand with New Order. I had originally been booked for a solo tour in Australia, then we figured that I could perform at more and bigger venues if we invited New Order to join the party. I always thought that I went out there on their bandwagon, but as Hooky (Peter Hook to you) reminded me quite recently, it was the other way round.

Me and New Order went back a long way. While a lot of the other punk-rock outfits were from south Manchester, they had a footing in Salford because of Hooky and Bernard Summer, aka Barney, and used to practise in a room above the Swan pub, so I would run into them quite a lot. There was also the football connection, because unlike most Manchester showbiz types like the Gallagher brothers, Bernard Manning, and Eddie Large, Hooky and Barney were fellow United fans.

Right back when I first knew them as Warsaw, I'd seen something in them. Or should I say, I didn't see anything different from the rest of the punk bands on the scene. Warsaw were no worse or better than anybody else, so why they attracted so much animosity was a mystery to me. I mean, none of them could play very much, but as I've said, limited technical proficiency was one of punk rock's strengths, *and* a large part of its charm. Then, to be fair, when Tony Wilson took them under the Factory wing and they changed their name to Joy Division, they deserved their success, because they departed from the punk template quite early on. They became more of a keyboard-driven event, with most of the guitar stuff supplied by Hooky, who didn't really play bass guitar like a bass guitar: he played melodies.

I'd been as shocked and saddened by Ian Curtis's death as anyone. On the strength of their critically acclaimed Factory output, they were headed for the States the next day. I thought, 'There's a guy with a big future.' How wrong can you be.

After Ian's death, the rest of the band had reinvented themselves out of necessity, throwing themselves headlong into the construction of their new corporate identity. When they came out with me to Australia, although they were showing great promise, they needed to establish themselves with Bernard Summer as their singer, and were obviously all very unsure of their direction. They were playing Joy Division stuff written just before Ian's death, while also forming their new sound as a sort of electronic pop outfit. Indeed, New Order were the frontrunners in that world. They'd become much more proficient as live performers, as you can imagine, but they were still very young and they weren't 'great musicians' in inverted commas. Nevertheless, as a band, New Order made it happen: they went from nobodies to somebody to somebody else, quite effortlessly, really.

The tour kicked off in Melbourne with shows at the Palais Theatre and the Seaview Ballroom. The journey had been terrible. I still had a stash of residual DF118s from the Elvis Costello and The Attractions Scandinavian trip, and a supply of Valium, but it had been a long flight and Iris and I were both a little off-colour.

As soon as we made it into our hotel room, number-one priority was obviously to stock up on narcotics. According to Peter Hook, we demanded that a supplier be urgently located, and refused to leave the room until a delivery arrived. I'm ashamed to say that this is probably true.

Once I had my MO sorted out, though, I discovered that getting gear wasn't a problem anywhere in Australia. Moreover, there was none of that filthy brown stuff. What you had here was the shoot-up-able item. Pink rocks straight out of Penang, Cambodia, and Vietnam. They couldn't stop it coming in, because it was such a lucrative trade and everybody was into it. Girls who worked in offices would even keep a syringe in their handbag. The must-have accessory was the Blue Lady, a hypodermic made almost entirely out of blue glass; a really fabulous piece of precision kit.

We were flying about, using planes like buses. I wasn't planning to leave any gear behind in Melbourne, so on the next flight to Sydney I had to resort to my old smuggling ruses. Getting through security was easier then than it is now – there weren't sniffer dogs in all the airports, for a start – but it was still always a risk and I got turned over a hell of a lot. Everybody else knew that anyone moving large amounts of narcotics probably looked like the managing director of a reputable company, but not these customs inspectors. Back then it was stop at first base; there was no second guessing about it: 'He looks the type, let's shake the fucker down.'

I used every trick in the book to get heroin across borders. I used to sew it into the waistbands of my trousers. Another reliable trick was the old shaving cream routine. Back then Erasmic shaving preparation came in a large tomato purée-style tube made out of some kind of tin. Like them, when you bought a new tube of Erasmic, the nozzle end had a protective metallic seal that you had to pierce with a spike in the lid. The closed bottom end was simply rolled over and crimped with a pair of pliers, and was therefore very easy to unravel. I'd then squeeze out a quantity of the shaving preparation, and replace it with a wrap of heroin and a syringe in a small plastic bag. Having done this I would re-roll the bottom and, finally, carefully re-crimp it with my pliers. Anybody searching me at airport security would look at that tube of Erasmic and see that the seal hadn't been broken; they could shake it about and nothing rattled. It didn't matter how much attention they paid to it – it looked like I'd just bought a new tube of shaving cream at the airport.

We had a bit of downtime in Sydney before the show at the Capitol Theatre. The big controversy over there at the time was nouvelle cuisine: 'Call that a meal?' and all that. The colour supplements were full of it. I was very interested in the trend. I liked the look of it; in the pictures I'd seen, the layouts reminded me of a Picasso or a Kandinsky. Plus, when you're a junkie you don't want to clog yourself up with too much bulk, or stuff yourself full of carbs all the time – I was never a weight-watcher or anything like that, but you know, what did I want energy for? On the other hand, one loves a snack, so I was all for it. Anyway, when we got to Sydney one of the tour promoters, a guy called Dennis Stoneman who ran a club called the Trade Union there, came over and said he wanted to take us out for dinner at the Bayswater Brasserie, the city's new go-to restaurant. 'They do that bloody nouvelle cuisine,' he said. 'Great! Bring it on, Dennis,' I replied. I was quite the contrarian like that; my take on things was that there must be something good about it if everybody else hated it. If it was that bad, how come it's such a Thing?

The Bayswater Brasserie did not disappoint. When my dinner arrived I realised that all those colour-supplement pictures had been deceptive: shot from above, you didn't have a perspectival view of the dish. My meal was just as artfully presented – all the food was in the middle of the plate, a drizzle here, a smear there – but, firstly, the plates were really big, and not only that, they were really deep, so although the food didn't cover much of the surface area, it was all piled up. As I found out by the time I'd knocked down the tower of ingredients, it was no less than a normal meal, and certainly not the meagre portions that the nouvelle cuisine naysayers would have had me believe. Plus, depth of flavour was everything: things were reduced rather than thickened, so the taste was very clean, intensively rendered down, and utterly delicious. I'd been right to be positive about it. I knew I'd like it, and I did.

Smithy had been out in Sydney the week before, playing the same venues as me, and as I was tucking in with evident enthusiasm, Dennis said to me, 'Your mate Mark Smith was out here last week. We booked a table here for the whole group.' 'Oh, yeah? How did that go?' I asked. 'Well,' Dennis replied, 'he took me to one side, and said, "Just you and me, mate. They wouldn't appreciate it. Get them a bag of chips." ' 'Yeah,' I told him. 'That's Smith all right. That's him all over.'

New Order got a really bad time in some parts of Australia, and the crowds were pretty hostile, especially in Sydney. The band followed the same script they had previously perfected as Joy Division, only now they were minus their charismatic frontman, and seemingly not even playing any actual instruments. They steadfastly omitted all the old Joy Division songs from the setlist, and because a lot of their new music was sequenced – all the electronic keyboard and drum-pad programming business was done on computers before they went on – to the audience, they didn't seem to be doing very much work. They didn't say a word; they barely moved, just stood there while the music played; and they didn't do an encore. On the contrary, they would just exit the stage in the middle of the last song while the automated pre-programmed music kept playing. They all found that highly amusing – they thought it was great, cutting edge and kind of futuristic. I agreed with them, but it didn't play into the hands of the Aussies, who still had that strong work ethic.

When it came to rock and roll, Australians were very meat and potatoes. Their bands were still very much whamalamma, proper spit and sawdust; if you were a guitarist, you had to be able to play, and to work up a proper sweat to prove it. I'm not having a go at them; I mean, some of their bands were great – The Saints, The Birthday Party, The HooDoo Gurus, and the Church, for instance – but to the Aussies, New Order seemed like elevator muzak.

To be honest, at that point New Order didn't have any fans in Australia, so to all intents and purposes it was just me who was pulling in the punters. For the Sydney Capitol show, therefore, we decided that I should sing an encore with them, to pull it all together and make it look like it was a Manchester Pop Art package.

For this 'Big Finale', I suggested that we do The Velvet Underground's 'Sister Ray'. I'd always wanted to do that number – it would be quite a different dynamic to the usual show. Plus, New Order were all really big on the Velvets themselves. I could just make up the bits I didn't know – Lou Reed never had a strong voice, and the band are really loud on that track, so no one could ever make out all the lyrics anyway – nobody would notice. Then we thought, yeah, but a twenty-minute encore with me ad-libbing? That might be taking the piss. People would be walking out before we'd got two minutes in. The show had to end somewhere, so we stuck with the Velvets, but went for 'Lady Godiva's Operation' instead.

Mid-tour, during the first week of December, New Order had some dates lined up in New Zealand, and for some unknown reason, Iris and I decided we'd go along and I'd support them. I don't remember a great deal about that trip; I gather from recent conversations with Hooky that they did shows in Auckland, Christchurch, and Wellington, and that he was worried about me because I was never around. His worries were not misplaced. I'd got mixed up with a bunch of gun-toting skinheads. I hadn't thought obtaining the needful supplies would be a problem, New

Zealand being so close to Vietnam and all, but heroin was slightly harder to get out there, and I had to deal with all sorts of fucking terrible people to get hold of even the tiniest amounts.

Things started looking up in Auckland when I met this nurse and her dealer boyfriend, who moved larger amounts of the stuff and wasn't quite as cut-throat as the skinheads. That was when I died for the first time, however. Thank God, the nurse happened to be around and brought me back to life – she punched my heart back into action and walked me around until I snapped out of it – so somebody up there likes me. But you know, dying is a fantastic feeling; ask anybody who's ever been brought back from the dead and they'll tell you the same thing. One minute, I'm in a fool's paradise and now this nurse with the shaking and the thumping of my idle heart, and I'm all like, 'What the . . .? Huh . . .? Don't worry about it, will ya?' It's a thankless task, saving the life of a junkie. Nobody is ever grateful. After that, everything is a bit of an anti-climax for a while. Anything short of flaking out is a total disappointment.

By this point, we'd been cut loose from New Order, who were heading back to Sydney for a few days of beer and barbies on the beach while Iris and I were forced to prolong our stay in New Zealand. I bet they were glad to see the back of us. Unfortunately, I'd been paying over the odds for the small amounts I'd squeezed out of the skinheads; something like NZ$1000 a gram. I'd run up a considerable bill, which I couldn't immediately pay. I was in their pocket until I made good the shortfall.

It had been a nice break for New Order, until Iris and I reappeared in Sydney in time to honour our shows at Selina's in Coogee Bay and the Manly Vale Hotel. The problem for me was that my luggage had missed the flight. All of my suitcases containing my best stage suits were lost, and I never got them back. I only had what I was standing up in: a pair of Levi's and my leather jacket. I couldn't go on stage dressed in that get-up and I didn't have time to go trawling round the shops, so I took myself down to the TV Channel Nine wardrobe department. It was vast, a whole floor of the studios, all the costumes stored according to historical period. I was right on it, and told the wardrobe assistant to take me straight to the Sixties – I was looking for a classic three-button Continental suit, ideally something in a silk and mohair. All the actors down under, however, must have been built like Hercules, because I tried on a good few and nothing fitted me. It's a well-known fact that back in history, people were smaller due to childhood trauma and poor nutrition. With this in mind, we moved to the nineteenth-century department.

My luck was in: I got this black needle-cord Doc Holliday-style frock coat that fitted me like a dream. It was like something that John Wesley would have worn, distressed and threadbare. I also got a white ruffled shirt out of them. They were dynamite clothes, beautifully made. I got really quite attached to that shirt. It looked pretty glam paired with the leather jacket; I always liked that frilly shirt and biker jacket look. I'll say it in one word: Chrissie Hynde.

Sadly, the costume department didn't have any trousers from any era that fitted me, so in an afternoon they cut me a pair of very tight black pants in some stretchy leatherette material. Coupled with a pair of RM Williams boots that I'd just acquired, it was a fucking great look – totally monochrome but nineteenth century – just perfect for the gig. New Order always avoided colour, so it looked like it had all been designed, what with the 'Lady Godiva' finale and everything.

After that, I was glad the airline had lost my clothes. Well, not glad exactly, that's going a bit far, but if it hadn't happened I would never have discovered this new look. In a sense, we all reinvented ourselves on that tour.

Chapter Fifty-Seven

TEN YEARS IN AN OPEN NECKED SHIRT

Iris and I flew back from Australia direct. We had briefly considered breaking our return journey and spending Christmas in Bali, where it was possible to obtain a made-to-measure two-piece suit in shantung silk in an afternoon for £25. Instead, we white-knuckled the horrible twenty-four-hour flight, with only Rohypnol and Scotch for company. Iris was by now fully ensnared, but as I never tired of trying to convince her, she wasn't as sick as I was. After all, women have a higher pain threshold; it's a medical fact.

Anyway, we landed at Heathrow early in the morning, got through customs and baggage (without baggage in my case), and hightailed it to Jackie Genova's. It had been nice weather when we left Sydney, the height of their summer; back in Blighty it was freezing cold and pissing it down. We staggered into this awful December dawn in our flimsy summer clothes, collected Iris's old Morris Marina from the long-stay car park, and drove straight to Stoke Newington.

Like any other commodity, the more you bought the cheaper it was. I had loads of money, so we copped a quarter-ounce and paid off our arrears. If it had been a gram or less, it would have been in a paper wrap, but with this amount, Jackie had bagged it up in plastic. As we were leaving, he handed me a quarter-ounce chunk of Afghani hashish, a gift from one of his customers. He didn't want it, so no charge. I didn't particularly want it either, but I could never throw anything like that away, so I stuck it in my side pocket and didn't think any more of it.

We were now living temporarily in Hammersmith with Iris's sister and her boyfriend, but we needed to get sorted, right now. We didn't have any of the necessary accoutrements at home – we'd been away for a month, and obviously weren't going to leave any tell-tale apparatus in our room. We therefore got back in the Marina and drove to Halls Chemist on Piccadilly. It was still pissing down, so Iris parked right outside and I ran into the shop.

Halls was just a junkie chemist, basically; being in Piccadilly, they cashed all the modern-jazz junkie prescriptions, and consequently they sold disposable 2ml syringes. I bought about twelve of these, and a roll of cotton wool.

As I stepped out onto the pavement with my purchases in a paper bag, I found the three paces to the waiting Marina obstructed by two uniformed cops who stopped me and asked what I had in the bag. One of them, who was very young, had a look for himself, so there was no arguing. He knew who I was; he'd heard my stuff on the radio, and was a fan, so he seemed personally disappointed to find out that I was a drug user. He asked me what else I had in my pockets. Luckily, I had that decoy piece of Afghani hash, so with a kind of 'It's a fair cop, guvnor, you've got the drop on me' attitude, I handed it over and, in one smooth motion, scooped the bag of heroin out with my other hand, dropped it onto the kerb, stepped on it and then, with the toe of the other foot, gently tapped the door of the car. Iris looked up and instantly worked out what was going on. I was arrested and taken to Bow Street police station, all the time praying that Iris had retrieved the precious £500 bag of heroin which I'd left lying in the gutter beside the near-side car door.

There's no law against having a bag of unused syringes, and all they could charge me with was marijuana possession. So I got out on bail, and as I was picking up my possessions, the desk sergeant handed me the bag and said, 'Don't forget your works.'

Of course they knew the score, having checked my arms, which were scarred by tracks and traumatised injection sites, but it was bad luck for the coppers on that occasion. If I hadn't been able to whip out that chunk of Afghani, I would have been nabbed for the far more serious offence of Class A possession – at the very least. Given the quantity I was carrying, I could have been up for intent to supply.

Lady Fortune had smiled on me that day, without a doubt. I made my way home to Hammersmith, and sure enough, Iris and our mega-stash were waiting for me, safe and sound.

I've been trying not to mention stuff I think is dreadful, but 20 November 1982 saw the world premiere of the long-awaited documentary *John Cooper Clarke – Ten Years in an Open Necked Shirt*, directed by Nick May and produced by the Arts Council of Great Britain and Channel 4.

For me, the whole film thing is weird. Even if I'm just being me, it always feels like I'm playing a part in any on-screen piece. Truthfully, I only watch anything I'm in once, and then I can't bear to see it ever again, so I honestly can't remember much about Nick May's flick. It featured cinéma-vérité footage of me on stage (filmed mainly on the road with Linton Kwesi Johnson), guest appearances from fellow poets including Linton himself, and bits of me being interviewed by Patrick Humphries of *Melody Maker*, and by a couple of Manchester students who were very nice but asked some really pretentious questions which I did my best to answer.

Then there were dramatised vignettes from my fake autobiography, based on the introduction to the forthcoming book of the same title, which was partly set in a strict closed-order convent school. My fictional headmistress, Mother Cyrene, was played by the great character actress Hilary Mason, who was really good. I was a big fan of hers, and had seen her in a lot of films, notably as the spooky blind psychic in *Don't Look Now*, so it was quite a thrill to get to actually meet her. That was one saving grace, I suppose. Another was the inclusion of my friend Jules Deelder.

I know it was supposed to be a documentary, but I would have been happy if the whole thing had been fictionalised and they'd got somebody else to play me. The way it ended up, however, as far as I could see, the entire affair was neither fish nor fowl. I thought they should have gone one way or the other with it, but what do I know? My one semi-excuse is that I had nothing to do with the production at all; I just fell in with somebody else's idea of who I am. It's the only way I know of dealing with these things: I have to be able to renounce all responsibility. Otherwise, if it had anything to do with me, I'd take the whole thing over. Like I say, I'm not a team player.

Nick May and I haven't spoken since; we fell out over the Arts Council. Apart from my two weeks on the sausage, I was very proud of the fact that I'd never relied on any state money. I begged him not to do so either, and to do a bit of product placement instead – anything but the Arts Council, please . . . but he did, and now I can't say I've never been in their pay. OK, it was publicity, and I didn't profit from it – move on. But my memory is long and my vengeance is total, and to this day I swear I'll embark on a life of crime rather than take any money from the lousy government again. I'm not saying nobody else can, but I wouldn't go to anything that had been financed from the public purse. Fuck off! Find some other patsy. Put it this way, if I had a pound for every Ken Loach film I've ever seen, I'd start watching them.

★   ★   ★

By this time John Arnison and I had called it a day, and I was ploughing my own lonely furrow once again. Other than that, the start of 1983 was more of the same, and then some. Shows, shows, and more shows, interspersed with the odd social engagement or an outing to see someone else perform on stage.

John had become Marillion's manager in 1982. He must have come across them the previous year when they'd appeared as my support at Friars in Aylesbury. To think that I had a hand in launching the awful Marillion onto the public! Then again, maybe that's the only favour I ever did John Arnison. I mean, I fucking hate that sort of music, but there's a fuck of a lot of people who disagree with me. Marillion got a major record deal, and sold a few million more records than I did. John must have made a few bob out of that signing at least, and when they started to get big and were selling out major tours all over the globe, I guess he realised he just didn't need my kind of earache.

I can't blame him for jumping at the main chance and getting out of my orbit as soon as he possibly could. To be honest, now that I was taking care of two habits, things had got a bit out of hand. My demands for money were unfeasible. I was always on at him to get me a fucking advance. It must have been awful for him. He didn't have any experience working with junkies – who did, back then? Obviously, he could only do so much, but I bombarded him with all manner of ultimatums, including threats to pull gigs, and eventually he called it down. It was that or a nervous breakdown, and I wouldn't wish that on anybody. After me, Marillion must have seemed like a doddle: they were real-ale types – easily sorted out.

With no John Arnison to escort me to shows, and Martin Hannett embroiled in legal disputes with Factory and rapidly succumbing to multiple addictions, I had a situation vacant to deal with before I next went out on the road. That's when I employed Jackie Genova as the designated driver. He had a Porsche, so he was doing all right. File Under: Seemed Like a Good Idea at the Time.

As with Martin before him, it didn't ever strike me as a problem that a junkie was driving me around, potentially nodding out; I just thought, 'Result!' In fact, having Jackie as my driver was OK, because it was more of a problem if the driver didn't have any stuff: involuntary muscular spasms are part of the withdrawal scenario – and you don't want that to be happening at the steering wheel of a muscle car in the outside lane. But, as I said, that never occurred to me at the time, nor did the equally alarming dangers of a doped-out driver.

I suppose it was around this time that I connected with Alan Wise again; I think it was via Nico, with whom I'd recently shared a band for a few shows in Europe, as I've said. Alan had been Nico's manager since around '81 when she and her harmonium arrived in Manchester, already firmly in the grip of morphia following a decade-long relationship with Philippe Garrel, the French art-house film director. She attracted artistic people, always. How, then, had Nico ended up with Alan Wise? You may well ask. Alan's dad Lionel was a pharmacist, with a chain of chemist's shops around town, so maybe that sweetened the deal. At the time, though, I had no idea how she had wound up living round the corner from Steve, nor how or why Al was looking after her career, but apparently Nigel Bagley,* Wisey's promotional sidekick, had got a call from an agency in London, so he booked her for Rafters.

Al was always one for taking in waifs and strays, so first of all he'd put her up in a Polish ex-servicemen's club before moving her into her own apartment in Sedgley Park. Spookily enough, Alan had his own removal business called Wise Moves, by whom

---

* Nigel is now a very rich man: he got involved early on with some area of computing and cleaned up.

grand pianos were utterly trashed, priceless mirrors irretrievably smashed, his payment cheques were seldom cashed (poetry – it never really leaves you). There was a level of ineptitude worthy of the Three Stooges. He was forever trying to claw back his lost removals revenue from the financially moronic world of punk rock, first as the booker/promoter at Rafters, at the Russell Club for Don Tonay, and then for Tony Wilson when it became the Factory at the Russell.

Now, although I never signed anything with him, Alan had become my manager by default. I don't really know how that happened, to be honest. I think Jackie Genova might have played some part in it, because along with his extra-legal caper, on my recommendation he was employed by Wise Moves, and Nico and I were the human furniture. Jackie expanded his client base, and delivered us on time and sorted. Everybody was happy.

I was finding it a bit of a job rattling the money out of the clubland chisellers, so I quizzed Jackie about Wisey. He had no complaints. Al always paid him on time, and Jackie seemed to be enjoying the old rock and roll lifestyle; one hand washes the other, as they say in 'this thing of ours'. He ventured that I was in need of representation. Wisey was getting Nico a lot of gigs, so maybe he could do the same for me. Why I took Jackie Genova's advice about anything other than fucking heroin, I don't know. I had known Wisey in Manchester, obviously. From 1976, I would run into him from time to time due to his efforts as a musical promoter. Al was a person you would orient towards because, no matter what you thought about him, he was fucking hilarious. He had a great sense of humour, but he was remarkable in many ways, really. He was a very intelligent and extremely literate person, but troubled and sensitive; psychologically delicate, shall we say, as were his twin brothers with whom I became good friends. They were a very neurasthenic family.

Wisey had an over-eating problem, and although he'd been on

prescription benzodiazepines for years, he had no personal experience of recreational drug use until he accidentally ate a hashish brownie from Nico's backstage rider. Permanently peckish, he had simply spotted a cake and swallowed it. Consequently, Wisey didn't know what was happening to him. Ambulances had to be called. Marijuana is quite an extreme drug, really. If you eat it, the effects come on when you're not expecting them, especially if you didn't know it was there in the first place. It would be like déjà vu and amnesia at the same time – as close to a nervous breakdown as makes no difference.

I don't know how Al conducted his bloody affairs, but he was always falling in love with prostitutes, and then he got married to a woman from central Europe, but she was only taking him for the patsy he already was. I tried to warn him. She must have been nagging at him to marry her, and he'd never even met the girl. He showed me a picture of her and asked me what I thought – should he marry her or was she just after him for a British passport or something? I said, 'No, she's in love with you.' I could see that the sarcasm was falling on deaf ears, so I said, 'Of course she's after a fucking passport, Al.' But you couldn't tell him fuck all; I mean, if you couldn't convince him that hookers don't fall in love with their customers, what hope did you have of talking him out of this marriage shit?

I thought Al was the funniest guy alive until he was involved with my money, and then it was no laughing matter. It was my own fault. Why should I think that somebody might be good with money just because he's a funny guy? 'That guy is a total nut. I know: I'll make him my manager!' What right-thinking person would make that step? To paraphrase Gary Lewis and the Playboys, 'Everybody loves a clown, so why not me?'

Wisey operated on a knife-edge. His policy was 'The higher you aim, the more likely you are to pull it off.' He would get all these big-name acts over from the States with this policy for what thus became a headline event. I figured, with a line-up like that, surely nobody could possibly get stiffed, but invariably Alan would overspend, and then have to scuttle around all over London arranging arrangements: barely promoted shows that were guaranteed to sell out. Meanwhile Nico and I were doing Dingwalls, the Half Moon in Putney, fucking Hammersmith Palais, you name it. We'd have to do all these additional nights in order to get paid for a gig we'd already done. That's how close to the wind Wisey sailed. A case of 'I'm ahead if I can quit while I'm behind.'

Al had creditors all over the shop, at all times. He got so behind with his books that a smart person would have just cut their losses and run, but there was always the chance that maybe this time he would pay out: and if, like me, you were in with him for a lot of dough, it would have been a big decision to kiss it goodbye. It was like when you've waited for a bus for forty-five minutes; any time now there'll be three at once.

Law of averages, I thought, it must come right sometimes with this guy, or why would the likes of New Order, Gil Scott-Heron, Chuck Berry, Bo Diddley, Jerry Lee Lewis, and Nico deal with him in the first place? And more than once, even.

In June, it was three sell-out nights with Nico at the Library Theatre in Manchester. That August we also did a show together in Birmingham at the Tin Can Club, an 'alternative' venue above the dingy Sunset Strip Club in Bradford Street, Digbeth, run by a couple of former managers from the Rum Runner, followed by three jammed-out shows at the Zap Club on Brighton's seafront.

In September, I did my thing at Leeds' Queens Hall as part of Futurama, 'The World's First Science Fiction Music Festival'. I didn't really get the sci-fi connection, because the night I was there, the headliners were the earthbound Bay City Rollers, but there might have been some stalls selling comics, videos, and various extra-terrestrial artefacts for any Jeff Albertson types. Billy

Bragg, Howard Devoto, Red Guitars, Sex Beat, The Chameleons, The Comsat Angels, and The Mekons were also on the bill, as were the Smiths, but they were a no-show on the night because, apparently, Morrissey refused to go on before the Rollers.

I didn't mind playing second banana to Les and the boys – after all, the Bay City Rollers had history and a few good tunes. The Futurama festival, however, attracted a lot of goths who didn't take kindly to the 'tartan teen sensations from Edinburgh', and things started to kick off a bit during their set. There were aggressive mutterings and empty beer cans were lobbed onto the stage. When a crumpled can got in the way of Les's jaunty side-stepping dance moves, he bent down and tossed it underhand back into the crowd.

I was backstage in my dressing room in the middle of the lengthy shooting-up process when they came off, and soon thereafter I could hear a bit of a commotion. I stuck my head out the door to see that the rozzers had arrived mob-handed. I had just enough time, and presence of mind, to dodge into a large cupboard where I managed to administer the injection while holding a torch between my teeth. It was pretty cosy in there, and I must have nodded off, because the next thing I knew, someone was tapping on the cupboard door: it was Dave Formula come to beckon me out of my hiding place. 'You're all right, Clarkey,' he said. 'You can come out now. They're not after you, for once.' Les McKeown, on the other hand, had been arrested for assault on account of the beer can incident.

In October, *Ten Years in an Open Necked Shirt* was finally published by Arena, with Steve's exquisite pencil drawings throughout. I'm very happy that I held firm in that respect. Over the years there were several reissues, and the pictures are an enduring part of the book's appeal. Whatever I paid Steve in the end, it probably wasn't enough: he never gained the level of recognition he deserved, but with talent like that, his posthumous day will surely come.

The collection didn't attract the blanket review coverage hoped for by Arena's publicity manager. In fact, I think it received a single, gnomic, four-line write-up from the slightly snooty *PN Review*: '[. . .] contains much raw verbal invention. One hopes he keeps in touch with his audience (this review copy of *Ten Years in an Open Necked Shirt* comes with a sheet of hype from which it is too depressing to quote). At the very least his work shows up the miserable lack of any real power of invective in contemporary writing.'

Well, I got off lightly compared to poor Jenny Joseph, reviewed as part of the same roundup thus: 'Jenny Joseph's *Beyond Descartes* contains work of such fey awfulness, it is at times almost beyond belief. In her persistent use of a *vers libre* for which she seems to have little ear she appears to deny the very essence of what one feels is an intrinsically formal elegiac gift.'

Chapter Fifty-Eight

I ONLY LIVE TWICE

In October 1983 I was off to Australia again for 'The Return of John Cooper Clarke' tour organised by promoters Ken West and Vivien Lees, who would later found Australia's biggest festival, The Big Day Out.

We started in Perth, at a venerable old establishment called the Old Melbourne Hotel in the city centre. Built during the gold rush of the 1890s, the building featured all the opulent architectural elements of the era: elegant facades, ornate cantilevered first-floor balconies, a grand central staircase, and a capacious high-ceilinged saloon bar which took up the entire ground floor, with a stage and everything. Outside there was a generous boardwalk behind a hitching rail: proper. Honestly, it was just like an Old West watering hole; outside, the cars were even parked at right angles to the kerb, in the way you'd hitch a horse to a post. Such a place, and everything was in-house, with the accommodation upstairs and the show taking place in the ground-floor saloon.

The Old Melbourne had obviously been a bit of an entertainment hub in the gold rush, and was now run by Kevin and Brett, identical twins who looked a bit like the Australian version of the Scouser brothers from Harry Enfield's TV show; they both wore that bubble perm/Zapata moustache combo. I'd just got there, straight off the twenty-six-hour flight, checked into my room, and was sitting on the bed wondering where I was going to cop something, when one of them, probably Kevin, knocked on my door to thank me for agreeing to do the gig and to check that everything was all right with the room. They were nice guys, proper chirpy, so I told him everything was lovely, very atmospheric. 'I bet this place has got some stories,' I ventured.

'Shit, yeah,' said Kevin, and blah blah blah, he gives me the potted history of the hotel. Then he started on his and Brett's life story.

'We're not from Perth. Me and my brother, we're new to this catering lark.' Then he said, 'I'm a competitive bodybuilder. I'm doing pretty good, I'm through to the weightlifting championships.' He pointed to his bedroom opposite and I could see through the open door that it was full of apparatus: chest expanders, weights, bullworkers, bar bells, and all of that.

'Feel free to work out,' he said. 'You don't need to ask; if you want to lift a few weights or something, Johnny, there it is. Knock yourself out, mate.'

'Thanks, Kevin. I'll remember that,' I replied, and I was just about to forget it when he continued, apropos of nothing:

'Yeah, me and Brett, we had a chain of pharmacies in Sydney, but we thought we'd get out of the big city and kiss goodbye to the competitive rat race. Start enjoying life. Look after ourselves.'

Well, I could quite understand them swapping the hectic regime of the apothecarist for the leisurely schedule of the hotelier, but then came one of my bright ideas.

Pharmacists, eh? I wonder if he's got any odds and sods lying about in his dressing-room drawers.

So, then I was straight back in there without missing a beat, 'Thanks very much, Kevin. I might take you up on your kind offer.'

I thought I could drop in and pump some iron – that would be the premise for being in his room. All very convenient. I waited until he'd got to the bottom of the stairs, and I was straight in there, rifling through his chest of drawers, and sure enough, pill city. Give it a name: phenobarbital: a whole two cards of this real knock-you-out shit.

'I'll fucking have them,' I thought; at least I'd get a night's sleep. But swallowing a ton of barbiturates was the worst thing I could have done. It's a terrible feeling: you'd like to think properly, but your brain is in shutdown and just refuses to operate. Anyway, it got me through to the next morning, when I quickly sorted myself out the usual way – by asking where the hookers hung out, then paying for their time and blagging an introduction to their inevitable dealer in lieu of any sexual activity.

From Perth, I flew to Brisbane. At that time, Queensland had more or less declared UDI under the leadership of a maverick called Joh Bjelke-Petersen. Premier Bjelke-Petersen clearly fancied himself as the Huey 'Kingfish' Long of Australia, and according to everybody I met over there, he was a redneck fascist scumbag who was going to throw me in jail simply for being John Cooper Clarke.

When I got to Queensland, however, it was like arriving in the Garden of Eden. Brisbane is a terrific town. From where I was sitting, it seemed like the very model of progressive liberalism. It was the first place in Australia where I saw any black people, for instance. Not only that, but among the first people I came across were a big-shot dealer and his wife who said I should move into their place. It was like arriving in paradise: a little bit out of town in this kind of jungle set-up, the frondescent garden looked like it had been landscaped by Henri Rousseau, with plentiful fruit trees and all manner of gorgeous tropical birds flying here and about, so there was constant birdsong which changed through the day with the prevalence of one species or another.

Heroin dealers though they were, Pancho and Shirley were lovely people, quite unlike any of the gangsters I was used to dealing with. To call them pushers would be a misrepresentation; they were also users, so it was a kind of heroin cooperative. Like with the Perretts, the more you got, the cheaper it was.

Everyone spends a lot of time outdoors in Australia, so they have this thing where they put all the white goods out on the veranda: the tumble dryer, the washing machine, the fridge, the freezer. We all just sat out there in the shade, fanning ourselves in the jungle breeze within arm's length of the fridge door. The soundtrack – as often as not Gregory Isaacs' latest album – was dead right. Also, Shirley was a world-class cook, and what with the pink rocks from Penang, it was luxury, pure unashamed luxury.

Forthcoming dates at the Sydney Seaview Ballroom, closely followed by three nights at the Trade Union Club, called an end to my fun, alas, and I bade farewell to Brisbane and the unforgettable hospitality of Pancho and Shirley. Sydney was a blast nevertheless, because the audiences were mad for my stuff down there; also, thanks to the connections I'd made on that first chaotic visit, this time round, the dope situation was sorted.

I say sorted, but I died again on that jaunt. I was in Melbourne for the last nights of the tour, and this time there was no nurse at hand, but somebody's girlfriend knew what to do. She punched me back into operation and walked me round the block. Madam, please accept my belated gratitude.

With the multiple deaths and the terrors of Alphabet City, I began at least to entertain the idea that I'd better quit. Tomorrow.

Back in London, Iris and I were now living with one of her sisters, a bunch of militant feminists, and their single-issue children in Victoria Mansions on the Holloway Road, quite close to where Joe Meek (the mad scientist of pop) murdered his landlady before turning the gun upon himself. It was closer to Jackie Genova's and I saved on cab fares, so it seemed like a good move at the time.

Although it was some kind of women's collective, we'd got in on account of Iris's sister, who had decided eighteen months previously that she was a lesbian, and had started dressing accordingly. As a self-identifying bloke, I wasn't exactly flavour of the month, but as I never left my room anyway unless it was to go out and cop, the ladies couldn't complain. The one time I did engage was when they were all going to this International Women's Day event. It was a serious political forum, and they didn't want to be distracted by the demands of their offspring, so they'd organised a creche, and needed someone to run it. They were going to interview candidates, but to make some chickenshit point, they'd decided it had to be a guy. I wasn't in the running for the role. When it comes to a gang of other people's kids, put me down as a well-wisher, in that I don't wish them any specific harm. But I couldn't help sticking my neck out, though.

'Are you sure you want your kid to be looked after by a guy who wants to look after kids?' I said. 'To me, that disqualifies them for the job.'

They didn't want to hear any of that. A few days later, I answered the door to applicant one and was met by this ungodly woof. A sweaty bad-body smell; the pheromones of Satan. I've never seen a more textbook specimen of a pervert child-molester: dirty mac, bald head with thumb prints. I thought this guy was a wrong 'un, so I said to one of my housemates that I hoped he wasn't in with a chance.

'He's an archetypal nonce,' I said. 'If I saw him within fifteen miles of any child, I'd call the police.'

'Well, actually he is a sex offender,' she replied.

She didn't believe that people should be judged on their sexuality, whereas in a case like this, I think they should.

Chapter Fifty-Nine

IN REHAB

Around this time, Iris and I were finally checked into a private detox facility.

Obviously, I didn't have any money to pay for this treatment – if I had, I would have bought heroin with it, and wouldn't have been kicking the habit in the first place: apart from the nagging guilt concerning Iris's habit, it was the money that was the problem.

I'd tried various walk-in walk-out National Health set-ups, but I was always wary of signing up fully to any kind of formal drug-rehabilitation programme. I didn't want to register as a heroin addict: I didn't believe them when they said it was confidential, and I was right – along with the criminal record I'd already accrued, being a registered user would bar me from the States for thirty-five years.

At the time, however, it felt like I had no choice but to be admitted somewhere in order to get clean. It was the only way it was going to work in my case and anyway, as I was already living in one room, the idea of being institutionalised held no terrors for me.

I don't recall the exact details of the arrangement, but I do know that Alan Wise was instrumental in sorting out the financial side. He must have talked the record company around somehow, because instead of CBS dropping me, they actually paid for this top-dollar drug-rehab clinic for both me and Iris. When I say CBS paid, of course, what I really mean is that they advanced me the cash. I may or may not have paid it back to this day.

The clinic didn't treat couples together because of co-dependency and all that, so Iris was in the Hampstead version while I was in the Chelsea branch just off the King's Road.

As addiction clinics go, it was five-star. The treatment followed the Betty Ford model, in which all addictions are treated as mental, physical, and spiritual diseases. I was in there with alcoholics, coke freaks, gamblers, sex hounds, and Valium victims. You are an addict, and every addict has to do the same things to get well.

It was an open-ended programme where each symptom was tackled individually and the Twelve Steps were rigidly policed. The treatment involved physical exercise, NA and AA meetings, plus hours and hours of group therapy. I'm reminded here of the late Peter Cook, himself a former inmate of this establishment, who in one televisual interview declared that he'd been treated in the Henry Ford clinic. 'Don't you mean the Betty Ford Clinic?' interjected the interviewer. 'No,' replied Peter. 'In this place they wouldn't let you out until you'd built a car.'

After a couple of the mandatory group sessions, my biggest revelation was that if you're a heroin addict, it doesn't make you a very sympathetic person. It was amazing how little tolerance there was amongst the opioid faction. I was the worst on that front, especially when it came to coke heads. I'd sit there in group, listening to them all moaning about how charlie had ruined their life, how they'd hoovered up a fortune, and had to sell their second home, and boo hoo hoo, and I was like, 'What? For cocaine? Blimey! You wanna leave it alone mate!'

If it's such a life and death issue why are coke heads so gregarious and eager to share their stash? There's no mileage in being a party animal with fucking heroin. What's in it for you? I mean, it's not going to make you popular or anything.

It's true to an extent that an addict is an addict is an addict, but I'm not that objective about it, and although we were encouraged to empathise, three months of group therapy didn't lead me to a greater understanding, except perhaps for the dipsomaniacs. Booze must be the most difficult thing to quit. It's everywhere. They even fucking advertise it on the telly. You go to any familial set piece – a wedding, a funeral, a fucking engagement party – and try to forswear intoxicating drinks: 'What do you mean, you're not having a glass of champagne at your sister's wedding? It's all about you, you miserable bastard!' Substitute heroin for champagne, and you get the idea: 'Your sister's just got engaged and we've got all this fucking gear in and you won't shoot it up? You miserable bastard. One wouldn't hurt, would it?' You see where I'm going with this? Some addictions are more disapproved of than others.

A couple of weeks in and I was beginning to get sentimental about my previous life. I was up to all the mental chicanery addicts will use to get their way. Somewhere en route between the clinic and an NA meeting at the nearby St Mary Abbot's Hospital, I managed to cop a £10 bag. I quickly snorted it, just to take the edge off for a while, but it was immediately apparent to the expert eyes of my fellow patients. Naturally this couldn't be tolerated in this safe environment, and I got kicked out. It was all very embarrassing.

Set loose in London, I was back to sofa-surfing. It was pretty miserable, if I'm honest, and it didn't take me long to see the error of my ways. I had a kind of epiphany, and realised I had to go back and give the treatment a proper chance. Anyway, I turned up two weeks after my eviction and managed somehow to beg my way back in.

When we weren't in group treatment there were various other activities to pass the time. Smoking, for example. A lot of people give up their drug of choice and embark upon a total reinvention of their personality, embracing health foods, physical exertion, yoga, and the abandonment of tobacco. In the clinic, however, this course of action was discouraged. Whatever we did, no one should try to quit smoking, and as a consequence the place was a permanent fog of nervous tobacco smoke.

There was a choice of displacement activities. We could choose between badminton or 'relaxation'. Naturally, being of an idle disposition, relaxation as a form of exercise sounded right up my street. I can't tell you how awful it was. I settled myself on a bean bag. Fine, I could dig that, but then the sotto voce torture began: 'Slowly, relax your muscles, one by one. Feel the tension leave your body. Breathe. That's it. Now, take yourself to your happy place. You're on a beach, the white sand stretches before you, a calm, brilliant blue sea reaches to infinity . . . a dot appears on the horizon . . .'

She'd lost me at 'slowly', already – my jaw was clenched, my teeth grinding, my entire body bathed in a foetid sweat. By the time she started cooing about the bloody dot on the horizon, I was tachycardic. Who the fuck is that Dot on the horizon, and what the fuck do they want? It was like the light at the end of the tunnel that turns out to be an oncoming train. Relaxation my fucking arse.

I was once cajoled into a badminton doubles match, but I have to say it is the most frustrating game. You can whack that shuttle-cock with every ounce of strength at your disposal, but it's never going to go any further than three feet. My proven lack of team spirit dictated that most of the time I would engage in solo basketball practice in the gym. After a while, I was a regular little Harlem Globetrotter.

Eating took up a considerable amount of time in the clinic. When you're using, anything corporeal becomes borderline abhorrent, to the point where nourishing your body is no longer a priority. I would get a bit peckish here and there, usually for sweets, doughnuts, and cakes. As soon as I got clean, however, I could have come top in any pie-eating contest. They had a world-class chef in there, and the canteen was never closed. I was eating about five meals a day, with snacks in between. Every time I sat down, it sounded like a sack of potatoes falling down the cellar steps; everything felt slower and chunkier. Normally I let my waistband police my diet, but because I was wearing pyjamas all day, I wasn't paying much attention to my physique. Then on one occasion I got dressed to go out to an AA meeting. When I got there, I sat down, and as I did so the centre button of my three-button blazer shot out like a bullet from a gun and hit somebody opposite me, about three yards away, right between the eyes. I couldn't have done it better if I'd tried.

It's the only time I've ever gained any weight. I'm not an obsessive weigher of myself, but whenever I do, which could be every ten years, I've always been eight stone twelve. After the near-blinding incident, however, I stepped on the scales and found I was knocking on ten stone. 'Blimey,' I thought, 'ease up on the linguine, will ya?'

You could also get involved with chicks. When you're in the throes of heroin addiction, you don't have the desires of other men, so you're very much sufficient unto yourself. Now that I'd quit, I was reacquainted with the empire of the flesh. I was getting all my feelings back, even to the point of sexual stimulation at times. I was banged up with all these ultra-gorgeous rich girls, delinquent aristocrats. They had that stuff that makes even a junkie look good. What's it called? Oh, yeah: money. Anyway, it was fantastic, because any dalliance of this nature was kept within reason owing to the strict laws against romance in rehab. So, with Iris over in Hampstead, I was falling head-over-heels in love left, right, and centre. I would lose my heart to every female inmate who walked into group therapy.

It was all very charged, high-intensity, super-sensitivity in there.

All of a sudden, some overwhelming emotion or other would come right at you, and it was boo hoo hoo. 'And all because the lady loves Milk Tray . . . boo hoo hoo. Does she really? Boo hoo hoo.' Everything becomes too much; real life becomes like a fabulous new kind of drug. Obviously, that level of intensity can only go bad, and then it's like Edgar Allan Poe put it in *The Fall of the House of Usher*, 'an utter depression of soul which I can compare to no earthly sensation more properly than to the after-dream of the reveller upon opium the bitter lapse into everyday life – the hideous dropping off of the veil. There was an iciness, a sinking, a sickening of the heart – an unredeemed dreariness of thought which no goading of the imagination could torture into aught of the sublime.' In this hyper-medicalised situation, however, it's terrific – but then you have to leave.

It was time well-spent, not just in the enjoyment of no-strings romance: I was writing again. *Face* magazine had commissioned a short piece: my take on what 1984 had actually turned out like. Naturally I hadn't got round to submitting it. I was way past the deadline, but in between therapy, snacks, and basketball practice, I'd sit in my ever-tightening pyjamas and write.

The 1984 story was informed by various attempts to visit my mum in her new high-rise apartment. The street-level intercom was usually out of order, making my entrance both difficult and impossible. The building somehow interfered with the air currents, so there was a constant tornado of garbage. It was like standing in a wind tunnel for what seemed like years in my futile attempts to gain admittance. In the piece, this council estate junkie called Clint McCrocodile has gone out to cop, unsuccessfully, so he goes and buys a load of cough mixture. He's trying to get home, relax, and get well after his exhausting trip to the chemist's, but he can't get in because the intercom is dead. Nothing happens, anyway, apart from a happy ending where he falls asleep in front of the telly watching a video of Bob Chinn's 1978 classic *Hot and Saucy Pizza*

Girls. I'm not sure they ever published it, but it was quite a laugh, with cultural reference points indicative of the zeitgeist circa 1984. I would feature it in my live act for the rest of that year.

Nearing the end of my three-month retreat, I was allowed out on bail for two evenings. At that time Alan Wise could often be found hanging around the Denmark Street office of Phil Jones, my current and long-term manager. Along with Stuart Lyons they used to put on a lot of great high-profile acts at Ronnie Scott's, where they had organised a weekend two-nighter for me and Gil Scott-Heron.

These shows had been on the books for ages, long before rehab. Given the exceptional circumstances, I was permitted to leave the clinic on condition that I be accompanied at all times by two nurses. Fucking great! I thought. That could be quite a spectacle: me turning up flanked by the white coats, redolent of James Brown in the aforementioned *T.A.M.I. Show*, so I laid the dress code on them. 'I don't want you turning up in a suit,' I said. 'It's white coats and stethoscopes all the way. Otherwise I might lose you in the crowd, and anything could happen . . .'

Immediately the two medics were all 'Gil Scott-Heron this, Gil Scott-Heron that, Gil Scott-Heron the other.' At least it got them out of group treatment supervision duties, and their presence lent an air of imminent tragedy that I thought worked in my favour.

'John can't stay around too long after his performance, I'm afraid. He won't be able to do it this time,' Al explained to Gil as soon as we got there. 'He's got a drug problem.'

Quick as a fucking flash, Gil replied, 'I can get him some.'

I mean, it's an old gag, but it was the deadpan speed with which he came straight back with it, like it was the only reasonable response.

Gil was great, a real funny guy. I miss him. After I got out, Wisey did a few more gigs with him, and we spent a lot of time travelling around in the same car. We bonded over cowboy movies.

He was a fellow John Wayne fan. Gil was a secular saint in the firmament of the liberal left, but as he said, 'I don't care what his politics were, motherfucker was tall in the saddle.'

On the second night, I met one of my idols for the first time: the late Bulee 'Slim' Gaillard, the man responsible for the afore-referenced 'Who put the Benzedrine in Mrs Murphy's Ovaltine?' He was a highly accomplished guy; in addition to English, he spoke five languages − Greek, Arabic, German, Spanish, and Armenian − and had also invented one of his own called Vout; a mixture of his own unique form of scat, hipster argot, and a whole new lexicon of previously unknown words. He even went to the point of bringing out a Vout dictionary. Take any word, and add -aroony or -oreeny to its back end − e.g. the old sack-a-rooney − and you're in the groove, Jackson. This is murder, you're telling me.

Vout had other linguistic tics. Carvoeiro = pork. Cheap gold = copper. Frame stasher = a bed. Globe-a-vootie = the world. Ground hump = a mountain. Ground spot = island. Germ transport = a fly. Dip dip = ink. The guy was right out there, I tell you. It had really caught on as the hip slang of the day. You'd hear Sinatra doing it all the fucking time in the Forties. Everybody did. It was a badge of sophistication. It even turned up in Tom and Jerry cartoons.

Slim had the most colourful history of anyone I ever knew. His dad was a merchant seaman who took him to sea on a world voyage. When the ship docked at Crete, twelve-year-old Slim got lost and the ship buggered off with his dad on it, after which he lived the life of an urchin, making shoes and hats as a living, and taught himself to speak Greek. He also worked on boats travelling to Beirut and Syria, until somehow he eventually found his way back to the States, where he got involved with the real sharp edge of the jazz crowd, the Dizzy Gillespies, the Milt Jacksons, the Chet Bakers, Duke Ellington, Count Basie, Peggy Lee: all the real big hitters.

For a while in the late 1930s and early 1940s he paired up with Leroy Eliot Stewart, known as 'Slam', on bass and vocals, while

Slim sang, also playing guitar, piano, and vibraphone. Slim and Slam: you may remember them from numbers such as 'Flat Foot Floogie (with a Floy Floy)', 'Cement Mixer (Puti Puti)', 'Dunkin' Bagel', and 'The Groove Juice Special (Opera in Vout)'.

Slim knew everybody worth knowing, and when he dropped a name, you knew for a fact he'd actually spent time with that person. He'd casually slip in something about that time when he went round to see Arthur and Marilyn on Long Island. He was on first-name terms with them all: Judy Garland, Bing Crosby, Bob Hope, the entire Rat Pack, Robert Mitchum, plus Jimmy Cagney, Jimmy Cagney, and Jimmy Cagney.

Fucking unbelievable the people he hung out with, and *they'd* be bragging about having spent time with *him*. I'm inordinately proud to say he was a friend of mine.

Slim was living in London now, and I got to know him through Molly Parkin, who I knew from the Poetry Olympics. They both turned up to Ronnie Scott's, and when I came off stage the first thing Slim said to me was, 'Hey man. You're a walking computer. You could teach the professors.' Imagine having him say that. A guy who invented a language and was already my hero. That was quite something. I mean, what a payoff.

The White Coats allowed me just enough time to absorb a club soda at Molly and Slim's table, then Moll's daughter Sophie came in. She was about twenty-two at the time, and she sat down and said, 'Hey, Mum, guess who I've just shagged?' Then she gave us the answer: 'Nina Simone.' Of course, Moll took it in her stride, but Slim nearly fell off his chair. Or, that's what I thought had happened until I recently gave Sophie a call to verify this vivid recollection, only to learn that it is a clear case of false-memory syndrome – some scandal-rag headline I've dredged up from the gutter press that is my imagination. What a shame. There goes the movie deal.

★   ★   ★

By this point I had realised that this whole rehab thing was unsustainable; I was paying for the fucking place, or somebody was, and I was already in enough debt to last five lifetimes. Eventually I had to call it, and I decided to check myself out.

I'm not going to wax one way or the other nor badmouth the twelve-step recovery programme, but for some reason that I can't know, it 'works for everyone but me'.

Over at the Hampstead branch meanwhile, thank God, thank God, thank God Almighty, the treatment had worked for Iris. In that respect, even though it cost me a fortune, and landed me with a debt to CBS that has dogged me the whole of my fucking life ever since, it was worth every penny.

When it came to checking-out time, I tried to put on the suit I'd worn when I entered the place, but I couldn't get the trousers up past my knees. I couldn't get into any of my clothes. When Wisey arrived with his brother David to move me out, I had to give them a couple of hundred quid and send them out to Johnson and Johnson's.

Johnson and Johnson's was down near World's End, round the corner from Malcolm and Vivienne's shop, and luckily it specialised in those overcut Fifties Johnnie Ray-style suits where the coat has a low break and padded shoulders, and the trousers have multiple zoot-suit pleats. Good schmutter like linen, sharkskin, mohair, slub silk or hopsack, but cut in a way that just wasn't really my usual slimline style. Still, they were perfect for my now more generous dimensions, and Al and David returned with two extra-large summer-weight versions in a sky-blue wool gaberdine. Light, but drapey. It was that or a muumuu.

Chapter Sixty

EFFRA ROAD, BRIXTON

After we came out of rehab Iris and I stuck together for a bit, then we kind of fell apart. I think she was seeing other people, but so was I; as I've said, we'd both been sort of falling in and out of love in our respective clinics.

Alan had found me an apartment occupying the top two floors of a house on Effra Road in Brixton. The place wasn't quite ready, so his twin brothers each offered temporary accommodation. Johnny and David were both English teachers, Johnny out east in Forest Gate, and David in the comparatively salubrious borough of Twickenham.

Johnny and David were even funnier than Al, if that was possible. They would launch without warning into comedy routines involving expert impersonations of the stars. They must have been a fucking handful growing up. Their powers of mimicry extended to their childhood neighbours in Cheetham Hill, and so they used to make these crank calls in the guise of Maurice Raines who lived close enough for them to be able to see the results of their pranks playing out. Maurice Raines led the kosher life, but was also assimilated almost to the point of deracination and by then he was just posh. He was a successful timber merchant and a pillar of the community.

Mr Raines had a terribly rich, slightly fruity baritone, a cross between Topol and the former Chief Rabbi Jonathan Sacks, and he worked very hard on his received pronunciation. The Wise brothers had his accent off perfect.

There was this local Beth Din-approved delicatessen and catering firm run by a guy called Basil Seremba, whose high-volume arguments with his wife provided a unique shopping experience. Basil was the go-to guy for any of the set pieces of the Jewish social calendar: bar mitzvahs, weddings, seders, and shivas. The terrible twins would take it in turns to ring up Basil Seremba's shop: 'Hello, Maurice Raines here. I'm having a little simcha. Yes, a little simcha for my daughter Stephanie.' Then they'd launch into this unfeasible bulk order from the deli counter:

'Give me eight gross babka, a hundred-weight bublitchki and huluptzes, eight hundred matzo balls, half a ton of lokshen puddings, seventy-two kishke, enough chopped liver for forty people, and a Victoria sponge.' They'd ask for it to be delivered that same afternoon, then they'd all be at the window, pissing themselves at the resultant argument two doors down. There they would be, the unsuspecting Maurice Raines and Basil Seremba's delivery driver, having it out on the gravel drive: 'Now, look here my good man, what's the meaning of this? I didn't order it. It's too much for me. My wife's on a diet. I don't want it . . . Simcha? What simcha? My daughter Stephanie is in Israel taking care of her own dietary arrangements. Who ordered this is a mystery. You have to take it back.' I don't know why I'm laughing; if it happened to me I'd be fucking livid.

First I moved into Forest Gate with Johnny and his wife Denny. My daily visits to the local newsagents quickly earned me my neighbourhood nickname: the Professor – Prof informally. This, I think, was purely down to the fact that I wore glasses. It's strange how, for some reason, bad eyesight marks you out as an intellectual, the assumption being, I suppose, that you've worn your eyes out reading important literature in badly lit public libraries. Equally incomprehensible is the idea that a hearing aid denotes borderline imbecility. Every morning I'd go to buy my paper, to be quizzed on matters of international importance: 'What do you think, Prof?' After a while, my unjustified position as the community sage became onerous, so I moved to David's place in Twickenham, where the wearing of spectacles was not so unusual.

My reflection in any shop window, however, still took me by surprise, provoking the question, 'Who's that fat guy in the sky-blue zoot suit?' Alas, it was me. What was I to do? I couldn't go on a diet: the pleasures of the table were all I had left. Luckily, soon after I arrived at David's house, a bad dose of influenza took care of the problem, as I shed the extraneous pounds just like that. I was back to my normal size, and could fit into all my own clothes again.

I was avoiding drugs and all the people I knew from that world, so the first person I met up with, for some reason, was a girl called Sandra Goodrich. No, not the barefoot chanteuse from Dagenham. This Sandra Goodrich I knew through a mutual friend in Moss Side. She herself grew up in nearby Whalley Range in Manchester, and was now living in Soho. We were both on the rebound – me from Iris, Sandra from a guy called Tim Pope, a very good music-video maker who worked with the likes of The Cure and Siouxsie and the Banshees. She'd found temporary solace in a sapphic love affair, but I talked her out of it and we had a thing for a while.

Sandra was quite the head-turner. A space-age punkette with a pretty face and a cheerful disposition. She looked like Marina,*

---

* Aqua Marina was clearly modelled on *Dr. No* Bond girl Ursula Andress.

Troy Tempest's underwater love-interest in the TV puppet series *Stingray*. Her silent allure is adequately conveyed by Gary Millar over the back credits:

'Marina, Aqua Marina,
What are these strange enchantments that start whenever you're near?'

Platinum hair with black roots, a walking work of art, she was a pop sensation waiting to happen. She once wore a bodysuit made entirely out of crepe bandages dyed black. Over this in lieu of a dress she wore a slip in plum-coloured parachute silk plus a pair of non-identical high-heeled shoes of the same colour.

She was really smart. She had this fabulous gaff on Frith Street – directly above the Bar Italia and facing onto the world-famous Ronnie Scott's and its distinctive neon saxophone sign. There we were in *The Small World of Sammy Lee*. It was the perfect location for her business. She ran a very successful kissogram agency. In fact, I think she possibly invented that particular form of enterprise. It became a real big deal. She was doing a roaring trade in bookings for sexy nuns in mascara, naughty nurses, and over-glamorised policewomen (see Stevenage nick). There was also a camp guy called Anthony who wore one of those leopard-print one-shoulder leotards and turned up for events as the Gay Tarzan. Back then, she would hang out in gay clubs because she wouldn't get mithered there.

Sandra was raking it in. She was doing so well that she had an accountant-cum-coke dealer. She was a right coke nut, but she didn't need no cocaine. She was a regular little coffee pot, up all hours of the day and night. She also enjoyed a drink. She was a troublemaker, always getting us slung out of places. She had this girlfriend called Velda, who she had the cheek to say she couldn't take anywhere, but Sandra was far worse than her. Every time, it was everybody else's fault but hers.

After I started seeing Sandra, I moved out of Twickenham and into the Chelsea Arts Club – Molly Parkin put me up for membership, and Slim Gaillard seconded my application. It was the perfect environment in which to ease myself into a life beyond addiction. I got into quite the gentleman's routine there, which the clinic had advised was very important in recovery. I had a sparsely furnished room overlooking the walled garden, and would wake each day to a choice of sensational cooked breakfasts from the entire range of British classics: devilled kidneys, kedgeree, kippers, the Full English, even an omelette Arnold Bennett. I was keeping to the recovery programme and attending the Rooms, sometimes going to meetings on a twice-daily basis, which took up most of my day. Full of good intentions, I also dealt with some unfinished business and got my finances into some kind of order, on a neighbourhood level anyway: I'd gone into treatment owing Jackie Genova a small fortune, and now that I'd quit, was in a position to pay it all off.

The rest of the time I whiled away at the club, monopolising the snooker table. I'd learned to play in the Jewish hospital when I'd had my tonsils and adenoids removed at the age of ten or so, and had carried my interest into adulthood. Eventually, other more established members started to complain about not being able to get a game in.

Fortunately, the place in Effra Road was ready before my snooker habit caused any real upset. It was a capacious self-contained duplex apartment in a very substantial three-storey house owned by the landlady, a Jamaican-Chinese woman called Mrs Chin who lived on the ground floor. It was a good location, on the corner of Mervan Road, close to the Ritzy movie theatre and Effra Road Chapel, from whence the sweet sounds of the Gospel Choir awoke me each Sunday morning.

In order to keep me on the programme – and business is business – Alan had been busy making bookings for me, so I had a couple of big shows lined up. One was a local gig at the Brixton Academy in March, again with Gil Scott-Heron, then in April, up to Liverpool for a high-profile show at the Neptune Theatre with Allen Ginsberg, plus local talent Jimmy Kelly.

That was the only show of mine that my mother ever came to, and I was obviously keen to look healthy and drug-free. She'd only found out about the heroin when I went into treatment. She may have had her worries about me before then, but as far as I was concerned she had no idea about the junk, because I had kept everything quiet up until then. The only reason she knew anything about it was because my original admission to the clinic made it into the showbiz column in the *Sun* newspaper. I was amazed they'd bothered to mention it; I would have thought I was well below their radar. It was quite a well-meaning 'Good luck to him' sort of piece, but, nevertheless, I was pretty pissed off. Still, I didn't go all Hugh Grant about it. It wasn't Rupert Murdoch's fault: I took some agency in my own predicament. But once my mum was in the know, it added a whole other dimension to my recovery. After that, even when I was using I'd always deny it to her, 'No, I've been in a clinic, Ma.' Every so often, I had to convince her that I was all right, and so inviting her to come and watch me perform along with Allen Ginsberg was the perfect opportunity.

As a lifelong card-carrying library member and great reader of books, to her credit my mum was quite contemporary when it came to literature, and she obviously knew who Allen Ginsberg was. This was a class gig – a legitimate literary sit-down theatre do; nothing to do with rock and roll or punk or any of that. I figured that if the old girl was going to enjoy anything I did, this would be it.

I got the firm to sort it all out so she had the complete VIP package. I said, 'Treat her like the queen she is, OK?' Wisey sent a limousine round for her and everything. Nico was still living in Manchester at the time, in Singleton Road, so the limo picked her up on the way and I met them at the theatre. Nico and my mother in the back of a limo bound for Merseyside. Somebody should have filmed that. Where's Andy Warhol when you need him?

I loved living in Brixton. It was a damn sight more neighbourly than Holloway Road, for a start. I used to mosey about in the market and go up Acre Lane, where I discovered some fantastic shopping opportunities. A particularly fortuitous find was the Big Apple, a hat shop that catered to the Rastafarian demographic.

Back in the days of Bob Marley and the Wailers, the Big Apple had done a roaring business with the trademark red, green, and gold flat caps, tam o' shanters, and snoods, but now it had started to adapt more established items of gentlemen's headgear, giving them a slightly higher crown in order to accommodate the wearer's ever-expanding dreadlocks. I was a great frequenter of the place for the same reason: I had a similar problem with my high-maintenance bouffant.

Who wants to be a milliner? They did. It wasn't like some cottage industry; they were perfectionists, offering a limitless choice of all the trad hats: fedoras, borsalinos, Milans, and leghorns, the bobble hat, the stingy brim, the beanie, and of course, the Gatsby, an eight-piece newsboy cap in tweeds and herringbones – all with extra headroom on top. I bought a couple of stingy brims there, the perfect look for me. I also got one of their Rastaficated yachting caps. That was another good look: I built a whole outfit round that motherfucker. I thought, why not go the whole fucking nautical hog, so I got hold of a double-breasted navy-blue blazer to match. The whole yacht club schtick. Ahoy there, shipmates! This look isn't as stupid as I'm making it sound. Put it this way, I've seen pictures of Lionel

Richie wearing the whole rig and I'm just saying, like, you know, that ain't nothing.

There were, however, other local speciality traders and it didn't take me long to sniff them out. When I moved to Brixton I was still quite weak and attending regular NA meetings. One day at a time, sweet Jesus. But then I started buying the odd little bit of weed. This was Brixton after all, which at the time was sensi central – sin semilla that is, from the Spanish for 'no seeds'. It was the most crackpot weed you could get back then, and as I've said, my copy of *MIMS* had reliably informed me of its non-addictive properties.

Because of the absence of seeds, nobody could grow it in this country, and if you didn't have a Jamaican contact, forget about it. I quickly found a regular guy outside the betting shop on Railton Road who knocked out £5 deals.

I was also living within earshot of a friend of mine called Ray Jordan, who I knew through Jake Riviera. Early on he worked with The Clash's road crew as their security man, and he was and is one of the best. He was always good company.

I kinda got kidnapped by him for an afternoon at the cricket. At school I hated cricket and everything it stood for; I even wrote one of my very first poems about it. Before Mr Malone came along, when I was twelve or thirteen, physical exercise lessons had been abandoned one day because of fog, which was the only thing that could get us off games. To keep us occupied, the teacher gave us the job of writing a poem about cricket. Not knowing anything about the game, and not being particularly interested, I just wrote, 'Rain stopped play', and then looked out of the window for an hour. It wasn't appreciated, and I was severely punished. I thought I was being succinct, but the powers that be saw it as skiving off poetry duty.

Understandably, then, when Ray suggested an outing to the Oval, I wasn't keen. 'Count me out, Ray,' I said, 'but leave me a pinch of that stuff.' I couldn't give a fuck about the cricket; however, he had this big bag of Sinsemilla, and he talked me into it.

It turned out to be a very pleasant day. A blinding one, in fact. It was the fifth and final Test of the West Indies' victorious 1984 series against England, in the days of Clive Lloyd, Viv Richards, Michael Holding, and Joel Garner. We sat in the West Indian end, and if you are only ever going to see one cricket match, that was it.

Then Nico moved in. She'd been on a six-week tour of Italy, but her manager hadn't managed to pay the rent on her swank apartment, high atop Manchester's stately Sedgley Park. Consequently, she'd been evicted in absentia, and came home to find everything she owned stacked in a room on the ground floor. Another little job for Wise Moves. She urgently needed somewhere to live, and I and my Brixton duplex were Al's first port of call. It would have seemed churlish to refuse, given that it was him who sorted the gaff out in the first place. And who would say no to Nico? For an international superstar, she was easy company. She had very few possessions: the harmonium, the capsule wardrobe in every shade of dark, plus a quantity of heroin from the Neapolitan Mob. She said it was fabulous, and she wasn't given to effusive claims.

Nico was self-contained, self-possessed; she somehow fully owned any space she wound up in. Even if it was for one night only at a Holiday Inn, she would convert the most anonymous accommodation into Nico World. This she achieved by virtue of various diaphanous Indian scarves which would be draped over the windows and lamps. The use of incense was also helpful. As a result of this mini-makeover her room would be bathed in a magenta light, and perfumed by the scent of Nag Champa.

When I think of Nico, I picture her in the cloak, motorbike boots, and black jeans ensemble she wore most of the time. I don't remember her wearing a dress, ever. There's a widely distributed photograph of her and me sitting on the doorstep on Effra Road. It's in monochrome: we were monochrome people. We both look pretty good. Nico's wearing black leather jeans, a fine black turtleneck sweater, and black Turkish boudoir slippers, me beside her in a charcoal-grey Continental suit and sporting a Gatsby, freshly acquired from the Big Apple.

Thanks to this photograph appearing in the music press, we were perceived as an item. Both our careers could have done with a bit of a push at this point, and to capitalise on this I floated the idea of bringing out an album of duet covers under the name 'Nico and Johnnie'. The track list would include numbers such as 'The Beat Goes On' by Sonny and Cher, 'Love is Strange' by Mickey and Sylvia, 'Welcome Home' by Peters and Lee, 'I Just Want to Stay Here' by Steve Lawrence and Eydie Gormé, and 'Thanks for the Memory' by Bob Hope and Shirley Ross. What a terrific repertoire. We practised at home, and got to be pretty good. I can't prove this, because sadly there is no recorded evidence, but you've gotta believe me.

Meanwhile, I was obviously on that Neapolitan dope like a shark on a bucket of chum; like a Jap on a bottle of Scotch. See where I'm going with this? I was enthusiastic. It wasn't Nico's fault. It was always going to happen – I blame her uncharacteristic use of the word 'fabulous'.

Brixton, I discovered then, was full of heroin addicts. There were big distribution operations taking place in Villa Road and the Barrier Block, a sort of sub-Corbusian, on-the-cheap council estate built in the early Eighties, often mistaken for Brixton Prison. It was rapidly ghettoised in that homogeneous boho fashion, with all that New York ersatz Jean-Michel Basquiat rattle-can artwork on the concrete walls.

The Barrier Block and the Villa Road squats were home to various embryonic goth bands and trainee addicts, all of them in thrall to The Velvet Underground and, especially, Nico; if they'd found out where she was living they would have been camping out on our doorstep, and I didn't want that to happen.

Many people find the idea of routine to be boring, but there's nothing more tedious than a life of chaos. Routine is the unattainable goal of the addict. Take the mundane yet crucial regularity of one's bodily functions. Even when I was back on the junk in Brixton, I had my little regime. As we know, the constipating properties of opiates are legendary; they put everything to sleep including the urge to void your bowels. After rising, this became my top priority. With that in mind, I'd have my breakfast in a cafe in Brixton market run by two Italian brothers, Franco and Toto, who did good quick Continental snacks: avocado on toast, a prune Danish, or one of those Portuguese custards, I think they're called *pastéis de nata*, along with a pint of espresso and some sort of soft fruit: for me, that fruit and coffee combo invariably provokes an efficient peristaltic response. I wouldn't want you to think I was an obsessive, but only then could I get straightened out.

Back in Effra Road, for the rest of the afternoon it was daytime television. There would be snacks around the house – a vanilla slice here, a doughnut there – but when it came to sensible food, my go-to meal of choice for years was a can of plum tomatoes on toast.

I'm happy to share my recipe here for the first time. I'd cut a couple of really thick slices of Hovis (for me, the only acceptable brown bread) and toast them. Then, in lieu of butter, I'd apply a sort of vinaigrette made with lemon juice, olive oil, and mustard, and maybe the odd crush of garlic. Meanwhile, I'd warm the tomatoes over a medium heat. I'd then pour them onto the Hovis doorsteps, add salt and pepper to taste, and a final drizzle of olive oil.

Without being aware of it, I actually had a pretty good diet. They've lately found out that tinned tomatoes are extremely good for you: canning them builds up the antioxidant properties, and in fact, in terms of lycopene content, they're better than the fresh ones. There were people with far worse diets than I had.

Other than my tomatoes on toast speciality, I didn't do much cooking in Effra Road. The only thing Nico ever cooked was dhal and rice; in fact, what she ate more than anything else was raw cubes of Rowntrees jelly. She'd break a chunk off, straight out of the packet, usually Mandarin Orange flavour, like some sort of jujube. I can see why – delicious. I guess it would have *some* protein, what with the gelatine, but she thought it was full of Vitamin C. She ate a lot of that.

Another of Nico's recipes involved the use of Crabtree & Evelyn rosewater in the injection process. When you shoot up, the unbearably bitter taste of heroin enters your mouth immediately via the bloodstream, far quicker than if you'd put it on your tongue. Nico's rosewater rendered it delicious; it was like eating Turkish Delight, full of Eastern promise. The scent would also come out on your skin: our very sweat was fragrant beyond belief.

We had the occasional visitor staying over: Johnny, David, and Alan Wise, Jackie Genova, of course, Sandra, and Michael Archangel, for example. Michael was a Trinidadian dreadie who lived locally. Michael had had a chequered career which had brought him into contact with notorious mobster Lucky Gordon, slum lord Peter Rachman, Michael de Freitas, aka Michael X, Christine Keeler, and Mandy Rice Davies, but emboldened by the success of Linton Kwesi Johnson and myself, he had recently determined to get into the poetry business. Forty-five minutes after his arrival at our gaff, there would be another knock on the door, and it would be any one of a harem of twelve posh chicks, delivering his lovingly prepared lunch: jerk chicken, rice and peas, a bit of fish, curry goat, okra. Anyway, it always smelled delicious.

Wisey had his own room in Effra Road for when he came down to London. We all used to go out to the movies at the

Ritzy. Nobody had a video player at the time, and the great thing about living in Brixton and being so near the Ritzy was that it had everything on celluloid. The Ritzy showed art movies and all the classics, and it also had really good cakes and ice cream sourced from some farm or other. Nico and I became such regular customers that we got to know the programmer, to the extent that we could order up any movies in advance for our Saturday all-nighters. They already did a late show anyway, but we'd be there until dawn. Movie after movie after movie. One time, for example, we had a Sam Fuller night, with a selection of the multi-generic gems of the late great director played end to end: *Forty Guns*, *House of Bamboo*, *China Gate*, *The Naked Kiss*, *The Steel Helmet*, *I Shot Jesse James*, *Gangs of the Waterfront*, *Bowery Boy*, and *Pickup on South Street*. They even had the more recent *White Dog*, released in 1982. Sam Fuller was awarded the Légion d'Honneur for his hard-boiled movies, which were always delivered on time and under budget; he would often save money on his leading actors by recruiting them from popular TV shows: people like Aldo Ray, Anthony Eisley, and Peter Breck.

Al was a terrible person to go to the movies with. He was a big guy and he couldn't sit still. He always seemed distracted: he'd be twitching, counting his loose change, blowing his nose and then inspecting the contents of his handkerchief, nipping off for yet another ice cream – anything but pay attention to what was on the screen. It drove me mad. Why bother going if you're not going to watch the film? But afterwards he could talk you through that movie, give you the subtext – no nuance had escaped his attention. Without seeming to do so, he memorised entire chunks of dialogue. He had an eidetic memory when it came to motion picture films.

Chapter Sixty-One

TWO-FIFTHS OF THE VELVET UNDERGROUND UNDER MY ROOF

In spring 1985 John Cale moved in with us for a month. He was over to produce Nico's album *Camera Obscura*. Now I had two-fifths of The Velvet Underground under my roof. I was utterly starstruck. He had the spare room which Al sometimes utilised, so we'd spent hours hoovering and tidying it up in readiness. Brand-new bedding, the full VIP.

John didn't pull his weight on the domestic front, but that wasn't part of his remit, and anyway, most of the time he was studio-bound. In that respect, as a houseguest he was fairly low maintenance, except on one unhappy occasion. He had returned to the flat after a hard day's graft at the controls and was ready to hit the sack, only to discover a sickening void where his pillow should have been. Somebody – one of our many uninvited visitors – must have gone into his room and borrowed it. He lost his rag. He stomped into the lounge, threatening to defenestrate the guilty party. He was a big guy and entirely capable of carrying out this threat. Given the altitude, the spiked railings, and the busy main road beyond, this would have resulted in an impalement and certain death. I immediately saw all the possibilities at once – it was Hell. John Cale was doing vodka for breakfast and the rest of the day it was cocaine all the way. That combo would make anybody a bit irritable.

As I've said, The Velvet Underground were like living saints to all those gothic junkies in the Villa Road squats and so, as with Nico, we were at pains to keep John Cale's presence a secret. No matter how hard we tried, however, we couldn't keep somebody like Nico under wraps for long. She'd done some deal in the neighbourhood and that let the cat out of the bag, and once they'd discovered where she lived it was yap yap yappity yap. Where you have junkies, as sure as night follows day, liberties will be taken. 'Lend a man your horse, he'll steal your wife,' as Machiavelli used to say. And sure enough – in no time our happy home became a twenty-four-hour shooting gallery.

The whole escapade is recounted in James Young's *Nico: Songs They Never Play on the Radio*, which I have to confess I've never read, although I have over the years absorbed its contents second-hand.

James was a part-time piano-botherer, plucked from an Oxford saloon bar by his old college compadre, Dr Alan Wise. He got lucky, joined Nico's band, travelled the world, kept his mouth shut most of the time, and wrote his book.

James gave everybody different names except Nico and me: Alan Wise is Dr Demetrius, Jackie Genova is Jackie Genova, Raincoat is Phil Rainford, a hairdresser turned Wise Moves operative. I hope he's better now. I'm just plain old John Cooper Clarke, so I guess that's why I have been heavily quizzed on certain points.

The level of squalor evoked therein, 'The walls splattered with blood, putrefying takeaways . . .', for example. That was none of our doing. We were hyper-hygienic and Nico didn't have enough stuff to make a mess with. And my only takeaways came from the cake shop and were never around long enough for the agents of putrefaction to kick in.

Another bit which always comes up is when he was staying at my gaff and he describes finding me asleep, or seeming to be asleep, in front of the television which featured nothing but the monochrome fuzz and that atmospheric crackle you used to get when transmission ended around 1am. The announcer even used to say goodnight and then *Kssshhh . . .* According to James Young, I was sitting there conked out and he came in and switched the telly off, and apparently I woke up and said, 'I was watching that.' This may well have been the case, because I had a piece of cardboard with a shirt template cut out of it and would design shirt-fabric patterns based on the random flickering pointillism provided by the vacant screen. Sometimes, I could still be stippling away until breakfast time. That said, I might have flaked out – admittedly, that is also entirely possible.

Whatever, it's not all about me. The clue is in the title, *Nico: Songs They Never Play on the Radio* – her elusive glamour remains unassailable.

Once all the goth reprobates started to make themselves at home, it became untenable in Effra Road and Nico moved back up to Manchester, only to return that August for a triple-treat spectacular at the Chelsea Town Hall starring Slim Gaillard, Nico, and me.

Sadly – I say sadly because she was a lot of fun – in the interim, my affair with Sandra had begun to collapse. The last time I'd seen her, I'd hit her up for £70 then left her standing in Old Compton Street in the pissing rain, characteristically shouting: 'I want it back this time, Johnny. I want this one back.' You know, unlike all the other seventy quids I'd 'borrowed' off her.

'Yeah, later, San,' I replied as I jumped into a black cab. 'Can you drop me off in Earls Court?' 'No, Sandra. Fuck off! It's right out of the way,' and I had zoomed off to Forest Hill, Sandra's furious complaints receding into the distance. Who can blame her. I hadn't even given her a fucking lift in my taxi.

On the night of the Chelsea Town Hall show, I got there early to sort myself out, and went into the dressing room to find guess who? It was Sandra and her male companion. Any animosity had died down – she didn't remind me of the outstanding £70, but she made a real point of introducing me to her new squeeze. 'You won't have met Zodiac,' she said. Zodiac? With Sandra, of course it was Zodiac. His real name, I later discovered, was Mark Manning.

Zodiac had greasy hair down to his arse and no shoes. 'Fucking hell,' I thought. 'Sandra's come down in the world.' It was pissing down that day as well and there she was with the noble savage here walking the streets of London barefoot in the rain. I had to bring it up with everyone I bumped into for the rest of the night – all like, 'Have you seen who Sandra's ended up with? What a fucking loser.' Still, it had been good to see her.

Next thing I knew, who should be toppermost of the poppermost but Zodiac Mindwarp and the Love Reaction with their current smash 'Prime Mover'. After that, all my friends just loved rubbing my nose in it: 'It's all over for you now, Johnny', 'What did you expect?', 'I don't blame the girl', 'You were well overdue, you liberty taking cunt' – and all sorts of sympathetic stuff like that.

Still, if she was happy, I was happy, but her appearance had introduced an unexpected minor chord of melancholy to a sensational night. That was the first time George Ivan Morrison ever came to one of my shows. Remember 'Here Comes the Night' and the epic heartbreak therein? How perfectly he expressed the misery of young love betrayed. And then there's his magnum opus, the aforementioned *Astral Weeks*. Since then I have been a total fan.

Slim was in the autumn of his years and this was a rare chance to catch Monsieur Gaillard live on stage. I had therefore obviously assumed that Van was there for him. If I thought that somebody like Van Morrison was even indifferent to my poetry, I would have been destroyed, and so I was happy to learn that he was there for the entire show. Some people I knew had been sitting near him and they later told me that Van seemed to be enjoying himself, even during my set. Obviously, right away I was fishing for specifics: Which bits did he seem to like? Did he laugh at any point? If so, what at?

Since then, he's been in the audience at my shows twice that I know of. Thanks, Van.

I'm very proud of that, because I know that Van Morrison is a poetry lover and a fine lyricist. Once, while in the town of Belfast, I had an allocated driver named Malcolm and a couple of hours to kill before we drove up to my show in Portrush. Malcolm asked me if there was anywhere I wanted to go, so I requested Cyprus Avenue. 'Don't tell me when we get there,' I said. And there it was. Cyprus Avenue. It was immediately iden- tifiable, identical to the mental image conjured by the poetry of Van Morrison in his song of the same name. A true exercise in psychogeography.

By then, I was the last man standing in Brixton. I still harboured ideas about cleaning up, but what with all my connections in London, things were going to end badly if I hung around, so I decided to move back up to Manchester for a bit. I no longer knew anyone in Manchester who sold narcotics, or maybe just one or two, and I figured this was my best chance. In the Rooms it's what they call 'doing a geographical'. I handed the keys to Al, who came down and stayed there until the end of the lease.

There was me back in Manchester, Sedgley Park even, thinking I'd knock things on the head for good. Instead, for the next five years it was only the story of junk, and my life just got increas- ingly squalid. I had to stand by and watch the disintegration of my entire personality. Dion DiMucchi put it best:

Well, if I ever told you
All about the things I have done
I can't remember having
Even one day of fun [. . .]
The things I like and wanna have
I can't even buy
But I know, yeah
That I was born to cry.

I had good intentions . . . At first. I got everybody – me, Nico, and a couple of other addicts in the Wisey firm – on a methadone regime. That didn't mean that I stuck to it religiously, however. Nico pretty much stayed off junk after that, but I still hadn't reached that point. For me, methadone was more of a safety net than a serious effort to quit: I simply became a commuting junkie, training it down to London all the time in order to get fixed. Then, once I'd been in Manchester for a while and started dropping in the Lifeline drop-in centre, I found that thanks to the Ayatollah, the city was full of the shit.

Lifeline was run by a bunch of junkies turned Mandrax casualties, or whatever – they were all on something or other, stumbling about trying to give you advice. It was fucking bollocks. If anything, all Lifeline did was introduce me to new local connections. I'd go there for help and find myself surrounded by all these people I'd seen around town, but whom I wouldn't ever have taken for heroin users, not in a million years. The times I'd been in their company, sick as a dog, when they could have fucking sorted me out with a guy who lived three streets away. And there was me going all the way to Moss Side.

Lifeline made it so easy. The minute I got my feet under the table there, all incentive to kick simply vanished. The way they had things organised you'd be a fool not to get a habit. So going to Manchester didn't do any good and now to make it even worse,

I was perceived as that clever cunt who'd gone to the smoke like he was Big Time Charley Potatoes and now was back like a whipped dog, and penniless. 'I heard he was living in a storm drain in Bowker Vale', and all that kind of gossip. And worst yet, I was condemned to the dreaded half-life of the 'local eccentric'.

The only people I had any contact with were other junkies and my contacts, both pharmaceutical and professional. I still had to work; in fact, more than ever, even if I was sick. Then, as now, I was always able to put any illness, drug-related or otherwise, aside for the duration of my set. Nobody would know it, but very often I've been smiling through the tears. What a trooper. Just call me Judy Garland.

Al was still getting me some pretty high-profile bookings. In November '85 I appeared again at Liverpool's Neptune Theatre, this time with Nico. There's always something better to do than write a poem, ask anybody, and I hadn't written any new stuff for yonks apart from the odd magazine commission here and there. There were also a few vain attempts at publication under the nom de plume Byron Slayne: a couple of self-help books, namely *Schtup Til you Plotz* and *How to Hurt your Own Feelings*. Somebody told me that there was money to be made in the field of children's literature, so I even pitched a series of murder mysteries aimed at the under-twelves: *Eat Lead Miss*, *Scarface Junior*, and *Hickory Dickory Dead*. Even so, my set had become longer and I was expected to be on stage for forty-five minutes, so I would do prolonged intros to the poems which would be a vehicle for gags. As time went on, with no new material to speak of, the intros and gags took over to the point where some nights people would be begging for poetry: 'Read us a poem. Enough already with the gags.' I wore my repertoire out.

By this stage, Wisey wasn't much help where I was concerned. He owed me money and was nowhere to be found, especially when I was looking for him. He was a very troubled person, a complete fuck-up really, and anyway Nico was more than he could deal with, so in the end I had to give him the old pink slip.

Once again without representation, I'd now have to spend a whole afternoon in a telephone box chasing down work in ever more unlikely towns, e.g. Milford Haven, Whitby, Grasmere, and Ashby-de-la-Zouch. I was performing in all sorts of khazis for nothing, just to get well, schlepping all over the place on every kind of public transport, because I could kiss goodbye to the luxury of a personal driver. Hard, hard, hard. It became a completely feral hand-to-mouth existence. I couldn't make any arrangements, even two days in advance – when it comes to dope, whatever your schedule, you can't have one.

As I have been at pains to point out, when it came to romance, potential girlfriends always had to make the first move. Apart from the Kia-Ora routine, I don't remember ever chatting a girl up in my life. It sounds kind of vain, but I've never really put the heat on anybody – except Evie, my wife, and even then I wasn't confident.

I met Evie on Friday 13 March 1987, in the house we still call home in Essex. I was in town for a show at the local arts centre. Evie had been to see Linton and me at the University of Essex in 1981, but although she speaks three languages, this hadn't quite prepared her for our poetic approach involving out-of-town accents and slang-ridden synaptic shortcuts at breakneck speed. She'd gone to the Arts Centre that night to see if my poetry made any more sense. She has since told me she didn't understand a word of it that time either.

As she was about to go to bed, she got a call from Anita Pacione, who ran the arts centre. Anita was a friend of Evie's and she said that I'd missed the last train, I was hungry, didn't have anywhere to go, and boo hoo hoo. She asked if Evie would be the Good Samaritan and put me up for the night, and thank God, thank God, thank God Almighty, Evie said yes.

I stayed the night in Evie's spare room and at some point discovered that she had a boyfriend, so for once I had to put the graft in. Anyway, the hard work obviously paid off because I'm proud to now call Evelyne Edith Plusse my wife. That happy event, however, was far from my imaginings then.

I went back to Manchester, where my phone had been cut off, so other than writing Evie a letter, I had no means of further pursuing this chance encounter. Evie, apparently, thought I was sweet. The fact that I was an addict was impossible for her, however. She wasn't having that. She was an adult with a mortgage and a proper job as a bilingual secretary at a firm of accountants: the last thing she needed was a junkie and his monkey on her back. Nevertheless, she asked Anita for my number, who immediately warned her off. I was 'trouble', Anita said. Evie should leave well alone but then she got in touch with me through my mum anyway.

My mother lived quite close by but I was keeping out of her way on account of my condition. I was all the time trying to convince her I was still clean, and never answered the door when she called by. Any messages for me she put in an envelope and posted through my letterbox.

Evie used to read the *NME* so she knew when I was going to be in London. She'd meet me at Euston Station and accompany me to my gig, which was usually in a pub like the Lady Owen Arms in Clerkenwell, the Half Moon in Putney, the Cricketers in Kennington, the Hope and Anchor in Islington, or the Edinboro Castle in Camden, but mainly it was the regular monthly appearance at the Sir George Robey in Finsbury Park.

The Sir George Robey, named after the well-known Edwardian music-hall performer, was for many years a jolly punk-rock venue, but also a local for a lot of sharp characters and just about the most disreputable pub in North London at the time. The Sir George Robey was one of the very few places where I was guaranteed a gig. It was a great place; a big Irish pub, run by Malcolm and Brian, two gentlemen from Belfast and friends across the religious divide who had come to London to seek their fortune in the non-sectarian world of rock and roll. They had an enlightened booking policy with a large rotation of regular acts: jobbing rockers like the Triads, an all-girl combo from round the corner, also the UK Subs, the Groundhogs, Screaming Lord Sutch and the Savages – and me. It was a lifeline, really; it was the nearest thing I had to a regular job and I could always get paid cash in advance of future bookings. They never washed the pumps out so it was always the same advice; only drink bottled beer.

It was a hang-out for the likes of Max Splodge, Eddie Tudor Pole, and Wellsy aka Frankie Mansfield, with whom I'm still good mates to this day. I would often run into Mark Smith there when he was in London. It was also the local for John Lydon and his oppo John Rambo Stephens. It was quite close to Highbury so Friday nights would involve pre-match lock-ins with sing songs, minor punch-ups, and all manner of hilarity. It was full of Irish lump labourers and gangsters and if your face didn't fit you were likely to get a good hiding. There was all sorts of side action going on in there, all overseen by Fat Tony, supplier to the stars.

It's hard to imagine that such a place would achieve the rosy aura of romance, yet this was the setting of our early courtship.

Meanwhile, back up North, I was living by night. I never had any money to speak of, so I barely left the house other than my obligatory trip out for breakfast. We had a lot of kosher shops in the area, where I'd get the regulatory morning shot of coffee with maybe a bagel or a little sugary knish. On the way home I'd rent a video from the garage. I racked up a massive fine for *Terminator*, the movie Schwarzenegger was born to play. Admittedly, I had had it for ages but the rental got jacked up to £25.00 before they sent the reminder. They could have told me earlier. I had it out with the manager and got a bit knocked off, but in fairness I had watched it quite a few times before then. I thought it was a terrific picture. Twenty-five quid, though! I could have bought the mother-fucker twice over at that price.

At some indeterminate point I'd become a speedball maniac: a speedball being cocaine and heroin in the same shot. That's as good as it gets. Don't do it. Not even once.

I obviously had caviar taste and fishpaste money, so the ideal was when one of a number of people came round to my place having been unable to cop anywhere in town. It had become known among the more affluent car-owning fellow-users that I had connections all over London and if someone gave me a lift down there, then one way or another I'd be able to come good.

It was a syndicate-type arrangement: they had a load of money, I could get large-ish amounts from one of my various suppliers and by way of a finder's fee, I bagged a fairly big chunk of it for myself. The roads were relatively empty at 2am, so we'd have a clear run. We'd fucking clog it down the M6 with a bit of music on the car stereo, straight there, do the business and straight back home, and no hanging about. It was a round trip of about ten hours tops and sorted for a week. Bingo. There was often some unforeseen shortage, which was only good news for me, because I like being in a car anyway.

By then I was reliant on shit like that happening. At the end of the day, I was a long-distance junkie hustler and if I got a gig that paid three figures, well, yippee.

Something would crop up out of the blue, on the rare occasion even involving foreign travel. At some point, for example, someone or other set me up with a short solo tour of Switzerland involving

Zurich, Geneva, Lausanne, I suppose. The truth is, I can't even remember where exactly I went or even which city I flew into, but then I didn't have to, because someone else sorted out all the logistics for me: they sent me the plane ticket and all I had to do was get on an airplane, then once I arrived in Switzerland all my transport and hotels were pre-arranged. (I could never have organised a tour abroad for myself. I'm lousy at anything like that; to this day I couldn't organise a family trip to Southend without help.) In any case, on this occasion I'd got myself somehow to Switzerland, but after that it didn't quite go according to plan because I got kidnapped.

I'd got a late-afternoon flight and when I came through customs onto the arrivals concourse it was almost empty and the usual guy holding up the cardboard sign with my name on it was nowhere to be seen. I loitered around for a bit, then eventually went over to the information desk to ask if they could do an announcement over the tannoy. I was in the middle of giving them my name etc., when a guy appeared out of nowhere and tapped me on the shoulder. 'Mr Clarke,' he said, 'allow me to introduce myself.' He told me his name, Dr Something or Other, let's say Müller, then he said, 'Please, Mr Clarke. Come with me. My car is parked outside. I've taken the liberty of cancelling your hotel booking. I will explain further on our drive.'

Understandably, at first I was all, 'What the . . . ? Huh? You've done what?' But he spoke perfect English with a European accent, he was well turned out, his apparel understatedly expensive with a cashmere overcoat and silk scarf, so I took one look at him and thought he looked kosher: he didn't look like a chancer or anything, not like a gangster or anybody who needed money, and so I gave him the benefit of the doubt. What else would I be doing anyway, at that hour, in the airport of a strange city, with no idea of which hotel I was supposed to be sleeping in, nor any clue how to get there, even if I had?

'Dr Müller' was driving a very large Mercedes 280SL in a nice dull gold with the softest pale-leather upholstery – a beautiful classic car that had been bought by a discerning aesthete, so again all this went in his favour and I got into the car and we set off. He then told me that he would be honoured if I would be his family's guest for that week. He also divulged that he had ascertained that I was chemically dependent, which took me aback because, at that point, I was still trying to keep this really private; it wasn't in my interest to be known internationally as a user of narcotics, after all. He said that he could help me in this regard: as a qualified doctor he was in a position to make my short stay in Switzerland as easy and comfortable as possible. He would provide accommodation, transport to and from my shows across the country, and a no-questions-asked supply of whatever drugs I required. In other words, I wouldn't have to get involved in any criminal activity, so naturally I thought, 'Bring it on, Doc.'

In the course of our journey, it became apparent that Dr Müller was a great lover of English poetry. It's one thing to be able to hold your own with the help of a phrase book, and that I admire, but it's quite another to apply yourself to the poetry of another language, and as such he was clearly anxious to talk to a fellow enthusiast, I suppose. He was extremely well read; not only familiar with the classics, he was also au fait with the contemporary scene and with this perspective he compared my stuff to the work of Alexander Pope. All I had to do was just have poetic conversations with him, and to consolidate it he was able to sort me out in return, so obviously I went along with it.

We drove along winding Alpine roads into a snow-covered Christmas-card landscape until eventually this amplified cuckoo clock of a chalet appeared in a valley in the distance, its windows all brightly illuminated. It couldn't have looked more archetypically chocolate-box Swiss. After a further half hour we arrived at last and

went into the generously proportioned and tastefully modernised
Swiss interior, the delicious smells of a hot meal wafting from a
huge stove, over which stood Dr M's gorgeous trophy wife, two
sleepy pyjama-clad and perfectly blonde Swiss children by her
side. It was almost too good to be true – Dr Müller was thirty
years old, tops, so he'd obviously done very well very early on
and had every reward the medical profession could bestow upon
a person at such an early age.

Mrs M welcomed me in, telling me to make myself at home
while she put the children to bed, and then we would sit down
to dinner. But first things first: her husband understood that I
would be anxious to get sorted ASAP, and so he led me into the
library. There, he pulled out a particular volume from a shelf and
pushed a button, upon which the bookshelves magically swivelled
round to reveal a fully equipped walk-in pharmacy. Before you
accuse me, believe me, this was *not* a product of my habitually
fevered imagination. It was exactly like something out of James
Bond, one of those 'we have been expecting you, Mr Clarke'
moments. We stepped into this pharmacy and Dr Müller talked
me through his pharmacopeia, saying that some of these preparations would have a different name to what I knew them as, but
of course this I already knew, thanks to my treasured copy of
MIMS. As he was listing all the different names to see what I
might be interested in, I thought, 'Why hold back?' I said I liked
a mixture of heroin and cocaine in the same shot, explaining,
unnecessarily it transpired, that we called it a speedball.

Long story short, my request was instantly met by the good
doctor and I very quickly straightened myself out before dinner.
With bells on. This was my introduction to Merck cocaine,
presented as a shoot-up-able clear liquid in an ampoule. The
moment the first hit of this Swiss speedball entered my vein, I
realised that this had nothing to do with what we understand as
cocaine, i.e., the derivative of the South American coca plant.

This was in an entirely different league; this was purely the produce of pharmaceutical experts, manufactured by white-coated scientists under world-class conditions in an up-to-the-minute, top-of-the-range, Swiss laboratory. Quite simply, it is the best cocaine known to man.

I went outside and looked at the stars high above in the clear Alpine sky and I could have sworn that my feet left the ground. I've heard tales of euphoria, but like they say in the M&S advertisement, this was not just any high – this was a Merck Switzerland high, a kind of spaced-out levitation. Later to be verified in Keith Richards' memoir in which he too marvels at the joys of Merck pharma, writing that cocaine-wise, this was the best shit that you will ever come across.

It wasn't all about me though. What with his enthusiasm for English poetry Dr Müller was enjoying himself as much as I was, believe me. That week we were like Sherlock Holmes and Dr Watson, driving across Switzerland, his little black bag on the back seat of the Mercedes at the ready whenever it was required. It was an amazing experience that I never repeated; I've never come across that shit since. I never saw Dr Müller and his family again either. He was a top fellow. It was a beautiful friendship based on a one-off encounter. I hope they are OK.

1988 brought a sudden respite from my penury thanks to Quaker Oats Ltd and Sugar Puffs. Out of the blue a letter was left for me in the dressing room at the Rock Garden in Covent Garden. It was from Jeanne Willis and Trevor Melvin of the advertising firm Young and Rubicam, who happened to be fans of mine, inviting me to turn up at the firm's London HQ. Jeanne and Trevor were real whizz-kid hotshots, a copywriter/art director double act who had been responsible for a number of hugely successful campaigns and therefore carried a lot of clout. They figured that the Honey Monster could do with an equally quirky sidekick, and that's where I came in. We filmed a couple of Sugar

Puff TV ads directed by Willy Smax,* which paid out big time. I got thousands and then some. Lately they have what they call 'a buyout': a flat fee upfront and it doesn't matter how many times the advert is shown. But back then, however, being in a TV advert was a recipe for making money. I got paid the Equity rate for all the filming time, *and* I was on a kind of royalty. Every time the adverts were shown, I'd get full whack again, just as if I'd done a full day's work all over.

I was treated like a king. First-class ticket down from Manchester, top-dollar room at the Tower Hotel; they covered all my expenses. All I had to do was keep my receipts. That cranked things up a bit.

I almost didn't make it out of the hotel to make the ads at all, however. I think that was the third time I could have died, and on this occasion it was fucking alarming, because I was on my own. As I said, the advertising firm was paying for everything, so obviously it was speedballs a-go-go, and luxury, pure unashamed luxury all the way. I had cocaine and heroin by the family bucket. I was trying to regulate my heroin intake, but only in order to shoot up more often. Soon after breakfast, I administered my first hit of the day, and I was in the bathroom with all the marble, glass, and sharp corners. What a place to collapse.

I woke up in a pool of my own claret. In a space of an instant it had been zoom! *BLAM!* Good night Vienna. Memo to self: Seek out a place of soft furnishings. I was due at the film studio any minute, so naturally when I came round in this crimson-black puddle, I checked myself in the mirror for any damage. If my face had got messed up I would have lost £££s. I couldn't find any wound or swellings of any kind, not on my visage anyway. I

---

* Willy Smax was responsible for the George Harrison 'Got My Mind Set on You' video in which a room full of inanimate household objects come to life.

must have biffed the bridge of my nose on the side on the way down, incurring a nasal haemorrhage, or something. I don't know, to this day it's a mystery.

After the Sugar Puff windfall, my habit went utterly through the roof, and what with my predilection for the speedballs, even too much money was not enough.

By winter 1989 the royalties had inevitably dried up. Christmas was just round the corner, and I was skint. I didn't have any gear in and didn't have any work. I was in full-on panic-buying mode because I knew that nobody would be available around the festive season, so unless something happened, I was in for a shit Christmas that year and no mistake. Then the aforementioned Douglas Firkin Flood stepped in, like some kind of Mickey Mouse fairy godfather.

Dougie owned a number of nightclubs in both Manchester and Merseyside, including my dad's old hang-out, the Dev. He was a mate of Degsy Hatton and I knew his kid brother Ronnie from past events at Eric's. Dougie was reputedly one of the self-styled Quality Street Gang;* a bunch of Manchester car dealers, leisure-industry operatives, retired boxers, scrap merchants, and 'businessmen', who had their fingers in various slightly dubious puddings. They were just star-fuckers pretending to be gangsters really; they liked to dress in nice clothes, live the glam life. Maybe the QSG moved a bit of charlie around, but they'd also do nice things like Sunday dinners and afternoon activities for OAPs in their clubs. They were bad, but they weren't evil.

Dougie was a fan of my stuff and it had somehow got back to him that I was in a bit of a jam. Wisey may have had a part in this – I have no idea, but anyway Dougie miraculously materialised and

---

* If you'd like to learn more about these characters, I would refer you to my younger brother Paul and his mate Gaz, who because of their anti-social working hours would hang out at the Cotton Club, the Badda Bing of Manchester.

asked if I was looking to make some money. I answered in the affirmative and he outlined his plan. I guess he knew all the other club owners across Merseyside, it isn't a big town after all. He would pick me up and drive me around to several different venues where I could do my thing. I was happy to oblige, thinking that unlike all my other get-rich-quick schemes, this scheme was gonna get me rich – and quick.

Sure enough, Dougie arrived outside my gaff in one of those state-of-the-art Sweeney-style Ford Granadas and we drove across to Liverpool. We stopped off at his house in what looked just like Brookside Close so I could freshen up a bit, and then did five club appearances, one after the other, all over the town, half an hour in each place. I think we went to Birkenhead even. Each place we went to, Dougie walked in like he owned the joint, on account of he probably owned the joint. 'Give him everything he asks for, look after him. Don't let him get into any bother,' and it was all, 'Yes, Mr Flood, No, Mr Flood. Yes, sir, Mr Flood.' And yadda, yadda, yadda. And in every case I was paid right on time.

Talk about selling my sorry ass, but it all worked out fine and dandy. And not only that, there was dope at the end of a quick phone call, my night's takings were instantly converted into gear. It was a good piece of business and Christmas was all wrapped up.

Chapter Sixty-Two

FREE AT LAST

After I'd met Evie, I had a very good reason to clean up. I had since signed up to any number of non-residential NHS programmes and I was sticking to the script – the methadone script, that is.

By this stage, I needed all the help I could get. I even got a hold of a black box, that Meg Patterson contraption that got Eric Clapton off the junk. It supposedly emits some kind of electric wave that promotes the production of endorphins. It didn't work for me, but it seemed to do the trick for Mr Clapton, although from what I've read, he'd only had a habit for about a fortnight.

I don't know what talked me into finally quitting, but if I'm truly honest, I always felt like it was for the benefit of others, and here one of Nico's oft-repeated phrases comes to mind: 'Why should I be the one to suffer?' In the Twelve Step programme they tell you that you won't do it with that reasoning: you have to do it for yourself, and I kind of agree with that. You have to lose *everything*. You've got to reach the point where you have nothing left that you can sell, steal, or borrow – whatever it takes, quitting has got to seem like the best option. Until that happens, you are not going to succeed. I still wasn't there yet: I hadn't lost everything. Instead, it was a case of not losing what I hadn't got. Now I had an overarching desire for something far more precious – a lifetime of happiness with the woman of my dreams – and heroin precluded its attainment.

I resolved to stick to the methadone programme. At the beginning, I was on a bottle the size of an aqualung every week, and then I started losing my teeth. The dental corrosion was rapid and relentless. Fucking hell, I could actually feel it stripping away the enamel. I had to go to my pharmacist and plead with him to make a bespoke preparation for me, one that was free from sugar, chloroform, and tartrazine. With all the added extras taken out, volume-wise it was easier to transport, but horribly bitter. I didn't care. Already I looked like my tongue was in jail and I didn't want it to get any worse.

In 1990, I moved in with Evie. I'd spent the past four years trying and failing to get clean, but that's when I finally stopped shooting up.

I was now on prescription Physeptone and was down to half a tablet per day, along with a side order of Valium. I knew there was a time where I had to put a final stop to it and wean myself off all substitutes. And so when I ran out after a couple of months, I didn't renew the prescription.

After I stopped taking the Physeptone completely, even though I'd been on such a minuscule dose, I was a fucking invalid for what felt like ages. My legs were like spaghetti. I had no energy at all. I couldn't even walk to the newsagents up the road – or if I had done, I would have had serious problems getting back without a cab. I had to suffer about six months of medium-range infirmity before I began to recover.

There is a theory that if you've been a non-therapeutic user of opiate drugs, it renders them useless as a panacea, so God forbid you should get cancer. You'd be better off taking a Panadol. But I haven't found this to be the case. I have recently been given morphine in a post-procedural context where its analgesic properties seemed to be effective.

Thank God, Thank God, Thank God Almighty, free at last, to paraphrase the late Dr Martin Luther King. Enslavement ain't too big a word for opiate addiction. I refer you to an excerpt from that well-known song, 'Junco Partner' from Louis Jordan and his Tympany Five:

Down the street come a junco partner
He was loaded with misery
Knocked out strung out and loaded
And he wobbled all over the street
I done pawned my watch and pistol
I'm gonna pawn my keys and chain
I would've pawned my peccadillo
She was mellow as a cello
But the poor gal wouldn't sign her name

Great song. But you know, looking back, it wasn't all bad – very few things are. If I'd had half a gallon of ale every time I'd shot up, I'd have been forty-eight fucking stone by the time I was twenty-three years old, and then where would I have been? A professional darts player – if I was lucky.

Chapter Sixty-Three

MOM AND POP OPERATION

Relentless tragedy is always hilarious, so at some point the laughter has to stop. Gone was the muted trumpet of disappointment. Bring on the arpeggiated harp of a lyrical new dawn.

Evie was and is my life's most precious prize. A gift from the heavens. Mon ange. As I said, Evie had overheads and consequently her concerns were that of an intelligent, developed member of society, a society far distant from the land of her childhood. Her adventurous spirit had led her to a place of exile where the luxury of sentimentality has never been available to her. She has instead a sophisticated sense of humour and the kindest heart imaginable. I pity the fool who would not lose his heart to such a woman.

As a junkie, everything is geared to stop you getting what you want. Of course it is. Now that I was a recovering addict, I began to realise that the world was not my number-one adversary and that all this time I had been cutting my own throat, making rods for my own back, shooting myself in the foot, often literally – in short, I was my own worst enemy.

Meanwhile, over in Essex Evie had quit her job as a bilingual secretary in a reinsurance firm in the City of London and was now a life model for Grey Friars Adult Community College.

The teacher was a charming man called Francis Plummer, a

typical Royal Academician who specialised in huge paintings of women each representing generosity, fertility, industry, patience, and other virtuous human qualities. He was tall and slender, with a high forehead and pale delicate features. Mr Plummer was quite smitten with Evie and would become enraged when his students failed to capture her elusive beauty. He was extremely sanguine and not given to outbursts of extreme emotion, but every now and then he would lose it: 'No! No! No! Start again!'

I was with him all the way on that. They were beginners but a couple of them made her look like those Easter Island statues. To see herself depicted thus on canvas must have been very discouraging for the girl. I would give her the facts; tell her she didn't look anything like that; that this person was a terrible artist; and the other was obviously visually impaired.

Career-wise, I was on my ass. I had made some bad management choices and got involved with some real losers in the latter years in Manchester. I'm not even going to go into it because it's not that interesting, but they were bad people – incompetent. It's my own fault for thinking for even one second that they were qualified to look after my affairs. Then again, what did I expect? 'William Morris here. I understand that you're a mainlining waste of space who hasn't written a sentence for a decade. Have you got a manager at all?' Success appends success and if anybody like me had shown up, asking me for any help, they would have been shot, executed, and sent to the Russian front.

To paraphrase the legal profession, anyone who acts as their own agent has a fool for a client. If anyone ever asks me for advice, I always tell them to get an agent. If you're an artist, the delicate-ego-personality-problems type, you don't want to hear a booker at a venue telling you that you've only got this many fans and are not worth the requested fee. Who wants to hear that? It would send you into a fucking spiral of depression that you'd never climb out of. People would rather sell themselves short, so I say get an agent – they'll always ask for more money than you'll ask for yourself.

At this point, therefore, I wasn't getting too much work in the broadcast media – or many work offers at all. No one was interested, apart from a couple of honourable exceptions, notably Mark Radcliffe, who has always been in my corner from his early days on Piccadilly Radio, to his BBC Radio 5's *Hit the North* show with Marc 'Lard' Riley, to the present day, taking in a period in the early Noughties when I had a semi-regular feature as his on-air Style Consultant and Doo Wop Correspondent. Thanks, Mark.

Also, the aforementioned Tim Wells, aka Wellsy, alias Frankie Mansfield, would always make the journey into London worth my while at one of his regular-ish poetry evenings under the blanket name 'Rising'. I'd be on the bill about once a month at these events (advertised with the tagline 'Tough on Poetry. Tough on the Causes of Poetry'), which took place in various rented venues in the West End of London, alongside a dazzling array of poetic talent such as Francesca Beard, Fiona Russell-Powell, Ivan Penaluna, Joe Cairo, Selina Godden, Sophie Parkin, Paul Birtill, Hugo Williams, George Tahta, Joe Dunthorne, Phill Jupitus, and more. It was a startling and humbling experience to finally witness the oeuvre of my immediate competitors.

Wellsy is from Stamford Hill, a big lad with a good tailor (he is always nicely turned out in suedehead suits or choice casual wear), a Leyton Orient FC fan who not only writes fine poetry but is also a self-confessed expert in vintage reggae, Northern Soul, and the minutiae of the lesser-known Kung Fu movies of Sir Run Run Shaw – put it this way: his knowledge didn't begin and end with Bruce Lee. Wellsy and I have always had an ongoing one-upmanship thing going on in the background – we're always dropping names to impress each other, and indeed even collect people who look like various celebrities in order to trick the other into believing it really is them. For example, one time I enlisted the help of an ambitious young scribbler in a good suit called Andrew, whom I'd met once or twice at the Tardis club, and tried to pass him off as Robert Downey Jnr, who at the time was 'battling his demons in his private drug hell' and all that 'Hollywood's Number One Bad Boy' shit.

Whenever one of us gets the upper hand, he then tucks his thumbs beneath the lapels of his coat, adopts an exaggerated position of superiority, and asks the question, 'Who's the don?' One time when I had to acknowledge Wellsy's superior rank was when, knowing my enthusiasm in this regard, he showed up with 'Karen Black'. Obviously, it wasn't Karen Black, star of such motion picture films as *Nashville*, *Five Easy Pieces*, and *Easy Rider*, but a dead ringer, nevertheless. Right down to the lazy eye. Another time he got a commission reviewing pies for a well-known magazine. He couldn't wait to tell me about that and, once again, I had to admit, 'You the don, Wellsy.' Thanks to his research, I learned that you should always use a plastic spoon to eat a Key Lime Pie as the citrus reacts to the metal of a regular shovel.

He didn't get it all his own way. On another occasion, I was in London for one of his Rising events, and had gone to the Mezzo Bar on Dean Street, one of only three places where you could get a decent martini at the time, the other two being the Groucho Club and the Atlantic Bar and Grill. There I ran into Sandra, who had just lost her old drinking partner Michael Elphick, and so she was going round the corner to Harry's Bar to pick up her new buddy – the actor Burt Kwouk. I was fucking impressed to fuck – I mean, *the* Burt Kwouk who featured in countless TV series including *The Saint*, *The Avengers*, *Minder*, and was the voice on the aforementioned *The Water Margin*, plus had a transatlantic movie career including roles in *You Only Live Twice*, *Casino Royale*, *Kiss of the Dragon*, but most famously as Cato, Clouseau's manservant in the Pink Panther franchise.

I was due at Wellsy's gig, however, so I couldn't hang about. As a lover of poetry Burt seemed surprised that there was even such a thing as a public recital in the capital and so Sandra talked me up and sold him on it. We all shared a cab round the corner to the venue in Covent Garden, and en route I asked if he'd do me a favour and do the Cato thing at the end of my set. We went through the routine in the cab. I would always finish with 'Kung Fu International' on account of the last line: 'Enter the dragon. Exit Johnny Clarke.' I instructed Burt to listen out for that couplet, upon which he should leap onto the stage and go into the karate routine he had immortalised in the Pink Panther movies. 'This is going to kill Wellsy,' I thought. 'The *real* Burt Kwouk. This will put the lid on it.' When we got there we sneaked in and got a ringside table. Burt kept his head down the whole time, then it was my time to finish the night's performances. He heard my cue and then BAM! He hit the stage right on time, throwing those famous shapes as he did so. What a sporting gentleman, and what a way to end a poetry evening – sometimes everything just falls into place at once. Afterwards Wellsy conceded my triumph, with a gratifying, 'Hats off, Clarkie.' It would be nice to think I was magnanimous in my victory, but I don't think I was.

Otherwise, throughout the early Nineties, in terms of poetry bookings, my phone wasn't exactly ringing off the hook. I could always whip up something to keep bread on the table – a show for a couple of hundred cash in hand here or there – but it was a subsistence-level way of doing business. People took advantage, understandably I suppose, thinking I must be in the shit if I was doing it for cash. It's a fucking cut-throat world. I had my limits, though, even then. My bottom line was £400, unless it was in Essex or London, then I might have knocked a bit off. Considering the amount of entertainment they got and the bar-take in these venues, they must have been laughing all the way to the Sherman Tank. Even so, business is business.

How could a poor man stand such times and live? I had to go on strike and turn down work for a year in order to double my fee. What else can an underpaid worker do other than withdraw his labour? No more Mr Nice Guy. We didn't starve or anything but it was really hard to do.

When I went back to work, I still hadn't written any new poetry to speak of, but my act had effortlessly transformed into that of a stand-up comic. There was nothing alternative about it – mother-in-laws, golf jokes, foreigners, divorce settlements, and lashings of smut. I can't recommend it enough.

Our daughter Stella was born in 1994. I was present at the birth, although it wasn't planned that way. I am quite squeamish and more suited to chain-smoking out in the corridor than as an active birth partner. I had called into the maternity ward for my routine daily visit armed with a bottle of Lucozade and a box of Evie's favourite Thorntons Continental Assortment. I was perched on the edge of her bed, watching a made-for-television movie of *The Count of Monte Cristo* on her personal TV set. Births are always the same, both gradual and sudden, and just as the film had got to the crucial scene, Evie alerted me to our infant's imminent arrival. My disappointment at missing the sweet vengeance of Edmond Dantès was rapidly assuaged by the dramatic appearance of our darling Stella whose weight I accurately gauged – 7lbs exactly.

If I'd have known how much fun being a dad is, I would have started way earlier than I did and would have possibly ended up like the old woman who lived in the shoe (the Catholic version, of course, where new life is always a mitzvah).

When Stella was around three years old, Evie acquired a classic VW camper van in an early-Seventies shade of orange. Happily, a loose chipping caught the windshield and we had to get the whole front of the vehicle replaced and at the same time took the opportunity to get a complete respray job in a pleasing

Mediterranean blue. The best thing about it was that any tailback, we were the ones in front. At top speed it did about 40mph, perfect for country driving, and as the late Edgar Degas once said, 'The pursuit of speed at the expense of all else is immoral.'

Once motorised, trips to the seaside and other Essex beauty spots were now within easy reach and with Stella we discovered many delights we would otherwise never have experienced. On just such a jaunt, we took Stella and Kaya, one of her classmates, to Fingringhoe, Britain's premier nature reserve. Its estuarine topography makes it a wonderland of avian activity. You could enjoy a very agreeable afternoon there with a pair of binoculars and a bag of sandwiches. Families welcome. Book early.

On the road home we spotted a blackboard advertising potatoes at a knock-down rate. Evie put the brakes on and we tumbled out into a deserted farmyard. We could see a gigantic heap of loose spuds in a corrugated-iron barn, but not a soul in sight. We had a look around to find the proprietor who finally reluctantly appeared with a shovel over his shoulder. We filled a sack and made our getaway. Back in the camper van, I began to delineate the dark fictitious history of the potato farmer. Several of his common-law wives had apparently disappeared quite suddenly, without trace, I told Stella and Kaya. He'd been under investiga-tion for multiple spousal homicide by the CID, but as no bodies had ever been discovered they had nothing to hold him on. Nevertheless, he was definitely on the radar of the Old Bill, and that's why it was known locally as Murder Farm. After this I never saw Kaya again. Stella flatly refused to eat any potatoes that had been grown by a murderer and henceforth there was a notable frisson in the van every time we drove past on the way to some-where else.

I always enjoyed filling Stella's head with made-up nonsense. Another favourite, which is so well known it probably qualifies as a folk memory, is that I told her that whenever you hear the chimes of an ice-cream van, it means he's run out of everything. I'm not that mean, I only pulled that one on her once.

Once we drove down to Brighton for a weekend. First stop, the funfair on Palace Pier. What is it about fairgrounds that evokes equal parts terror and delight? In the days of my convalescence in Rhyl, I wouldn't go within a hundred yards of the mirror maze, believing it to be populated by the corpses of those customers who'd never found their way out, all in various stages of corruption. There I immediately bought tickets for the ghost train, and dared Stella to join me for the ride. I talked it up real good and gave her the full rundown on the horrors she could expect to encounter within: 'If you think you've been scared before,' I said, 'think again, Stella, and prepare to be *properly* terrified: zombies, ghouls, headless cadavers, belligerent skellingtons. And spooks.' Evie had opted out of this one, so Stella and I boarded the train ready for departure. She was already white as a sheet then, just as our carriage lurched towards the gaping doors with the jagged teeth and the darkness that lay beyond, the poor child registered her unease, saying: 'I wanna get off.' I promptly insisted that they put the brakes on the entire excursion in order that the Clarke party could make good its disembarkation.

On our various family forays into the surrounding countryside, we visited the guinea-pig town at Jimmy's farm, As Seen On TV. Yes, that Jimmy. A model village populated entirely by guinea pigs. The day we visited the inhabitants had gathered in the town centre where the food trays were situated and, I assume, at the end of the day each of them then retired to their respective residence. There were some fine houses, some of which had satellite dishes on the chimneys, and an elegant Palladian-style town hall worthy of Robert Adam himself – this building seemed very busy with a lot of comings and goings – a couple of sun-drenched piazzas, and a central water feature: every amenity they could possibly desire in miniature. I heard the town hall caught fire one time and the flames could be seen five feet away! Seriously though, one day all guinea pigs will live this way.

And then there were the Essex backwaters, home to several seal colonies. Who knew?

Stella was six at the turn of the millennium and at 11pm that New Year's Eve we embarked on a tour of street parties and firework displays. Stella immediately dropped off in the back of the van but was awoken by cheering, drunken crowds, honking car horns, plus the whistling and banging of the fireworks, 'What's all this?' she grumpily enquired. 'It's a very special occasion,' replied Evie. 'It won't be repeated for a thousand years.' 'Thank God for that!' Stella said, and went back to sleep.

As I said, I was away a lot when Stella was little. If I had a show beyond London, to do a single night often meant that I was absent for two or three whole days, using trains and taxis to get around the country.

The one exception was Essex to Aberdeen in mid-December when I booked an air ticket. It was a pre-terrorist domestic flight, so I hadn't reckoned on being searched for any reason. This was a big mistake. I had half an ounce of weed and a flick knife in my hand luggage and the blade set the metal detectors off as I went through security. It was a great little knife – a real commando number with a knurled metal handle in an olive drab colour. It even had a little stylised hilt which made it all the more dagger-like; then etched in relief along the haft: 'NATO MILITARY'. I'd bought it in a French supermarket for about a hundred francs while visiting Evie's sister Arlette and her husband Tayeb. Anyway, I was arrested for possession of a knife and the weed, charged and then bailed all on that same day. I took the next possible flight out and completed my part of the contract at Aberdeen's Lemon Tree Arts Centre. Professional or what?

In advance of my impending appearance at Harlow magistrates' court I got a lawyer called Mr Caldwell from nearby Saffron

Walden, an Ulsterman and a fan of mine, who said I could forget about the weed, that would be the usual fine etc. The flick knife, on the other hand, carried an automatic custodial sentence. I wasn't expecting that – it was more the kind of knife you'd use for getting the stones out of a horse's hoof, a bit of whittling perhaps, changing a plug, maybe the odd emergency tracheotomy, but you wouldn't have tried to kill somebody with it. I mean, there are far deadlier weapons available to the casual shopper on any high street – those Sabotage kitchen knives, for example, or a ratchet screwdriver – how would you like one of them up the nostril? And one I've thought about a lot: if you took a bite out of a McVitie's digestive biscuit and then dragged the bitten edge across somebody's eyeball – well, I wouldn't want to be responsible for the consequences.

'I'll do what I can,' Mr Caldwell said, 'but a flick knife carries a lot of emotional baggage beyond the amount of damage you could inflict with it.'

Rearrange these words into a well-known phrase: the bottom fell out of my world.

That cast a pall over my Christmas that year. Every time I put the telly on it was another bandit going to jail in a border town – I had it hanging over me the whole time. Then I started to resign myself to my sentence and decided to look on the bright side. After all, I was a cinch for that cushy job in the library, what with my spectacles and everything. I even began to envisage myself as some kind of prison-reform crusader, changing the plight of the convict from the inside. I'd be the prison scribe, dashing off florid love odes on behalf of my sub-literate fellow inmates who'd really miss me when I'd served my time. They'd be all like, sad to see me go, 'This place is going to hell since the untimely parole of Professor Johnnie Four Eyes.'

In early January, therefore, I headed off to Harlow with a pair of pyjamas and my toothbrush, fully prepared for my long stretch.

Instead, Mr Caldwell convinced the judicial panel of my unimpeachable character, my high standing in the literary world, and how it would damage society if my good name was called into question and I got off with a fine and a conditional discharge. My punishment was, however, that this addition to my criminal record prolonged my exile from the United States of America. What a chump I was.

There were other episodes of good fortune here and there. In 1998, when Simon Kelner became editor of the *Independent*, I did a series of commercials for the paper. Simon and his fellow-journalist brother Martin are from Manchester and, unbeknownst to me, were long-time fans. It was quite a lucrative gig and a welcome stream of income. Once a month for ages, I'd be delivered to one of the many voice-over studios in Soho, and we nailed it in no time. It was a great campaign; indeed, the first advert won an award (as did the earlier Sugar Puffs campaign, incidentally). They were all written in my style, but right from the start the advertising creatives instructed me to customise where necessary. There was no need: the copywriters at the firm really knew my work, so it was like I'd written them myself. Those people were experts. I never had to change a word. It's such a compliment when somebody gets it so right.

Also that year I had a bit-part in the movie *Middleton's Changeling*, a costume drama set in Counter-Reformation Spain and based on the seventeenth-century Jacobean tragedy by Thomas Middleton and William Rowley. This semi-modernisation was flamboyantly directed by Marcus Thompson, who describes the piece as 'a vortex of lust, corruption and murder, that culminates in an orgy of madness, sex and death.' Something for everyone, as they say, plus resplendent costumes by Elizabeth Emanuel, who famously designed Lady Diana's wedding dress.

I joined a cast which included Ian Dury, Billy Connolly, Vivian Stanshall, Richard Mayes, Leo Wringer, and Julia Tarnoky. I was only on screen for a nanosecond, but it was being filmed in a proper studio: give it a name – Pinewood! Movies and their manufacture involve a kind of magic that I don't care to interfere with, so this backroom glimpse was uncharacteristic. I was, however, anxious to see the world-famous Albert R. Broccoli 007 Stage, that humongous hangar built in 1976 to house the interior of the *Liparus* supertanker in *The Spy Who Loved Me*. That's why I agreed to do it.

The walls in the canteen were covered with framed hand-coloured period mugshots of all the post-war screen hunks: John Gregson, Kenneth More, Richard Burton, Anthony Quayle, you name it, all with the wavy Brylcreemed hair. While I was taking it all in, one of the old proprietors had suddenly appeared, a slightly dissolute Rank Charm School graduate – regimental blazer, cravat, and suede shoes, with the first pink gin of the morning in his grasp. Offering me a cigarette from a ten-pack of Senior Service he gave me a running commentary. At each picture, his opinion was the same: 'Lovely chap, terrible drinker.'

On the set of *The Changeling*, there was one scene involving everybody in full costume, the entire cast jammed into this marquee, then a handler came in with a black panther on a leash! He was flanked by two assistants – one had half a raw cow on the end of a ten-foot pole, while the other hopefully had a heavy-duty stun gun. What if it started acting up? It was gigantic, with the face of a congenital murderer, and it was looking around, making the odd snarling sound. I've never been a cat person and I'm quite cowardly, so for one reason or another I didn't want to get slashed up. Anyway, then it started really grumbling and the side of beef seemed to be of no interest to the beast. It was then that all the women were instructed to leave the tent. Why only the ladies? Ian Dury and I asked around and it was apparently because somebody was menstruating – I don't want to be sexist about it, but it was probably a woman. Obviously, they couldn't go round quizzing every woman about her cycle, 'Here, Julia. Is it your bad time at the moment, because if it is, fuck off. It's winding the panther up.' So it was a case of 'Ladies, please make your way calmly to the exit.' I've said it before and I'll say it again: 'Crikey!'

Joe Strummer and I went back a few years, and in November 2001 he kindly got me involved in a month of one-night stands with the Mescaleros including Pablo Cook, Tymon Dogg, Scott Shields, and Martin Slattery. Then they were off to the States, without me obviously, but I continued with the UK dates up until the following Christmas when Joe's sudden death cancelled out all future dates. As I've said, with no new poems to speak of, I had morphed into a stand-up comic and genuinely thought that my poetic muse had handed in her notice. Comedy is a cool medium, more observational, casual, conversational, whereas my poetry has more in common with the 'hot' medium of a live event; it's more declamatory, more urgent, more irresistibly rhythmic. In the same way as way back with Elvis Costello, the Mescaleros was a hot rock and roll date. The opportunity to perform in big venues – Manchester Academy, Glasgow Barrowlands, Birmingham Academy, Bristol Colston Hall, Brixton Academy – reactivated that rock and roll side of my approach. Needs must, and it's thanks to Joe and that tour, really, that I started writing again.

At some point in the Nineties three of my poems had been added to the GCSE English Literature syllabus: 'I Wanna Be Yours', 'Beasley Street', and 'Twat'. In 2002, when Stella was about eight, I was back on the road again – the railroad that is. I'd been signed up for a kind of school-trip package tour of the major cities, along with the likes of Simon Armitage, Carol Ann Duffy, Liz Lochhead, Fleur Adcock, Tom Leonard, Benjamin Zephaniah, and John Agard and his wife, the lovely Grace Nicholls. We'd pitch up at the town hall in the early afternoon and they bussed in a bunch of GCSE students from the immediate vicinity. A strange experience for me because I wasn't used to doing shows in the daylight hours.

It also involved rail excursions on a daily basis, and often it would turn into a major expedition. I remember one of the first of these gigs, when I left Essex the day before in order to get to Newcastle for a show the following afternoon. The journey was taking forever, with hundred-mile stretches where the train never went faster than a crawl. At 3am it ground to a halt at Newark and we were detrained. I don't know if you've ever been to Newark, but it's in the flatlands of Lincolnshire. There was nothing between us and Siberia, just a clear run from the polar desert. There was Arctic rain coming at us horizontally and the only waiting room was locked. It was a life-threatening situation – there were crying babies, heavily pregnant women, pensioners, and wheelchair users, all just stranded there, freezing to death on this deserted platform in the middle of a glacial plain.

When I finally crawled into the venue the following afternoon and somebody mentioned my late arrival, the use of profane language was called for. That GCSE tour went on for months and months and months. Still, I had nothing else going on at the time and even though it didn't pay much, it was regular, and it turned out to have been the right thing to do.

In February 2004, I went on a tour of Scotland as the 'very special guest' of The Fall. I like to think that Smithy and I had parallel careers in the magic realisation of Manchester and we had perfected our thing in tandem. Out on the road again, listening to the subjects of his new songs served as a reawakening of something I already knew, i.e., the more everyday the subject matter the better.

In 'Steak Place', for example, the first-person narrative dwells on the ambiance of this banal eatery and it becomes apparent that he's only here for the beer. It's the only place he can get a pint without getting mithered. So, that's when I started on the repertoire that would feature in my latest collection, *The Luckiest Guy Alive*, and wrote 'The Paperboy's Wife'. Here's a couple of outtakes:

The paperboy's wife was right
Forswear that Schwinn Bat Bike
There's something I don't like
About mudguards made out of Pittsburgh steel
Sharpened into spikes

On this occasion, I was hitching a ride with Dougie 'Soul Train' James, with whom Wisey was sharing an apartment in a gated development. On this tour, Dougie featured with Smithy on a call-and-response number called 'Open the Box'. In truth, you couldn't get more different to The Fall than Dougie – as musicians the Soul Train had a level of competence below which they never sank, so they were good,* with a cheesy edge. With the Soul Train Dougie had shared the bill with Frank Sinatra, the Jackson Five, Bill Haley and the Comets, Edwin Starr, Doris Troy, Norman Wisdom, Tommy Cooper, and last but not least, the aforementioned Stan Boardman. Dougie had become quite friendly with Tito Jackson with whom he had struck an unbelievable bargain – every couple of months he would receive a large package containing five pristine hand-me-down Jackson Five jumpsuits – freshly laundered, they were almost as good as new, perfect for the venues on the Seventies northern circuit, or any event where the Gamble and Huff songbook was required.

After the Scottish leg we had a couple of east-coast dates including one at the Newcastle Opera House. It was sub-zero that February, even the Geordies wore long-sleeved T-shirts. In the early hours after the gig, Mark slipped on the icy pavement outside our hotel and fractured his femur. A woman had apparently tried to help him up, but then she fell over and

---

* Indeed, most of them featured in The Invisible Girls at one point or another.

dragged Mark down for a second time, breaking his hip in the process, and bringing the tour to a premature and painful end.

Mark did however make an appearance in March for a 'Words and Music' event at the Manchester Bridgewater Hall. It was the early days of the crystal-meth craze and I'd asked Mark to sort me out in this regard, but thanks to the accident it had never happened. I was enjoying a cigarette by the stage door before the show when an ambulance arrived and Smithy was wheeled out. He handed me a wrap, saying, 'Bloody hell, Johnnie. Have you been here all night?' But seriously folks, I was genuinely concerned about the state of the game regarding his femoral trauma.

Manchester-wise it was an all-star cast with Pete Shelley, Howard Devoto, Smithy, and myself, and a general emphasis on lyrics. With me, that's all there is, so it was my night what with everybody else right outside their comfort zone and me just doing my thing. I was up last doing some new numbers along with the obligatory golden oldies which were received with thunderous appreciation. I was the only one who got any kind of civilised reception at the end of my set instead of a verbal bashing. Howard Devoto's adaptation of 'Hound Dog' was met with cries of 'You're taking the piss!', Pete Shelley's performance with shouts of 'Where's Orville?!' Smithy's got 'Fuck off! You're shit.' But the Hall director got the worst of it with a 'Fuck off, you fat B★ST★RD!' For me, it was a very enjoyable night: in the words of the late Genghis Khan, 'It's not enough that I should succeed – everybody else must fail.' Does that make me a bad person?

In July 2004 I was up in Manchester for the weekend and ran into Wisey. He was putting on a show at the Opera House with Jerry Lee Lewis and Chuck Berry. Unmissable. I told him straight. A show of this calibre requires a Master of Ceremonies with the hyperbolic vocabulary of the true fan, i.e. ME.

Before the show, I was in the crowded communal green room when through the open door I caught sight of Chuck Berry. He wore sharp slacks, a shimmering shirt, and two-tone footwear. He was heading up the corridor towards the stage, already into the duck walk with his low-slung Gibson 335. Taking two steps back, he gave me that cartoon-style doubletake and said, 'Hey, how you doin?' I'm not a humble person, but let's be reasonable, why would Chuck Berry know who I was? I looked over my shoulder and that's when I realised he was talking to *me* and I introduced myself as his MC that evening.

I was wearing a Bobby McGee-style dirty red bandana at the time, because my roots were out, so afterwards I went round all his troupe asking 'Who does Chuck think I am?' They were Americans and, as such, very polite, so they just said, 'He knows who you are.' But I didn't think he did. I was absolutely fucking positive it was a case of mistaken identity and Chuck had mistaken me for a member of the Rolling Stones – give it a name: Keith Richards. But Keith is one of those people I've always wanted to look like, so I wasn't bothered. I figured, 'Whoever Chuck thinks I am, I'll be that guy.'

Jerry Lee was up first that night. I went on in my candy-stripe Carnaby Street blazer, dark blue drainpipe trousers, and black suede flamenco boots and said, 'Ladies and gentlemen, introducing the greatest piano player that ever lived. 99lbs of pure industrial strength radioactive rock and roll dynamite, all the way from Ferriday, Louisiana. They call him the killer. His name is Jerry Lee Lewis.' He was wearing a black suit with white seam detailing and crescent moon pockets, and a black silk shirt worn with a bolas necktie, the slide on which was a solid gold fanned-out four-card poker hand. His slicked-back hair was white, and his face was whiter still.* Then I did the same thing for Chuck: 'Ladies

---

* His bass player was a guy called B.B. Cunningham, former gonzoid lyricist and singer with the Hombres, responsible for the hit tune 'Let it All Hang Out'.

and gentlemen, the rock and roll poet, the guy who wrote everything first. I oughta know – I've got a library card.' Or something, like that.

After Jerry Lee and Chuck heard my build-up, I had them eating out of my hand. Jerry Lee had been giving me the bad eye – they didn't call him 'The Killer' for nothing – but he turned quite avuncular and even complimented me on the cut of my clothes.

In fact, the following April when Wisey wanted to organise a tour of Spain for Chuck Berry, he agreed on condition that Alan booked 'that guy' to MC every night. He liked the way I'd talked him up and wanted me on the firm. *Ay carumba!*

We had the time of our lives. Wisey had a great security guy in the form of Yankee Bill, who had travelled all over the world with him. Say what you like about Al, but he always had good people around him – let's face it, they had to be. Yankee Bill looked like Howlin' Wolf. He had two families – I don't know whether he was an actual bigamist, but he had a wife and kids in Brooklyn, and in South Manchester, ditto. Consequently, Christmas and birthdays were a constant preoccupation for him.

He was always coming out with these fabulous and unarguable pearls of wisdom and was responsible for some indelible lines. Wisey consistently had his heart broken. He'd fall in love with a hooker, convince himself that she returned his affections, and then determine to rescue her from her life of vice, only to find cruelly that it was never going to happen – time after time after time the hooker was taking him for a mug like any other punter. On one occasion I overheard Yankee Bill commiserating with him: 'It's the pussy, man. They gots it. You wants it. They knows you wants it. They knows they gots it.' You can't argue with that.

On another occasion, when we were on the tour bus en route for Girona where we were meeting up with Chuck, we were driving along the coast. Yankee Bill asked me and Wisey if we'd

brought our swimwear. 'Not me, Bill,' I replied, 'how about you?'
He hadn't packed his trunks either and we got talking about the
moody nature of the sea and the dangers of swimming therein.
How you can wade in and it could be like a mill pond, but give
it five minutes and it's all riptides and treacherous currents. I said
I didn't bother going in the sea anywhere because I couldn't (and
still can't) swim, and then we let it drop. There ensued one of
those long periods of silence you often have on long car journeys,
each of us off in our own little musings, and then Yankee Bill
piped up: 'Yeah man, the sea. It'll kill you when it's ready.' Worthy
of Joseph fucking Conrad, better even, and it's not often you hear
an improvement on Conrad, who put it this way: 'The sea has
never been friendly to man. At most it has been the accomplice
of human restlessness.' I preferred Bill's version, in fact, I immediately jotted it down and it cropped up years later in my 'Ode
to the Coast', a poem commissioned by the National Trust.

In 2007 *The Sopranos* came to its conclusion. In my book,
when it comes to the superlative of televisual experience, it's got
to be the three S's — *The Simpsons*, *Seinfeld* and *The Sopranos* —
TV's finest hours. To hear 'Evidently Chicken Town' playing out
the end credits of 'Stage 5'— the second episode of the second
half of the sixth and final series of *The Sopranos* — was one of the
highlights of my career, no doubt about it. The back credits
featured a genuinely imaginative musical mix, featuring Frankie
Valli, Etta James, Johnny Thunders, Ray Charles, Bobby Darin,
Frank Sinatra, and me. Not all at the same time, obviously. Whoever
did that for me, thank you so very much. I am proud to be associated with that series, but I'm still holding out for my cameo in
The Simpsons. Then again, I can't help thinking that there is a
little bit of me in Sideshow Bob, what with the unruly hair, the
English accent, the rich vocabulary, and the slightly misanthropic
temperament.

Also in 2007 I actually did make a cameo appearance in *Control*, the biopic of Joy Division directed by Anton Corbijn.. I was filmed performing 'Evidently Chicken Town' in a yacht club in landlocked (huh?) Nottingham, which was then cut in and out as part of the ongoing narrative drive. Everyone else was played by an actor – Sam Riley as Ian Curtis, Samantha Morton as Deborah Curtis, and Ben Naylor as Martin Hannett – but I was playing myself, and the thing was, I still looked exactly the same. Indeed, my strikingly youthful profile and figure twenty years after the event actually got mentioned in dispatches in reviews of the film!

Before that film, I had been approached by Michael Winterbotham to appear in the 2002 release *24 Hour Party People*. If anyone asks me to be in a film, the first thing I always ask is, 'Who else is in it?' And if I'm the big name, my self-doubt is nagging at me, and I think the project is destined straight for the fucking bargain bin and I am not fucking interested. So, when Michael Winterbotham rang me up, and told me that Peter Kay was playing Don Tonay, Steve Coogan playing Anthony B. Wilson, Andy Serkis was Martin Hannett, and Howard Devoto was playing a cleaner, I thought that's not fair! So everybody else was being played by an actor and I had to play myself? Where's the class in that? I thought it would look like instead of them finding a suitable actor to portray me, I'd just mooched in like somebody who's too available and so I turned it down.

I was really looking forward to watching that film because I was dead curious to see who they'd cast as me, then when it came out I was so fucking disappointed because they'd written me out of the piece entirely. If only they'd said Smithy was in it as himself, I would have done it, and even he was just featured standing in the queue to get into the Hacienda, with only the one line: 'All right, Tony?' So I was written out of history! I have only myself to blame.

By 2011, I had been reacquainted with Phil Jones, who was now my manager. Once Phil took charge of my affairs, I started to appear more frequently on the mainstream radar and some lucrative side action presented itself in the form of various advertising campaigns. Domino's pizza, McCain oven chips, also try-outs for Ribena and Gordon's gin. In the case of Gordon's gin I lost out to Ian 'Star of TV's *Lovejoy*' McShane. Who could compete with his vulpine good looks? Actually, his vulpine good looks were not an issue, it was a voice-over only, and as a gifted impressionist I do a pretty convincing Ian McShane as it happens: 'The G in G and T.' I could have saved them £££s. I've always enjoyed doing adverts, though not everyone seemed to approve of me 'selling out'. There are certain artistic types who are very snarky when a poet makes money. I have to say, though, on this issue I can retain the high moral ground, if I wanted to, because I've never advertised anything that I wouldn't eat myself. They've all been quite innocent, tasty products that we all might enjoy: Sugar Puffs, Domino's pizza, McCain oven chips, as opposed to the Waitrose line-caught salmon promoted by the silver fox. Me, I know my place in the poetry food chain: I'm with the oiks, man o' the people, written in as the hot dog to Roger McGough's Pacific Rim salad. Actually, reading that back, apologies for any unintended homoerotic content.

Another highlight in 2011 was being part of Ray Davies's Meltdown festival at the Southbank Centre alongside a great music line-up including Nick Lowe, Madness, Lydia Lunch, the Sonics, Arthur Brown, the Legendary Pink Dots, the Alan Price Set, and spoken wordsmith Monty Python's Terry Jones, plus el zorro plateado, yes, Roger McGough.

I really wanted to see the only-recently-reformed Sonics, whose career had been revived due to the BMW Olympic ad campaign featuring their cover of James Berry's song 'Have Love Will Travel'*

---

* James Berry, singer in a doo-wop band called the Flares, also wrote 'Louie Louie'.

— but they were on at the same time as me. The best thing about doing Meltdown, though, was hearing later on that, the way Ray saw it, when he'd picked me up and put me on at Meltdown, I was nothing. He had recognised a fellow poet and pulled me out of the gutter, and out of the kindness of his heart stuck me on one of the best stages of London, single-handedly reviving my career. Better than the mere facts. Seriously though, thanks Ray. I owe you one. He left me a really nice thank-you note backstage in my dressing room afterwards. He has been an ongoing source of inspiration to me since 1964, so call me sentimental but that piece of paper is a treasured possession to this day.

In 2012 I had the pleasure of working with Ben Drew, aka Plan B. He got in touch with me through a friend called Pauline who runs the George Tavern in Whitechapel, where she used to put on an annual event called the Gomad festival. As a result of our conversation I made a cameo appearance in his movie *Ill Manors* – 'a hip hop musical for the twenty-first century'. I didn't want to be the light relief in what is a very hard-hitting film, so rather than simply declaiming one of my old poems, I performed a poem which I wrote specifically for the piece called 'Pity the Plight of Young Fellows', which is also featured on the smash hit Mercury Prize nominated soundtrack LP. I wanted to encapsulate the flavour of Ben's movie, which was a challenge and I was a bit nervous at first, because I'm not au fait with that whole East London hip hop gangsta argot – I didn't want to look like some old twat running to keep up with the kids of today but, at the same time, I didn't want to look like yesterday's news, either, so I thought it was better to be obviously out of step and somehow consciously 'unreal'. As it turned out, the content and delivery of 'Pity the Plight' was almost Dickensian. I'm really proud of that one.

Pity the plight of young fellows
Too long a-bed with no sleep
With their complex romantic attachments
O look on their sorrows and weep
They don't get a moment's reflection
There's always a crowd in their eye
Pity the plight of young fellows
Regard all their worries and cry
Their Christian mothers were lazy perhaps
Leaving it up to the school
Where the moral perspective is hazy perhaps
And the climate oppressively cool
Give me one acre of cellos
Pitched at some distant regret
Pity the fate of young fellows
And their anxious attempts to forget.

Plan B is a lovely fellow, a real hard worker. As he said himself, 'Anyone who puts 110% into their work deserves as much success as they can get.'

Then in 2012, BBC Four and Radio Six kicked off their *Punk Britannia* season with *Evidently . . . John Cooper Clarke*, an hour-long film devoted to me, me, me, directed by John Ross and Scotty Clark, and featuring the likes of Steve Coogan, Bill Bailey, Stewart Lee, Pete Shelley, Paul Farley, Alex Turner, Mark Radcliffe, and Craig Charles, who lined up to express admiration and say some extremely generous things about my contribution to poetry, reasserting my lofty status as 'one of the greatest voices' of my generation. Hearing such adulation, it was difficult not to believe that I had actually died. But what an obituary! I'll be honest with you, I couldn't have been happier. To hear people saying such nice things about me is obviously a wonderful thing.

Epilogue

SUNDAY NIGHT AT THE LONDON PALLADIUM

By 2013 I'd become reacquainted with Johnny Green. I'd known him since way back when he was road manager for the Clash, and in the intervening years would run into him from time to time at various festivals and literary events. In 1997 he had published *A Riot of Our Own*,* his acclaimed memoir about his time on the road with the group, and he was now a columnist for *Rouleur* magazine. Over the years our respective social circles have had points of overlap and we have always been easy company for each other. We share a relentlessly off-colour sense of humour, respective former habits, a tendency to the cerebral, and a deep love of Elvis.

I always enjoyed our chance encounters and so was delighted when I bumped into him with his massive family at Latitude, where I was performing as part of Keith Allen's late-night anti-social variety event. Afterwards he came backstage. He'd been knocked out by my current schtick. He wasn't interested if it was a legacy act and he told me so; he'd always been involved with dynamic people; the Clash, Joe Ely, Waylon Jennings, and Willie

---

* *A Riot of Our Own* is, in my opinion, the best book written about the Clash; because Johnny was involved, he tells the human story.

Nelson – yes, Willie Nelson! – and I think he was pleasantly surprised to hear that I wasn't just some old hack churning out yesterday's news. I was doing new stuff. I was an active artist who was shifting his sorry ass on public transport, so the next step was for Johnny to become my gentleman travelling companion, with the only two provisos being 1.) according to Johnny, 'the minute it gets formulaic I'm bailing out', and 2.) no snacking in the car.

The horrors of social media are unknown to us – what a team. Think Freebie and the Bean, Thunderbolt and Lightfoot, Pancho and Lefty, Snitch and Snatch, Deaf Smith and Johnny Ears – in fact, the Zebra Kid and Horace Batchelor. When it comes to any professional discourse with any difficult third party, Johnny is happy when it comes to high-volume profanity and menaces, whereas you know me: anything for a quiet life. He's a cunt so I don't have to be.

In July 2013 I was awarded an Honorary Doctorate from Salford University. Now that my full title was Dr John Cooper Clarke, at long last I could open that cosmetic surgery business I'd dreamt about for so long.

In September came the release of *AM*, the fifth album by The Arctic Monkeys, featuring their sensational reworking of 'I Wanna Be Yours'. I'd met the lads after a show at the Boardwalk, a popular venue in Sheffield, their hometown. This was about two weeks before they went global. I'd been halfway out the door when the proprietor told me that some young men in a band wanted a word because they'd done my poetry at school. I asked him what they were called, and he said The Arctic Monkeys. The name of a group is important and that one is unforgettable. They were speaking my language. There's a whole wide world in those two words; it calls up an emotional response. Think about it; the North Pole is no place for the higher primates. That's terrible. I mean, crikey! Get that monkey out of there!

That's the thing about those GCSE tours with Simon Armitage

et al. and getting my poems on the syllabus back in the Nineties. As I've said, it didn't pay much and at the time those train journeys were pure hell, so you can imagine how down I was on the whole thing. But in the long term it paid out big time. Every teacher I've met since then, whoever I was on with, has told me that the kids were actually dropping off, but I was the guy that woke them up. It brought me a whole new generation of fans, to a point where I have the audience I have today. There is no typical Johnny Clarke demographic any more, if there ever was. Now it's sixteen to eighty-five, male and female, black and white. It's quite amazing really. I cross a lot of territories and I wouldn't have that if I hadn't been on the radar of school kids up and down the country, kids like Ben Drew, Alex Turner, Matt Helders, Jamie Cook, Nick O'Malley, and Andy Nicholson.

Yes, I've had just about every reward a society could bestow upon a half-arsed grafter with a rich vocabulary and I thank God for my life on a daily basis. And now I'm a tax-paying pillar of society with a store-bought haircut and excellent posture, also I've got an office full of top-flight hustlers in my corner and a driver with a clean sheet.

Poetry is not something you have to retire from. There is no heavy lifting involved and I have no intention of ever quitting. I pray every day for my health and that of my family. After that, what? As they used to say at the start of the aforementioned *Stingray*, 'anything can happen in the next half hour.' With that in mind, I try to live every day as if it were my last – crying and shitting myself. Ha ha ha, seriously though, I got the world on a string and I'm sitting on a rainbow.

Well, gotta go, on account of you remember the London Palladium? The place that presented such high-end sensations as the Andrews Sisters, Carmen Miranda, Judy Garland, Mel Tormé, Sarah Vaughan, Bobby Darin, Sophie Tucker, Bing Crosby, Jack Benny, Danny Kaye, Rosemary Clooney, Mario Lanza, did I say the Andrews Sisters? Bob Hope, Lena Horne, Ella Fitzgerald, Peggy Lee, FRANK SINATRA, Sammy Davis Jnr., Johnnie Ray, and The Beatles? Yes, that London Palladium. Well, tonight it's the venue for a star-studded evening of poetry and who's the headliner? Yes, the bargain-basement Baudelaire himself, Dr John Cooper Clarke.

Anyway, I might as well end the story here; after this it's more of the same and then some – Stateside even – that's the plan, anyway. I'll be coming to a town near you, so catch me while I'm alive. Meanwhile these are some of the facts as I remember them. Any complaints, mail them to last Tuesday when I might have cared.